Probability, Statistics and Econometrics

Probability, Statistics and Econometrics

Oliver Linton
University of Cambridge
United Kingdom

ACADEMIC PRESS

An imprint of Elsevier
elsevier.com

Academic Press is an imprint of Elsevier
125 London Wall, London EC2Y 5AS, United Kingdom
525 B Street, Suite 1800, San Diego, CA 92101-4495, United States
50 Hampshire Street, 5th Floor, Cambridge, MA 02139, United States
The Boulevard, Langford Lane, Kidlington, Oxford OX5 1GB, United Kingdom

Notices

Knowledge and best practice in this field are constantly changing. As new research and experience
broaden our understanding, changes in research methods, professional practices, or medical treatment
may become necessary.

Practitioners and researchers must always rely on their own experience and knowledge in evaluating and
using any information, methods, compounds, or experiments described herein. In using such information
or methods they should be mindful of their own safety and the safety of others, including parties for
whom they have a professional responsibility.

To the fullest extent of the law, neither the Publisher nor the authors, contributors, or editors, assume any
liability for any injury and/or damage to persons or property as a matter of products liability, negligence
or otherwise, or from any use or operation of any methods, products, instructions, or ideas contained in
the material herein.

Library of Congress Cataloging-in-Publication Data
A catalog record for this book is available from the Library of Congress

British Library Cataloguing-in-Publication Data
A catalogue record for this book is available from the British Library

ISBN: 978-0-12-810495-8

For information on all Academic Press publications
visit our website at https://www.elsevier.com/books-and-journals

Working together
to grow libraries in
developing countries

www.elsevier.com • www.bookaid.org

Publisher: Nikki Levy
Senior Acquisition Editor: Graham Nisbet
Editorial Project Manager: Susan Ikeda
Senior Production Project Manager: Priya Kumaraguruparan
Designer: Victoria Pearson

Typeset by VTeX

To my Family.

Contents

List of Figures   xiii
About the Author   xv
Preface   xvii
Acknowledgment   xix

Part I
Probability and Distribution

1.   Probability Theory

1.1 Introduction   3
1.2 Definition of Probability   4
1.3 Some Counting Problems   7

2.   Conditional Probability and Independence

2.1 Conditional Probability   11
2.2 Bayes Theorem   12
2.3 Independence   14

3.   Random Variables, Distribution Functions, and Densities

3.1 Random Variables   21
3.2 Distribution Functions   23
3.3 Quantile   27
3.4 Density and Mass Functions   31

4.   Transformations of Random Variables

4.1 Distributions of Functions of a Random Variable   35
4.2 Probability Integral Transform   40

5. The Expectation

    5.1 Definition and Properties 43
    5.2 Additional Moments and Cumulants 49
    5.3 An Interpretation of Expectation and Median 52

6. Examples of Univariate Distributions

    6.1 Parametric Families of Distributions 55
        6.1.1 Discrete Distributions 55
        6.1.2 Continuous Distributions 58

7. Multivariate Random Variables

    7.1 Multivariate Distributions 63
    7.2 Conditional Distributions and Independence 66
    7.3 Covariance 69
    7.4 Conditional Expectation and the Regression Function 72
    7.5 Examples 81
    7.6 Multivariate Transformations 85
        7.6.1 Some Special Cases Where $q = 1$ and $p = 2$ 87
        7.6.2 Copula 90

8. Asymptotic Theory

    8.1 Inequalities 93
    8.2 Notions of Convergence 96
    8.3 Laws of Large Numbers and CLT 100
        8.3.1 Gambling Model 103
    8.4 Some Additional Tools 105

9. Exercises and Complements

Part II
Statistics

10. Introduction

    10.1 Sampling Theory 135
    10.2 Sample Statistics 136
        10.2.1 Properties of Descriptive Statistics 138
        10.2.2 Exact Properties Specific to the Normal Distribution 140
    10.3 Statistical Principles 142
        10.3.1 Some Important Concepts 144
        10.3.2 Bayesian Methods 146

11. Estimation Theory

11.1 Estimation Methods   151
    11.1.1 The Original Method of Moments or Analogy Principle   151
    11.1.2 Maximum Likelihood   155
    11.1.3 Computation   160
11.2 Comparison of Estimators and Optimality   163
    11.2.1 Asymptotic Properties   170
11.3 Robustness and Other Issues with the MLE   172

12. Hypothesis Testing

12.1 Hypotheses   175
12.2 Test Procedure   176
12.3 Likelihood Tests   181
12.4 Power of Tests   184
    12.4.1 Neyman Pearson Optimal Testing   186
    12.4.2 Consistency of Tests and Local Power   189
    12.4.3 Nonparametric Testing   193
12.5 Criticisms of the Standard Hypothesis Testing Approach   196

13. Confidence Intervals and Sets

13.1 Definitions   199
    13.1.1 General Large Sample Setting   201
13.2 Likelihood Ratio Confidence Interval   203
    13.2.1 A Bayesian Interval   208
13.3 Methods of Evaluating Intervals   209

14. Asymptotic Tests and the Bootstrap

14.1 Simulation Methods   211
14.2 Bootstrap   212
    14.2.1 Subsampling   219

15. Exercises and Complements

Part III
Econometrics

16. Linear Algebra

16.1 Matrices   231
    16.1.1 Linear Spaces   236
    16.1.2 Eigenvectors and Eigenvalues   237
    16.1.3 Applications   244
16.2 Systems of Linear Equations and Projection   249

17. The Least Squares Procedure

17.1 Projection Approach   251
17.2 Partitioned Regression   255
17.3 Restricted Least Squares   257
    17.3.1 Backfitting in Linear Regression   259
    17.3.2 Goodness of Fit   261

18. Linear Model

18.1 Introduction   263
18.2 The Model   263

19. Statistical Properties of the OLS Estimator

19.1 Properties of OLS   267
    19.1.1 Alternative Estimators   271
19.2 Optimality   271

20. Hypothesis Testing for Linear Regression

20.1 Hypotheses of Interest   277
20.2 Test of a Single Linear Hypothesis   278
20.3 Test of Multiple Linear Hypothesis   280
20.4 Test of Multiple Linear Hypothesis Based on Fit   281
20.5 Likelihood Based Testing   285
20.6 Bayesian Approach   287

21. Omission of Relevant Variables, Inclusion of Irrelevant Variables, and Model Selection

21.1 Omission of Relevant Variables   289
21.2 Inclusion of Irrelevant Variables/Knowledge of Parameters 291
21.3 Model Selection   292
    21.3.1 Problems and Issues   293
21.4 Lasso   294

22. Asymptotic Properties of OLS Estimator and Test Statistics

22.1 The I.I.D. Case   297
22.2 The Non-I.I.D. Case   302

23. Generalized Method of Moments and Extremum Estimators

23.1 Generalized Method Moments   313

23.2 **Asymptotic Properties of Extremum Estimators**   316
    23.2.1 Consistency   316
    23.2.2 Asymptotic Normality   322
23.3 **Quantile Regression**   327

24. A Nonparametric Postscript

25. A Case Study

26. Exercises and Complements

Appendix
  A Some Results from Calculus   357
  B Some Matrix Facts   358
    B.1   Matrix Operations Satisfy Certain Mathematical Laws   358
    B.2   Transpose of a Matrix   358
    B.3   Inverse   358
    B.4   Trace of a Matrix   358
    B.5   Determinant of a Matrix   358
    B.6   Rank of a Matrix   359
    B.7   Eigenvalues of Real Symmetric Matrix   359
    B.8   Positive Definiteness   359
Bibliography   361
Index   363

List of Figures

Fig. 3.1	c.d.f. of the logit distribution	24
Fig. 3.2	c.d.f. of the single die experiment	24
Fig. 3.3	Comparison between two c.d.f.s	28
Fig. 3.4	Quantile function of logit distribution	29
Fig. 3.5	c.d.f. and density function of example	33
Fig. 5.1	This density $\exp(-|x|^3)/1.786$ looks like the "Samsung distribution"	51
Fig. 7.1	Shows different linear approximations to a nonlinear regression function	79
Fig. 8.1	Shows argument in proving Markov's inequality	95
Fig. 8.2	Simulations illustrating the CLT	101
Fig. 10.1	Shows the empirical c.d.f. of a subsample of the dataset of size 100	137
Fig. 10.2	Kernel density estimate of daily stock returns alongside the standard normal density function	137
Fig. 11.1	Shows the lack of in sample identification	157
Fig. 11.2	Likelihood function of uniform example	159
Fig. 11.3	Score function of the Cauchy MLE	161
Fig. 12.1	Variation of income by star sign	180
Fig. 12.2	Comparison of distribution of test statistic under the null hypothesis and under an alternative hypothesis	185
Fig. 12.3	Power of the test	185
Fig. 13.1	Confidence interval for correlogram of daily S&P500 return series	202
Fig. 13.2	Correlogram of daily return series with Bartlett confidence bands	203
Fig. 13.3	Correlogram and confidence bands for absolute value of daily return series	203
Fig. 13.4	Confidence interval for binary parameter	207
Fig. 14.1	Results of simulation	212
Fig. 14.2	Distribution of statistic	214
Fig. 14.3	Distribution of T^*	214
Fig. 14.4	Comparison of density of T and T^*	217
Fig. 16.1	Shows $\lambda_i / \sum_{i=1}^d \lambda_i$, which is the percentage of total variance explained: 0.422, 0.044, 0.026, etc. $d = 441$ stocks, $n = 2700$ sample observations	247
Fig. 25.1	Medal count against athletes	337
Fig. 25.2	Alternative regression models	338

About the Author

Professor Oliver Linton (Professor of Political Economy, Trinity College, Cambridge University) has been a Co-editor of *Econometric Theory* since 2000, the *Journal of Econometrics* since 2014, was Co-Editor of *Econometrics Journal* from 2007-14. He is an Elected Fellow of the Econometric Society, the Institute of Mathematical Statistics, and the British Academy. He has published over 130 articles in statistics, econometrics, and in empirical finance. He is particularly interested in nonparametric and semiparametric methods and financial econometrics.

Preface

This book is intended to provide an intermediate level coverage of material suitable for advanced undergraduates and graduate students in economics, finance and other disciplines. I wanted to bring the essential material into one place for systematic study rather than shunt a lot of stuff to the appendix and start with the end product. I also wanted to make this a short and succinct book without too many digressions and motivations, but I am not sure I have succeeded in either direction. The intention is not to cover everything in detail. I have not covered time series nor have I adequately covered instrumental variables, especially not the practical aspects of their employment, although I do give some relevant theoretical results relevant for these topics. Nor, apologies to my Dutch friends, do I cover the Kronecker product or matrix differential calculus. Rather, I try to cover a broad range of mathematics suitable for this level of study and to provide applications that well motivate the theory and put it in a relevant practical context. The book contains some harmful econometrics, but also perhaps some harmless material.

It is hard to make any book an exhaustive treatment, and there are so many additional sources of information out there. The bold face words in the text suggest possible further reading, e.g., through internet search. The intention is to help focus additional study not to just punt on the difficult material.

Oliver Linton
Cambridge, UK
September 2016

Acknowledgment

I would like to thank the people who have had an influence on my research career; even though they may not have been directly involved in the development of this book, I have drawn heavily on my interactions with them throughout this project: Haya Friedman, Jan Magnus, Tom Rothenberg, Jens Perch Nielsen, Peter Bickel, Wolfgang Härdle, Enno Mammen, Peter Robinson, Don Andrews, Peter Phillips, Xiaohong Chen, Arthur Lewbel, Yoon-Jae Whang, Jean-Marie Dufour, Greg Connor, Andrew Harvey, Andrew Chesher, and Richard Smith.

I would like to thank Miguel Delgado, Alexei Onatski, Seok Young Hong, Arthur Lewbel, Peter Phillips, Steve Satchell, Katja Smetanina, Sorawoot Srisuma, and Haihan Tang for comments.

Part I

Probability and Distribution

Chapter 1

Probability Theory

1.1 INTRODUCTION

Uncertainty or *variability* are prevalent in many situations. It is the purpose of probability theory to provide the tools to understand and quantify this notion. The material is basic to all sciences as well as to econometrics and statistics. The basic situation is an experiment whose outcome is unknown to the experimenter before it takes place, i.e., any procedure with more than one outcome. For example:

1. Coin tossing
2. Outcome of an election
3. Grade at end of this class
4. The decimal expansion of the number $\pi = 3.1415926\ldots$.

In each case *we* don't know for sure what the outcome will be. Example 1 is the simplest case. We are pretty sure that the only outcomes are H or T and that they are equally likely. Although we know what the possible outcomes are in 2. and 3. we are very unlikely to agree on how likely each possible outcome is. Example 4 doesn't appear to be random – π is what it is, so there is no before and after. However, effectively it is random, since no-one can know the full decimal expansion of this number. To be concrete, what is the 111,111,113,738,222nd term of the expansion?[1]

We start out by describing the **sample space** or outcome space S, which is the set of all possible relevant outcomes. For example, in examples (1) and (2) we have

$$S = \{H, T\}, \quad S = \{\text{Bush, Clinton, Also Rans}\}.$$

Both these examples have a finite sample space; neither of them are numerical. Consider now example 4. In this case, the sample space consists of all infinite sequences $(3, 1, 2, 3, \ldots)$, which is a countable infinity. Suppose you ask someone to choose a number in $[0, 2\pi]$ at random, in which case the outcome space is an uncountable infinity. Neither of these experiments can physically be performed,

---

1. Actually, it is known that the relative frequencies of the digits of the decimal expansion of π is approximately "uniform", see for example http://www.eveandersson.com/pi/precalculated-frequencies.

Probability, Statistics and Econometrics. http://dx.doi.org/10.1016/B978-0-12-810495-8.00002-6

but so what − it can be interpreted as just an approximation. Some calculations turn out to be much easier when using uncountable infinities − e.g., the normal distribution is much easier to work with than a discrete distribution that has many points of **support** (that is, the set of different values that can occur).

1.2 DEFINITION OF PROBABILITY

An event A is any subset of S; it is essentially a question that we could answer with a yes or no. Probability is concerned with measuring given events and comparing them, and to do this we will need to use set theoretic mathematics in the sequel. Here is a brief revision.

Set notation. $\in$, $\notin$, ϕ, $A \subseteq B$, $A \cap B$, $A \cup B$, A^c

$$A^c = \{x \in S, \; x \notin A\}$$
$$A = B \text{ if } A \subseteq B \text{ and } A \supseteq B, \; A \cup B = \{x : x \in A \text{ or } x \in B\}.$$

Basic properties:

(1)	$A \cup B = B \cup A;$ $A \cap B = B \cap A$	Commutativity
(2)	$A \cup (B \cup C) = (A \cup B) \cup C;$ $A \cap (B \cap C) = (A \cap B) \cap C$	Associativity
(3)	$A \cap (B \cup C) = (A \cap B) \cup (A \cap C);$ $A \cup (B \cap C) = (A \cup B) \cap (A \cup C)$	Distributive
(4)	$(A \cup B)^c = A^c \cap B^c;$ $(A \cap B)^c = A^c \cup B^c$	DeMorgan's

The proof of these properties can best be seen by a Venn's Diagram.

We must work with sets of sets. Consider a collection of sets A_α with index $\alpha \in \Gamma$, which we denote by

$$\{A_\alpha : \alpha \in \Gamma\}.$$

We can define for an index set Γ of arbitrary cardinality the union and intersection:

$$\bigcup_{\alpha \in \Gamma} A_\alpha = \{x \in S : x \in A_\alpha \text{ for some } \alpha \in \Gamma\}$$
$$\bigcap_{\alpha \in \Gamma} A_\alpha = \{x \in S : x \in A_\alpha \text{ for all } \alpha \in \Gamma\}.$$

A collection of sets is **exhaustive** if $\bigcup_{\alpha \in \Gamma} A_\alpha = S$, and is **pairwise exclusive** or **disjoint** if $A_\alpha \cap A_\beta = \phi$, $\alpha \neq \beta$. A **partition** of S is an exhaustive disjoint collection of sets.

We need some further structure before we can define probability. It turns out that when S is very big (in terms of the number of elements), such as the real line, we can't just define probability for all subsets of S, because there are some sets on the real line whose probability cannot be determined, i.e., they are unmeasurable. For example, the **Cantor set**. Such sets are usually quite complicated to construct, and play no role in our applications, so we just refer the reader to any advanced probability book like Chung (1974) or Billingsley (1986) for further discussion. We shall define probability on a family of subsets of S that possess the following structure.

Definition 1.1. Let $\mathcal{A}$ be a non-empty class of subsets of S. $\mathcal{A}$ is an *algebra* (or field) if

1. $A^c \in \mathcal{A}$, whenever $A \in \mathcal{A}$
2. $A_1 \cup A_2 \in \mathcal{A}$, whenever $A_1, A_2 \in \mathcal{A}$.

Definition 1.2. $\mathcal{A}$ is a sigma-algebra (or σ-**algebra** or σ-field) if in addition to 1 and 2

2'. $\bigcup_{n=1}^{\infty} A_n \in \mathcal{A}$, whenever $A_n \in \mathcal{A}$, $n = 1, 2, \ldots$

Note that since $\mathcal{A}$ is nonempty, (1) and (2) imply that $(\Rightarrow)$ $\phi \in \mathcal{A}$ and $S \in \mathcal{A}$ because if

$$A \in \mathcal{A} \Rightarrow A^c \in \mathcal{A} \Rightarrow A \cup A^c = S \in \mathcal{A} \Rightarrow S^c = \phi \in \mathcal{A}.$$

Note also that (1) and (2') imply that $\bigcap_{n=1}^{\infty} A_n \in \mathcal{A}$.

The largest sigma-algebra is the set of all subsets of S, (the **power set**), denoted $\mathcal{P}(S)$, and the smallest is the trivial sigma algebra $\{\phi, S\}$. We can generate an algebra or sigma-algebra from any collection of subsets by adding to the set the complements and unions of its elements. A simplest such sigma algebra is $\{\phi, A, A^c, S\}$, which can be generated by the set A.

Exercise. If $\mathcal{A}_1$ and $\mathcal{A}_2$ are sigma algebras, prove that $\mathcal{A}_1 \cap \mathcal{A}_2$ is a sigma algebra. Is $\mathcal{A}_1 \cup \mathcal{A}_2$ necessarily a sigma algebra?

Example 1.1. Let $S = \{1, 2, 3, 4, 5, 6\}$. Then let $\mathcal{A} = \mathcal{P}(S)$, which contains 64 elements (see below) including all the singletons $\{1\}, \{2\}, \ldots, \{6\}$, and all the pairs $\{1, 2\}$, etc. Note that the power set can be generated by the set of all singletons $\{\{1\}, \{2\}\{3\}\{4\}\{5\}\{6\}\}$, meaning that any subset of S can be written as the union of the singletons of its members, since in this case S has finite cardinality. An alternative sigma algebra is $\{\varnothing, S, \{2, 4, 6\}, \{1, 3, 5\}\}$. This is a coarser sigma-algebra than the power set.

Example 1.2. Let $S = \mathbb{R}$, and let

$$\mathcal{B} = \{(a, b), \ a, b \in \mathbb{R}\}.$$

Then let $\mathcal{A} = \sigma(\mathcal{B})$ consist of all countable unions of members of $\mathcal{B}$ and complements thereof. This is called the **Borel** sigma-**algebra** and is the usual sigma-algebra we work with when $S = \mathbb{R}$. The sigma algebra $\mathcal{A}$ is a strict subset of $\mathcal{P}(\mathbb{R})$, that is, there are sets in $\mathcal{P}(\mathbb{R})$ that are not in $\mathcal{A}$. Note that any closed interval may be obtained by intersecting a suitable countable number of open intervals

$$\cap_{n=1}^{\infty} (a - \frac{1}{n}, b + \frac{1}{n}) = [a, b].$$

It follows that $\mathcal{A}$ contains all closed intervals, and half open intervals and countable unions and complements thereof.

We next give the definition of probability measure, which is due to Kolmogorov.

Definition 1.3. Given a sample space S and a sigma-algebra $\mathcal{A}$ defined on S, a probability measure P is a set function from $\mathcal{A} \to \mathbb{R}$ such that

1. $P(A) \geq 0$ for all $A \in \mathcal{A}$
2. $P(S) = 1$
3. If $A_1, A_2, \ldots$ are pairwise disjoint, i.e., $A_i \cap A_j = \phi$ for all $i \neq j$, then

$$P\left(\bigcup_{i=1}^{\infty} A_i\right) = \sum_{i=1}^{\infty} P(A_i). \tag{1.1}$$

The probability measure P will depend on the problem, we will see many examples later. When S has finite cardinality, we usually take P to be such that primitive outcomes (singleton sets) are **equally likely**, i.e., $P(\{x\}) = 1/n$, where n is the number of elements of S; this is certainly the case in the coin tossing example. When S is an interval of the real line, say $[a, b]$, the counterpart of this would be to take P such that $P([c, d]) = (d - c)/(b - a)$ for intervals $[c, d] \subset [a, b]$. The weaker concept of **measure** dispenses with property 2 (and replaces it by $P(\phi) = 0$), that is, a measure μ is a set mapping $\mathcal{A} \to \mathbb{R}$ such that 1. and 3. hold. For example, Lebesgue measure, usually denoted λ, satisfies $\lambda([c, d]) = d - c$ for any $c < d \in \mathbb{R}$. Lebesgue measure does not satisfy the normalization condition that the whole space should have measure one. The key property of measures and probability measures is that of countable additivity, property 3. This allows to extend the definition of probability from a relatively simple class of sets, say intervals, to a much bigger class generated by forming countable unions.

We next collect some properties of probability measure.

Theorem 1.1. PROPERTIES OF P

1. $P(\phi) = 0$;
2. $P(A) \leq 1$;
3. $P(A^c) = 1 - P(A)$;
4. $P(A) = P(A \cap B) + P(A \cap B^c)$;
5. If $A \subset B$, then $P(A) \leq P(B)$;
6. $P(A \cup B) = P(A) + P(B) - P(A \cap B)$;
7. $P\left(\bigcup_{i=1}^{\infty} A_i\right) \leq \sum_{i=1}^{\infty} P(A_i)$ for any set $A_1, A_2, \ldots$

Proof. The proofs of these properties involve manipulating sets to obtain disjoint sets and then apply the axioms. For example, A and A^c are mutually exclusive and exhaustive so that

$$1 = P(S) = P(A \cup A^c) = P(A) + P(A^c),$$

which establishes property 3. A measure such as Lebesgue measure needs not satisfy 1, 2, and 3, but does satisfy the other properties.

Property 7 is called Bonferroni's inequality and is very useful. Property 6 implies the sometimes useful bounds

$$P(A \cap B) \geq P(A) + P(B) - 1. \qquad (1.2)$$

Exercise. After a very fierce battle, 72% of soldiers have lost an eye, 85% have lost an arm, and 63% have lost a leg. Therefore, no less than 20% of them are missing: an eye, an arm, and a leg? We have

$$P\left(A \cap \overbrace{B \cap C}^{\text{combine}} \right) \geq P(A) + P(B \cap C)) - 1 \geq P(A) + P(B) + P(C) - 2$$

We conclude *that* $P(A \cap B \cap C) \geq 0.20$ as stated.

Sets of measure zero include the empty set but may also include nontrivial sets that can be important. Two measures P and Q may disagree on the valuation given to some sets A, but they may agree on whether a set A has measure zero. In such a case, we say that they are **mutually absolutely continuous**. That is, $P(A) = 0$ if and only if $Q(A) = 0$. In finance a common application is to change probability measures from the so-called objective measure P to the risk-neutral measure Q. □

1.3   SOME COUNTING PROBLEMS

Some more sophisticated discrete problems require counting techniques. For example:

(a) What is the number of subsets of a given set?

(b) What is the probability of getting four of a kind in five card poker?

(c) What is the probability that two people in this room have the same birthday?

(d) If your birthday is the 13th, what is the probability you will have a birthday on Friday?

(e) What is the probability of winning the lottery?

The sample space in both cases, although discrete, can be quite large and it may not be feasible to write out all possible outcomes.

Permutation. How many different ways of *rearranging* a set $A = \{a_1, \ldots, a_n\}$ with regard to the order, i.e., (a_1, a_2) counts as separate from (a_2, a_1). In general, there are $n! = n(n-1) \times \cdots \times 2 \times 1$ permutations of n symbols. Now, how many different permutations $P(n, r)$ of subsets of size $r \leq n$ are there? For example, $A = \{1, 2, 3\}$, $n = 3$, $r = 2$, we have six different permutations

$$(1, 2), (2, 1), (1, 3), (3, 1), (3, 2), (2, 3).$$

In general

$$P(n, r) = n(n-1) \times \cdots \times (n - r + 1) = \frac{n!}{(n-r)!}.$$

Combinations. Now suppose that you want to treat, for example, (a_1, a_2) as indistinguishable from (a_2, a_1). In general, the number of combinations is

$$C(n, r) = \frac{P(n, r)}{r!} \quad [r! \text{ is the number of permutations each } r\text{-set}$$

$$= \frac{n!}{(n-r)!r!} = \binom{n}{r}.$$

To summarize:

	with replacement	without replacement
ordered	n^r	$\frac{n!}{(n-r)!}$
unordered	$\binom{n+r-1}{r}$	$\binom{n}{r}$.

Solution to (a). For a given set $\{1, 2, \ldots, n\}$ there are $\binom{n}{r}$ different subsets of size r. The answer is

$$\binom{n}{1} + \binom{n}{2} + \ldots + \binom{n}{n} = 2^n - 1, \tag{1.3}$$

so if we include the empty set there are a total of 2^n subsets. This follows from the **Binomial Theorem**, which regards a general formula for $(a + b)^n$, where a, b are real numbers.

Solution to (b). The card game of Poker: five cards are deal in sequence without replacement from a 52 card deck. The objective is to get as high a hand as possible. Here, we don't care about the order in which we receive the cards. Furthermore, the dealing is done without replacement. There are $\frac{52!}{5!47!}$ "different" hands $= 2,598,960$. We assume that each such hand is equally likely. What is the probability of receiving four of a kind? There are 13 different ways of getting four. The last card can be chosen in 48 ways, so that

$$\text{Pr(Four of a kind)} = \frac{13 \cdot 48}{2,598,960}.$$

Solution to (c). Let A be the event that *at least* two people in the room have the same birthday. We calculate $P(A^c)$. There are 365 possible birthdays, if we ignore leap years, which gives that

$$P(A^c) = \frac{365 \times \cdots \times (365 - r + 1)}{365^r}.$$

Then use $P(A) = 1 - P(A^c)$. When $n = 23$, $P(A) = 0.507$. When $n = 32$, $P(A) = 0.753$. When $n = 56$, $P(A) = 0.988$.

Regarding (d) you might think that 1/7 is the correct answer, but in fact this is not exactly correct. If one looks at any four hundred year period (our calendar has a cycle of 400 years or 20,871 complete weeks), say between 1600 and 2000, there are 4800 days that were the 13th day of some month. One can enumerate that: 687 were Sundays or Wednesdays; 685 were Mondays or Tuesdays, 684 were Thursdays or Saturdays; and 688 were Fridays. So Friday the 13ths are relatively common. See Brown (1933). Of course, for most practical purposes 1/7 is a pretty good answer.

Solution to (d) will be discussed later.

Chapter 2

Conditional Probability and Independence

2.1 CONDITIONAL PROBABILITY

In many statistical applications we have events A and B and want to explain or predict A from B, i.e., we want to say how likely A is, given that B has occurred.

Example 2.1. In university admissions, we might be interested in

$$A = \{\text{got g.p.a. 4.0 in college}\}$$
$$B = \{\text{got g.p.a. 4.0 in High School}\}.$$

Example 2.2. Investment professionals might be interested in the case

$$A = \{\text{stocks up Today}\}$$
$$B = \{\text{stocks up Yesterday}\}.$$

We are interested not just in **marginal** probabilities, but also in **conditional** probabilities, that is, we want to incorporate some information into our predictions.

Definition 2.1. The probability of an event $A \in \mathcal{A}$ given an event $B \in \mathcal{A}$, denoted $P(A|B)$, is given by

$$P(A|B) = \frac{P(A \cap B)}{P(B)}, \tag{2.1}$$

when $P(B) > 0$.

The exclusion of the case $P(B) = 0$ has important ramifications later on. If A and B are mutually exclusive events, then $P(A|B) = 0$. If $A \subseteq B$, then $P(A|B) = P(A)/P(B) \geq P(A)$ with strict inequality unless $P(B) = 1$. If $B \subseteq A$, then $P(A|B) = 1$. We will later have interest in the special case where $P(A|B) = P(A)$.

Note that $P(\cdot|B)$ is a probability measure that maps $\mathcal{A} \to \mathbb{R}_+$. In particular, we have:

Probability, Statistics and Econometrics. http://dx.doi.org/10.1016/B978-0-12-810495-8.00003-8

11

Theorem 2.1. *Suppose that* $B \in \mathcal{A}$. *Then*

1. *For any* $A \in \mathcal{A}$, $P(A|B) \geq 0$;
2. $P(B|B) = 1$
3. $P\left(\bigcup_{i=1}^{\infty} A_i | B\right) = \sum_{i=1}^{\infty} P(A_i|B)$ *for any pairwise disjoint events* $\{A_i\}_{i=1}^{\infty}$.

This follows directly from the definitions and properties of P.

Example 2.3. We have 100 stocks and we observe whether they went up or down on consecutive days, the information is given below

		Today		
		up	down	
	up	53	25	78
Y'day				
	down	15	7	22
		68	32	100

The information given here is effectively: $P(A \cap B)$, $P(A \cap B^c)$, $P(B \cap A^c)$, and $P(B^c \cap A^c)$, where $A = \{$up Y'day$\}$ and $B = \{$up T'day$\}$. It is an easy exercise to convert these "joint probabilities" to marginal and conditional probabilities using the **Law of total probability**. Specifically, the equation

$$P(A) = P(A \cap B) + P(A \cap B^c)$$

determines the marginals, and then definition (2.1) gives the conditionals. Thus

$$P(\text{Up Y'day}) = \frac{78}{100}$$

$$P(\text{Down Y'day}) = \frac{22}{100}$$

$$P(\text{Up Today}|\text{Up Y'day}) = \frac{53/100}{78/100} = \frac{53}{78}.$$

2.2 BAYES THEOREM

We next give the famous **Bayes Rule** (or Formula, Lemma or Theorem depending on the source), which is an important result in probability and statistics. Often we have prior information about a marginal probability and about a conditional probability, but we are interested in the reverse direction conditional probability, i.e., in making an **inference**. This can be obtained from this rule.

Theorem 2.2. *(Bayes Rule). Let A and B be two events with $P(A) \neq 0$. Then*

$$P(B|A) = \frac{P(A|B) \times P(B)}{P(A)} = \frac{P(A|B) \cdot P(B)}{P(A|B) \cdot P(B) + P(A|B^c) \cdot P(B^c)}. \quad (2.2)$$

Proof. This follows from the definition of conditional probability and the law of total probability:

$$P(A \cap B) = P(A|B) \cdot P(B) = P(B|A) \cdot P(A)$$
$$P(A) = P(A \cap B) + P(A \cap B^c) = P(A|B) \cdot P(B) + P(A|B^c) \cdot P(B^c).$$

$\square$

The probability $P(B)$ is frequently called the **prior** probability and $P(A|B)$ is called the **likelihood**, while $P(B|A)$ is called the **posterior**. We next give some examples.

Example 2.4. Suppose we want to know what is the probability a person is telling the truth given the results of a Polygraph test. Let a positive reading on the Polygraph be denoted by $(+)$, and a negative reading be denoted by $(-)$; T denotes the person is telling truth and L denotes the person is lying. We have information on $P(\pm|L)$ and $P(\pm|T)$ from lab work (we are using a shorthand but obvious notation here). Suppose we get $+$ readout

$$P(T|+) = \frac{P(+|T)P(T)}{P(+|T)P(T) + P(+|L)P(L)}$$

If we believe that $P(T) = 0.99$, say, and know that $P(+|L) = 0.88$, $P(+|T) = 0.14$, then

$$P(T|+) = 0.94.$$

This is perhaps a bit surprising, see **Prosecutor's Fallacy**.

Example 2.5. We next consider an example from economic theory, called the **sequential trading** model. A stock price can take two possible values

$$V = \begin{cases} V_H & \text{with prob } 1 - \delta \\ V_L & \text{with prob } \delta, \end{cases}$$

where $V_L < V_H$ and $\delta \in [0, 1]$. This is the prior distribution on value. The investor is chosen randomly from two possible types

$$T = \begin{cases} I & \text{with prob } \mu \\ U & \text{with prob } 1 - \mu \end{cases}$$

The timeline is: first, a value is chosen, and then a type of investor is chosen, and that investor carries out his strategy. The strategies of the investors are as follows. The informed traders (I), will buy if the value is high V_H, and sell if the value is low V_L, provided the quoted prices lie in the interval $[V_L, V_H]$. The uninformed traders (U), buy or sell with probability 1/2. Suppose that a buy order is received (but it is not known from whom), what does that tell us about the value of the stock? Let $A = \{V = V_L\}$ and $B = \{buy\ order\ received\}$. We can calculate $P(B|A)$ directly from the knowledge of the traders strategies and the distribution of trader types. That is

$$P(B|A) = \frac{1}{2}(1 - \mu)$$

because if the value is low the informed trader will not buy and the uninformed trader will buy one half of the time. Likewise

$$P(B|A^c) = \frac{1}{2}(1 - \mu) + \mu$$

because when the value is high the informed trader will always buy. We want to know $P(A|B)$ as this tells us the updated value distribution. By Bayes rule, we can calculate the updated distribution (**posterior**) of V

$$\underbrace{P(A|B)}_{posterior} = \frac{\overbrace{P(B|A)}^{likelihood}\overbrace{P(A)}^{prior}}{P(B)}$$

$$= \frac{P(buy|V = V_L)P(V = V_L)}{P(buy|V = V_L)P(V = V_L) + P(buy|V = V_H)P(V = V_H)}$$

$$= \frac{\frac{1}{2}(1 - \mu) \times \delta}{(1 + \mu(1 - 2\delta))/2}$$

$$= \frac{1 - \mu}{1 + \mu(1 - 2\delta)} \times \delta$$

$$\leq \delta$$

$$P(V = V_H|buy) = P(A^c|B) = 1 - P(A|B) = \frac{(\mu + 1)}{(1 + \mu(1 - 2\delta))}(1 - \delta) \geq 1 - \delta$$

The information that a buy order has been received is useful and increases our valuation of the asset. On the other hand, if a sell order were received, this would lower our valuation of the asset.

Example 2.6. Why most published research findings are false, Ioannidis (2005).

2.3 INDEPENDENCE

We next define the notion of independence, which is a central property in much of statistics. This concerns a special case of conditional probability that makes many calculations simpler.

Definition 2.2. Independence. Suppose $P(A), P(B) > 0$, then A and B are independent events if:

(1) $P(A \cap B) = P(A) \cdot P(B)$

(2) $P(A|B) = P(A)$

(3) $P(B|A) = P(B)$

These are equivalent definitions. Definition (1) is symmetric in A and B; the value of property (1) is that given knowledge of $P(A)$ and $P(B)$, we can directly determine $P(A \cap B)$, whereas without independence all we can say is the bound (1.2). Definitions (2) and (3) are perhaps easier to interpret. In (2) we are saying that knowledge of B does not change our assessment of the likelihood of A, and essentially B is useless for this purpose. We can in principle allow $P(A)$ and/or $P(B)$ to be zero in all three definitions provided we assign $0/0 = 0$.

If A and B are mutually exclusive events, i.e., $P(A \cap B) = 0$, then A and B cannot be independent unless either $P(A) = 0$ or $P(B) = 0$. If $A \subseteq B$, then A and B cannot be independent (unless $P(A) = 0$). Independence is a **symmetric** relationship, so that A is independent of B, if and only if B is independent of A. Furthermore, if A is independent of B, then: A is independent of B^c, A^c is independent of B, and A^c is independent of B^c. If you know B, then you know B^c. However, it is not a **transitive** relationship, i.e. A is independent of B and B is independent of C does not imply that A is independent of C.

Example 2.7. A counterexample: in the six-sided die example $S = \{1, 2, 3, 4, 5, 6\}$, take $A = \{2, 4, 6\}$, $B = \{1, 2, 3, 4\}$, and $C = \{1, 3, 5\}$.

Independence is an important property that is often assumed in applications. For example:

(a) Stock returns are independent from day to day;

(b) Different household spending decisions are independent of each other;

(c) Legal cases such as **Sally Clark/Roy Meadow**. Expert Meadow testified that the odds against two cot deaths occurring in the same family was 73,000,000:1, a figure which he obtained by squaring the observed ratio of live-births to cot deaths in affluent non-smoking families (approximately 8,500:1), which would be valid under independence of these two events. He testified under oath that: "one sudden infant death in a family is a tragedy, two is suspicious and three is murder unless proven otherwise" (**Meadow's law**). See Dawid (2002) expert witness statement in the retrial.

Although independence is a central case, in practice dependence is common in many settings. One can measure the amount of dependence and its direction (positive or negative) between two events in several ways:

$$\alpha(A, B) = P(A \cap B) - P(A) \cdot P(B)$$

$$\beta(A, B) = P(A|B) - P(A) = \frac{P(A \cap B)}{P(B)} - P(A)$$

$$\gamma(A, B) = \frac{P(A \cap B)}{P(A)P(B)} - 1,$$

where α, β, γ can be positive or negative indicating the direction of the mutual dependence. For example, if $\beta > 0$ this means that event A is more likely to occur when B has occurred than when we don't know whether B has occurred or not. We may show that $\alpha \in [-1, 1/4]$, $\beta \in [-1, 1]$, and $\gamma \in \mathbb{R}$. These measures allow us to rank cases according to the degree of dependence. Suppose that $A \subseteq B$, then clearly, knowing B gives us some information about whether A has occurred whenever B is a strict subset of S. In this case

$$\alpha(A, B) = P(A)(1 - P(B))$$

$$\beta(A, B) = \frac{P(A)}{P(B)} - 1$$

$$\gamma(A, B) = \frac{1}{P(B)} - 1.$$

Example 2.8. In the stock example, we have very mild negative dependence with:

$$\alpha(A, B) = 0.53 - 0.78 \times 0.68 = -0.0004$$

$$\beta(A, B) = -0.000588$$

$$\gamma(A, B) = -0.000754.$$

Example 2.9. An example of conditional probability and independence. Suppose you deal two cards without replacement.

$$A = \left\{ \begin{array}{c} \text{first card} \\ \text{is Ace} \end{array} \right\}, \ B \left\{ \begin{array}{c} \text{second card} \\ \text{is King} \end{array} \right\}, \ C = \left\{ \begin{array}{c} \text{first card} \\ \text{is King} \end{array} \right\}.$$

We have

$$P(A) = 4/52, \ P(B|A) = 4/51$$

$$P(B) = P(B|C) \cdot P(C) + P(B|C^c)P(C^c).$$

Furthermore, $P(C) = 4/52$, $P(C^c) = 48/52$, $P(B|C) = 3/51$, $P(B|C^c) = 4/51$. This implies that

$$P(B) = \frac{3}{51} \cdot \frac{4}{52} + \frac{4}{51} \cdot \frac{48}{52} = \frac{12 + 192}{51 \cdot 52} = \frac{204}{51 \cdot 52} = \frac{4}{52} < \frac{4}{51}$$

So $P(B) < P(B|A)$, i.e., A and B are not independent events. In this case $\beta(A, B) = 1/51 > 0$ meaning there is positive dependence.

We next consider the more general case with more than two events.

Definition 2.3. A general definition of independence. Events $A_1, \ldots, A_n$ are said to be mutually independent if

$$P\left(\bigcap_{j=1}^{k} A_{i_j}\right) = \prod_{j=1}^{k} P(A_{i_j}), \text{ for all } A_{i_1}, \ldots, A_{i_k}, \ k = 2, \ldots, n$$

For example, independence of events A, B, C requires the following conditions to hold:

1. $P(A \cap B) = P(A)P(B)$
2. $P(A \cap C) = P(A)P(C)$
3. $P(B \cap C) = P(B)P(C)$
4. $P(A \cap B \cap C) = P(A)P(B)P(C)$.

Example 2.10. The **infinite monkey theorem** says that if one had an infinite number of monkeys randomly tapping on a keyboard, with probability one, at least one of them will produce the complete works of Shakespeare. If one has a finite set of characters on the typewriter K and a finite length document n, then the probability that any one monkey would type this document exactly is K^{-n}. If there are 47 keys on the standard typewriter, and 884,421 words, so perhaps 5 million characters, in which case the probability is so low that a given monkey will produce the documents. Let $A_i = \{$Monkey i nails it$\}$. Then

$$P(A_i) = K^{-n}$$

However, the probability that no monkeys would produce it is (assuming that the monkeys are mutually independent agents and don't interfere with other monkeys)

$$\lim_{M \to \infty} P\left(\cap_{i=1}^{M} A_i^c\right) = \lim_{M \to \infty} \left(1 - K^{-n}\right)^M = 0.$$

This can be strengthened to say that with probability one an infinite number of monkeys would produce the complete works of Shakespeare. Consider the sets $B_1 = \{1, 2, \ldots, M\}$, $B_2 = \{M + 1, M + 2, \ldots, 2M\}$, etc. There was an Arts council grant that was commissioned to investigate the infinite monkey theorem.[1]

We give two further independence concepts.

Definition 2.4. Pairwise independence. Events $A_1, \ldots, A_n$ are said to be pairwise independent if for all A_i, A_j

$$P(A_i \cap A_j) = P(A_i) \cdot P(A_j).$$

We can have pairwise independence but not independence, i.e., pairwise independence is the weaker property.

Example 2.11. Suppose that $S = \{1, 2, 3, 4\}$, $A = \{1, 2\}$, $B = \{1, 3\}$, and $C = \{1, 4\}$. Then $P(A \cap B \cap C) = 1/4$ but $P(A) = P(B) = P(C) = 1/2$ and $P(A \cap B) = P(A \cap C) = P(B \cap C) = 1/4$.

There is a further concept of interest in many applications.

Definition 2.5. Conditional Independence. Suppose that $P(A)$, $P(B)$, $P(C) > 0$, then A and B are independent events given C if either:

(1) $P(A \cap B|C) = P(A|C)P(B|C)$;
(2) $P(C)P(A \cap B \cap C) = P(A \cap C) \cdot P(B \cap C)$.

Note that independence of A and B does not imply conditional independence of A and B given C, and vice versa, conditional independence of A and B given C does not imply independence of A and B.

Example 2.12. You toss two dice

$$A = \left\{ \begin{array}{c} \text{Your first die} \\ 6 \end{array} \right\}, B \left\{ \begin{array}{c} \text{Your second die} \\ \text{is 6} \end{array} \right\}, C = \left\{ \begin{array}{c} \text{Both dice are} \\ \text{same} \end{array} \right\}$$

A and B here are independent. However, A and B are conditionally dependent given C, since if you know C then your first die will tell you exactly what the other one is.

There are many examples where conditional independence holds but not independence. Likewise, the direction of dependence or association can change

---

1. In 2003, lecturers and students from the University of Plymouth MediaLab Arts course studied the literary output of real monkeys. They left a computer keyboard in the enclosure of six Celebes crested macaques in Paignton Zoo in Devon in England for a month, with a radio link to broadcast the results on a website. The monkeys produced nothing but five total pages largely consisting of the letter S, the lead male began by bashing the keyboard with a stone, and the monkeys continued by urinating and defecating on it.

depending on whether you are in the conditional distribution or unconditional. This is called **Simpson's Paradox**: the reversal of the direction of an association when data from several groups are combined (aggregated) to form a single group. That is, we may have $\Pr(A|B) > \Pr(A|B^c)$ but both $\Pr(A|B, C) < \Pr(A|B^c, C)$ and $\Pr(A|B, C^c) < \Pr(A|B^c, C^c)$ for events A, B, C.

Example 2.13. A common application of conditional independence is in time series. We have a sequence of outcomes on the stock market observed over time, either up or down. Each outcome is random at time t, and there is a probability p_t of an Up and $1 - p_t$ of a Down and this probability may depend on past outcomes. We assume that only what happens yesterday is relevant for today, i.e., the future is independent of the past given the present

$$P(\text{Outcome}_t | \text{Outcome}_{t-1} \cap \cdots \cap \text{Outcome}_{-\infty}) = P(\text{Outcome}_t | \text{Outcome}_{t-1}).$$

This is called a **Markov Chain**. A special case of this is when p_t is time invariant as in our next example.

Example 2.14. Gambler's ruin. Each period there is a probability p of an up and probability $1 - p$ of a down, and this does not depend on past outcomes. Suppose that you have \$1 and take \$1 positions in the stock market indefinitely [when the market is up, you gain \$1, and when it is down you lose \$1], or until you become bankrupt. What is the probability you become bankrupt? You can write out a table showing all the possible paths you can take to the destination \$0. An important thing to note in this problem is the symmetry. Let $P_{j,k}$ be the probability of going from \$j to \$k. Clearly, $P_{j+\ell,k+\ell}$ for any ℓ, i.e., just adding \$\ell to your total doesn't change anything real. Now note that

$$P_{1,0} = 1 - p + p P_{2,0}.$$

Furthermore, $P_{2,1} = P_{1,0}$ and so $P_{2,0} = P_{2,1} P_{1,0} = P_{1,0}^2$. Therefore, we have a quadratic equation

$$P_{1,0} = 1 - p + p P_{1,0}^2,$$

which has solutions

$$P_{1,0} = 1 \quad ; \quad P_{1,0} = \frac{1 - p}{p}.$$

The first solution is relevant when $p \leq 1/2$, while the second is relevant otherwise. This says that for example even if you have a fifty fifty chance of success, you will become bankrupt with probability one. This shows the advantage of the principle "quit while you are ahead".

Chapter 3

Random Variables, Distribution Functions, and Densities

3.1 RANDOM VARIABLES

We have defined a probability space $(S, \mathcal{A}, P)$ and introduced various concepts in this setting. This is a very general setting, but isn't particularly easy to work with. In practice, we often need to work with mathematical spaces with some structure (e.g., distance and algebra). Also, we often want to answer several different questions about the same experiment. It is convenient therefore to work with a cardinalization of S by using the notion of **random variables**.

Definition 3.1. A random variable X is a mapping from the sample space to the real line,[1] i.e.,

$$X : S \to S_X \subset \mathbb{R},$$

with certain properties. Specifically it is a **measurable** $[\mathcal{B} \backslash \mathcal{A}]$ mapping, i.e.,

$$\mathcal{A}_X = \{A \subset S : X(A) \in \mathcal{B}\} = \{X^{-1}(B) : B \in \mathcal{B}\} \subseteq \mathcal{A}, \qquad (3.1)$$

where $\mathcal{B}$ is a sigma algebra on S_X and $\mathcal{A}$ is the sigma algebra on S. Here,

$$X(A) = \{X(a) : a \in A\} \quad ; \quad X^{-1}(B) = \{a \in S : X(a) \in B\}.$$

It is a straightforward exercise to show that $\mathcal{A}_X$ is a sigma algebra whenever $\mathcal{B}$ is [do it]; it is called the sigma algebra generated by X, and is sometimes denoted by $\sigma(X)$. The probability measure P_X can then be defined by

$$P_X(B) = P(X^{-1}(B)), \qquad (3.2)$$

where P is the original probability measure on S. Therefore, P_X is a probability measure obeying Kolmogorov's axioms. We have transferred $(S, \mathcal{A}, P) \to (S_X, \mathcal{B}, P_X)$. We could just start out with $(S_X, \mathcal{B}, P_X)$ as our basic experiment, but in many cases we will want to define multiple random variables and it is convenient to have them coming from the same source.

---

1. We can also consider multivariate random variables and even random variables with outcome the extended real line.

Probability, Statistics and Econometrics. http://dx.doi.org/10.1016/B978-0-12-810495-8.00004-X
21

The sigma algebra $\mathcal{A}_X$ is induced by the mapping X. When S_X is finite, we usually take $\mathcal{B}$ to be the power set $\mathcal{P}(S_X)$. When $S_X = \mathbb{R}$, we usually take $\mathcal{B}$ to be the Borel sigma algebra defined above.

Example 3.1. The simplest form of random variables are the indicators $X = I_A$

$$I_A(s) = \begin{cases} 1 & \text{if } s \in A \\ 0 & \text{if } s \notin A \end{cases}$$

We may take $\{\phi, \{0\}, \{1\}, \{0, 1\}\}$ as the sigma algebra on S_X. This has associated sigma algebra $\{\phi, S, A, A^c\}$ in S. In this case, $P_X(\{1\}) = P(A)$ and $P_X(\{0\}) = P(A^c) = 1 - P(A)$.

Example 3.2. We toss two dice in which case the sample space is

$$S = \{(1, 1), (1, 2), \ldots, (6, 6)\}.$$

The natural sigma algebra on S would be the power set, let's say, $\mathcal{A}$, which contains $2^{36} - 1$ elements (excluding the empty set). We can define three random variables: the Sum (X), the Product of the outcomes (Y), and the first outcome (Z), which have associated outcomes:

$$S_X = \{2, 3, 4, 5, 6, 7, 8, 9, 10, 11, 12\}$$
$$S_Y = \{1, 2, 3, 4, 5, 6, 8, 9, 10, \ldots, 36\}$$
$$S_Z = \{1, 2, 3, 4, 5, 6\}.$$

The associated sigma algebra of X can be defined as the sigma algebra generated by the set

$$\left\{ X^{-1}(\{2\}), X^{-1}(\{3\}), \ldots, X^{-1}(\{12\}) \right\} \subset \mathcal{A}.$$

Note that this sigma algebra will not contain all the elements of $\mathcal{A}$. For example, consider

$$X^{-1}(\{3\}) = \{(1, 2), (2, 1)\}.$$

Although we will combine this set with its complement and take unions with other sets similarly defined, we will not be able to split $(1, 2)$, $(2, 1)$ apart, i.e., we will not see the singleton $\{(1, 2)\}$ in $\mathcal{A}_X$. Similar comments apply to Y. Now consider the random variable W with $W((1, 1)) = 1$, $W((1, 2)) = 2$, etc., for which

$$S_W = \{1, 2, 3, \ldots, 36\}.$$

In this case, $\mathcal{A}_W$ is the power set of S since there is a one to one relation between S and S_W. We have $\mathcal{A}_X \subset \mathcal{A}_W$, i.e., $\mathcal{A}_X$ is a coarser sigma algebra than $\mathcal{A}_W$, which is another way of saying that knowing W tells us more than knowing X. In fact, one can show that if $\mathcal{A}_X \subset \mathcal{A}_W$, then there is a measurable function f such that $X = f(W)$ and vice versa, Tucker (1967).

In the sequel we will distinguish between two polar cases: **discrete** and **continuous**. A discrete random variable takes values in a set that is equivalent to a subset of $\{0, 1, 2, \ldots\}$, i.e., has finite or countable cardinality, whereas a continuous random variable takes values in a set that is equivalent to $\mathbb{R}$ or to some interval $[a, b] \subset \mathbb{R}$. A more precise definition is given below.

3.2 DISTRIBUTION FUNCTIONS

Associated with each random variable X or probability measure P_X, there is its cumulative distribution function (c.d.f.)

$$F_X(x) = P_X((-\infty, x]) = P(\{a : X(a) \le x\}), \tag{3.3}$$

which is defined for all $x \in \mathbb{R}$. This function effectively replaces P_X. In the sequel, we only need this (apparently) less complete information to describe fully the random variable. Note how we can reconstruct P_X from F_X. For example $P_X([a, b]) = F_X(b) - F_X(a)$. We can then use the properties of probability measure to determine the probability of any Borel set on S_X.

In the sequel we will often denote probability by the causal notation $\Pr(X \le x)$ when it is not important to emphasize the specific probability measure.

Example 3.3. The logistic c.d.f. is defined for all $x \in \mathbb{R}$

$$F_X(x) = \frac{1}{1 + e^{-x}}. \tag{3.4}$$

It is continuous everywhere and asymptotes to 1 and 0 at $\pm\infty$ respectively. It is strictly increasing on $\mathbb{R}$. See Fig. 3.1.

Example 3.4. The die example ($X \in \{1, 2, 3, 4, 5, 6\}$ with equal probability), see Fig. 3.2

$$F(x) = \begin{cases} 0 & x < 1 \\ \frac{1}{6} & 1 \le x < 2 \\ \frac{2}{6} & 2 \le x < 3 \\ \frac{3}{6} & 3 \le x < 4 \\ \frac{4}{6} & 4 \le x < 5 \\ \frac{5}{6} & 5 \le x < 6 \\ 1 & 6 \le x \end{cases}$$

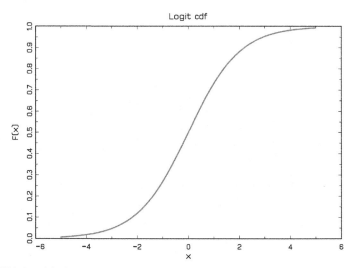

FIGURE 3.1 c.d.f. of the logit distribution

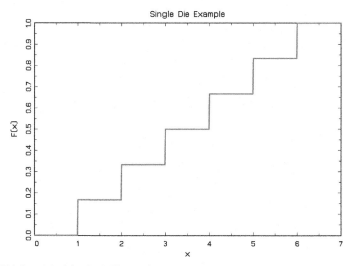

FIGURE 3.2 c.d.f. of the single die experiment

For any random variable X we have the following properties.

Theorem 3.1. *A function $F(\cdot)$ is the c.d.f. of a random variable X if and only if the following three conditions hold:*

1. $\lim_{x \to -\infty} F(x) = 0$ *and* $\lim_{x \to \infty} F(x) = 1$

2. F is a nondecreasing function of x, i.e., $F(x') \geq F(x)$ whenever $x' \geq x$

3. F is everywhere right-continuous, i.e., for all $x_0 \in \mathbb{R}$, $\lim_{x \downarrow x_0} F(x) = F(x_0)$.

Proof. Property (2) follows by the fact that

$$P(A) \leq P(B) \text{ if } A \subseteq B.$$

Properties (1) and (3) are consequences of the following result.

Lemma 3.1. *Let $A_n \subseteq A_{n+1} \subseteq \cdots$ [i.e., $A_n \uparrow$] with $\lim_{n \to \infty} A_n \equiv \bigcup_{n=1}^{\infty} A_n$. Let $B_n \supseteq B_{n+1} \supseteq \cdots$ [i.e., $B_n \downarrow$] with $\lim_{n \to \infty} B_n \equiv \bigcap_{n=1}^{\infty} B_n$. Then*

$$P(\lim_{n \to \infty} A_n) = \lim_{n \to \infty} P(A_n) \quad ; \quad P(\lim_{n \to \infty} B_n) = \lim_{n \to \infty} P(B_n).$$

Proof of Lemma. Define a sequence of sets

$$A_1' = A_1, \ A_2' = A_2 \backslash A_1, \ A_3' = A_3 \backslash A_2, A_1, \ldots$$

Then A_n' are disjoint sets such that for all m

$$\bigcup_{n=1}^{m} A_n' = \bigcup_{n=1}^{m} A_n.$$

It follows that

$$P\left(\bigcup_{n=1}^{m} A_n'\right) = \sum_{n=1}^{m} P(A_n').$$

Pass to the limit

$$P\left(\bigcup_{n=1}^{\infty} A_n\right) = P\left(\bigcup_{n=1}^{\infty} A_n'\right) = \sum_{n=1}^{\infty} P(A_n')$$

$$= \lim_{m \to \infty} \sum_{n=1}^{m} P(A_n') = \lim_{m \to \infty} \sum_{n=1}^{m} P(A_n) = \lim_{m \to \infty} P(A_m). \quad \square$$

We return to the proof of property (1). Define a sequence of decreasing sets $B_n = \{s : X(s) \leq -n\}$. Then

$$\bigcap_{n=1}^{\infty} B_n = \phi$$

so that $\lim_{x \to -\infty} F(x) = \lim_{n \to \infty} \Pr[B_n] = \Pr[\phi] = 0$ as required.

Proof of (3). Let $A = \{s : X(s) \leq x_0\}$, where $P(A) = F_X(x_0)$. Define also

$$A_n = \{s : X(s) \leq x_0 + \tfrac{1}{n}\} = A \cup B_n,$$

where $B_n = \{s : X(s) \in (x_0, x_0 + \frac{1}{n})\}$. Then, $P(A_n) = P(A) + P(B_n)$, where

$$\lim_{n \to \infty} P(B_n) = 0 \text{ because } \bigcap_{n=1}^{\infty} B_n = \phi. \qquad \square$$

A consequence of property 3 is that F is continuous except possibly at a countable set of points, which we now show. Let D be the set of discontinuity points of F. For each $x \in D$, let q_x be the rational number such that

$$\Pr(X < x) < q_x < \Pr(X \le x). \qquad (3.5)$$

Such an q_x exists by the properties of any two distinct real numbers. If $x, y \in D$, with $x < y$, then $q_x < q_y$. This says that there is a one to one relationship between the set of discontinuity points and a subset of the set of rational numbers, which says that the set of discontinuity points is itself countable.

We may say that a random variable is continuous if its distribution function $F_X(x)$ is a continuous function everywhere. We say that a random variable is discrete if its distribution function is a step function, which is continuous from the right but discontinuous (it jumps) from the left. We next give a formal way of measuring the contribution of continuous and discontinuous components to a distribution.

Definition 3.2. Let $D = \{x_i, i = 1, \ldots, \infty\}$ denote the countable set of points of discontinuity of F_X. Define the following

$$\tau_X = \sum_{i=1}^{\infty} \Pr(X \le x_i) - \Pr(X < x_i). \qquad (3.6)$$

A continuous random variable has $\tau_X = 0$. A discrete random variable has $\tau_X = 1$. A mixed random variable (with both continuous and discrete components) would have $0 < \tau_X < 1$. We will see later some examples of these different types of random variables.

For a continuous random variable we have

$$\Pr(a < X < b) = \Pr(a < X \le b) = \Pr(a \le X < b)$$

for any a, b. Furthermore, for any **countable** set, say $\mathbb{Q} = \cup_{i=1}^{\infty} \{x_i\}$, we have

$$\Pr(X \in \mathbb{Q}) = \Pr\left(X \in \cup_{i=1}^{\infty} \{x_i\}\right) = \sum_{i=1}^{\infty} \Pr(X \in \{x_i\}) = 0.$$

This says for example that the probability that a continuous random variable equals a rational number is zero. This may be hard to swallow, but it is a consequence of the definitions we have given. In fact, events of probability zero happen all the time. What is meant here is that after the fact $X = x$ for some value x so that one could say that the event $\{x\}$ had occurred even though **ex ante** it could only happen with probability zero.[2] This is taking the logic of probability to extremes.

Definition 3.3. X and Y are **identically distributed** if

$$P(X \in A) = P(Y \in A) \text{ for all } A \in \mathcal{A}$$
$$\Leftrightarrow F_X(x) = F_Y(x) \ \forall x \in \mathbb{R}.$$

This doesn't mean that $X = Y$, only that their distributions are equal. In cases where distributions are not equal we may be interested in ordering them, i.e., saying which one is "bigger". Let X and Y be two random variables (incomes, returns/prospects at either two different points in time, or for different regions or countries, or with or without a program (treatment)).

Definition 3.4. We say that X **First Order Stochastically Dominates** Y, denoted $X \succeq_{FSD} Y$, if for all x

$$F_X(x) \leq F_Y(x) \quad \text{or} \quad 1 - F_X(x) \geq 1 - F_Y(x)$$

with strict inequality for some x. This has an interpretation in terms of expected utility theory, see below. This is only a **partial order** on the set of distribution functions.

Fig. 3.3 shows two distributions where blue dominates red.

3.3 QUANTILE

The quantile function $Q_X : [0, 1] \to \mathbb{R}$ is intended to be the inverse of the c.d.f., specifically, $Q_X(\alpha)$ should be the real number that solves the equation

$$\Pr(X \leq Q_X(\alpha)) = F_X(Q_X(\alpha)) = \alpha. \tag{3.7}$$

Note that $Q_X(1/2)$ is called the **median**, and sometimes denoted by M, while $Q_X(3/4)$ is the **upper quartile**, and $Q_X(1/4)$ is the **lower quartile**.

In fact, there may be: (a) no solution to (3.7); (b) a unique solution; or (c) many solutions. When F_X is continuous and strictly increasing at the point

---

2. Similarly, every week someone wins the lottery even though ex ante their probability of winning was very small.

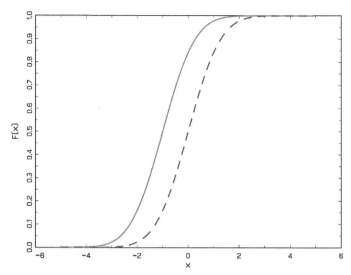

FIGURE 3.3 Comparison between two c.d.f.s. (For interpretation of the references to colour in this figure, the reader is referred to the web version of this article.)

$x = Q_X(\alpha)$, then the quantile exists and is uniquely defined. Since in this case, $Q_X = F_X^{-1}$ exists, we can alternatively write for example $M = F_X^{-1}\left(\frac{1}{2}\right)$.

Example 3.5. For the logit case (3.4) we have

$$Q_X(\alpha) = \ln\left(\frac{\alpha}{1-\alpha}\right)$$

for all $\alpha \in [0, 1]$ and in particular $M = Q_X(1/2) = 0$ (the distribution is actually symmetric about zero). See Fig. 3.4.

For discrete random variables, there may be many values that satisfy this equation or there may be none. Suppose that

$$X = \begin{cases} 0 & 1/3 \\ 1 & 1/3 \\ 2 & 1/3. \end{cases}$$

Then there does not exist an M with $F_X(M) = 1/2$. Also, in the die case any $3 \le M < 4$ is a median according to the above definition.

The case (c), where (3.7) has many solutions, can occur for both continuous and discrete random variables. In this case, F_X has a flat spot at the point of interest.

We modify the definition of quantile below to ensure that there always is a unique value.

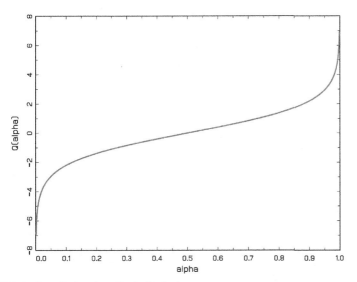

FIGURE 3.4 Quantile function of logit distribution

Definition 3.5. For any $\alpha \in [0, 1]$, let

$$Q_X(\alpha) = \inf\{x : F_X(x) \geq \alpha\}.$$

Then we can see that this quantity is well defined for all c.d.f.'s F_X. In general, $F_X(Q_X(\alpha)) \geq \alpha$. In the case that F_X is strictly increasing, then this definition coincides with the previous one, namely $F_X(Q_X(\alpha)) = F_X(F_X^{-1}(\alpha)) = \alpha$.

Some alternative definitions of the quantile function are (for all $\alpha \in [0, 1]$):

$$Q_X^*(\alpha) = \sup\{x : F_X(x) \leq \alpha\} \quad ; \quad Q_X^\dagger(\alpha) = \frac{Q_X^*(\alpha) + Q_X(\alpha)}{2}.$$

In the die example, $Q_X(1/2) = 3$, $Q_X^*(1/2) = 4$, while $Q_X^\dagger(1/2) = 3.5$. Therefore, $F_X(Q_X(1/2)) = 1/2$ but $F_X(Q_X^*(1/2)) = 2/3$.

Example 3.6. Suppose that

$$X = \begin{cases} 0 & 1/3 \\ 1 & 1/3 \\ 2 & 1/3 \end{cases},$$

we have

$$Q_X(\alpha) = Q_X^*(\alpha) = Q_X^\dagger(\alpha) = \begin{cases} 0 & \alpha \leq 1/3 \\ 1 & 1/3 < \alpha \leq 2/3 \\ 2 & 2/3 < \alpha. \end{cases}$$

In this case,

$$F_X(Q_X(\alpha)) = \begin{cases} 1/3 & \alpha \leq 1/3 \\ 2/3 & 1/3 < \alpha \leq 2/3 \\ 1 & 2/3 < \alpha. \end{cases}$$

Theorem 3.2. *Properties of Q_X.*

1. $\lim_{\alpha \to 0} Q_X(\alpha) = L$ *and* $\lim_{\alpha \to 1} Q_X(\alpha) = U$, *where L, U are the lower and upper bounds on the support of the random variable, e.g., $L = -\infty$ and $R = \infty$*

2. Q_X *is a nondecreasing function of α, i.e., $Q_X(\alpha') \geq Q_X(\alpha)$ whenever $\alpha' \geq \alpha$*

3. Q_X *is everywhere left-continuous, i.e., for all α_0, $\lim_{\alpha \uparrow \alpha_0} Q_X(\alpha) = Q_X(\alpha_0)$.*

When X is continuously distributed, the quantile function is not necessarily continuous. Specifically, when the c.d.f. has a flat spot, the generalized inverse will have a jump at the right end of the flat spot. If F_X is strictly increasing, then the quantile function is continuous.

We are often interested in tail quantiles such as $Q_X(\alpha/2)$ and $Q_X(1 - \alpha/2)$ for α quite small.

Definition 3.6. A random variable X is symmetrically distributed about the point M if

$$M - Q_X(\alpha/2) = Q_X(1 - \alpha/2) - M$$

for all $\alpha \in [0, 1]$. Clearly, $M = Q_X(\alpha/2)$. For example, when $M = 0$, we have $Q_X(\alpha/2) = -Q_X(1 - \alpha/2)$. This property is used in testing and inference questions.

The **Lorenz curve** of a random variable is defined (provided the integrals exist) as

$$L(\alpha) = \frac{\int_0^\alpha Q_X(t)dt}{\int_0^1 Q_X(t)dt},$$

which is widely used in measuring inequality, when X is income or some other well-being measures. The **Gini coefficient** can be defined as

$$G = 1 - 2\int_0^1 L(\alpha)d\alpha.$$

This is a number between zero and one with one indicating complete inequality and zero indicating complete equality. For example, in 2012, the UK had $G = 0.32$, while China has $G = 42.1$.

3.4 DENSITY AND MASS FUNCTIONS

Suppose that the probability measure P_X of the random variable X (or equivalently the c.d.f. F_X) is absolutely continuous with respect to a measure μ, that is: for any set A, $P_X(A) = 0$, whenever $\mu(A) = 0$. Then the **Radon–Nikodym Theorem** guarantees that there exists a function f_X, called the density of F_X with respect to μ, that is measurable with respect to μ such that

$$F_X = \int f_X d\mu, \tag{3.8}$$

where the integral is the **Lebesgue integral**. This is more general than the ordinary **Riemann integral** that one learns in high school calculus, but the sequence of steps to defining it is similar.[3] We write $f_X = dF_X/d\mu$; note that the density is uniquely defined by this except on sets of measure zero according to μ because such points cannot change the value of the integral (3.8). We may instead define f_X explicitly as

$$f_X(x) = \lim_{\epsilon \downarrow 0} \frac{P_X([x - \epsilon, x + \epsilon])}{\mu([x - \epsilon, x + \epsilon])} \tag{3.9}$$

when this limit exists. Note that the limit may be infinite at a point, and we will see an example of this later.

There are two leading cases regarding μ. In the purely discrete case with support the set $\{x_1, x_2, \ldots\}$, we may take μ to be the **counting measure** with $\mu(\{x_i\}) = 1$ for $i = 1, 2, \ldots$. In that case, we obtain

$$f_X(x) = \Pr(X = x),$$

which is called the **probability mass function** (p.m.f.). This gives the height of jumps in the c.d.f., that is, $f_X(x) = \Pr(X \leq x) - \Pr(X < x)$, which is equal to zero except at $x \in \{x_1, x_2, \ldots\}$.

In the purely continuous case, with support (a, b) with $-\infty \leq a < b \leq \infty$, we take μ to be the Lebesgue measure on (a, b). In that case, we obtain the **probability density function** (p.d.f. or density for short) f_X, which is a measurable mapping from $\mathbb{R} \to \mathbb{R}_+$ such that

$$F_X(x) = \int_a^x f_X(t)dt, \tag{3.10}$$

where this is a Riemann integral.

---

3. First define it for simple functions (indicator functions), then for linear combinations of these, and then passing to a limit.

We continue the discussion for the purely continuous case. If the c.d.f. $F_X(\cdot)$ is differentiable at the point x, then

$$f_X(x) = \frac{dF_X(x)}{dx},$$

which follows from the **fundamental theorem of calculus**. However, F_X need not be differentiable everywhere.

Example 3.7. Consider the following c.d.f. on $[0, 1]$

$$F_X(x) = \begin{cases} ax & \text{if } x < m \\ b + cx & \text{if } m \leq x \leq 1, \end{cases}$$

where $m \in [0, 1]$ and $a, c > 0$. In fact, we must have $b + c = 1$ for F_X to be a c.d.f. We suppose that $am = b + cm$, which ensures that F_X is continuous everywhere, and is absolutely continuous with respect to Lebesgue measure. However, F_X may not be differentiable at $x = m$, although it is differentiable everywhere else on $[0, 1]$. In this case we can define the density function as

$$f_X(x) = \begin{cases} a & \text{if } x < m \\ \lambda & \text{if } x = m \\ c & \text{if } m < x \leq 1, \end{cases}$$

where according to (3.9) $\lambda = (a + c)/2$. However, since it is only a single point it doesn't really matter what value we take for λ in the sense that it does not affect the value of integrals. Fig. 3.5 shows the case $m = 1/2$ and $a = 0.2$ where we take $\lambda = c$.

It can be shown that the set of points at which F_X is not differentiable is countable. Therefore, we can define the density function by differentiation almost everywhere except for a countable set of points. This countable set of points does not affect the value of integrals of otherwise continuous functions. At those tricky points we can set the density to some arbitrary value.

Theorem 3.3. *Properties of $f_X(x)$*

1. $f_X(x) \geq 0$ *for both continuous and discrete*
2. $f_X(x) \leq 1$ *for discrete only*
3. $\sum_x f_X(x) = 1$ *or* $\int_{-\infty}^{\infty} f_X(x)dx = 1$.

The density function may be discontinuous and it may be unbounded at certain points (see the Beta distribution below), although most examples we encounter are bounded and continuous on their domains.

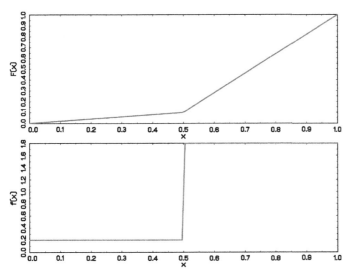

FIGURE 3.5   c.d.f. and density function of example

Specifying the density is often the starting point in modelling. An important related quantity is the **hazard** function (or failure rate), $\lambda(x)$, which is defined as

$$\lambda(x) = \frac{f(x)}{S(x)},$$

where $S(x) = 1 - F(x)$ is called the **survivor function**. This satisfies $\lambda(x) \geq 0$, but does not necessarily lie between zero and one and does not integrate to one. If X were the age of death of an individual or the time of failure of an engineering system, then $\lambda(x)$ measures the rate at which failure occurs given that failure has not yet occurred. Human mortality has a sort of a v shaped hazard: infant mortality rate is high followed by a reduction throughout childhood and then an increase during teenage years with a plateau followed by a sustained increase through later life. That is, initially there is negative **duration dependence** ($\lambda'(x) < 0$) followed by positive duration dependence ($\lambda'(x) > 0$). Failure rates are important factors in the insurance, finance, biostatistics, commerce and regulatory industries and fundamental to the design of safe systems in a wide variety of applications.

Chapter 4

Transformations of Random Variables

4.1 DISTRIBUTIONS OF FUNCTIONS OF A RANDOM VARIABLE

In this chapter we will focus on the continuous case (i.e., $F_X(\cdot)$ is absolutely continuous with respect to Lebesgue measure) and the discrete case (absolutely continuous with respect to counting measure). In the continuous case we can use the ordinary **Riemann integration**

$$\int_a^b f_X(x)dx,$$

which only requires the function f to be continuous on the interval $[a, b]$. In this case, we can apply the standard tools of calculus. A proper treatment of more general situations requires Lebesgue integration theory in which we achieve a unification of the continuous and discrete cases, but we shall not pursue this further here.

If X is a random variable with c.d.f. $F_X(x)$, then any real-valued **measurable** function of X (in the sense of (3.1)), say $Y = g(X)$, is also a random variable, and we can define

$$P_Y(B) = \Pr(Y \in B) = \Pr(g(X) \in B)$$

for any set B in the relevant sigma-algebra. Specifically, we have $P_Y((-\infty, y]) = \Pr(g(X) \le y)$. This probability depends on P_X and $g(X)$. Continuous functions are measurable, but measurable functions need not be continuous. For example the function $g(x) = 1(x > 0)$ is not continuous at $x = 0$, but it is a measurable mapping.

Often we want to work with a normal distribution which has support the entire real line. If $X > 0$ [e.g., price] or $X \in [0, 1]$ [e.g., infant mortality], then this would be logically inconsistent, i.e., X could not have a normal distribution. But if we take $Y = \ln X$ (in the case where $X > 0$), and $Y = \ln \frac{X}{1-X}$ (in the case where for $X \in (0, 1)$), then in both cases the transformed random variable Y may have support $\mathbb{R}$, and therefore be consistent with a normal distribution. These transformations are often used in modelling.

Probability, Statistics and Econometrics. http://dx.doi.org/10.1016/B978-0-12-810495-8.00005-1

What we want to do is to express $\Pr(Y \le y)$ in terms of F_X and g, likewise to find a nice expression for the density function f_Y of the random variable Y. This is important for many applications in statistics, especially models where we specify distribution for unobservable error terms ε, but are interesting in the distribution of the observed variables Y, which are functions of ε. In some cases, the answer can be found immediately.

Example 4.1. Suppose that

$$Y = a + bX$$

where a, b are constants and X is a scalar random variable. Then

$$\Pr(Y \le y) = \Pr(a + bX \le y)$$
$$= \Pr\left(X \le \frac{y - a}{b}\right)$$
$$= F_X\left(\frac{y - a}{b}\right),$$

provided $b > 0$. When $b < 0$, $\Pr(Y \le y) = 1 - F_X\left(\frac{y-a}{b}\right)$. The density function can be found from the fact that $f_Y(y) = \partial \Pr(Y \le y)/\partial y$, which gives

$$f_Y(y) = \frac{1}{|b|} f_X\left(\frac{y - a}{b}\right)$$

for any $b \ne 0$.

Example 4.2. Normal distribution. Suppose that

$$f_X(x) = \frac{1}{\sqrt{2\pi\sigma^2}} \exp\left(-\frac{1}{2}\left(\frac{x - \mu}{\sigma}\right)^2\right)$$

we say that $X \sim N(\mu, \sigma^2)$. Then it follows that

$$Y = \frac{X - \mu}{\sigma} \sim N(0, 1)$$

i.e.,

$$f_Y(y) = \frac{1}{\sqrt{2\pi}} \exp\left(-\frac{1}{2}y^2\right).$$

Conversely, $X = \mu + \sigma Y \sim N(\mu, \sigma^2)$ when Y is standard normal.

Example 4.3. Uniform distribution. Suppose that $X \sim U[0, 1]$ meaning that

$$f_X(x) = \begin{cases} 1 & \text{if } x \in [0, 1] \\ 0 & \text{else.} \end{cases}$$

Then

$$Y = a + bX \sim U[a, a+b]$$

in which case

$$f_Y(y) = \begin{cases} \frac{1}{b} & \text{if } y \in [a, a+b] \\ 0 & \text{else.} \end{cases}$$

For the same example. What about $Y = X^\alpha$ for any $\alpha \neq 0$? We have

$$\Pr(Y \leq y) = \Pr(X^\alpha \leq y) = \Pr(X \leq y^{1/\alpha}) = y^{1/\alpha}.$$

Therefore,

$$f_Y(y) = \begin{cases} \frac{1}{\alpha} y^{1/\alpha - 1} & \text{if } y \in [0, 1] \\ 0 & \text{else.} \end{cases}$$

A linear function is an example of a **strictly monotonic** function. Another monotonic function is the logarithm $y = \ln X$ for $X > 0$. In this case,

$$\Pr(Y \leq y) = \Pr(\ln X \leq y) = \Pr(X \leq e^y) = F_X(e^y)$$

because $\ln X \leq y \Leftrightarrow X \leq e^y$. The density function is

$$f_Y(y) = f_X(e^y)e^y.$$

Example 4.4. Suppose that $y = X^2$ with $X \in \mathbb{R}$. This is not a monotonic function on $\mathbb{R}$, but it is monotonic on the two subsets $\mathbb{R}_+$ and $\mathbb{R}_-$, which together constitute $\mathbb{R}$. We have by the law of total probability

$$\Pr(Y \leq y) = \Pr(X^2 \leq y) = \Pr(X^2 \leq y, \ X > 0) + \Pr(X^2 \leq y, \ X < 0).$$

But on the set $x > 0$, $y = x^2$ is monotonic with inverse $x = \sqrt{y}$. Therefore,

$$\begin{aligned} \Pr(X^2 \leq y) &= \Pr(X \leq \sqrt{y}, X > 0) + \Pr(-X \geq \sqrt{y}, \ X < 0) \\ &= \Pr(-\sqrt{y} \leq X \leq \sqrt{y}) \\ &= F_X(\sqrt{y}) - F_X(-\sqrt{y}). \end{aligned}$$

The density function is

$$f_Y(y) = \frac{1}{2\sqrt{y}} f_X(\sqrt{y}) + \frac{1}{2\sqrt{y}} f_X(-\sqrt{y}). \tag{4.1}$$

Example 4.5. Suppose that $X > 0$ and consider $Y = X^{-1}$. Then

$$F_Y(y) = \Pr(Y \le y) = \Pr\left(X \ge \frac{1}{y}\right) = 1 - F_X\left(\frac{1}{y}\right)$$

$$f_Y(y) = \frac{1}{y^2} f_X\left(\frac{1}{y}\right).$$

We try now to provide some results for the general case $Y = g(X)$. We must be more precise about the **domain** and **range** of the function. Define

$$S = \{x \in \mathcal{X} : f_X(x) > 0\} \text{ and } \mathcal{Y} = \{y : y = g(x) \text{ for some } x \in S\}.$$

These sets are called the support of the random variables X and Y. For example, suppose that $Y = X^2$, where $X \in \mathcal{X} = \mathbb{R}$. Then, $\mathcal{Y} = [0, \infty)$. Now consider the function

$$g : \mathcal{X} \to \mathcal{Y}.$$

If g is **one-to-one** and **onto**, then $g^{-1} : \mathcal{Y} \to \mathcal{X}$ is well-defined, but in general,

$$g^{-1} : \text{elements of } \mathcal{Y} \to \text{subsets of } S$$

$$g^{-1}(y) = \{x \in S : g(x) = y\}, \ y \in A.$$

We talk about $g^{-1}(A) = \{x \in S : g(x) \in A\}$, which is well-defined as a set-valued mapping. Now we say

$$P_Y(A) = P_X(g^{-1}(A)) = \Pr(g(X) \in A).$$

We have already done the same thing when we defined random variables. We can show that $P_Y(\cdot)$ is a probability measure, e.g., it is countably additive. This formula will not generally lead to a density function for Y unless additional structure is present.

Monotonic functions [or functions that are monotonic within a partition] allow a more developed theory that gives the density function $f_Y(y)$ of the random variable $Y = g(X)$ using the standard theory of change of variables for integration.

Theorem 4.1. *1. Suppose that the density f_X and the inverse function $g^{-1}(\cdot)$ are well-defined and continuously differentiable. Then*

$$F_Y(y) = \begin{cases} F_X(g^{-1}(y)) & \text{if } g \text{ is increasing} \\ 1 - F_X(g^{-1}(y)) & \text{if } g \text{ is decreasing} \end{cases}$$

$$f_Y(y) = f_X(g^{-1}(y)) \left| \frac{d}{dy} g^{-1}(y) \right|$$

is defined for $y \in \mathcal{Y}$.

2. *Suppose that there is a partition $\{S_i\}_{i=0}^k$ of S such that $\Pr(X \in X_0) = 0$ and f_X is continuous on each S_i. Further suppose that there exist functions g_i defined on S_i with $g_i(x) = g(x)$ for $x \in S_i$ such that the inverse functions $g_i^{-1}(\cdot)$ are well defined and continuously differentiable. Then,*

$$F_Y(y) = \sum_{i=1}^{k} \Pr(X \le g_i^{-1}(y), X \in X_i)$$

$$f_Y(y) = \sum_{i=1}^{k} f_X(g_i^{-1}(y)) \left| \frac{d}{dy} g_i^{-1}(y) \right|.$$

We give some examples and discussion.

Example 4.6. $Y = X^2$, then $k = 2$, $S_1 = (-\infty, 0]$, $S_2 = (0, \infty)$, $\mathcal{Y} \in [0, \infty)$. Furthermore,

$$\left. \begin{array}{l} g_i(x) = x^2, \ i = 1, 2 \\ g_i^{-1}(y) = \sqrt{y} \end{array} \right\},$$

and $f_Y(y)$ is as defined in (4.1).

Example 4.7. Suppose that $Y = aX^2 + bX + c$. The function is monotonic on the two sides of the point $x = -b/2a$. The g_i^{-1} functions are found as the solutions to a quadratic equation, i.e.,

$$g_i^{-1}(y) = x = \frac{-b \pm \sqrt{b^2 - 4a(c - y)}}{2a}.$$

Example 4.8. The Box–Cox transform

$$y = \begin{cases} \frac{x^\lambda - 1}{\lambda} & \lambda > 0 \\ \log x & \lambda = 0 \end{cases},$$

which is defined for $x > 0$. The inverse transform g^{-1} is defined and monotonic for $y \ge -1/\lambda$. This is an important transformation in econometrics and statistics.

$$f_Y(y) = \begin{cases} f_X((y\lambda + 1)^{1/\lambda})(y\lambda + 1)^{(1-\lambda)/\lambda} & \lambda > 0 \\ f_X(\exp(y)) \exp(y) & \lambda = 0 \end{cases}.$$

Example 4.9. In option pricing theory, one is interested in transformations such as

$$Y = \max\{X - K, 0\},$$

where X is a continuously distributed random variable, the stock price, and K is a fixed number. In this case, Y has a distribution that has both discrete and continuous features. Specifically, $\Pr(Y = 0) = \Pr(X \leq K) > 0$, while for $y > 0$

$$F_Y(y) = F_X(y - K) \quad ; \quad f_Y(y) = f_X(y - K).$$

Example 4.10. Finally, suppose that $X \in \mathbb{R}$ and

$$Y = 1(X \in A) = \begin{cases} 1 & \text{if } X \in A \subseteq \mathbb{R} \\ 0 & \text{otherwise} \end{cases}.$$

We can't apply the density theory here, since Y is discrete while X was continuous. Nevertheless, the distribution of Y is obvious,

$$P_Y(\{1\}) = \Pr(X \in A) = P_X(A).$$

4.2 PROBABILITY INTEGRAL TRANSFORM

Theorem 4.2. *Let X have a continuous c.d.f. $F_X(x)$ and let $Y = F_X(X)$. Then Y is uniformly distributed on $[0, 1]$, that is for all $y \in [0, 1]$*

$$\Pr(Y \leq y) = y.$$

Proof. Although this is true for any continuous c.d.f. we just give the proof in the case that $F_X(\cdot)$ is strictly increasing. We have

$$\begin{aligned} \Pr(Y \leq y) &= \Pr(F_X(X) \leq y) \\ &= \Pr(F_X^{-1}[F_X(X)] \leq F_X^{-1}(y)) \\ &= \Pr(X \leq F_X^{-1}(y)) \\ &= F_X(F_X^{-1}(y)) \\ &= y. \end{aligned} \qquad \square$$

Corollary 4.1. *Suppose that X has a continuous c.d.f. F_X and that U is uniformly distributed on $[0, 1]$. Then the random variable $Y = F_X^{-1}(U)$ has the distribution of X.*

This result is used a lot in doing simulations: most programs give you a uniform random number generator and a normal random number generator, but for more exotic distributions you are on your own. For example, suppose you want to generate Logistic random variables. We have $F_X(x) = 1/(1 + \exp(-x))$ so that $F_X^{-1}(y) = \ln(y/(1 - y))$. Therefore, $\ln(U/(1 - U))$ has the logit distribution when U is uniform.

Corollary 4.2. *Suppose that X, Y are continuous random variables with strictly increasing c.d.f.'s F_X, F_Y respectively. Then we can write $Y = h(X)$, where $h = F_Y^{-1}(F_X)$.*

Chapter 5

The Expectation

5.1 DEFINITION AND PROPERTIES

The expectation of a random variable with bounded support, meaning $|X| \leq M$, always exists and is finite. Suppose that the probability measure P_X of the random variable X is absolutely continuous with respect to a measure μ, then the expectation is in general defined through the Lebesgue integral

$$E(X) = \int x \, dF_X(x). \tag{5.1}$$

This is also often denoted by $\int X(s) \, dP(s)$. We will focus on the two leading cases where we can give simpler more explicit definitions.

In the continuous case we have

$$E(X) = \int x f_X(x) \, dx, \tag{5.2}$$

where f_X is the p.d.f., whereas in the discrete case

$$E(X) = \sum_x x f_X(x), \tag{5.3}$$

where f_X is the p.m.f. We sometimes forget to include the brackets and write EX for example.

We now consider the general case when the support of the random variable is unbounded. In this case, one must take limits of a sequence of cases with bounded supports, and one may find that the limit is not necessarily finite and may not even be **well-defined**. We will briefly make a distinction between these cases.

Definition 5.1. If $\int_{-\infty}^{\infty} |x| f_X(x) \, dx < \infty$, then we say that the expectation of X exists, and is denoted by $E(X)$. If $\int_0^{\infty} x f_X(x) \, dx = \infty$ and $\int_{-\infty}^{0} x f_X(x) \, dx > -\infty$, then we say that the expectation exists but $E(X) = \infty$. If $\int_0^{\infty} x f_X(x) \, dx < \infty$ and $\int_{-\infty}^{0} x f_X(x) \, dx = -\infty$, then we say that the expectation exists but $E(X) = -\infty$. If $\int_0^{\infty} x f_X(x) \, dx = \infty$ and $\int_{-\infty}^{0} x f_X(x) \, dx = -\infty$, then $E(X)$

Probability, Statistics and Econometrics. http://dx.doi.org/10.1016/B978-0-12-810495-8.00006-3

43

is not defined, i.e., it does not exist. When the expectation exists, we define it as

$$E(X) = \int_{-\infty}^{\infty} x f_X(x) dx,$$

noting that it can be plus or minus infinity. If X is discrete, we replace integrals by sums in the above.

For a general random variable $X \in \mathbb{R}$ we can decompose it into its positive and negative parts

$$X = X_+ - X_-,$$

where $X_+ = \max\{X, 0\} \geq 0$ is called the positive part and $X_- = \max\{-X, 0\} \geq 0$ is called the negative part. We then say that the expectation of X exists if the expectation of X_+ and X_- are both finite or if only one or other but not both is infinite.

Expectation is a measure of the average value or "central tendency" of a random variable or distribution.

We next give some examples

Example 5.1. Uniform distribution $X \sim U[0, a]$ i.e.,

$$f_X(x) = \begin{cases} \frac{1}{a} & \text{if } 0 \leq x \leq a \\ 0 & \text{else.} \end{cases}$$

This has

$$E(X) = \int_0^a x f_X(x) dx = \frac{1}{a} \int_0^a x dx = \frac{1}{a} \left[\frac{x^2}{2} \right]_0^a = \frac{a}{2}.$$

Example 5.2. Normal or Gaussian distribution. Suppose that

$$f_X(x) = \frac{1}{\sqrt{2\pi\sigma^2}} \exp\left(-\frac{1}{2} \left(\frac{x - \mu}{\sigma} \right)^2 \right)$$

we say that $X \sim N(\mu, \sigma^2)$. This has

$$E(X) = \int_{-\infty}^{\infty} x f_X(x) dx = \mu.$$

For the special case $\mu = 0$ and $\sigma^2 = 1$ we have

$$
\begin{aligned}
E(X) &= \frac{1}{\sqrt{2\pi}} \int_{-\infty}^{\infty} x \exp\left(-\frac{1}{2}x^2\right) dx \\
&= \frac{1}{\sqrt{2\pi}} \int_{-\infty}^{0} x \exp\left(-\frac{1}{2}x^2\right) dx + \frac{1}{\sqrt{2\pi}} \int_{0}^{\infty} x \exp\left(-\frac{1}{2}x^2\right) dx \\
&= -\frac{1}{\sqrt{2\pi}} \int_{0}^{\infty} x \exp\left(-\frac{1}{2}x^2\right) dx + \frac{1}{\sqrt{2\pi}} \int_{0}^{\infty} x \exp\left(-\frac{1}{2}x^2\right) dx \\
&= 0,
\end{aligned}
$$

by symmetry; or use a change of variables $u = x^2/2$.

Example 5.3 (Cauchy). Suppose that for all x

$$
f_X(x) = \frac{1}{\pi} \frac{1}{1+x^2}.
$$

This density is symmetric about zero, and so $\int_{-a}^{a} x f_X(x)dx = 0$ for all a. One is tempted to say that $E(X) = \lim \int_{-a}^{a} x f_X(x)dx = 0$, but

$$
\int_{0}^{\infty} x f_X(x)dx = \infty \text{ and } \int_{-\infty}^{0} x f_X(x)dx = -\infty,
$$

so $E(X) = \lim \int_{-a}^{b} x f_X(x)dx$ is not well defined. However, $E|X| = \infty$ (it does exist but is equal to infinity; we just say for simplicity the expectation does not exist). The median is zero, because the distribution is symmetric about zero.

We also wish to define higher moments, say $E(X^4)$, and we use the following definition.

Definition 5.2. We define for any (measurable) function g such that $\int_{-\infty}^{\infty} |g(x)| f_X(x)dx < \infty$

$$
E(g(X)) = \int_{-\infty}^{\infty} g(x) f_X(x)dx. \tag{5.4}
$$

We may also consider the random variable $Y = g(X)$ and obtain its density function $f_Y(y)$ or mass function and then define its expectation by the definition $E(Y) = \int_{-\infty}^{\infty} y f_Y(y)dy$. These two definitions can be shown to be the same, which can be proven by a change of variables argument.

Whether the moments of a random variable exist or not is a question with some practical implications, because it relates to the likelihood of observing extreme values. For example, some authors have argued that for daily stock returns $E(|X|^4) = \infty$, but $E(|X|^3) < \infty$. A sufficient condition for $EX^k < \infty$

for positive random variable X is that $1 - F_X(x) \leq Cx^{-(j-1)}$ for some constant C and $j > k + 1$.

Example 5.4. ST. PETERSBURG PARADOX. Suppose you toss a fair coin until the first head shows up in which case you win $\$2^{k-1}$, where k is the number of tosses until the first head shows up. Your expected winnings are

$$E(X) = \sum_{k=1}^{\infty} 2^{k-1} \times \frac{1}{2^k} = \infty.$$

An alternative version of this is the well known Doubling strategy for coin tossing. First bet \$1 on heads, if lose, bet \$2 on heads; if lose, bet \$4 etc. If one assumes one can continue indefinitely, you always make \$1. Although you always win, the expected amount of capital needed to play is infinite. In fact, for finite capital one can show that the probability of going bankrupt is one.

However, Bernoulli showed in 1738 that

$$E(\log X) = \sum_{k=1}^{\infty} \log(2^{k-1}) \frac{1}{2^k} = \log(2) < \infty.$$

This says that the value of the game for logarithmic utility is $\log(2)$. However, for log utility there exist other games that would have infinite expectation.

Theorem 5.1. *Expectation has the following properties:*

1. [Linearity] For measurable functions g_1, g_2, and constants α_1, α_2, and α_3

$$E(\alpha_1 g_1(X) + \alpha_2 g_2(X) + \alpha_3) = \alpha_1 E(g_1(X)) + \alpha_2 E(g_2(X)) + \alpha_3.$$

2. [Monotonicity] If $g_1(x) \geq g_2(x)$ for all $x \Rightarrow Eg_1(X) \geq Eg_2(X)$.
3. Jensen's inequality. If $g(x)$ is a (weakly) convex function, i.e., $g(\lambda x + (1 - \lambda)y) \leq \lambda g(x) + (1 - \lambda)g(y)$ for all x, y, and all λ with $0 \leq \lambda \leq 1$, then

$$E[g(X)] \geq g[E(X)].$$

Conversely, if $g(x)$ is a (weakly) concave function, then $E[g(X)] \leq g[E(X)]$.

Proof. Let $a + bx$ be the tangent line to the curve $g(x)$ at the point $g(E(X))$. Then $g(x) \geq a + bx$, for all x by the definition of convexity. It follows from property (2) that

$$E[g(X)] \geq a + bE(X) = g(E(X)). \qquad \square$$

Remarks. 1. Two important examples for property (3). First, $E|X| \geq |EX|$, in fact $|EX|$ is exactly zero for any random variable with zero mean, whereas $E|X| > 0$ unless $X = 0$ with probability one. Consider $\log X$. In this case $-\log X$ is convex (i.e., log is concave). Therefore,

$$E(-\log X) = -E(\log X) \geq -\log EX \Leftrightarrow \log EX \geq E \log X.$$

2. Utility functions are (usually) assumed to be concave, which means that

$$E[U(X)] \leq U(E(X))$$

for any random variable X for which the expectations are well-defined, i.e., you prefer a sure thing with the same expected value to an uncertain prospect with the same expected value but some risk of losing, aka **risk aversion**.

3. More generally, $Eg(X)$ and gEX may not be related. In fact one could exist while the other does not, e.g., if

$$g(x) = \frac{x}{1 + |x|},$$

then $E[|g(X)|] < \infty$ for any random variable X because g is a bounded function, but if X is Cauchy, EX does not even exist.

4. Property 2 implies that for $X \geq 1$, $EX^k < \infty \Longrightarrow EX^j < \infty$ for all $j \leq k$, because $x^j \leq x^k$. This is also true for $X \geq 0$ because $\int_0^1 x^j f(x)dx \leq \int_0^1 f(x)dx < \infty$ for any j. In general for $j \leq k$, we have

$$E\left(|X|^k\right) < \infty \Rightarrow E\left(|X|^j\right) < \infty.$$

5. We have

$$F_X(x) = E[1(X \leq x)], \qquad (5.5)$$

where $1(.)$ denotes the indicator function.

The median can be compared with the mean, as it also measures "central tendency". However, the median is not linear in the sense that we can't guarantee that

$$M(\alpha_1 g_1(X) + \alpha_2 g_2(X) + \alpha_3) = \alpha_1 M(g_1(X)) + \alpha_2 M(g_2(X)) + \alpha_3. \qquad (5.6)$$

On the other hand it possesses a useful property called **monotone equivariance** or equivariance with respect to a monotonic transformation.

Theorem 5.2. *Suppose that g is an increasing transformation (if $t \geq s$, then $g(t) \geq g(s)$). Then we have*

$$M(g(X)) = g(M(X)). \qquad (5.7)$$

For example, if $g(X) = aX + b$ where a, b are constants with $a > 0$, then

$$M(aX + b) = aM(X) + b.$$

If $X > 0$, then $M(\log(X)) = \log(M(X))$. The result (5.7) is a simple consequence of the fact that for any real number m and increasing transformation g, the following two events are identical

$$\{a : X(a) \leq m\} = \{a : g(X(a)) \leq g(m)\}. \tag{5.8}$$

We next connect the notion of stochastic dominance with expected utility. Let $\mathcal{U}_1$ denote the class of all von Neumann–Morgenstern type utility functions, u, such that $u' \geq 0$, (increasing).

Theorem 5.3. *X First Order Stochastic Dominates Y if and only if*

$$E[u(X)] \geq E[u(Y)]$$

for all $u \in \mathcal{U}_1$, with strict inequality for some u.

Proof. We give a rough argument for the equivalence of the two definitions of first order stochastic dominance. We suppose for simplicity that both random variables have compact support $[a, b]$ and that $F_j(a) = 0$ and $F_j(b) = 1$ for $j = X, Y$. Let f_j be the density of F_j. By integration by parts

$$
\begin{aligned}
Eu(X) - Eu(Y) &= \int_a^b u(x)[f_X(x) - f_Y(x)]dx \\
&= [(F_X(x) - F_Y(x))u(x)]_a^b - \int_a^b [F_X(x) - F_Y(x)]u'(x)dx \\
&= -\int_a^b [F_X(x) - F_Y(x)]u'(x)dx,
\end{aligned}
$$

which has the opposite sign of $F_X(x) - F_Y(x)$. To prove the necessity, one constructs a special utility function that coincides with the interval of c.d.f. domination. See Levy (2016) for the full argument. □

This says that whether X is preferred to Y for all individuals with increasing utility is equivalent to whether the c.d.f. of X is dominated by the c.d.f. of Y.

Finally, the c.d.f. and the expectation operation are connected through the following result.

Theorem 5.4. *Let X be a positive (continuous) random variable. Then we have*

$$E(X) = \int_0^\infty (1 - F_X(x))\, dx.$$

Proof. This follows by a change of variable $y = 1 - F(x)$. □

In fact, this gives an alternative way of defining expectation. For a random variable $X \geq 0$, provided $\sum_{k=0}^{\infty} \Pr(X \geq k) < \infty$, we have

$$E(X) = \lim_{\epsilon \to 0} \sum_{k=1}^{\infty} k \Pr((k-1)\epsilon < X \leq k\epsilon). \tag{5.9}$$

5.2 ADDITIONAL MOMENTS AND CUMULANTS

The **variance** of a random variable X, denoted σ_X^2, is defined as

$$\begin{aligned} \mathrm{var}(X) &= E[\{X - E(X)\}^2] \\ &= E[\{X^2 - 2XE(X) + E^2(X)\}] \\ &= E(X^2) - E^2(X). \end{aligned}$$

We have

$$0 \leq \mathrm{var}(X) \leq E(X^2)$$

so that a sufficient condition for the existence of the variance is: $E(X^2) < \infty$.

Exercise. Prove that $\mathrm{var}(aX + b) = a^2 \mathrm{var}(X)$ for all a, b.

The **standard deviation** $\sigma_X = \sqrt{\sigma_X^2}$, sometimes called *SD*. This satisfies $SD(aX + b) = |a| SD(X)$, i.e., $SD(X)$ changes proportionally. Variance measures dispersion, so that higher variance corresponds to the random variable being more spread out. In financial applications variance is a common measure of risk, and much research is devoted to modelling this quantity. In statistics, the variance of an estimator is important because it gives some understanding of the precision with which the quantity being estimated has been measured. Define the random variable

$$Z = \frac{X - E(X)}{SD(X)}. \tag{5.10}$$

This "standardized" quantity has $E(Z) = 0$ and $\mathrm{var}(Z) = 1$.

The **interquartile range** [i.e., the range of the middle half]

$$IQR(X) = Q_X(3/4) - Q_X(1/4)$$

always exists (when X is continuously distributed with a strictly increasing c.d.f.) and is an alternative measure of spreadoutness. For the standard normal distribution $IQR(X) = 1.349$, which justifies the use of $IQR/1.349$ as an alternative to the standard deviation as a general measure of scale. For the standard Cauchy, $IQR = 2$. Note that $Z = (X - M(X))/IQR(X)$ has median zero and interquartile range of 1, and this Z is an alternative standardization of X.

Skewness and **Kurtosis**. Suppose that $EX^4 < \infty$, then we may define the skewness and excess kurtosis:

$$\kappa_3(X) = \frac{E(X - E(X))^3}{\text{var}^{3/2}(X)}$$

$$\kappa_4(X) = \frac{E(X - E(X))^4}{\text{var}^2(X)} - 3.$$

For a normal distribution, $\kappa_3(X) = \kappa_4(X) = 0$. In general, $\kappa_3(X) \in \mathbb{R}$. Both quantities are invariant to location and scale changes, that is $\kappa_j(aX + b) = \kappa_j(X)$ for any constants a, b and any random variable X. Skewness is one measure of (lack of) symmetry of the distribution, albeit imperfect. If X is symmetric about $E(X)$, then $\kappa_3 = 0$, but if $\kappa_3 = 0$, then one cannot conclude that X is symmetric. In high school, one is often taught that when mean > median, the distribution is said to be right skewed, otherwise left skewed. An alternative measure of skewness is called the **nonparametric skewness**

$$\varrho_X = \frac{E(X) - M(X)}{\sigma_X}. \tag{5.11}$$

It can be shown that $-1 \le \varrho_X \le 1$ for any random variable X, with $\varrho_X > 0$ corresponding to "positive skewness". Note however that there is no necessary logical relationship between ϱ_X and $\kappa_3(X)$ in the sense that we could have $\varrho_X > 0$ and $\kappa_3(X) < 0$ and vice versa.

Typically, income distributions are right skewed (because there are some very high income individuals and lots of low income ones). Some investment strategies tend to have payoff distributions that are left skewed (meaning that for much of the time they make a small positive return, but every now and then they suffer a wipeout. This may be to the fund managers advantage because in the good times they get a payoff, and if it all goes pear shaped they just leave).

Kurtosis measures the thickness of the tails [and consequently the peakedness of the middle] of a distribution relative to the normal [which has $\kappa_4 = 0$]. Heavy tails correspond to the **leptokurtic** case [$\kappa_4 > 0$], while thin tails correspond to the **platykurtic** case [$\kappa_4 < 0$]. Note that in any case $\kappa_4 \ge -3$. Typically, income distributions are right skewed (because there are some very high income individuals and lots of low income ones). Likewise income distributions and stock returns are Leptokurtic. The "Samsung distribution" is platykurtic (by this I mean the distribution used in some of their advertising). See Fig. 5.1.

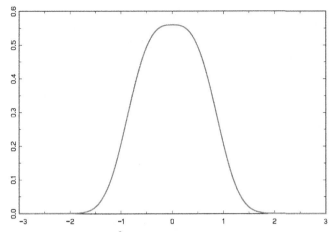

FIGURE 5.1 This density $\exp(-|x|^3)/1.786$ looks like the "Samsung distribution"

Finally, we turn to the **moment generating function** [m.g.f.] and the characteristic function [c.f.]. The m.g.f. is defined (for continuous random variables) as

$$M_X(t) = E e^{tX} = \int_{-\infty}^{\infty} e^{tx} f_X(x) dx \qquad (5.12)$$

for any $t \in \mathbb{R}$, provided this integral exists in some neighbourhood of $t = 0$. It is the Laplace transform of the function f_X with argument $-t$. We have the useful inversion formula

$$f_X(x) = \int_{-\infty}^{\infty} M_X(t) e^{-tx} dt, \qquad (5.13)$$

when the m.g.f. exists. The moment generating function is of limited use, since it does not exist for many random variables (although it does exist for normal random variables and any variable with bounded support). The **characteristic function** is applicable more generally, since it always exists, although in general it is complex valued:

$$\varphi_X(t) = E e^{itX}, \text{ real } t, i = \sqrt{-1}$$
$$= \int_{-\infty}^{\infty} e^{itx} f_X(x) dx$$
$$= \underbrace{\int_{-\infty}^{\infty} \cos(tx) f_X(x) dx}_{\text{real}} + i \underbrace{\int_{-\infty}^{\infty} \sin(tx) f_X(x) dx}_{\text{imaginary}}.$$

This takes the value one at $t = 0$. This is essentially the **Fourier transform** of the density function $f_X(x)$ and there is a well-defined inversion formula

$$f_X(x) = \frac{1}{2\pi} \int_{-\infty}^{\infty} e^{-itx} \varphi_X(t) dt. \tag{5.14}$$

If X is symmetric about zero, the complex part of φ_X is zero and $\varphi_X(t)$ is a real valued function. Also,

$$\frac{\partial^r}{\partial t^r} \varphi_X(0) = E(i^r X^r e^{itX})\Big|_{t=0} = i^r E(X^r), \ r = 1, 2, \ldots$$

Thus the moments of X are related to the derivative of the characteristic function at the origin.

5.3 AN INTERPRETATION OF EXPECTATION AND MEDIAN

We claim that $E(X)$ can be given the interpretation of the unique minimizer of the function $E(X - \theta)^2$ with respect to θ.

Theorem 5.5. *Suppose that $E(X^2)$ exists and is finite. Then $E(X)$ is the unique minimizer of $E(X - \theta)^2$ with respect to θ.*

Proof. For any $\theta \in \mathbb{R}$, write (**completing the square**)

$$\begin{aligned} E(X - \theta)^2 &= E(X^2) - 2\theta E(X) + \theta^2 \\ &= \theta^2 - 2\theta E(X) + E^2(X) + E(X^2) - E^2(X) \\ &= (\theta - E(X))^2 + E(X^2) - E^2(X) \\ &= (\theta - E(X))^2 + \text{var}(X) \\ &\geq \text{var}(X). \end{aligned}$$

The lower bound in the last expression is achieved by taking $\theta = E(X)$ in the last but one line. One can also show this constructively using calculus applied to the function $Q(\theta) = E(X - \theta)^2$. Specifically, the first order condition is

$$E(X - \theta) = 0, \tag{5.15}$$

which yields the same solution. $\square$

This theorem says that the expectation of X is the closest constant to the random variable X in terms of the **mean squared error**.

We next show that the median minimizes the **mean absolute error** $E|X - \theta|$. This is a bit more tricky to establish since we can't expand out the function $E|X - \theta|$ as we did for $E(X - \theta)^2$. Furthermore, the function $|x - \theta|$

is not differentiable at $x = \theta$, so that one can't just obtain a first order condition directly by differentiating inside the integral sign.

Theorem 5.6. *Suppose that X is continuously distributed with strictly increasing c.d.f. and $E(|X|) < \infty$. Then the median minimizes uniquely the Least Absolute Error criterion, that is,*

$$M(X) = \arg\min_{\theta \in \mathbb{R}} E\,|X - \theta|\,.$$

We may define M equivalently as the minimizer of the function $E D(X, \theta)$ with respect to θ, where

$$D(x, \theta) = |x - \theta| - |x - M|$$

is a bounded function of θ for all x, in which case the requirement that $E(|X|) < \infty$ is not needed.

Proof. The fact that $D(x, \theta)$ is bounded can best be seen by drawing a graph. As a consequence, we do not require any moments of X to exist for the solution of the minimization problem to exist. Let $Q(\theta) = E D(X, \theta)$. We have

$$Q(\theta) = \int_{-\infty}^{\infty} |x - \theta|\, f_X(x)dx - \int_{-\infty}^{\infty} |x - M|\, f_X(x)dx$$

$$= \int_{\theta}^{\infty} ((x - \theta) - |x - M|)\, f_X(x)dx$$

$$- \int_{-\infty}^{\theta} ((x - \theta) - |x - M|)\, f_X(x)dx.$$

The function Q is differentiable in θ with (total) derivative

$$Q'(\theta) = -\int_{\theta}^{\infty} f_X(x)dx + \int_{-\infty}^{\theta} f_X(x)dx = -E[\text{sign}(X - \theta)],$$

where $\text{sign}(x) = 1(x > 0) - 1(x < 0)$. The second derivative is $-2f_X(\theta)$, which is always negative. In conclusion, a minimizer of Q satisfies

$$E[\text{sign}(X - M)] = 0. \tag{5.16}$$

Now note that $\text{sign}(x - \theta) = 1(x - \theta > 0) - 1(x - \theta < 0)$ so that the above equation says that

$$E[1(X - M > 0)] = E[1(X - M < 0)], \text{ i.e.,}$$
$$\Pr(X > M) = \Pr(X < M),$$

which is the defining property of the median of a continuous random variable. $\square$

Example 5.5. Suppose that X is standard normal. Then

$$
\begin{aligned}
E\,|X - \theta| &= \int_\theta^\infty (x - \theta)\,\phi(x)dx + \int_{-\infty}^\theta (\theta - x)\phi(x)dx \\
&= \int_\theta^\infty x\phi(x)dx - \int_{-\infty}^\theta x\phi(x)dx - \theta \int_\theta^\infty \phi(x)dx + \theta \int_{-\infty}^\theta \phi(x)dx \\
&= \frac{1}{\sqrt{2\pi}} \int_\theta^\infty x \exp\left(-0.5x^2\right) dx - \frac{1}{\sqrt{2\pi}} \int_{-\infty}^\theta x \exp\left(-0.5x^2\right) dx \\
&\quad + \theta\,(2\Phi(\theta) - 1) \\
&= \frac{1}{\sqrt{2\pi}} \int_{\frac{1}{2}\theta^2}^\infty \exp(-u)du - \frac{1}{\sqrt{2\pi}} \int_{-\infty}^{\frac{1}{2}\theta^2} \exp(-u)du + \theta\,(2\Phi(\theta) - 1) \\
&= \frac{2}{\sqrt{2\pi}} \exp(-\frac{1}{2}\theta^2) + \theta\,(2\Phi(\theta) - 1) \\
&\geq \sqrt{\frac{2}{\pi}} = E|X|
\end{aligned}
$$

with equality if and only if $\theta = 0$. We used the change of variable $x \mapsto u = x^2/2$ (or Mathematica). This function although complicated is differentiable in θ for all values of θ and in fact infinitely times differentiable. It has a well defined minimum at $\theta = 0$ (we know that the median of the standard normal is zero) in which case $E|X| = \sqrt{2/\pi}$.

If the density is symmetric about M, then $E(X) = M(X)$. Finally, for any k such that the absolute moment exists, we have for continuous random variables

$$
E(X^k) = \int_0^1 Q_X^k(\alpha)d\alpha. \tag{5.17}
$$

This follows by a change of variables argument, letting $y = F_X^{-1}(\alpha)$.

Chapter 6

Examples of Univariate Distributions

6.1 PARAMETRIC FAMILIES OF DISTRIBUTIONS

We consider families of distributions $\{f_X(x|\theta); \ \theta \in \Theta\}$, where each member $f_X(\cdot|\theta)$ for $\theta \in \Theta$ is a p.d.f. or p.m.f. The properties of f_X [and the underlying random variable] are influenced by the value of θ. We just discuss some of the main examples.

6.1.1 Discrete Distributions

Example 6.1. BINOMIAL DISTRIBUTION. This distribution is important in modelling binary choices as occur in many economics datasets.

$$\text{Bernoulli } X = \begin{cases} 1 & \text{with prob } p \\ 0 & \text{with prob } 1-p \end{cases}, \ 0 \le p \le 1.$$

Then

$$EX = p \cdot 1 + (1-p) \cdot 0 = p$$
$$\text{var}(X) = p \cdot 1 - p^2 = p(1-p)$$

The Binomial arises when you repeat Bernoulli trials n times. The sample space is $\{0, 1\}^n$. We may define the random variable $Y =$ number of 1's in n trials. This has sample space $\{0, 1, 2, \ldots, n\}$. We have

$$\Pr(Y = y|n, p) = \binom{n}{y} p^y (1-p)^{n-y}, \ y \in \{0, 1, \ldots, n\}.$$

The probability of each sequence of y ones's and $n - y$ zero's can easily be determined and we then multiply by the number of possible ways of rearranging this particular set of values. Mean and variance $EY = np$, var $Y = np(1-p)$. The moment generating function is $M_Y(t) = [pe^t + (1-p)]^n$.

Example 6.2. GEOMETRIC DISTRIBUTION. Consider the number of trials until first success. This has the frequency function

$$f(x) = (1-p)^{x-1}p, \quad x = 1, 2, \ldots,$$

Probability, Statistics and Econometrics. http://dx.doi.org/10.1016/B978-0-12-810495-8.00007-5

which has mean $1/p$. This distribution has a number of applications in economics and finance. For example, the classic model of non-trading. Each period there is a trade with probability π and no trade with probability $1 - \pi$. Then we may be interested in the number of time periods between successive trades, which can be modelled by this distribution.

Example 6.3. NEGATIVE BINOMIAL DISTRIBUTION. Let X be the number of Bernoulli trials to get a fixed number of successes r for $r = 1, 2, \ldots$. Now r is the parameter and $X = n$ is the random variable with

$$\Pr(X = x | r, p) = \binom{x-1}{r-1} p^r (1-p)^{x-r}, \ x = r, r+1, \ldots$$

We have $X = x$ iff $r - 1$ successes in the first $x - 1$ trials and a success in the xth trial; this has probability

$$\binom{x-1}{r-1} p^{r-1} (1-p)^{x-r} \times p,$$

which is as stated. We have

$$E(X) = r + \frac{r(1-p)}{p} = \frac{r}{p} \ ; \ \text{var}(X) = \frac{r}{p} \times \frac{1-p}{p}.$$

Example 6.4. DISCRETE UNIFORM OR MULTINOMIAL. Suppose that for $j = 1, 2, \ldots, J$

$$\Pr(X = x_j) = p_j, \quad j = 1, \ldots, J$$

where $\{x_1, x_2, \ldots, x_J\} = S$ is the support. Then

$$E(X) = \sum_{j=1}^{J} x_j \Pr(X = x_j) = \sum_{j=1}^{J} x_j p_j$$

$$\text{var}(X) = \sum_{j=1}^{J} p_j x_j^2 - \left(\sum_{j=1}^{J} p_j x_j \right)^2.$$

The c.d.f. here is

$$\Pr[X \le x] = \sum_{j=1}^{J} p_j 1(x_j \le x).$$

For example, the dice example is of this sort with $x_j = j/6$, $j = 1, 2, \ldots, 6$, and $p_j = 1/6$.

Example 6.5. ZIPF'S LAW. The support is $\{1, 2, \ldots, J\}$, where J may be a large finite number or $J = \infty$, and

$$\Pr(X = j) = \frac{j^{-\alpha}}{\sum_{j=1}^{J} j^{-\alpha}} = \frac{j^{-\alpha}}{H_J(\alpha)}$$

for some parameter $\alpha > 0$, where $H_J(\alpha) = \sum_{j=1}^{J} j^{-\alpha}$ (this quantity is hard to express simply, but it is well defined – in the case where $J = \infty$ this is known as Riemann's zeta function). The distribution of words ranked by their frequency in a random text corpus is approximated by Zipf's law with $\alpha \sim 2$. We have

$$E(X) = \frac{\sum_{j=1}^{J} j \times j^{-\alpha}}{\sum_{j=1}^{J} j^{-\alpha}} = \frac{H_J(\alpha - 1)}{H_J(\alpha)}$$

$$\mathrm{var}(X) = \frac{H_J(\alpha) H_J(\alpha - 2) - H_J(\alpha - 1)^2}{H_J(\alpha)^2}.$$

Note that for $J = \infty$ and large j we can approximate

$$\Pr(X > j) \sim C j^{-\xi} \tag{6.1}$$

with $\xi = \alpha - 1$ and C some positive constant, provided $\alpha > 1$.

Example 6.6. POISSON DISTRIBUTION. This arises in a number of situations: (a) waiting times between events (e.g., arrivals of traders in a market); (b) number of occurrences in a given time interval, e.g., Tornadoes per year in Massachusetts; (c) Prussian Cavalry: number of deaths by horse kick per year in a given corps (19th century); (d) patents

$$\Pr(X = x | \lambda) = \frac{e^{-\lambda} \lambda^x}{x!}, \ x = 0, 1, 2, \ldots$$

Calculations with the Poisson distribution make use of the fact that for any t, $e^t = \sum_{j=0}^{\infty} \frac{t^j}{j!}$. For example:

$$E(X) = \sum_{x=0}^{\infty} \frac{x e^{-\lambda} \lambda^x}{x!} = e^{-\lambda} \sum_{x=1}^{\infty} \frac{\lambda^x}{(x-1)!} = \lambda e^{-\lambda} \sum_{x=1}^{\infty} \frac{\lambda^{x-1}}{(x-1)!}$$

$$= \lambda e^{-\lambda} \sum_{y=0}^{\infty} \frac{\lambda^y}{y!} = \lambda$$

$$E(X(X-1)) = \sum_{x=0}^{\infty} \frac{x(x-1)e^{-\lambda}\lambda^x}{x!} = e^{-\lambda} \sum_{x=2}^{\infty} \frac{\lambda^x}{(x-2)!}$$

$$= \lambda^2 e^{-\lambda} \sum_{x=2}^{\infty} \frac{\lambda^{x-2}}{(x-2)!} = \lambda^2 e^{-\lambda} \sum_{y=0}^{\infty} \frac{\lambda^y}{y!} = \lambda^2$$

$$\text{var}(X) = E(X(X-1)) + E(X) - E^2(X) = \lambda.$$

We consider the relationship between the Binomial and Poisson distributions. The m.g.f.'s are respectively $M_X(t) = [pe^t + (1-p)]^n$ and $M_X(t) = e^{\lambda(e^t-1)}$.

Consider a sequence of Binomial distributions with parameter $p(n) = \lambda/n$. Then the Binomial m.g.f. is

$$M_X(t) = \left[\frac{\lambda}{n}e^t + 1 - \frac{\lambda}{n}\right]^n$$

$$= \left[1 + \frac{\lambda(e^t - 1)}{n}\right]^n$$

$$\to e^{\lambda(e^t-1)} \text{ as } n \to \infty.$$

This holds for all $t \in \mathbb{R}$. This says roughly that the Poisson distribution may be used as an approximation to the Binomial distribution when p is small and n is large.

6.1.2 Continuous Distributions

Example 6.7. UNIFORM on $[a, b]$. The distribution and c.d.f. are

$$f(x|a,b) = \begin{cases} \frac{1}{b-a} & \text{if } x \in [a,b] \\ 0 & \text{otherwise} \end{cases}$$

$$F(x|a,b) = \int_a^x f(z|a,b)dz = \frac{x-a}{b-a},$$

and the moments are:

$$E(X) = \frac{b+a}{2}, \text{ median} = \frac{b+a}{2}$$

$$\text{var}(X) = \frac{(b-a)^2}{12}, \text{ } SD(X) = \frac{b-a}{\sqrt{12}},$$

$$IQR = \frac{b-a}{2}.$$

Note also that if $X \sim U[a, b]$, then $X - a \sim U[0, b - a]$, and furthermore

$$\frac{X - a}{b - a} \sim U[0, 1].$$

We next consider the Normal or Gaussian distribution as it is sometimes called. There are many reasons for the popularity of this distribution:

(a) Empirically it seems to work well, for example human height and weight;
(b) Mathematically, it is easy to work with;
(c) The central limit theorem means that it approximates many other distributions.

Example 6.8. GAUSSIAN NORMAL DISTRIBUTION. We say that $X \sim N(\mu, \sigma^2)$ when

$$f(x|\mu, \sigma^2) = \frac{1}{\sigma\sqrt{2\pi}}e^{-(x-\mu)^2/2\sigma^2}, \quad -\infty < x < \infty.$$

For this distribution $E(X) = \mu$, $\mathrm{var}(X) = \sigma^2$. The distribution is symmetric about μ, i.e., $f(x) = f(2\mu - x)$. It is also unimodal so that mean = median = mode. It is positive everywhere; and tends to zero as $x \to \pm\infty$. We have

$$\frac{X - \mu}{\sigma} = Z \sim N(0, 1), \quad \phi(z) = \frac{1}{\sqrt{2\pi}}e^{-z^2/2}, \quad -\infty < z < \infty,$$

where Z is called the standard normal distribution whose density function and c.d.f. are commonly denoted by ϕ and Φ respectively. The Gaussian density has very thin tails, so can integrate any polynomial, i.e., $E(Z^n) < \infty$ for all n, and in fact $E(e^{tZ}) = \exp\left(\mu t + \sigma^2 t/2\right) < \infty$ for all t. Note that

$$\Pr(|Z| \le 3) = .9974$$

so that most of the mass is found within three standard deviations of the mean.

One can approximate the Binomial distribution with large n and fixed p by a normal distribution with mean $\mu = np$ and variance $\sigma^2 = np(1 - p)$. This was in fact proven by Abraham de Moivre in 1738 and is the first central limit theorem.

There are various offspring of the normal distribution like the χ^2-distribution, the t-distribution, and the F-distribution, which were central to the development of exact sampling theory for estimation of means and variances of the normal distribution. We define the χ^2, t, and F random variables in terms of normal random variables as follows.

Definition 6.1. (a) Let $Z_1, \ldots, Z_p \sim N(0, 1)$ and mutually independent then

$$\sum_{i=1}^{p} Z_i^2 \sim \chi^2(p).$$

Definition 6.2. (b) $t(k) = U/\sqrt{V/k}$, where U is independent of V, $U \sim N(0, 1)$, $V \sim \chi^2(k)$

Definition 6.3. (c) $F(k, m) = \frac{U/k}{V/m}$, $U \sim \chi^2(k)$, $U \sim \chi^2(m)$, U independent of V.

Let $\chi_\alpha^2(k)$, $t_\alpha(k)$, and $F_\alpha(k, m)$ denote the $1 - \alpha$ quantile of these distributions, i.e., for random variable $X \sim F(k, m)$ we have

$$\Pr(X > F_\alpha(k, m)) = \alpha.$$

The lognormal distribution is widely used for income distributions and stock prices and more recently city sizes (**Gibrat's Law**): X is lognormal if $\ln(X) \sim N(\mu, \sigma^2)$.

Example 6.9. CAUCHY. A general Cauchy density is

$$f(x|\theta, \gamma) = \frac{1}{\pi \gamma} \frac{1}{1 + \left(\frac{x-\theta}{\gamma}\right)^2},$$

with the standard Cauchy having $\gamma = 1$ and $\theta = 0$. This distribution is the prototypical bad guy being wheeled out to violate standard assumptions such as finite variance.

Example 6.10. GAMMA. The general form of the p.d.f. is

$$f(x|\alpha, \beta) = \frac{1}{\Gamma(\alpha)\beta^\alpha} x^{\alpha-1} e^{-x/\beta}, \ 0 < x < \infty, \ \alpha, \beta > 0$$

α is shape parameter, β is a scale parameter. Here $\Gamma(\alpha) = \int_0^\infty t^{\alpha-1} e^{-t} dt$ is the Gamma function, $\Gamma(n) = (n-1)!$. The $\chi^2(k)$ distribution is a special case when $\alpha = k$, $\beta = 1$.

Example 6.11. BETA

$$f(x|\alpha, \beta) = \frac{1}{B(\alpha, \beta)} x^{\alpha-1} (1-x)^{\beta-1}, \ 0 < x < 1, \ \alpha, \beta > 0$$

where $B(\alpha, \beta) = \int_0^1 x^{\alpha-1}(1-x)^{\beta-1} dx$ is the beta function. When $\alpha = \beta = 1$ we have uniform on $[0, 1]$. For any $\alpha, \beta < 1$, the density $f(x|\alpha, \beta)$ is unbounded at $x = 0$ and $x = 1$. The special case $\alpha = 1/2$, $\beta = 1/2$ is of interest in the study of chaotic dynamics.

Example 6.12. LOGISTIC. It is more convenient here to specify the c.d.f., which is

$$F(x) = \frac{e^x}{1 + e^x}, \quad -\infty < x < \infty.$$

This is often used in **Binary choice** modelling because it has some nicer properties than the normal; specifically its c.d.f. is in closed form and is easy to compute.

Example 6.13. PARETO. For $x \geq L$

$$f(x|\theta, L) = \theta L^\theta x^{-(\theta+1)} \quad ; \quad F(x|\theta, L) = 1 - (x/L)^{-\theta}.$$

This distribution is the continuous analogue of Zipf's distribution. It is widely used for modelling income distributions and stock returns. Note that $EX^k < \infty$ if and only if $k > \theta + 1$.

Example 6.14. GOMPERTZ–MAKEHAM. This is a family of random variables that has been used to describe human mortality. The density function is

$$f(x|\alpha, \beta, \lambda) = \left(\alpha e^{\beta x} + \lambda\right) \exp\left(-\lambda x - \frac{\alpha}{\beta}\left(e^{\beta x} - 1\right)\right),$$

for $x > 0$, where the parameters: $\alpha, \beta, \lambda > 0$. The hazard function for the Gompertz–Makeham distribution is much simpler

$$\lambda(x|\alpha, \beta, \lambda) = \alpha e^{\beta x} + \lambda. \tag{6.2}$$

Chapter 7

Multivariate Random Variables

7.1 MULTIVARIATE DISTRIBUTIONS

We now consider the extension to multiple random variables, i.e., we have a population random variable $X = (X_1, \ldots, X_k) \in \mathbb{R}^k$. This introduces some additional concepts about how the coordinate random variables relate to each other.

Definition 7.1. A vector random variable X is a measurable mapping from the sample space S

$$X : S \to S_X \subset \mathbb{R}^k$$

such that $\mathcal{A}_X = \{A \subset S : X(A) \in \mathcal{B}\} = \{X^{-1}(B) : B \in \mathcal{B}\} \subseteq \mathcal{A}$, where $\mathcal{B}$ is the sigma algebra on S_X and $\mathcal{A}$ is the sigma algebra on S.

Example 7.1. Let $S_X = \mathbb{R}^k$, and let

$$\mathcal{B} = \{(a_1, b_1) \times \cdots \times (a_k, b_k), \ a_i, b_i \in \mathbb{R}, \ i = 1, \ldots, k\}.$$

Then let $\mathcal{A} = \sigma(\mathcal{B})$ consist of all countable unions of members of $\mathcal{B}$ and complements thereof. This is called the product Borel sigma-algebra. The coordinate random variables X_i have the usual Borel sigma algebra derived by marginalization.

We may define the probability measure of X as before; we concentrate on the c.d.f.

Definition 7.2. The multivariate joint c.d.f. is defined for all $x = (x_1, \ldots, x_k) \in \mathbb{R}^k$

$$F_X(x) = \Pr(X_1 \leq x_1, X_2 \leq x_2, \ldots, X_k \leq x_k).$$

We will work with this quadrant version extension of the univariate c.d.f.[1] The Multivariate c.d.f. has similar coordinate-wise properties to a univariate c.d.f.

---

1. In the multivariate case, there are a number of alternatives to 'the c.d.f.' that also contain essentially the same information, i.e., knowing the function is equivalent to knowing P. For example, **hyperplane** probabilities: $F_X(c, t) = \Pr(X \in H(c, t))$, where $H(c, t) = \{x : \sum_{l=1}^{k} x_l c_l \leq t\}$, do the job. That is, if we know $F_X(c, t)$ for all c and all t, then we know $F_X(x)$ and hence P.

Probability, Statistics and Econometrics. http://dx.doi.org/10.1016/B978-0-12-810495-8.00008-7

Theorem 7.1. *The following properties hold:*
(i) $F_X(x) \leq F_X(x')$ whenever $x \leq x'$ in the multivariate sense, i.e., $x_i \leq x_i'$ for $i = 1, \ldots, k$;
(ii) It is right continuous: take any sequence $x_n \geq x$ with $x_n \to x$, then $F_X(x_n) \to F_X(x)$ as $n \to \infty$;
(iii) $F_X(x) \to 0$ as $x \to (-\infty, -\infty, \ldots, -\infty)$ and $F_X(x) \to 1$ as $x \to (+\infty, +\infty, \ldots, +\infty)$.

Suppose that $X = (X_1, X_2)$, where $X_1 \in \mathbb{R}^{k_1}$ and $X_2 \in \mathbb{R}^{k_2}$, where $k_1 + k_2 = k$. The **Marginal** c.d.f. (marginal distributions) of the subset X_1,

$$F_{X_1}(x_1) = \Pr(X_1 \leq x_1),$$

has a relationship with the joint c.d.f., $F_X(x)$. In particular

$$F_{X_1}(x_1) = \lim_{x_2 \to (+\infty, +\infty, \ldots, +\infty)} F_X(x_1, x_2). \tag{7.1}$$

This follows because we may write $\Pr(A) = \Pr(A \cap B) + \Pr(A \cap B^c)$, where $B = \{X_2 \leq x_2\}$. Taking the limit as $x_2 \to \infty$, the event B increases to the whole sample space, while B^c shrinks to zero. Therefore, the joint probability $\Pr(A \cap B)$ converges to the marginal probability $P(A)$.

We next turn to the joint p.m.f. and p.d.f. It is possible to define the density function in a general way with respect to some measure on $\mathbb{R}^k$, but we shall just consider the two polar cases.

In the discrete case the p.m.f. is defined as before

$$f_X(x) = \Pr(X = x) \tag{7.2}$$

for $x \in \mathbb{R}^k$. In the continuous case, we may define the p.d.f. through its relation with the c.d.f. as follows

$$F_X(x) = \int_{-\infty}^{x_1} \cdots \int_{-\infty}^{x_k} f_X(z_1, \ldots, z_k) dz_1 \cdots dz_k.$$

We can then compute this integral recursively by first computing $g_1(x_2, \ldots, x_k) = \int_{-\infty}^{x_1} f_X(x) dx_1$ and then repeating the process. Under technical conditions [**Fubini's Theorem**], we can reverse the order of integration, which may be useful for some computations.

Theorem 7.2. *Suppose that the joint c.d.f. F is k-times partially differentiable at the point $x = (x_1, \ldots, x_k) \in \mathbb{R}^k$. Then, the joint density function f satisfies*

$$f_X(x) = \frac{\partial^k F_X(x_1, \ldots, x_k)}{\partial x_1, \ldots, \partial x_k}.$$

Proof. This is shown recursively. For $\ell = 1, 2, \ldots, k$, let,

$$g_{1\ldots\ell}(x) = \int_{-\infty}^{x_{\ell+1}} \cdots \int_{-\infty}^{x_k} f_X(x_1, \ldots, x_\ell, z_{\ell+1}, \ldots, z_k) dz_{\ell+1} \cdots dz_k.$$

Then

$$F_X(x) = \int_{-\infty}^{x_1} g_1(z_1, x_2, \ldots, x_k) dz_1$$

$$\frac{\partial F_X}{\partial x_1}(x) = g_1(x) = \int_{-\infty}^{x_2} \cdots \int_{-\infty}^{x_k} f_X(x_1, z_2 \ldots, z_k) dz_2 \cdots dz_k$$

$$= \int_{-\infty}^{x_2} g_{12}(x_1, z_2, x_3, \ldots, x_k) dz_2.$$

Therefore,

$$\frac{\partial^2 F_X}{\partial x_1 \partial x_2}(x) = \frac{\partial g_1(x)}{\partial x_2} = g_{12}(x),$$

and so on. □

Note that Lebesgue measure on $\mathbb{R}^k$ puts zero volume on all sets that are of **lower dimension**. It follows that for a continuous random variable X (that is absolutely continuous with respect to Lebesgue measure on $\mathbb{R}^k$) $\Pr(X = x) = 0$ for any point $x \in \mathbb{R}^k$, but even more holds. In fact,

$$\Pr(X \in \{x : f_1(x_1, \ldots, x_k) = 0, \ldots, f_r(x_1, \ldots, x_k) = 0\}) = 0 \qquad (7.3)$$

for any measurable functions $f_j : \mathbb{R}^k \to \mathbb{R}$ for $j = 1, \ldots, r$ with $r \geq 1$.

Example 7.2. Suppose that $X = (X_1, X_2)$ are continuously distributed on $\mathbb{R}^2$, i.e., absolutely continuous with respect to Lebesgue measure on $\mathbb{R}^2$. Then

$$\Pr\left(X_1^2 + X_2^2 = r\right) = 0$$

for any $r > 0$. The probability that X lies on the circumference of a circle is zero.

Suppose that $X = (X_1, X_2)$, where $X_1 \in \mathbb{R}^{k_1}$ and $X_2 \in \mathbb{R}^{k_2}$, where $k_1 + k_2 = k$. The marginal densities of the subset X_1 have a relationship with the joint densities.

Theorem 7.3. *For any joint p.m.f. or p.d.f. function, the functions*

$$f_{X_1}(x_1) = \sum_{x_2} f_X(x_1, x_2)$$

$$f_{X_1}(x_1) = \int_{-\infty}^{\infty} \cdots \int_{-\infty}^{\infty} f(x_1, x_2) dx_2$$

are themselves mass functions or density functions, and are called the marginals.

The proof of this result is straightforward. This result emphasizes that a random variable X_1 might be part of a bigger picture involving other random variables X_2. It is easy to go from the joint distribution to the marginal but not in the other direction. The joint distribution can not be determined from the marginals alone: knowing f_{X_1} and f_{X_2} does not determine f_X uniquely unless X_1 and X_2 are independent.

Example 7.3. We return to a population version of the stock example. Suppose that X is yesterdays stock market outcome and Y is today's outcome with $X = +1$ or $X = -1$ and $Y = +1$ or $Y = -1$ with the following probabilities

	$Y = 1$	$Y = -1$
$X = 1$	$\pi_{1,1}$	$\pi_{1,-1}$
$X = -1$	$\pi_{-1,1}$	$\pi_{-1,-1}$

The table shows us

$$\Pr(X = i, Y = j) = \pi_{i,j},$$

which satisfy $\pi_{i,j} \in [0, 1]$ for all i, j, and $\pi_{1,1} + \pi_{1,-1} + \pi_{-1,1} + \pi_{-1,-1} = 1$. The marginal probabilities are

$$p_1 = \Pr(X = 1) = \pi_{1,1} + \pi_{1,-1}$$
$$p_{-1} = \Pr(X = -1) = \pi_{-1,1} + \pi_{-1,-1} = 1 - p_1$$
$$q_1 = \Pr(Y = 1) = \pi_{1,1} + \pi_{-1,1}$$
$$q_{-1} = \Pr(Y = -1) = \pi_{1,-1} + \pi_{-1,-1} = 1 - q_1.$$

On the other hand, knowing p_1, p_{-1}, q_1, and q_{-1} does not determine $\pi_{1,1}$, $\pi_{1,-1}, \pi_{-1,1}$, and $\pi_{-1,-1}$ uniquely. This can be seen by a straight count. There are three freely varying quantities in the π's but only two freely varying quantities amongst the p_1, p_{-1}, q_1, and q_{-1}.

7.2 CONDITIONAL DISTRIBUTIONS AND INDEPENDENCE

We defined conditional probability $P(A|B) = P(A \cap B)/P(B)$ for events A, B with $P(B) \neq 0$. We now want to define the **conditional distribution** of $Y|X$. A general definition would be

$$P(A|X = x) = \lim_{\epsilon \to 0} \frac{P(A \cap B_\epsilon)}{P(B_\epsilon)} \quad , \quad B_\epsilon = \{X \in [x - \epsilon, x + \epsilon]\}. \quad (7.4)$$

We focus on the two leading cases where simple definitions are available. In the case where both Y and X are discrete we may define the conditional p.m.f. as

$$f_{Y|X}(y|x) = \Pr(Y = y|X = x) = \frac{f_{Y,X}(y,x)}{f_X(x)},$$

when the event $\{X = x\}$ has non-zero probability. Likewise, we can define the conditional c.d.f. as

$$F_{Y|X}(y|x) = \Pr(Y \leq y|X = x) = \frac{\sum_{y \leq y} f(y,x)}{f_X(x)}$$

Note that $f_{Y|X}(y|x)$ is a p.m.f. and $F_{Y|X}(y|x)$ is a c.d.f., i.e.,

Theorem 7.4. *For all* x

(1) $f_{Y|X}(y|x) \geq 0$ *all* y;

(2) $\sum_y f_{Y|X}(y|x) = \frac{\sum_y f(y,x)}{f_X(x)} = \frac{f_X(x)}{f_X(x)} = 1.$

In the continuous case, it appears a bit anomalous to talk about the $\Pr(y \in A|X = x)$, since $\{X = x\}$ itself has zero probability of occurring. Still, we define the conditional density function

$$f_{Y|X}(y|x) = \frac{f_{Y,X}(y,x)}{f_X(x)} \tag{7.5}$$

in terms of the joint and marginal densities. It turns out that $f_{Y|X}(y|x)$ has the properties of a p.d.f.:

Theorem 7.5. *For all* x,

(1) $f_{Y|X}(y|x) \geq 0$ *for all* y;

(2) $\int_{-\infty}^{\infty} f_{Y|X}(y|x)dy = \frac{\int_{-\infty}^{\infty} f_{Y,X}(y,x)dy}{f_X(x)} = \frac{f_X(x)}{f_X(x)} = 1.$

We may define the conditional c.d.f. through the conditional density as

$$F_X(y|x) = \int_{-\infty}^{y} f_{Y|X}(y'|x)dy'.$$

We may also start with a conditional c.d.f. and infer the existence of the conditional density through the integration formula. We may show $\Pr(Y \in [a,b]|X = x) = F_X(b|x) - F_X(a|x)$.

The relationship between the joint density and the conditional density

$$f_{Y,X}(y,x) = f_{Y|X}(y|x)f_X(x) \tag{7.6}$$

turns out to be very useful in modelling and time series in particular. It generalizes to any number of random variables so that

$$f_{Y,X,Z}(y,x,z) = f_{Y|X,Z}(y|x,z) f_{X|Z}(x|z) f_Z(z)$$

etc. In some case we may specify a model for the conditional density and the
marginal density and this relation implies the joint density, which itself is of
central interest. It also shows a way that we might simulate outcomes on y, x
by first simulating x from its marginal and then drawing y from the conditional
distribution. This sequential approach is very convenient in complicated situations.

We may also define a version of Bayes theorem for densities:

$$f_{X|Y}(x|y) = \frac{f_{Y|X}(y|x) f_X(x)}{f_Y(y)} = \frac{f_{Y|X}(y|x) f_X(x)}{\int f_{Y,X}(y,x)dx}. \tag{7.7}$$

This formula is very useful in statistical inference questions. It is also useful
for the sort of signal extraction and learning problems widely encountered in
economics.

Definition 7.3. INDEPENDENCE. We say that Y and X are **independent** [de-
noted $Y \perp\!\!\!\perp X$] if

$$\Pr(Y \in A, X \in B) = \Pr(Y \in A) \Pr(x \in B)$$

for all events A, B in the relevant sigma-algebras. This is equivalent to the following definition in terms of the c.d.f.'s, which is simpler to state and apply:

$$F_{YX}(y,x) = F_Y(y) \cdot F_X(x)$$

for all $x, y \in \mathbb{R}$.

Example 7.4. Stock market example again. The condition for independence is

$$\Pr(X = i, Y = j) = \Pr(X = i) \Pr(Y = j) \tag{7.8}$$

for all $i, j \in \{-1, 1\}$. This requires

$$\pi_{i,j} = \left(\pi_{i,j} + \pi_{i,-j}\right) \times \left(\pi_{i,j} + \pi_{-i,j}\right)$$

for all i, j, although given the other restrictions it is sufficient to check this
condition for only one combination. Under independence, there are only two
free parameters in the π's, say $\pi_{1,1}$ and $\pi_{-1,-1}$, since then

$$\pi_{1,-1} = \left(\pi_{1,1} + \pi_{1,-1}\right) \times \left(\pi_{1,-1} + \pi_{-1,-1}\right)$$
$$= \pi_{1,-1}\left(\pi_{-1,-1} + \pi_{1,1}\right) + \pi_{-1,-1}\pi_{1,1} + \pi_{1,-1}^2$$

so that $\pi_{1,-1}$ satisfies the quadratic equation

$$\pi_{1,-1}^2 + \pi_{1,-1}\left(\pi_{-1,-1} + \pi_{1,1} - 1\right) + \pi_{-1,-1}\pi_{1,1} = 0. \qquad (7.9)$$

Note that $\pi_{-1,-1} + \pi_{1,1} - 1 \le 0$. In fact, $\pi_{-1,-1} + \pi_{1,1} - 1 < 0$, otherwise X and Y cannot be independent. Eq. (7.9) has a unique solution if and only if there is independence. For example, suppose that $\pi_{-1,-1} = \pi_{1,1} = 1/4$, then the unique solution to (7.9) is $\pi_{1,-1} = 1/4$.

A special case of interest for sampling is where Y and X are **independent and identically distributed (i.i.d.)**, i.e., $F_Y(x) = F_X(x) = F(x)$, say, so that $F_{YX}(y, x) = F(y)F(x)$.

We sometimes work with the density (or p.m.f. for discrete random variables) version of this concept.

Definition 7.4. We say that Y and X are **independent** if either of the following conditions hold:
(1) $f(y, x) = f_Y(y) \cdot f_X(x)$ for all y, x;
(2) $f_{Y|X}(y|x) = f(y)$ for all x;
(3) $f_{X|Y}(x|y) = f(x)$ for all y.

Note that if Y is independent of X, then $g(X)$ is independent of $h(Y)$ for any measurable functions g and h.

Suppose that $Y = g(X)$ for some measurable transformation g, then Y is "perfectly dependent" on X, in the sense that knowledge of X determines Y. Of course it may be that knowledge of Y does not perfectly determine X: for example, if $g(x) = \cos(x)$ or if $g(x) = 1(x > 0)$.

We now consider the relationship between two (or more) random variables when they are not independent. In this case, conditional densities $f_{Y|X}$ and c.d.f.'s $F_{Y|X}$ in general vary with the conditioning point x. Likewise for the conditional mean $E(Y|X)$, the conditional median $M(Y|X)$, conditional variance $\text{var}(Y|X)$, conditional characteristic function $E(e^{itY}|X)$, and other **functionals**, all of which characterize the relationship between Y and X. We first consider the notion of covariance.

7.3 COVARIANCE

Definition 7.5. Let X, Y be random variables with finite variance. Then

$$\overbrace{\text{cov}(X, Y)}^{\sigma_{XY}} = E[\{X - \overbrace{E(X)}^{\mu_X}\}\{Y - \overbrace{E(Y)}^{\mu_Y}\}] = E(YX) - \mu_X\mu_Y.$$

If X or Y are constant, then $\text{cov}(X, Y) = 0$. Note that

$$\text{cov}(aX + c, bY + d) = ab\,\text{cov}(X, Y),$$

so that covariance is affected by a, b but not by c, d. The covariance measures how much X and Y move together: $\sigma_{XY} > 0$ corresponds to positive movement, $\sigma_{XY} < 0$ corresponds to negative movement.

The covariance is related to variance in the following way. We have

$$
\begin{aligned}
\text{var}(X + Y) &= E\left[(X - EX + Y - EY)^2\right] \\
&= E\left[(X - EX)^2\right] + E\left[(Y - EY)^2\right] + 2E\left[(X - EX)(Y - EY)\right] \\
&= \text{var}(X) + \text{var}(Y) + 2\text{cov}(X, Y). \tag{7.10}
\end{aligned}
$$

If $\text{cov}(X, Y) = 0$, then $\text{var}(X + Y) = \text{var}(X) + \text{var}(Y)$. If $\text{cov}(X, Y) > 0$, then $\text{var}(X + Y) > \text{var}(X) + \text{var}(Y)$. If $\text{cov}(X, Y) < 0$, then $\text{var}(X + Y) < \text{var}(X) + \text{var}(Y)$. For example, suppose that X represents stock returns today and Y represents stock returns tomorrow. Then, the argument above says that the variance of two period returns is greater than, equal to, or lesser than the sum of the variances of the one period returns, depending on the covariance between the two random returns. Under the efficient markets hypothesis we would have the implication that $\text{cov}(X, Y) = 0$, and the variance of the sum is the sum of the variances.

An alternative measure of association is given by the **correlation coefficient**.

Definition 7.6. Let X, Y be random variables with finite variance. Then

$$
\rho_{XY} = \text{corr}(X, Y) = \frac{\text{cov}(X, Y)}{\sigma_X \sigma_Y}.
$$

This satisfies $-1 \leq \rho_{XY} \leq 1$. The correlation coefficient is invariant, in magnitude, to the scale in which X, Y are measured, so that

$$
\rho_{aX+b, cY+d} = \text{sign}(a)\text{sign}(c)\rho_{XY}
$$

for any a, b, c, d. However, the correlation coefficient is not invariant to nonlinear transformations, i.e.,

$$
\rho_{g(X), h(Y)} \neq \rho_{XY} \text{ for arbitrary } X, Y.
$$

Theorem 7.6. *We have* $\text{corr}(X, Y) = \pm 1$ *if and only if* $Y = aX + b$ *for some constants* a, b *with* $a \neq 0$.

Proof. If $Y = aX + b$, then it is straightforward to show that $\text{corr}(X, Y) = \pm 1$ with the sign determined by the sign of a. What about the converse? This will be a consequence of the Cauchy–Schwarz inequality, which we give below. $\square$

This says that nonlinear functions of X can't be perfectly correlated with X itself. The intuition is that correlation is about linear relationships, so any nonlinear function must have an imperfect correlation with its argument.

Covariance is a weaker property than independence, since independence is equivalent to the lack of covariance between any functions of the two random variables.

Theorem 7.7. *X and Y are independent random variables if and only if*

$$\text{cov}(g(X), h(Y)) = 0,$$

for all functions g, h for which the covariance is defined. Specifically, if X and Y are independent random variables, then $\text{cov}(X, Y) = 0$.

Proof. The second claim follows because:

$$E(g(X)h(Y)) = \int_{-\infty}^{\infty} \int_{-\infty}^{\infty} g(x)h(y)f(y,x)dydx$$

$$= \int_{-\infty}^{\infty} \int_{-\infty}^{\infty} g(x)h(y)f(y)f(x)dydx$$

$$= \int_{-\infty}^{\infty} g(x)f_X(x)dx \cdot \int_{-\infty}^{\infty} h(y)f_Y(y)dy = E(g(X))E(h(Y)).$$

The reverse direction is not proved here. $\qquad\qquad\square$

Here is an example that illustrates the fact that uncorrelated random variables need not be independent.

Example 7.5. Suppose that $X = \cos\theta$ and $Y = \sin\theta$, where θ is uniform on $[0, 2\pi]$. Then $Y^2 = 1 - X^2$ so X and Y are functionally related and not independent. However,

$$\text{cov}(X, Y) = \int_0^{2\pi} \cos(\theta)\sin(\theta)d\theta - \int_0^{2\pi} \cos(\theta)d\theta \times \int_0^{2\pi} \sin(\theta)d\theta = 0$$

so that the two random variables are uncorrelated. In this case, $f_{Y|X}$ is discrete with

$$f_{Y|X}(y|x) = \begin{cases} \frac{1}{2} & \text{if } y = \sqrt{1 - x^2} \\ \frac{1}{2} & \text{if } y = -\sqrt{1 - x^2} \\ 0 & \text{else} \end{cases}$$

Example 7.6. Correlation is a useful and widely used concept, but it is important to distinguish correlation from causation. There are many examples of **spurious correlations**. http://www.tylervigen.com/spurious-correlations US spending on science, space, and technology correlates (99.8%) with Suicides by hanging, strangulation and suffocation.

7.4 CONDITIONAL EXPECTATION AND THE REGRESSION FUNCTION

The conditional expectation of the random variable Y given the random variable X is an important quantity in much applied statistics/econometrics. Later we will spend a lot of time on empirical regression. We are concerned here with the population quantity. We first give a very general definition of a conditional expectation of a random variable given a sigma field, and then specialize that.

Definition 7.7. A random variable Z is called the conditional expectation of Y given the sigma-algebra $\mathcal{A}$ (we write $E(Y|\mathcal{A})$) if
(1) The sigma algebra generated by Z is contained in $\mathcal{A}$.
(2) Z satisfies for all $A \in \mathcal{A}$

$$E\left(Y 1_A\right) = E\left(Z 1_A\right).$$

One can show the existence and uniqueness of the random variable Z using measure theoretic arguments. This is not a very constructive definition but it does apply very generally to any kind of random variable and any kind of sigma algebra. We are mostly concerned here with the case where the sigma field $\mathcal{A}$ is generated by some random variable X, in which case we write $E(Y|X)$. Note that unlike covariance, regression is not symmetric in X and Y, so that $E(X|Y)$ is potentially totally different from $E(Y|X)$, just like $P(A|B)$ may not equal $P(A|B)$.

We will next specialize the theory to the polar cases we have mostly considered so far. In general X could be multivariate ($\in \mathbb{R}^k$) but we just focus on the scalar $k = 1$ case. We can classify the problem into several cases: (1) Y, X discrete; (2) Y is discrete and X is continuous; (3) Y is continuous and X is discrete; (4) Y, X are both continuously distributed. We mostly focus on case (4) for simplicity of presentation. Case (1) contains nothing substantially different and can be analyzed by replacing the integrals by sums and the densities by probability mass functions in the sequel. The case (3) is mostly covered by our analysis below. The case (2) is important and is worth a short additional discussion at the end.

We can define expectations within the (continuous) conditional distribution as follows

$$m(x) = E(Y|X = x) = \int_{-\infty}^{\infty} y f_{Y|X}(y|x)dy = \frac{\int_{-\infty}^{\infty} y f(y, x)dy}{\int_{-\infty}^{\infty} f(y, x)dy}, \qquad (7.11)$$

provided the integrals are well defined. We let $E(Y|X) = m(X)$ denote the conditional expectation evaluated at the random conditioning variable X, so that

$E(Y|X)$ is a random variable, while $E(Y|X = x)$ is a particular realization of that random variable.

Conditional expectation obey similar monotonicity and linearity properties as expectation:

Theorem 7.8. *For random variables* Y_1, Y_2, X:
(1) If $Y_1 \leq Y_2 \Longrightarrow E(Y_1|X = x) \leq E(Y_2|X = x)$;
(2) For constants $\alpha_1, \alpha_2, \alpha_3$

$$E(\alpha_1 Y_1 + \alpha_2 Y_2 + \alpha_3|X = x) = \alpha_1 E(Y_1|X = x) + \alpha_2 E(Y_2|X = x) + \alpha_3.$$

Note however that $E(X|\alpha_1 Y_1 + \alpha_2 Y_2)$ may have no relation to $\alpha_1 E(X|Y_1) + \alpha_2 E(X|Y_2)$, the linearity property is only on the left hand side.

When the expectation is defined, we can write for any such random variables Y, X

$$Y = \overbrace{E(Y|X)}^{m(X)} + \overbrace{(Y - E(Y|X))}^{\varepsilon}, \tag{7.12}$$

$$\underbrace{}_{\text{systematic part}} \underbrace{}_{\text{random part}}$$

where $m(x) = E(Y|X = x)$ is called the regression function. By the linearity property of conditional expectations, the random variable ε satisfies $E(\varepsilon|X) = 0$, but ε is not necessarily independent of X. For example, $\text{var}(\varepsilon|X) = \text{var}[Y - E(Y|X)] = \text{var}(Y|X) = \sigma^2(X)$ can be expected to vary with X as much as $m(X) = E(Y|X)$. Note that the quantities $E(Y|X)$, $E(\varepsilon|X)$, and $\text{var}(\varepsilon|X)$ are random variables depending on the realization of the random variable X, and so we should say that $E(\varepsilon|X) = 0$ with probability one or $E(\varepsilon|X = x) = 0$ for all x in the support of X, and we shall sometimes remember to do this. One could equally write $Y = m(X)\eta$, where $E(\eta|X) = 1$, except that we should require $m(.) \neq 0$ otherwise $\eta = Y/m(X)$ may not be well defined. We are taking a **top down** approach here working from the random variables Y, X to define ε or η; often the reverse **bottoms up** approach is taken where (7.12) is assumed with say ε being independent of X, so that given X and ε one determines Y. A lot of thinking about regression proceeds from this conceptualization. Indeed, a convenient and popular simplification is to assume that the regression function is linear and the error term is

$$Y = \alpha + \beta X + \varepsilon, \tag{7.13}$$

where ε is independent of X with variance σ^2. This follows from joint normality of (Y, X), although normality is not necessary. We may have any kind of nonlinear function for example $m(x) = \sin(x^\beta)\exp(-x)$.

We have the following results about conditional expectations.

Theorem 7.9. *Law of iterated expectations. Suppose that $E(|Y|) < \infty$. Then we have the following property:*

$$E(Y) = E(E(Y|X)).$$

Proof. We suppose continuous random variables. Write $f_{YX}(y,x) = f_{Y|X}(y|x)f_X(x)$.

$$E(Y) = \int yf_Y(y)dy = \int y\left\{\int f_{YX}(y,x)dx\right\}dy$$

$$= \iint yf_{YX}(y,x)dydx = \int \left\{\int yf_{Y|X}(y|x)dy\right\}f_X(x)dx$$

$$= \int \{E(Y|X=x)\}f_X(x)dx = E(E(Y|X)). \qquad \square$$

Example 7.7. For example Y is temperature and $X \in \{day, night\}$. This says the average temperature is the average of average nighttime temperature and average daytime temperature. Say $E(Y|X = day) = 25$ and $E(Y|X = night) = 15$, then $E(Y) = 20$.

More generally, we have

$$E(Y|X) = E[E(Y|X,Z)|X] \qquad (7.14)$$

for any Y, X, Z. If I have more information, (X, Z), than you, X, then your forecast is the average of mine over my additional information.

Note that $E(Y|X = x)$ may exist for all x, while $E(Y)$ does not exist. For example $Y = X + \varepsilon$, where X is Cauchy and ε is normal. Then $E(Y|X = x) = x$ for all x but $E(Y)$ is not well defined. However, if $E(|Y|) < \infty$, then we must have $E(|Y||X = x) < \infty$ except at a countable number of points. For example, suppose that $Y = 1/X + \varepsilon$, where X has the density $f_X(x) = |x|1(|x| \le 1)$ and ε is normal. In this case

$$E(Y|X = x) = \frac{1}{x}$$

for any $x \ne 0$. Therefore,

$$E(Y) = \lim_{\epsilon \to 0}\int_\epsilon^1 \frac{1}{x}xdx + \lim_{\epsilon \to 0}\int_{-1}^{-\epsilon} \frac{1}{x}(-x)dx = \int_{-1}^1 \frac{1}{x}|x|dx = 2\int_0^1 dx = 2.$$

However, $E(Y|X = 0)$ is not well defined since

$$\infty = \lim_{n \to \infty} E\left(Y|X = \frac{1}{n}\right) \ne \lim_{n \to \infty} E\left(Y|X = \frac{-1}{n}\right) = -\infty.$$

Theorem 7.10. *Analysis of Variance formula. Suppose that $E(Y^2) < \infty$. Then we have the following property*

$$\text{var}(Y) = \overbrace{\text{var}(E(Y|X))}^{\text{Explained "sum of squares"}} + \overbrace{E(\text{var}(Y|X))}^{\text{Residual "sum of squares"}} \ .$$

Proof. We have

$$\text{var}(Y) = E[\{Y - E(Y)\}^2] = E(\{Y - E(Y|X) + E(Y|X) - E(Y)\}^2)$$
$$= E[\{Y - E(Y|X)\}^2] + E[\{E(Y|X) - E(Y)\}^2]$$
$$+ 2E[(Y - E(Y|X))[E(Y|X) - E(Y)]]$$
$$= I + II + III.$$

The first term is

$$E[\{Y - E(Y|X)\}^2] = E\left[E\{(Y - E(Y|X))^2|X\}\right] = E\,\text{var}(Y|X)$$

The second term is

$$E[\{E(Y|X) - E(Y)\}^2] = \text{var}\,E(Y|X)$$

The third term is zero, because $\varepsilon = Y - E(Y|X)$ is such that $E(\varepsilon|X) = 0$ and $E(Y|X) - E(Y)$ is measurable with respect to X, i.e., is just a function of X. So use earlier Theorem

$$E(\varepsilon h(X)) = E[E(\varepsilon h(X)|X)] = E[h(X)E(\varepsilon|X)] = 0. \qquad \square$$

Example 7.8. In the temperature example, say $\text{var}(Y|X = day) = 5$ and $\text{var}(Y|X = night) = 10$, then

$$\text{var}(Y) = \frac{1}{2}(5 + 10) + \text{var}(E(Y|X)) = 32.5$$
$$\text{var}(E(Y|X)) = \frac{1}{2}(25 - 20)^2 + \frac{1}{2}(15 - 20)^2 = 25.$$

Example 7.9. Consider the linear regression example

$$Y = \alpha + \beta X + \varepsilon,$$

where ε is independent of X with variance σ^2. Then

$$\text{var}(Y) = E(\text{var}(Y|X)) + \text{var}(E(Y|X))$$
$$= E(\sigma^2) + \text{var}(\alpha + \beta X)$$
$$= \sigma^2 + \beta^2 \text{var}(X).$$

Only in the special case where $E(Y|X)$ is constant with respect to X is it the case that $\text{var}(Y) = E(\text{var}(Y|X))$.

We next introduce the concept of mean independence.

Definition 7.8. We say that Y is mean independent of X if $E(Y|X) = \mu$ for all x.

Theorem 7.11. *Suppose that $E(Y|X) = \alpha = E(Y)$ with probability one. Then* $\text{cov}(Y, X) = 0$, *but not vice versa.*

Proof. We have

$$
\begin{aligned}
\text{cov}(Y, X) &= E(XY) - \mu_X \mu_Y = E([XE(Y|X)]) - \mu_X \mu_Y \\
&= E[XE(Y)] - \mu_X \mu_Y = \mu_X \mu_Y - \mu_X \mu_Y \\
&= 0. \qquad\qquad\qquad\qquad\qquad\qquad\qquad\qquad\quad \square
\end{aligned}
$$

We have a hierarchy of dependence concepts. Independence is strongest and implies mean independence, which in turn implies lack of correlation. In the normal distribution they are equivalent.

We next give a further interpretation of the regression function as being the best mean squared error predictor and compare it with the best linear such predictor.

Theorem 7.12. *Suppose that $EY^2 < \infty$ and $EX^2 < \infty$. Then we have the following properties:*
(a) $E(Y|X)$ minimizes $E[(Y - g(X))^2]$ over all measurable functions $g(\cdot)$;
(b) The linear function $E_L(Y|X) = \alpha_o + \beta_o X$, where $\alpha_o = E(Y) - \beta_o E(X)$ and $\beta_o = \text{cov}(Y, X)/\text{var}(X)$, minimizes $E[(Y - \alpha - \beta X)^2]$, and

$$
E[(Y - E(Y|X))^2] \leq E[(Y - E_L(Y|X))^2].
$$

Proof of (a). Using the Law of Iterated Expectations we write

$$
E[(Y - g(X))^2] = E\left[E[(Y - g(X))^2 | X] \right].
$$

Then by completing the square we obtain

$$
\begin{aligned}
E[(Y - g(X))^2 | X] &= (g(X) - E(Y|X))^2 + \text{var}(Y|X) \\
&\geq \text{var}(Y|X)
\end{aligned}
$$

for all functions g and all realizations X with equality if and only if $g(X) = E(Y|X)$ with probability one, which establishes the result. $\qquad\square$

Proof of (b). Let $\widetilde{Y} = Y - E(Y)$ and $\widetilde{X} = X - E(X)$. Then we consider the problem to minimize with respect to α, β the objective function

$$E[(\widetilde{Y} - \alpha - \beta\widetilde{X})^2] = E(\widetilde{Y})^2 + \alpha^2 + \beta^2 E(\widetilde{X}^2) - 2\beta E(\widetilde{X}\widetilde{Y}).$$

Clearly, $\alpha = 0$ is minimal, and since $E(\widetilde{Y})^2$ does not depend on the parameters we minimize $\beta^2 E(\widetilde{X}^2) - 2\beta E(\widetilde{X}\widetilde{Y})$ with respect to β. Then dividing through by $E(\widetilde{X}^2)$ (assuming this is non-zero) this is equivalent to minimizing

$$(\beta - \beta_o)^2 - \beta_o^2,$$

which can be achieved only by setting $\beta = \beta_o$ as claimed. It follows that α_o, β_o minimize $E[(Y - \alpha - \beta X)^2]$.

The second result follows from the property of conditional expectation, since $E_L(Y|X)$ is just another measurable function of X to be compared with the regression function. Note that in general the regression function $E(Y|X) \neq E_L(Y|X)$. □

Note that we may define conditional expectation and best linear prediction without reference to the second moment of Y although the above theorem uses that property.

Example 7.10. Suppose that

$$Y = X + \varepsilon,$$

where $X \sim N(0, \sigma_X^2)$ and $\varepsilon \sim N(0, \sigma_\varepsilon^2)$ with ε independent of X. Then

$$E_L(Y|X) = \frac{\text{cov}(X, Y)}{\text{var}(X)} X = X = E(Y|X).$$

But what about $E(X|Y)$? We have

$$E_L(X|Y) = \frac{\text{cov}(X, Y)}{\text{var}(Y)} Y = \frac{\sigma_X^2}{\sigma_X^2 + \sigma_\varepsilon^2} Y = E(X|Y),$$

where the final equality follows from Bayes rule applied to the bivariate normal (X, Y). Suppose instead that $X \sim U[-\sqrt{3}\sigma_X, \sqrt{3}\sigma_X]$ and $\varepsilon \sim U[-\sqrt{3}\sigma_\varepsilon, \sqrt{3}\sigma_\varepsilon]$, so that (X, Y) are no longer normal. Then we have the same variances and covariances as before so that

$$E_L(X|Y) = \frac{\text{cov}(X, Y)}{\text{var}(Y)} Y = \frac{\sigma_X^2}{\sigma_X^2 + \sigma_\varepsilon^2} Y,$$

but $E(X|Y) \neq E_L(X|Y)$ by the following argument. Suppose that $Y = \sqrt{3}(\sigma_X + \sigma_\varepsilon)$, which is the maximal value that Y could achieve, then $E(X|Y) =$

$\sqrt{3}\sigma_X$, because in that case we know that X has to be at its maximum. This does not coincide with the best linear predictor evaluated at the same Y. In this case, the best predictor of X by Y has to be nonlinear.

We discuss here the relationship between the regression function and the best linear fit. Suppose that Y, X are scalar random variables and that

$$E(Y|X) = g(X)$$

for some differentiable function g. The effect of X on Y could be measured by the derivative of g, $g'(x)$, which varies with the point of evaluation. The average **marginal effect** is

$$\delta = E\left[g'(X)\right] = \int g'(x)f_X(x)dx = \int \left\{\frac{\partial}{\partial x}\int yf_{Y|X=x}(y|x)dy\right\}f_X(x)dx.$$
(7.15)

This quantity is widely used in nonlinear models to summarize the effect of the X's on the y. In the case where the regression function is linear, i.e., $g(x) = \alpha + \beta x$ for constants α, β, then $\delta = \beta$. Consider the general nonlinear case. In general we do not expect $\delta = \beta$.

Many authors argue heuristically, that the linear approximation to the regression function obtained by finding the **Taylor Approximation** to m at its mean. So consider the second order Mean Value Theorem

$$m(X) = m(\mu) + (X - \mu)m'(\mu) + \frac{1}{2}(X - \mu)^2 m''(X^*),$$

$$\simeq m(\mu) + (X - \mu)m'(\mu),$$
(7.16)

where X^* is a value that lies between $\mu = E(X)$ and X. In effect they argue that $\beta = m'(\mu)$ and $\alpha = m(\mu) - \mu m'(\mu)$, i.e., the best linear fit is providing a linear approximation to m. This is not true in general.

Example 7.11. Suppose that

$$Y = 1 + X^3 + \varepsilon$$

where $X \sim U[0, 1]$ and ε standard normal. We have

$$E_L(Y|X) = \frac{16}{20} + \frac{9}{10}X$$

$$\delta = 3EX^2 = 1 \quad ; \quad \beta = \frac{9}{10} \quad ; \quad m'(E(X)) = \frac{3}{4}.$$
(7.17)

In general, all three quantities in (7.17) are different, and the best linear approximation to Y and hence to $m(X)$ is not given by the Taylor approximation. See Fig. 7.1.

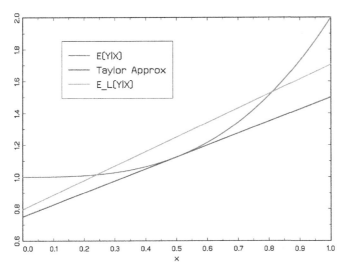

FIGURE 7.1 Shows different linear approximations to a nonlinear regression function

When is the linearization (7.16) a good approximation? We can show that

$$E\left[\left|\left(m(X) - m(\mu) - (X - \mu)m'(\mu)\right)\right|\right] \le \frac{1}{2}\mathrm{var}(X)\sup_x |m''(x)|,$$

so that if $\mathrm{var}(X)$ or $\sup_x |m''(x)|$ is "small" and the other quantity not offsettingly large then the approximation error can be small enough such that the linear approximation is good and the α and β are essentially as argued. Clearly, if m is linear then $m'' = 0$ but otherwise there will be approximation error.

There is one special case where the slope of the best linear fit β measures the marginal effect.

Theorem 7.13. *Suppose that $X \sim N(\mu_X, \sigma_X^2)$ and that $Y = g(X) + \varepsilon$, where $E(\varepsilon|X) = 0$. Then $\delta = \beta$.*

Proof. For any normally distributed random variables, **Stein's Lemma** (essentially integration by parts) says that

$$\mathrm{cov}(X, g(X)) = \mathrm{var}(X)E\left[g'(X)\right]. \tag{7.18}$$

Furthermore,

$$\mathrm{cov}(X, Y) = \mathrm{cov}(X, g(X) + \varepsilon) = \mathrm{cov}(X, g(X)) + \mathrm{cov}(X, \varepsilon) = \mathrm{cov}(X, g(X)).$$

Therefore,

$$E\left[g'(X)\right] = \frac{\mathrm{cov}(X, Y)}{\mathrm{var}(X)} = \beta,$$

the slope of the best linear fit to Y.   □

This says that for normally distributed random covariates the linear regression slope measures the average marginal effect even when the regression function is nonlinear.

We conclude with a discussion of the case where Y is continuous and X is discrete. This case is rather simple, and a lot of the above discussion is not needed because the regression function is very simple and possibly linear. Consider the case where $X \in \{0, 1\}$ and $X = 1$ with probability p. Then we have two conditional densities $f_{Y|X=0}$ and $f_{Y|X=1}$ and the conditional expectation is either $\int y f_{Y|X=0}(y) dy \equiv \alpha_1$ or $\int y f_{Y|X=1}(y) dy \equiv \alpha_2$ and we can therefore equivalently write

$$E(Y|X) = \alpha + \beta X$$

with $\alpha = \alpha_1$ and $\beta = \alpha_2 - \alpha_1$.

We next turn to a discussion of the conditional median and its interpretation. The conditional median can be defined similarly through the conditional distribution. Specifically, $M(Y|X = x) = F_{Y|X}^{-1}(0.5|x)$. We may also write

$$Y = M(Y|X) + \overbrace{Y - M(Y|X)}^{\eta},$$

where $M(\eta|X) = 0$ because $M(Y|X)$ is a constant in the conditional distribution.

Theorem 7.14. *Suppose that the distribution of Y given X is continuous. Then $M(Y|X)$ minimizes the objective function $E[|Y - g(X)|]$ over all measurable functions $g(\cdot)$.*

This follows by similar arguments given for the unconditional case. Finally, does the following equality (Law of the Iterated Median) hold?

$$M(Y) = M(M(Y|X)). \tag{7.19}$$

This statement is not always true, although for example in the bivariate normal case it is, see below.

Example 7.12. Suppose that

$$Y = X + \eta,$$

where $\eta|X = x \sim U[-x, x]$, which has conditional median zero, and $X \sim U[0, 1]$. Thus $M(Y|X) = X$ and so $M(M(Y|X)) = M(X) = 1/2$. So now we have to check whether

$$\Pr[Y \le 1/2] = \Pr[X + \eta \le 1/2] = 1/2.$$

The left hand side is equal to

$$E\left[1(X + \eta \le 1/2)\right] = E\left(E\left[1(X + \eta \le 1/2)|X\right]\right) = E\left(\Pr[X + \eta \le 1/2|X]\right)$$

by an application of the law of iterated expectation. We have

$$\Pr[X + \eta \le 1/2|X = x] = \Pr[\eta \le 1/2 - x|X] = \begin{cases} 1 & x \le 1/4 \\ \frac{1}{4x} & x > 1/4 \end{cases}.$$

Taking expectations

$$E\left(\Pr[X + \eta \le 1/2|X]\right) = \frac{1}{4} + \int_{1/4}^{1} \frac{dx}{4x} = \frac{1}{4}(1 + \log 4) \simeq 0.6.$$

In fact the median of Y is about 0.37. To conclude we have shown that $M(M(Y|X)) \ne M(Y)$.

7.5 EXAMPLES

Example 7.13. MULTINOMIAL. We can think of this as a vector of k binary outcomes, thus we can define random variables X_i such that

$$(X_1, \ldots, X_k) = \begin{cases} (1, 0, \ldots, 0) & \text{with probability } p_1 \\ (0, 1, \ldots, 0) & \text{with probability } p_2 \\ \vdots & \vdots \\ (0, 0, \ldots, 1) & \text{with probability } p_k \end{cases} \quad \sum_{j=1}^{k} p_j = 1.$$

The random variables X_i are themselves Bernoulli random variables with respective parameters p_i. Can $X_1, \ldots, X_k$ be mutually independent? No, because $\sum_{i=1}^{k} X_i = 1$. There is perfect dependence between the random variables, and the conditional distributions are degenerate. Now suppose we repeat the multinomial n times. We get $(n_1, \ldots, n_k) = Y$

$$\Pr(Y = (n_1, \ldots, n_k)) = \frac{n!}{n_1! \cdots n_k!} p_1^{n_1} \times \cdots \times p_k^{n_k} \text{ for any } \sum_{j=1}^{k} n_j = n.$$

Letting $Y = (Y_1, \ldots, Y_k)$, the marginals Y_ℓ, $\ell = 1, \ldots, k$, are Binomial(n, p_ℓ). They are no longer perfectly dependent. Knowing that $Y_1 = n_1$ does not pinpoint $Y_2, \ldots, Y_n$ for me although it does tell you $\sum_{\ell=2}^{n} Y_\ell$.

Example 7.14. EUROMILLIONS LOTTERY. The outcome is a set of 5 numbers between 1 and 50 chosen equally likely but without replacement (you can't have the same number). That is

$$X = (Y_1, Y_2, Y_3, Y_4, Y_5),$$

where $Y_1 \in I$, where $I = \{1, 2, \ldots, 50\}$ with $\Pr(Y_1 = i) = 1/50$ for $i = 1, 2, \ldots, 50$, while $Y_2|Y_1 = i \in I \setminus \{i\}$ with probability $1/49$ etc. The support of X is the product of $(I \times I \times I \times I \times I) \setminus T$, where T is the set of all ties such that $Y_i = Y_j$ for any $i \neq j$. The probability of winning is

$$\frac{1}{50} \times \frac{1}{49} \times \frac{1}{48} \times \frac{1}{47} \times \frac{1}{46}$$

How would you test whether the lottery is truly random?

Example 7.15. Let $Y_j \sim Po(\lambda)$, $j = 1, 2$, be independent Poisson random variables with parameter λ and let

$$X = \frac{Y_1}{Y_1 + Y_2}$$

with $0/0 = 0$. Verify that X is a random variable whose support is the set of rational numbers on the interval $[0, 1]$, i.e.,

$$\Pr(X = x) > 0 \text{ for all } x \in \mathbb{S} = \mathbb{Q} \cap [0, 1].$$

Example 7.16. BIVARIATE NORMAL. We say that X, Y is bivariate normal if

$$f_{X,Y}(x, y | \mu_X, \mu_Y, \sigma_X^2, \sigma_Y^2, \rho) = \frac{1}{2\pi \sigma_X \sigma_Y \sqrt{1 - \rho^2}} \exp\left(-\frac{u(x, y)}{2(1 - \rho^2)}\right),$$

$$u(x, y) = \left(\frac{x - \mu_X}{\sigma_X}\right)^2 + \left(\frac{y - \mu_Y}{\sigma_Y}\right)^2 - \left(\frac{2\rho(x - \mu_X)(y - \mu_Y)}{\sigma_X \sigma_Y}\right)$$

where $\mu_X = E(X), \mu_Y = E(Y), \sigma_X^2 = \mathrm{var}(X), \sigma_Y^2 = \mathrm{var}(Y)$, and $\rho = \mathrm{corr}(X, Y)$.

Theorem 7.15. *(a) If X, Y are bivariate normal as above, then $X \sim N(\mu_X, \sigma_X^2)$, which is shown by integration of the joint density with respect to the other variables.*
(b) The conditional distributions of X are Gaussian too

$$f_{Y|X}(y|x) \sim N(\mu_{Y|X}, \sigma_{Y|X}^2)$$

where the conditional mean vector and conditional covariance matrix are given by

$$\mu_{Y|X} = E(Y|X) = \mu_Y + \frac{\sigma_{XY}}{\sigma_X^2}(X - \mu_X)$$

$$\sigma_{Y|X}^2 = \sigma_Y^2 - \frac{\sigma_{XY}^2}{\sigma_X^2}.$$

In fact, we may write for the bivariate normal case

$$Y = \mu_Y + \frac{\sigma_{XY}}{\sigma_X^2}(X - \mu_X) + \varepsilon, \tag{7.20}$$

where ε is independent of X with mean zero and variance $\sigma_{Y|X}^2$. Note that the conditional median is equal to the conditional mean. In fact, when $\mu_X = \mu_Y = 0$ and $\sigma_Y^2 = \sigma_X^2 = 1$ we have

$$Y = \rho X + \sqrt{1 - \rho^2}Z, \tag{7.21}$$

where Z is standard normal independent of X. Note that the conditional median is equal to the conditional mean. If (X, Y) are jointly normally distributed, they are independent if and only if $\text{cov}(X, Y) = 0$.

Bayes rule combines very well with normal distributions to yield simple solutions to **signal extraction** problems.

Theorem 7.16. *Suppose that $X \sim N(\mu_x, \sigma_x^2)$ and $Y|X \sim N(X, \sigma_u^2)$. Then*

$$X|Y = y \sim N(m(y), v(y))$$

$$m(y) = \frac{\sigma_u^2}{\sigma_u^2 + \sigma_x^2}\mu_x + \frac{\sigma_x^2}{\sigma_u^2 + \sigma_x^2}y$$

$$v(y) = \frac{\sigma_x^2 \sigma_u^2}{\sigma_u^2 + \sigma_x^2}.$$

Proof. We have $Y \sim N(\mu_x, \sigma_x^2 + \sigma_u^2)$, so that

$$f_X(x) = \frac{1}{\sqrt{2\pi\sigma_x^2}} \exp\left(-\frac{1}{2}(x - \mu_x)^2/\sigma_x^2\right)$$

$$f_{Y|X}(y|x) = \frac{1}{\sqrt{2\pi\sigma_u^2}} \exp\left(-\frac{1}{2}(y - x)^2/\sigma_u^2\right)$$

$$f_Y(y) = \frac{1}{\sqrt{2\pi\sigma_x^2 + \sigma_u^2}} \exp\left(-\frac{1}{2}(y - \mu_x)^2/(\sigma_x^2 + \sigma_u^2)\right).$$

Bayes Theorem says that

$$f_{X|Y}(x|y) = \frac{f_{Y|X}(y|x)f_X(x)}{f_Y(y)}.$$

We have by combination of the terms that the exponent of $f_{X|Y}(x|y)$ is minus one half times

$$\frac{(y-\mu_x)^2}{\sigma_u^2+\sigma_x^2} - \frac{(y-x)^2}{\sigma_u^2} - \frac{(x-\mu_x)^2}{\sigma_x^2}$$

$$= -\frac{1}{\sigma_u^2\sigma_x^2\left(\sigma_u^2+\sigma_x^2\right)}\left(x\left(\sigma_u^2+\sigma_x^2\right) - y\sigma_x^2 - \sigma_u^2\mu_x\right)^2$$

$$= -\frac{\left(\sigma_u^2+\sigma_x^2\right)}{\sigma_u^2\sigma_x^2}\left(x - \frac{\sigma_x^2}{\left(\sigma_u^2+\sigma_x^2\right)}y - \frac{\sigma_u^2}{\left(\sigma_u^2+\sigma_x^2\right)}\mu_x\right)^2.$$

Therefore, this is the density of a normal with the stated mean and variance.   □

We next consider the class of Mixture Models, which provide a simple way of generalizing the classical distributions, and allowing for **heterogeneity**. That is, individuals may have difference preference parameters for example and one might think of these **hyperparameters** as coming from some distribution across individuals and then given the preference parameter some other outcome is realized.

Example 7.17. NORMAL MIXTURES. For example,

$$Y|\mu,\sigma^2 \sim N(\mu,\sigma^2), \qquad \text{where } (\mu,\sigma^2) \sim P_{\mu,\sigma^2}$$

for some distribution P_{μ,σ^2}. We can write $Y = \mu + \sigma Z$, where Z is standard normal and independent of (μ,σ^2). This says essentially that within a certain subgroup you have a normal distribution, but that the unconditional distribution is some average over subgroups indexed by μ,σ^2, with proportions determined by the distribution P_{μ,σ^2}. The unconditional distribution of Y is not normally distributed and can be asymmetric. Consider a special case of this, a scale mixture of normals, in which:

$$Y|\sigma^2 \sim N(0,\sigma^2),$$

where σ^2 has some density p. The density function f_Y of a scale mixture Y is

$$f_Y(y) = \int \phi_\sigma(y)p(\sigma^2)d\sigma^2.$$

In this case, Y is symmetric about zero, but can be leptokurtic. We can write $Y = \sigma Z$, where $Z \sim N(0, 1)$ and σ are mutually independent. It follows that $\text{var}(Y) = E\sigma^2$, and

$$EY^4 = E(\sigma^4)EZ^4 = 3E(\sigma^4) \geq 3\text{var}(Y)^2 = 3E^2\sigma^2,$$

because $\text{var}(\sigma^2) = E\sigma^4 - E^2\sigma^2 \geq 0$ with strict inequality unless σ^2 is constant with probability one.

We give an example for a discrete random variable.

Example 7.18. POISSON MIXTURE. Suppose that $Y|\lambda$ is Poisson (λ) and λ is a continuous random variable on $(0, \infty)$ with density f. Then Y is a discrete random variable with support the non-negative integers with

$$\Pr(Y = y) = E_\lambda[\Pr(Y = y|\lambda)] = E_\lambda \left[\frac{e^{-\lambda}\lambda^y}{y!} \right] = \int_0^\infty \frac{e^{-\lambda}\lambda^y}{y!} f(\lambda)d\lambda.$$

This frees up the Poisson from the restriction that the mean is equal to the variance. This is important in practice, because many datasets report quite different values for these moments. We have

$$\text{var}(Y) = E(\lambda) + \text{var}(\lambda) \geq E(\lambda),$$

and we say that Y has **overdispersion**.

7.6 MULTIVARIATE TRANSFORMATIONS

Suppose we have some transformation

$$g : \mathbb{R}^p \to \mathbb{R}^q, \ q \leq p$$
$$Y = g(u) = g(u_1, \ldots, u_p) = [g_1(u), \ldots, g_q(u)].$$

Starting from the p.m.f. or p.d.f. of $u_1, \ldots, u_p$, we would like to calculate the p.m.f. or p.d.f. of Y. We state a general transformation result that under some conditions gives the joint density function of the transformed random variables. This generalizes the univariate result and is essentially the change of variables formula for multivariate calculus. We just consider the case $p = q = 2$ here because the full result requires matrix theory, which is treated later. What is $q < p$, then we can't directly apply the transformation result. However, we may complete the system by adding some redundant transformations, apply the theorem, and then integrate out those components not of interest.

Example 7.19. The **simultaneous equations model**

$$B_{11}Y_1 + B_{12}Y_2 + C_{11}X_1 + C_{12}X_2 = u_1$$
$$B_{21}Y_1 + B_{22}Y_2 + C_{21}X_1 + C_{22}X_2 = u_2,$$

which often is used to represent the interaction of supply and demand. Often assume that (u_1, u_2) is bivariate normal with parameters $(0, 0, \sigma_1^2, \sigma_2^2, \rho_{12})$ and that X *is fixed* [or, more precisely, every calculation is made in the conditional distribution given X]. We would like to calculate the distribution of Y_1, Y_2 condition on X_1, X_2.

Example 7.20. A more general class of models allow nonlinear transformations. For example,

$$\begin{bmatrix} \frac{y_1^{\lambda_1} - 1}{\lambda_1} \\ \frac{y_2^{\lambda_2} - 1}{\lambda_2} \end{bmatrix} = \begin{bmatrix} \mu_1 \\ \mu_2 \end{bmatrix} + \begin{bmatrix} u_1 \\ u_2 \end{bmatrix}$$

is an example of a nonlinear simultaneous equation. What is the distribution of $y = (y_1, y_2)$ given the distribution of $u = (u_1, u_2)$.

We give following result for transformations from $\mathbb{R}^2$ to $\mathbb{R}^2$. A more general result can be expressed in terms of matrix algebra, which we treat later.

Theorem 7.17. *Suppose that $p = q = 2$ and that $X \in \mathbb{R}^2$ is continuously distributed with density function f_X. Suppose that*

$$S = \{x : f_X(x) > 0\} = \bigcup_{j=1}^{m} S_j,$$

where $g_j = (g_{j1}, g_{j2}) : \mathbb{R}^2 \to \mathbb{R}^2$ with

$$y_1 = g_{j1}(x_1, x_2), \quad y_2 = g_{j2}(x_1, x_2)$$

is a one-to-one transformation of S_j into $g_j(S_j) = Y_j \subset \mathbb{R}^2$ for $j = 1, \ldots, m$. Let

$$x_1 = g_{1j}^{-1}(y), x_2 = g_{2j}^{-1}(y)$$

denote the inverse transformation of $Y_j \to S_j$. Suppose that all the partial derivatives are continuous on Y_j and the quantities

$$J_j(y) = \frac{\partial g_{j1}^{-1}}{\partial y_1} \frac{\partial g_{j2}^{-1}}{\partial y_2} - \frac{\partial g_{j1}^{-1}}{\partial y_2} \frac{\partial g_{j2}^{-1}}{\partial y_1} \tag{7.22}$$

are non-zero. Then

$$f_Y(y) = \sum_{j=1}^{m} |J_j(y)| f_X(g_{j1}^{-1}(y), g_{j2}^{-1}(y))$$

for any $y \in \mathcal{Y} = \bigcup_{j=1}^{m} \mathcal{Y}_j$.

Example 7.21. In the simultaneous equations case with no X, the transformation is one-to-one for all u_1, u_2 provided

$$J = B_{11}B_{22} - B_{12}B_{21} \neq 0.$$

We have

$$\frac{\partial u_i}{\partial Y_j} = B_{ij},$$

so that

$$f_Y(y) = |B_{11}B_{22} - B_{12}B_{21}| \, f_u(B_{11}Y_1 + B_{12}Y_2, B_{21}Y_1 + B_{22}Y_2).$$

Example 7.22. In the Box–Cox case

$$J = \frac{\partial \theta_1(y_1)}{\partial \lambda_1} \cdot \frac{\partial \theta_2(y_2)}{\partial y_2},$$

so that

$$f_Y(y) = \frac{\partial \theta_1}{\partial \lambda_1}(y_1) \frac{\partial \theta_2}{\partial \lambda_2}(y_2) f_u(\theta_1(y_1), \theta_2(y_2)).$$

7.6.1 Some Special Cases Where $q = 1$ and $p = 2$

We can solve some questions without the general transformation theorem.

Example 7.23. Suppose that $Y = X_1 + X_2$, where X_1, X_2 are continuously distributed with joint density $f_{X_1 X_2}$. We have

$$
\begin{aligned}
\Pr[Y \leq y] &= \Pr[X_1 + X_2 \leq y] \\
&= \iint_{x_1 + x_2 \leq y} f_{X_1 X_2}(x_1, x_2) dx_1 dx_2 \\
&= \int_{-\infty}^{\infty} \left[\int_{-\infty}^{y - x_2} f_{X_1 X_2}(x_1, x_2) dx_1 \right] dx_2 \\
&= \int_{-\infty}^{\infty} \left[\int_{-\infty}^{y} f_{X_1 X_2}(u - x_2, x_2) du \right] dx_2,
\end{aligned}
$$

which we denote by $F_Y(y)$. Here, we use the change of variables $x_1 \to u = x_1 - x_2$. Then

$$f_Y(y) = \frac{d}{dy} F_Y(y) = \frac{d}{dy} \int_{-\infty}^{y} \int_{-\infty}^{\infty} f_{X_1 X_2}(u - x_2, x_2) dx_2 du$$

$$= \int_{-\infty}^{\infty} f_{X_1 X_2}(y - x_2, x_2) dx_2,$$

by symmetry. When $X_1 \perp\!\!\!\perp X_2$,

$$F_Y(y) = \int_{-\infty}^{\infty} F_{X_1}(x_1) f_{X_2}(y - x_1) dx_1$$

$$f_Y(y) = \int_{-\infty}^{\infty} f_{X_1}(x_1) f_{X_2}(y - x_1) dx_1,$$

which is called the **convolution** of f_{X_1} with f_{X_2}. We denote $f_Y(y)$ by $(f_{X_1} * f_{X_2})(y)$. This is quite a difficult expression to work with in general. The characteristic function is easier to work with, at least in the independent case. Recall that

$$\varphi_Y(t) = E e^{it Y_1} = E e^{it(X_1 + X_2)} \overset{\text{independence}}{=} E e^{it X_1} E e^{it X_2} = \varphi_{X_1}(t) \cdot \varphi_{X_2}(t),$$

where $\varphi_{X_j}(t) = E e^{it X_j}$, $j = 1, 2$. In other words, convolution is just multiplication in the Fourier domain.

In the special case that X_2 has zero mean, Y is a mean preserving spread of X_1, and one can see that $\text{var}(Y) \geq \text{var}(X_1)$. In fact, one can show that $\int_{-\infty}^{y} F_Y(y') dy' \leq \int_{-\infty}^{y} F_{X_1}(y') dy'$ for all y.

An alternative method is to apply the transformation theorem. In this case we add a redundant transformation. Specifically, let

$$Y_1 = X_1 + X_2 \quad ; \quad Y_2 = X_1 - X_2,$$

which has well defined inverse

$$X_1 = \frac{1}{2}(Y_1 + Y_2) \quad ; \quad X_2 = \frac{1}{2}(Y_1 - Y_2).$$

We obtain the joint distribution of Y_1, Y_2 by applying the formula, with $|J| = 1/2$, and then obtain the marginal distribution of Y_1 by integrating out over Y_2. The choice of redundant transformation is arbitrary. Instead one could take

$$Y_1 = X_1 + X_2 \quad ; \quad Y_2 = X_1 - 2X_2,$$

which has well defined inverse

$$X_1 = \frac{1}{3}(2Y_1 + Y_2) \quad ; \quad X_2 = \frac{1}{3}(Y_1 - Y_2).$$

Although the joint distribution of Y_1, Y_2 is different in this case, the marginal distribution of Y_1 is the same.

Example 7.24. Let $Y = X_1 X_2$, where $X_i \geq 0$. Then we have

$$\Pr[Y \leq y] = \iint_{x_1 x_2 \leq y} f_{X_1 X_2}(x_1, x_2) dx_1 dx_2$$

$$= \int_0^\infty \left[\int_{y/x_2}^\infty f_{X_1 X_2}(x_1, x_2) dx_1 \right] dx_2.$$

Substitute $u = x_1 x_2 \Rightarrow du = x_2 dx_1$, i.e., $dx_1 = \frac{du}{x_2}$. Then

$$F_Y(y) = \int_0^y \int_0^\infty \frac{1}{x_1} f_{X_1 X_2}\left(x_1, \frac{u}{x_1}\right) dx_1 du,$$

so that

$$f_Y(y) = \int_0^\infty \frac{1}{x_1} f_{X_1 X_2}\left(x_1, \frac{y}{x_1}\right) dx_1.$$

In this case, applying the transformation theorem, we might add the redundant transformation

$$Y_1 = X_1 X_2 \quad ; \quad Y_2 = X_1/X_2,$$

which has well defined inverse

$$X_1 = \sqrt{Y_1 Y_2} \quad ; \quad X_2 = \sqrt{Y_1/Y_2}.$$

Example 7.25. Suppose that $Y = \max\{X_1, X_2\}$. This quantity is of interest in many applications from competing risks models to value at extreme risk models. We have

$$F_Y(y) = \Pr[Y \leq y] = \Pr[X_1 \leq y \text{ and } X_2 \leq y]$$

$$= \int_{-\infty}^y \int_{-\infty}^y f_{X_1 X_2}(x_1, x_2) dx_1 dx_2.$$

The density $f_Y(y) = \frac{d}{dy} F_Y(y)$, and we take the total derivative of the integral to obtain that

$$f_Y(y) = \int_{-\infty}^y f_{X_1 X_2}(y, x_2) dx_2 + \int_{-\infty}^y f_{X_1 X_2}(x_1, y) dx_1. \tag{7.23}$$

In the special case that $X_1 \perp\!\!\!\perp X_2$,

$$F_Y(y) = \int_{-\infty}^{y} f_{X_1}(x)dx \int_{-\infty}^{y} f_{X_2}(x)dx = F_{X_1}(y) \cdot F_{X_2}(y)$$

$$f_Y(y) = F_{X_1}(y)f_{X_2}(y) + F_{X_2}(y)f_{X_1}(y).$$

In this case, applying the transformation theorem is a little tricky. Perhaps we might complete the system by

$$Y_1 = \max\{X_1, X_2\} \quad ; \quad Y_2 = \min\{X_1, X_2\}.$$

We then divide $\mathbb{R}$ into two regions $S_1 = \{(x_1, x_2) : x_1 > x_2\}$ and $S_2 = \{(x_1, x_2) : x_1 < x_2\}$; we may ignore the case that $x_1 = x_2$, since this is a set of measure zero on the plain. On the set S_1, $Y_1 = X_1$ and $Y_2 = X_2$, and the inverse transformation is $X_1 = Y_1$ and $X_2 = Y_2$ with $|J| = 1$, while on the set S_2, $Y_1 = X_2$ and $Y_2 = X_1$ etc. It follows that

$$f_{Y_1,Y_2}(y_1, y_2) = \begin{cases} f_{X_1,X_2}(y_1, y_2) + f_{X_1,X_2}(y_2, y_1) & \text{if } y_1 \geq y_2 \\ 0 & \text{else.} \end{cases}$$

The marginal density is obtained by integrating y_2 out from $-\infty$ to y_1 to obtain (7.23).

7.6.2   Copula

Suppose that $Y_1 = F_{X_1}(X_1)$ and $Y_2 = F_{X_2}(X_2)$, then Y_1 and Y_2 are uniformly distributed. The function

$$C(u_1, u_2) = \Pr(Y_1 \leq u_1, Y_2 \leq u_2)$$

is called the **Copula** of X_1, X_2; it is a bivariate distribution function on $[0, 1] \times [0, 1]$. The joint distribution of X_1, X_2 is equivalently described by the copula $C(u_1, u_2)$ and the two marginal distribution functions F_{X_1} and F_{X_2}. This allows separate modelling of the dependence (by modelling C) from the marginal distributions.

Theorem 7.18. *(Sklar) Suppose that X_1, X_2 are continuously distributed. Then the joint distribution of X_1, X_2 can be written uniquely as*

$$\Pr(X_1 \leq x, X_2 \leq x_2) = C\left(F_{X_1}(x_1), F_{X_1}(x_2)\right)$$

for some distribution function $C : [0, 1]^2 \longrightarrow [0, 1]$.

This approach converts marginal distributions into a standard scale, which allows modelling of the dependence in a common framework. If $C(u_1, u_2) = u_1 u_2$, then X_1 and X_2 are independent. A leading example is the so-called Gaussian copula

$$C(u_1, u_2) = \Phi_2 \left(\Phi^{-1}(u_1), \Phi^{-1}(u_2); \rho \right) \qquad (7.24)$$

where Φ is the standard univariate normal c.d.f., while $\Phi_2(s, t; \rho)$ is the c.d.f. of the standard bivariate normal distribution (with mean vector zero and variances equal to one) with correlation parameter ρ. This implies the model for the bivariate c.d.f. and density function

$$F(x_1, x_2) = \frac{1}{2\pi \sqrt{1 - \rho^2}}$$

$$\times \int_{-\infty}^{\Phi^{-1}(F_1(x_1))} \int_{-\infty}^{\Phi^{-1}(F_1(x_2))} \exp \left(-\frac{s^2 + t^2 - 2\rho st}{2 \left(1 - \rho^2 \right)} \right) ds \, dt$$

$$(7.25)$$

$$f(x_1, x_2) = \frac{1}{\sqrt{1 - \rho^2}} \exp \left(-\frac{\rho \Phi^{-1}(F_1(x_1)) \Phi^{-1}(F_2(x_2))}{2 \left(1 - \rho^2 \right)} \right) \times f_1(x_1) f_2(x_2).$$

$$(7.26)$$

This has been called **The formula that killed Wall Street**, and not because it is too complicated;[2] it is because it was widely used in credit risk modelling, because it is very flexible with regard to the marginal distributions not being Gaussian and so had the veneer of respectable generality. The weakness was that not only are extreme events likely but when they happen for one risk they tend to happen to all risks.

---

2. Needless to say, the rumours of its death were greatly exaggerated.

Chapter 8

Asymptotic Theory

8.1 INEQUALITIES

This section gives some inequalities that are useful tools in establishing a variety of probabilistic results.

Theorem 8.1. TRIANGLE INEQUALITY. *For random variables* X, Y

$$E|X + Y| \leq E|X| + E|Y|.$$

Proof. This just follows from the property of real numbers and the additivity of expectation. □

Theorem 8.2. CAUCHY–SCHWARZ INEQUALITY. *For random variables* $X, Y,$

$$(E(XY))^2 \leq E\left(X^2\right) \times E(Y^2)$$

with equality if and only if $Y = aX$ *for some a.*

Proof. Let

$$0 \leq h(t) = E[(tX - Y)^2] = t^2 E(X^2) + E(Y^2) - 2t E(XY). \quad (8.1)$$

Then, $h(t)$ is a quadratic function in t which increases as $t \to \pm\infty$. It has a minimum at

$$h'(t) = 2t E(X^2) - 2E(XY)$$

$$\Rightarrow t = \frac{E(XY)}{E(X^2)}.$$

Substituting into $h(t)$ we obtain

$$0 \leq \frac{E^2 XY}{E(X^2)} + E(Y^2) - \frac{2E^2(XY)}{E(X^2)},$$

which implies that

$$0 \leq E(Y^2) - \frac{E^2(XY)}{E(X^2)},$$

which implies the result. □

Probability, Statistics and Econometrics. http://dx.doi.org/10.1016/B978-0-12-810495-8.00009-9
93

The CS inequality is also used in other nonprobabilistic contexts, so that for numbers a_i, b_i

$$(\Sigma a_i b_i)^2 \leq (\Sigma a_i^2) \cdot (\Sigma b_i^2),$$

and for functions f, g

$$\left(\int fg\right)^2 \leq \int f^2 \cdot \int g^2.$$

Theorem 8.3. HÖLDER'S INEQUALITY. *For any p, q satisfying $\frac{1}{p} + \frac{1}{q} = 1$, we have*

$$E|XY| \leq (E|X|^p)^{1/p}(E|Y|^q)^{1/q}.$$

For example

$$E|XY| \leq (E|X|^8)^{1/8}(E|Y|^{8/7})^{7/8}.$$

Theorem 8.4. MARKOV'S INEQUALITY. *For $\eta > 0$*

$$\Pr[|X| \geq \eta] \leq \frac{E|X|}{\eta}.$$

Proof. First, we have

$$\Pr[|X| \geq \eta] = \int_{|x| \geq \eta} f(x)dx = \int 1(|x| \geq \eta)f(x)dx = E1(|X| \geq \eta)$$

Clearly (see Fig. 8.1),

$$\overbrace{1(|X| \geq \eta)}^{indicator} \leq \frac{|X|}{\eta}.$$

This implies that

$$E1(|X| \geq \eta) \leq \frac{E|X|}{\eta}. \qquad \square$$

Theorem 8.5. CHEBYCHEV'S INEQUALITY. *For $\eta > 0$*

$$\Pr[|X - EX| \geq \eta] \leq \frac{\text{var}(X)}{\eta^2}.$$

Proof. Assume that $EX = 0$ and compare

$$1(|X| \geq \eta) \text{ with } \frac{X^2}{\eta^2}. \qquad \square$$

The Markov and Chebychev inequalities have many statistical applications, but they have also been useful in investment theory.

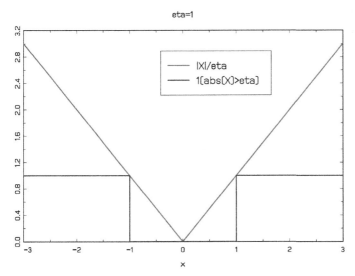

FIGURE 8.1 Shows argument in proving Markov's inequality

Example 8.1. Roy (1952) proposed the safety first rule of investment, which involved minimizing the probability of disaster. If d is the disaster level and X is the investment return (which can be controlled up to a point by portfolio choice decisions), then Roy advocated minimizing the disaster probability

$$\Pr(X < d).$$

If X were normally distributed, then $\Pr(X < d) = \Phi((d - \mu)/\sigma)$, where $\mu = E(X)$ and $\sigma^2 = \text{var}(X)$, and in that case, the portfolio X that maximizes $(\mu - d)/\sigma$ also minimizes the disaster risk. When d is chosen to be the risk free rate r, the prescription is to maximize the **Sharpe ratio**. When X is not normally distributed we can infer from Chebychev's inequality that

$$\Pr(|X - \mu| \geq \mu - d) \leq \frac{\sigma^2}{(\mu - d)^2},$$

from which we obtain

$$\Pr(X < d) \leq \frac{\sigma^2}{(\mu - d)^2}.$$

Roy proposed to minimize this upper bound, which is valid for any distribution with finite variance.

These inequalities can be quite "conservative". Suppose that $X \sim N(0, 1)$, then we know that $\Pr(|X| \geq 1.96) = 0.05$, whereas Chebychev's inequality says only that $\Pr(|X| \geq 1.96) \leq 0.26$.

8.2 NOTIONS OF CONVERGENCE

Asymptotic theory involves generalizing the usual notions of convergence for real sequences to allow for random variables.

Definition 8.1. We say that a sequence of real numbers $\{x_n\}_{n=1}^{\infty}$ converges to a limit x_{∞}, $x_n \to x_{\infty}$, also denoted

$$\lim_{n \to \infty} x_n = x_{\infty},$$

if for all $\epsilon > 0$ there exists an integer n_0 such that $|x_n - x_{\infty}| < \epsilon$ for all $n \geq n_0$.

Example 8.2. $x_n = 1/n$, $\lim_{n \to \infty} x_n = 0$.

Example 8.3. $x_n = \sin(\pi n)$ or $x_n = \sin(\pi/n)$ do not converge, i.e., $\lim_{n \to \infty} x_n$ does not exist.

In the case where a sequence does not converge there are always subsequences that converge. The lim inf is the smallest possible limit and lim sup is the largest possible limit. In the previous example, $\liminf_{n \to \infty} \sin(\pi n) = -1$ and $\limsup_{n \to \infty} \sin(\pi n) = 1$.

Random variables are more complicated than real numbers, and for sequences of random variables there are several different notions of convergence.

Definition 8.2. We say that a sequence of random variables $\{X_n\}_{n=1}^{\infty}$ converges with probability one (or almost surely) to a random variable X, denoted,

$$X_n \xrightarrow{a.s.} X,$$

if

$$\Pr\left(\lim_{n \to \infty} X_n = X\right) = 1.$$

We might ask what to say if $X_n \longrightarrow X$ with probability one half, say, but this is not possible according to the **zero-one law**, i.e., either a sequence of random variables converges with probability one or with probability zero.

A real-valued random variable X satisfies for all $\epsilon > 0$ there exists an M such that

$$\Pr(|X| > M) \leq \epsilon,$$

that is, it is **stochastically bounded**.

Definition 8.3. A sequence $\{X_n\}_{n=1}^{\infty}$ of random variables is stochastically bounded if for all $\epsilon > 0$ there exists an M and n_0 such that for all $n \geq n_0$

$$\Pr(|X_n| > M) \leq \epsilon.$$

In this case we write $X_n = O_p(1)$.

Example 8.4. Suppose that $X_n \sim N(\sin(n), 1)$ for each n. This sequence does not converge in any useful way but it is stochastically bounded.

Definition 8.4. We say that a sequence of random variables $\{X_n\}_{n=1}^{\infty}$ converges in probability to a random variable X, denoted,

$$X_n \xrightarrow{P} X,$$

if for all $\epsilon > 0$,

$$\lim_{n \to \infty} G_n(\epsilon) = 0,$$

where $G_n(\epsilon) = \Pr(|X_n - X| > \epsilon)$. The limit X could be a constant or a random variable. We sometimes write

$$p \lim_{n \to \infty} X_n = X$$

or $X_n = X + o_p(1)$.

Convergence in probability is weaker than convergence almost surely (convergence almost surely implies convergence in probability) and easier to establish. The quantity $G_n(\epsilon)$ depends on the joint distribution of X_n and X.

Example 8.5. Suppose that

$$X_n = \begin{cases} 1 & \text{with probability } \frac{1}{n} \\ 0 & \text{with probability } 1 - \frac{1}{n} \end{cases}.$$

Then, for any $\epsilon > 0$

$$\Pr(X_n \geq \epsilon) = \frac{1}{n} \to 0,$$

so that $X_n \xrightarrow{P} 0$,

Example 8.6. $X_n \sim U[0, 1/n]$. We have for any $\epsilon > 0$ that there exists an n_0 such that $\epsilon > 1/n_0$. Then for all $n \geq n_0$

$$\Pr(X_n \geq \epsilon) = 0,$$

so that $X_n \xrightarrow{P} 0$.

Suppose that

$$X_n = X + R_n,$$

where $R_n \xrightarrow{P} 0$. Then

$$\Pr(|X_n - X| > \epsilon) = \Pr(|R_n| > \epsilon) \to 0,$$

and it follows that the random variable X is the probability limit of X_n, i.e., $X = p \lim_{n \to \infty} X_n$.

Definition 8.5. We say that a sequence of random variables $\{X_n\}_{n=1}^{\infty}$ converges in mean square to a random variable X, denoted $X_n \xrightarrow{m.s.} X$, if

$$\lim_{n \to \infty} E[(X_n - X)^2] = 0.$$

This presumes of course that $EX_n^2 < \infty$ and $EX^2 < \infty$. When X is a constant,

$$E[(X_n - X)^2] = E[(X_n - EX_n)^2] + (EX_n - X)^2 = \text{var}(X_n) + (EX_n - X)^2,$$

and it is necessary and sufficient that $EX_n \to X$ and $\text{var}(X_n) \to 0$.

Mean square convergence implies convergence in probability. This follows from the Chebychev inequality. Convergence in probability does not imply convergence in mean square.

Example 8.7. Suppose that

$$X_n = \begin{cases} n & \frac{1}{n} \\ 0 & 1 - \frac{1}{n} \end{cases}.$$

Then for any $\epsilon > 0$

$$\Pr(X_n \geq \epsilon) = \frac{1}{n} \to 0.$$

But

$$E(X_n^2) = n^2 \cdot \frac{1}{n} = n \to \infty.$$

Definition 8.6. We say that a sequence of random variables $\{X_n\}_{n=1}^{\infty}$ converges in distribution to a random variable X, denoted,

$$X_n \xrightarrow{D} X,$$

if for all x at which $F(x) = \Pr[X \leq x]$ is continuous,

$$\lim_{n \to \infty} F_n(x) = \Pr(X \leq x),$$

where $F_n(x) = \Pr(X_n \leq x)$.

Specifically, we often have

$$\sqrt{n}(\widehat{\theta} - \theta) \overset{D}{\longrightarrow} X \sim N(0, \sigma^2), \overbrace{\sqrt{n}(\widehat{\theta} - \theta) \overset{D}{\longrightarrow} N(0, \sigma^2)}^{\text{shorthand notation}}.$$

The limiting normal distribution is continuous everywhere and so in this case we must check the convergence for all $x \in \mathbb{R}$.

Convergence in distribution does not restrict at all the relationship between X_n and X: specifically, X_n and X could be independent in which case

$$\Pr(|X_n - X| > \epsilon)$$

does not go to zero.

Note that convergence in probability is stronger than convergence in distribution, but they are equivalent when X is a constant (i.e., not random).

Theorem 8.6. *Suppose that the sequence of random variables $\{X_n\}_{n=1}^{\infty}$ satisfies $X_n \overset{P}{\longrightarrow} X$ for some random variable X. Then $X_n \overset{D}{\longrightarrow} X$. If X is constant, then vice versa.*

Proof. Let x be a point of continuity of X, i.e., $\Pr(X = x) = 0$. For any $\epsilon > 0$ we have by the law of total probability that

$$\Pr(X_n \leq x) \leq \Pr(X_n \leq x, |X_n - X| \leq \epsilon) + \Pr(|X_n - X| \geq \epsilon)$$
$$\leq \Pr(X \leq x + \epsilon) + \Pr(|X_n - X| \geq \epsilon).$$

Similarly we obtain a lower bound to yield

$$\Pr(X \leq x - \epsilon) - \Pr(|X_n - X| \geq \epsilon) \leq \Pr(X_n \leq x)$$
$$\leq \Pr(X \leq x + \epsilon) + \Pr(|X_n - X| \geq \epsilon).$$

Then letting $n \to \infty$ and $\epsilon \to 0$ we obtain the result. □

Example 8.8. Suppose that

$$X_n = \begin{cases} \frac{1}{n} & \frac{1}{2} \\ \frac{-1}{n} & \frac{1}{2} \end{cases}.$$

Then $X_n \overset{P}{\longrightarrow} 0$ and so $X_n \overset{D}{\longrightarrow} 0$, i.e.,

$$\Pr(X_n \leq x) \to \begin{cases} 1 & x \geq 0 \\ 0 & x < 0. \end{cases}$$

But note that for all n, $\Pr(X_n = 0) = 0$.

8.3 LAWS OF LARGE NUMBERS AND CLT

We now come to the two main theorems, the **Law of Large Numbers** (LLN), and the **Central Limit Theorem** (CLT).

Theorem 8.7. *(Kolmogorov) Let* $X_1, \ldots, X_n$ *be independent and identically distributed (i.i.d.). Then a necessary and sufficient condition for*

$$T_n = \frac{1}{n} \sum_{i=1}^{n} X_i \xrightarrow{a.s.} \mu \equiv E(X_1)$$

is that $E(|X_i|) < \infty$.

This is called the strong law of large numbers and implies the weak law of large numbers (convergence in probability). The hypothesis that $E(|X_i|) < \infty$ is necessary, i.e., if $E|X| = \infty$, for example X is Cauchy, then the LLN does not hold. What happens in that case? In fact, we may show in that case that $\sum_{i=1}^{n} X_i / a_n$ converges in distribution to a random variable, called a stable distribution for some sequence a_n with $a_n / \sqrt{n} \to \infty$.

Under stronger moment conditions we can establish the CLT.

Theorem 8.8. *(Lindeberg–Levy) Let* $X_1, \ldots, X_n$ *be i.i.d. with* $E(X_i) = \mu$ *and* $\mathrm{var}(X_i) = \sigma^2$. *Then*

$$\frac{1}{\sqrt{n}} \sum_{i=1}^{n} (X_i - \mu) \xrightarrow{D} N(0, \sigma^2).$$

A proof of the result can be based on the characteristic function. Thus

$$\varphi_n(t) = E(e^{it\overline{X}/\sqrt{n}}) = \varphi(t/\sqrt{n})^n,$$

where $\varphi(t) = E(e^{itX_i})$. We may expand the right hand side as follows

$$\varphi(t/\sqrt{n})^n = \left[\varphi(0) + \frac{t}{\sqrt{n}}\varphi'(0) + \frac{t^2}{2n}\varphi''(0) + \ldots \right]^n,$$

where $\varphi(0) = 1$, $\varphi'(0) = iE(X) = 0$, and $\varphi''(0) = i^2 E(X^2) = -\sigma^2$. Therefore,

$$\varphi_n(t) = \left[1 - \frac{t^2\sigma^2}{2n} + o(t^2/n^2) \right]^n \to e^{-t^2\sigma^2/2},$$

which is the characteristic function of a normal random variable. This is a bit heuristic.

The LLN and CLT are important results because they show that no matter what the distribution of X_i, the average of the X's has a distribution that can

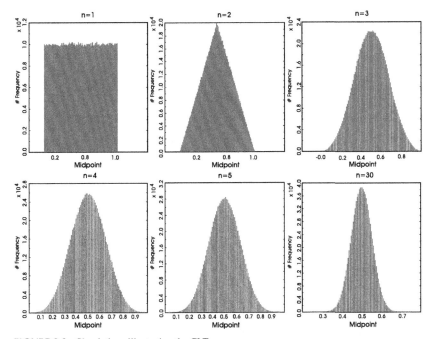

FIGURE 8.2 Simulations illustrating the CLT

be approximated by a potentially much simpler normal distribution. Example suppose $X_i \sim U[0, 1]$, Fig. 8.2 is distribution of $\frac{1}{n} \sum_{i=1}^{n} X_i$ from 1000000 simulations.

There are now many generalizations of LLN and CLT for data that are not i.i.d., e.g., heterogeneous, dependent weighted sums. We will consider **triangular arrays** of random variables $\{X_{ni}\}_{i=1}^{n}$, which allow a little more generality than sequences; this generality is needed in a number of situations.

Theorem 8.9. *Chebychev. Let $X_{n1}, \ldots, X_{nn}$ be pairwise uncorrelated random variables, i.e., $\mathrm{cov}(X_{ni}, X_{nj}) = 0$ for all $i \neq j$ for all n, with $EX_{ni} = 0$ and $\mathrm{var}(X_{ni}) \leq C < \infty$. Then*

$$T_n = \frac{1}{n} \sum_{i=1}^{n} X_{ni} \xrightarrow{P} 0.$$

Proof. We have

$$E(T_n^2) = \mathrm{var}\left(\frac{1}{n} \sum_{i=1}^{n} X_{ni}\right)$$

$$= \frac{1}{n^2} \sum_{i=1}^{n} \text{var}(X_{ni}) + \frac{1}{n^2} \sum_{i=1}^{n} \sum_{\substack{j=1 \\ i \neq j}}^{n} \text{cov}(X_{ni}, X_{nj})$$

$$= \frac{1}{n^2} \sum_{i=1}^{n} \text{var}(X_{ni}) \leq \frac{C}{n} \rightarrow 0.$$

This establishes mean square convergence, which implies convergence in probability. $\square$

Theorem 8.10. *(Lindeberg–Feller) Let $X_{n1}, \ldots, X_{nn}$ be independent random variables with $E(X_{ni}) = 0$ and $\text{var}(X_{ni}) = \sigma_{ni}^2$, and let $s_n^2 = \sum_{i=1}^{n} \sigma_{ni}^2$. Suppose also that Lindeberg's condition*

$$\frac{1}{s_n^2} \sum_{i=1}^{n} E\left[X_{ni}^2 1\left(X_{ni}^2 > \epsilon s_n^2\right)\right] \rightarrow 0 \quad \text{for all } \epsilon > 0$$

holds. Then

$$\frac{1}{\sqrt{s_n}} \sum_{i=1}^{n} X_{ni} \xrightarrow{D} N(0, 1).$$

A sufficient condition is that $\sum_{i=1}^{n} E[|X_{ni}|^3]/s_n^3 \rightarrow 0$ (Lyapunov condition). In the case that s_n^2 is bounded away from zero and infinity, the Lindeberg condition implies that $\max_{1 \leq i \leq n} \text{Pr}\left(|X_{n,i}| > \epsilon\right) \rightarrow 0$ for all $\epsilon > 0$; this is a version of asymptotic negligibility, i.e., it says that individual terms in the sum are small compared to the sum itself. If X_i is i.i.d. then the Lindeberg condition is automatically satisfied.

Example 8.9. Suppose that $U_i \sim U[-1/2, 1/2]$

$$X_i = \sqrt{i} \times U_i.$$

Then X_i are independent with $EX_i = 0$ but not identically distributed. In fact,

$$s_n^2 = \sum_{i=1}^{n} \sigma_i^2 = \frac{1}{12} \sum_{i=1}^{n} i = \frac{n(n+1)}{24}$$

$$\frac{1}{s_n^2} \sum_{i=1}^{n} E\left[X_i^2 1\left(X_i^2 > \epsilon s_n^2\right)\right] = \frac{24}{n(n+1)} \sum_{i=1}^{n} i E\left[U_i^2 1\left(U_i^2 > \epsilon \frac{n(n+1)}{24i}\right)\right]$$

$$\leq \frac{24}{n(n+1)} \sum_{i=1}^{n} i E\left[U_i^2 1\left(U_i^2 > \epsilon \frac{(n+1)}{24}\right)\right]$$

$$= 0 \text{ for all } n > 6/\epsilon - 1.$$

So Lindeberg's condition is satisfied.

Not all sequences of random variables satisfy the CLT.

Example 8.10. Suppose that $\{X_i\}_{i=1}^n$ are independent with

$$
X_i = \begin{cases} m^2 & p_m \\ -m & 1 - p_m, \end{cases}
$$

where $p_m = m/(m^2 + m)$. Then $E X_i = 0$ for all i and $\mathrm{var}(X_i) = m^4 p_m + m^2(1 - p_m)$. If the CLT were to hold, the sample average should be less than zero approximately half the time when the sample size is large. This is not the case. We have

$$
\Pr\left(\frac{1}{\sqrt{s_n}} \sum_{i=1}^n X_i < 0 \right) \geq (1 - p_m)^n,
$$

where $s_n^2 = n\mathrm{var}(X_i)$. If we take $m = c \times n$, then $(1 - p_m)^n \geq \exp(-c^{-1})$, which can be arbitrarily close to one for some c. So the CLT can't hold in this case. Intuitively, the sequence is dominated by the $-m$ value.

8.3.1 Gambling Model

Suppose that you have initial wealth W_0 that you can divide into a risky asset with payoff $\mathcal{R} \geq 0$ per dollar invested and a riskless asset that pays off $R_f \geq 1$ per dollar invested. You choose a fraction $\omega \in [0, 1]$ to invest in the risky asset. The wealth next period is

$$
W_1 = W_0 \left(\omega \mathcal{R} + (1 - \omega) R_f \right).
$$

The payoff at period n if the same proportion is invested every period and if the risky asset payoffs are i.i.d. is

$$
W_n = W_0 \prod_{i=1}^n \left(\omega \mathcal{R}_i + (1 - \omega) R_f \right),
$$

where $\mathcal{R}_i$ is the risky payoff in period i. We take logs and assume "without loss of generality" that $W_0 = 1$, then

$$
\log W_n = \sum_{i=1}^n \log \left(\omega \mathcal{R}_i + (1 - \omega) R_f \right).
$$

Let

$$
X_i(\omega) = \log \left(\omega \mathcal{R}_i + (1 - \omega) R_f \right)
$$

and suppose that $E|X_i(\omega)| \leq C < \infty$ exists and let $\mu(\omega) = E(X_i(\omega))$. It follows that by the law of large numbers that

$$\frac{1}{n} \log W_n \xrightarrow{P} \mu(\omega).$$

If also $E|X_i^2(\omega)| \leq C < \infty$ exists and let $\sigma^2(\omega) = \text{var}(X_i(\omega))$. It follows that by the CLT that

$$\sqrt{n} \left(\frac{1}{n} \log W_n - \mu(\omega) \right) \xrightarrow{D} N(0, \sigma^2(\omega)).$$

There are three cases:

1. If $\mu(\omega) > 0$, then $W_n \to \infty$ with probability one.
2. If $\mu(\omega) < 0$, then $W_n \to 0$ with probability one.
3. If $\mu(\omega) = 0$, then actually provided $E\left[X_i(\omega)^2\right] < \infty$

$$\frac{1}{\sqrt{n}} \log W_n \xrightarrow{D} N\left(0, \text{var}\left[X_i(\omega)\right]\right).$$

What is the condition for $\omega \in (0, 1)$? We optimize

$$E\left[\log\left(\omega \mathcal{R}_i + (1 - \omega)R_f\right)\right]$$

with respect to ω. The first order condition and second order condition

$$E\left[\frac{\mathcal{R}_i - R_f}{\omega(\mathcal{R}_i - R_f) + R_f}\right] = 0$$

$$-E\left[\frac{\left(\mathcal{R}_i - R_f\right)^2}{\left(\omega \mathcal{R}_i + (1 - \omega)R_f\right)^2}\right] < 0.$$

If $E(\mathcal{R}_i) > R_f$, then $\omega = 0$ would coincide with a positive value to the first derivative of the objective function so that $\omega = 0$ could not be a solution. If $E(\mathcal{R}_i^{-1}) < R_f$, then $\omega = 1$ would coincide with a negative value to the first derivative of the objective function so that $\omega = 1$ could not be a solution. So provided these two conditions are satisfied the investor will put some money in both stocks and bonds.

For example, suppose that $R_f = 1$ and

$$\mathcal{R} = \begin{cases} \theta & \text{with probability } 1/2 \\ \frac{1}{\theta} & \text{with probability } 1/2, \end{cases}$$

for $\theta \in (0, 1)$. Then $E(\mathcal{R}) = (1 + \theta^2)/2\theta$ and $\text{var}(\mathcal{R}) = \left(1 - \theta^2\right)^2/4\theta^2$. The first order condition is

$$\frac{1 - \theta}{\omega(\theta - 1) + 1} = \frac{\frac{1}{\theta} - 1}{\omega(\frac{1}{\theta} - 1) + 1},$$

which has a unique solution $\omega = 1/2$. In this case

$$\mu = \frac{1}{2} \ln (\theta + 1) + \frac{1}{2} \ln \left(\frac{1}{\theta} + 1\right) - \ln(2),$$

which is decreasing in θ. In fact, $\mu \geq 0$, and $\mu \to 0$ as $\theta \to 1$ because in that case one just has a riskless asset paying off 1.

8.4 SOME ADDITIONAL TOOLS

The following results are very useful in conjunction with the LLN and CLT:

Theorem 8.11. *Mann–Wald or Continuous Mapping Theorem. Suppose that* $X_n \xrightarrow{D} X$ *and that g is continuous. Then* $g(X_n) \xrightarrow{D} g(X)$. *If* $X_n \xrightarrow{P} \alpha$, *then* $g(X) \xrightarrow{P} g(\alpha)$.

Proof. We show the second result. Let $\epsilon > 0$ be given. By continuity of g at α, $\exists \eta > 0$ such that if

$$|x - \alpha| < \eta \Rightarrow |g(x) - g(\alpha)| < \epsilon.$$

Let $A_n = \{|X_n - \alpha| < \eta\}$ and $B_n = \{|g(X_n) - g(\alpha)| < \epsilon\}$. But when A_n is true, we know that B_n is true, i.e., $A_n \subset B_n$. Since $\Pr[A_n] \to 1$, we must have $\Pr[B_n] \to 1$. $\qquad \square$

In the Gamblers ruin problem. We can apply the Mann–Wald theorem to obtain the limiting behaviour of W_n. Specifically,

$$W_n^{1/n} = \exp(\frac{1}{n} \log W_n) = \exp(\log W_n^{1/n}) \xrightarrow{P} \exp(\mu(\omega)).$$

There are three cases:

1. If $\mu(\omega) > 0$, then $W_n \simeq \exp(n\mu(\omega)) \xrightarrow{P} \infty$.
2. If $\mu(\omega) < 0$, then $W_n \simeq \exp(n\mu(\omega)) \xrightarrow{P} 0$. You are ruined in probability.
3. If $\mu(\omega) = 0$, then see below

Theorem 8.12. *Slutsky. Suppose that* $X_n \xrightarrow{D} X$, $Y_n \xrightarrow{P} \alpha$. *Then:*
(i) $X_n + Y_n \xrightarrow{D} X + \alpha$;

(ii) $X_n Y_n \xrightarrow{D} \alpha X$; *and*

(iii) $X_n / Y_n \xrightarrow{D} X / \alpha$, *provided* $\alpha \neq 0$.

This result is a natural generalization of the corresponding properties of real sequences.

Example 8.11. Suppose that $X_n = \sum_{i=1}^{n} A_i / \sqrt{n}$ and $Y_n = \sum_{i=1}^{n} B_i / n$, where A_i, B_i are i.i.d. with $E(A_i) = 0$, $\text{var}(A_i) = \sigma_A^2$ and $E(B_i) = \mu_B$. Then

$$
X_n + Y_n = \frac{1}{\sqrt{n}} \sum_{i=1}^{n} A_i + \frac{1}{n} \sum_{i=1}^{n} B_i \xrightarrow{D} X + \mu_B \sim N(\mu_B, \sigma_A^2)
$$

$$
X_n Y_n = \left(\frac{1}{\sqrt{n}} \sum_{i=1}^{n} A_i \right) \left(\frac{1}{n} \sum_{i=1}^{n} B_i \right) \xrightarrow{D} X \times \mu_B \sim N(0, \mu_B^2 \sigma_A^2)
$$

$$
\frac{X_n}{Y_n} \xrightarrow{D} X / \mu_B \sim N \left(0, \frac{\sigma_A^2}{\mu_B^2} \right).
$$

Finally, we point out that when dealing with a vector $X_n = (X_{n1}, \ldots, X_{nk})$, we have the result that

$$
\sum_{j=1}^{k} \left(X_{nj} - X_j \right)^2 \xrightarrow{P} 0,
$$

if and only if for all $j = 1, \ldots, k$:

$$
|X_{nj} - X_j| \xrightarrow{P} 0.
$$

The if part is no surprise and follows from the continuous mapping theorem. The only if part follows because if $\sum_{j=1}^{k} \left(X_{nj} - X_j \right)^2 < \epsilon^2$ then $|X_{nj} - X_j| < \epsilon$ for each j. In this case, we say $X_n \xrightarrow{P} X$.

As regards convergence in distribution, we have the **Cramér–Wald** Theorem

Theorem 8.13. *A vector X_n converges in distribution to a random vector X, i.e.,*

$$
\lim_{n \to \infty} \Pr(X_n \leq x) = \Pr(X \leq x),
$$

for any $x \in \mathbb{R}^k$ a continuity point of the c.d.f. of X, if and only if $c^{\mathsf{T}} X_n$ converges in distribution to $c^{\mathsf{T}} X$ for every vector c.

It is not sufficient that each marginal distribution converges in distribution because this does not restrict the joint distribution.

Example 8.12. Suppose that $X_n \sim N(0, 1)$ and $Y_n = -X_n$ for all n, then $X_n \xrightarrow{D} X$ and $Y_n \xrightarrow{D} Y$, where $X, Y \sim N(0, 1)$, but $(X_n, Y_n) \xrightarrow{D} (X, -X)$, which is a degenerate distribution. In this case $c_1 X_n + c_2 Y_n = (c_1 - c_2) X \sim N(0, (c_1 - c_2)^2)$ for all (c_1, c_2).

Theorem 8.14. *Suppose that $\sqrt{n}(\widehat{\theta} - \theta_0) \xrightarrow{D} X$, where X is some random variable and suppose that f is differentiable at $\theta_0 \in \mathbb{R}$ with $f'(\theta_0) \neq 0$. Then*

$$\sqrt{n}(f(\widehat{\theta}) - f(\theta_0)) \xrightarrow{D} \left(f'(\theta_0)\right) \times X.$$

Proof. The function f is differentiable at θ_0, which means that for all $\epsilon > 0$ there exists $\delta > 0$ such that

$$|\theta - \theta_0| \leq \delta \Longrightarrow |f(\theta) - f(\theta_0) - f'(\theta_0)(\theta - \theta_0)| \leq \epsilon |\theta - \theta_0|.$$

Since $\widehat{\theta} \xrightarrow{P} \theta_0$, we have for any $\delta > 0$, $\Pr(|\widehat{\theta} - \theta_0| \leq \delta) \to 1$.
Define the events

$$A_n = \left\{ |\widehat{\theta} - \theta_0| \leq \delta \right\} \quad ; \quad B_n = \left\{ |\sqrt{n} R_n| \leq x \right\},$$

where $R_n = f(\widehat{\theta}) - f(\theta_0) - f'(\theta_0)(\widehat{\theta} - \theta_0)$. It follows that

$$\Pr\left(|\sqrt{n} R_n| \leq x\right) = \Pr(B_n) = \Pr(B_n \cap A_n) + \Pr\left(B_n \cap A_n^c\right)$$
$$\leq \Pr(B_n \cap A_n) + \Pr\left(A_n^c\right)$$

by the law of total probability and the fact that $B_n \cap A_n^c \subset A_n^c$. We have

$$\Pr(B_n \cap A_n) \leq \Pr\left(\epsilon \sqrt{n} |\widehat{\theta} - \theta_0| \leq x\right) \to F_Y(x/\epsilon),$$

where F_Y is the c.d.f. of the random variable $Y = |X|$ so that $F_Y(x/\epsilon)$ is arbitrarily close to one as $\epsilon \to 0$ for any $x > 0$ (the c.d.f. of Y is continuous on $\mathbb{R}_+$). Then $\Pr\left(A_n^c\right) \to 0$ by the fact that $\sqrt{n}(\widehat{\theta} - \theta_0) \xrightarrow{D} X$.
We have shown that

$$\sqrt{n}(f(\widehat{\theta}) - f(\theta_0)) = f'(\theta_0)\sqrt{n}(\widehat{\theta} - \theta_0) + \sqrt{n} R_n,$$

where $\sqrt{n} R_n \xrightarrow{P} 0$. The result now follows. $\qquad \square$

Corollary 8.1. *Suppose that $D_n(\widehat{\theta} - \theta_0) \xrightarrow{D} X$, where X is some random variable and $D_n \to \infty$. Suppose that f is twice differentiable at $\theta_0 \in \mathbb{R}$ with $f'(\theta_0) = 0$ and $f''(\theta_0) \neq 0$. Then*

$$D_n^2(f(\widehat{\theta}) - f(\theta_0)) \xrightarrow{D} \frac{1}{2} f''(\theta_0) \times X^2.$$

Proof. Follows by similar arguments to the theorem.   □

In the Gamblers ruin problem, let

$$\widehat{\theta} = \frac{1}{n} \log W_n \quad ; \quad \theta_0 = \mu(\omega).$$

Then we have

$$\sqrt{n}\left(\widehat{\theta} - \theta_0\right) \xrightarrow{D} N(0, \sigma^2(\omega)).$$

By the Delta method we have

$$\sqrt{n}\left(\exp(\widehat{\theta}) - \exp(\theta_0)\right) \xrightarrow{D} N(0, \exp(2\theta_0)\sigma^2(\omega)),$$

where $\exp(\widehat{\theta}) = \exp(\log(W_n^{1/n})) = W_n^{1/n}$.
Suppose that $\mu(\omega) = 0$. Then this says that

$$\sqrt{n}\left(W_n^{1/n} - 1\right) \xrightarrow{D} N(0, \sigma^2(\omega)),$$

$$W_n \simeq \left(1 + \frac{N(0, \sigma^2(\omega))}{\sqrt{n}}\right)^n.$$

Exact distribution theory is limited to very special cases [normal i.i.d. errors plus linear estimators], or involves very difficult calculations. This is too restrictive for applications. By making approximations based on large sample sizes, we can obtain distribution theory that is applicable in a much wider range of circumstances. It is important to note that infinity is an abstract mathematical concept, and that no known physical mechanism can ever entertain infinity. We use the theorems to provide approximations, that is all.

Finally, we give an advanced inequality, called Bernstein's inequality.

Theorem 8.15. *Suppose that X_i are i.i.d. with mean zero, variance σ^2, and satisfy $|X_i| \leq M < \infty$. Then*

$$\Pr\left(\left|\frac{1}{\sqrt{n}} \sum_{i=1}^{n} X_i\right| > x\right) \leq 2\exp\left(-\frac{1}{4}\frac{x^2}{\sigma^2 + xM/\sqrt{n}}\right). \tag{8.2}$$

We do not provide a proof of this result. It can be useful in some contexts. Specifically, it gives an explicit bound on the c.d.f. of the sample average, which holds for all n. Suppose that we take $x = (c \log n)^{1/2}$ in this formula, then the right hand side of (8.2) is

$$2\exp\left(-\frac{1}{4}\frac{c\log n}{\sigma^2 + (c\log n)^{1/2}M/\sqrt{n}}\right) \sim 2\exp\left(-\frac{c}{4\sigma^2}\log n\right) \sim 2n^{-c/4\sigma^2}, \tag{8.3}$$

which goes to zero rapidly for $c > 4\sigma^2$. Suppose that $X_i \sim N(0, 1)$, then $\frac{1}{\sqrt{n}} \sum_{i=1}^{n} X_i$ is also standard normal and we have by symmetry that

$$\Pr\left(\left|\frac{1}{\sqrt{n}} \sum_{i=1}^{n} X_i\right| > x\right) = 2\Pr(Z > x),$$

where Z is a standard normal random variable. The following bound can be shown by elementary arguments: for all $x > 0$

$$\frac{x \exp\left(-\frac{1}{2}x^2\right)}{\left(1 + x^2\right)\sqrt{2\pi}} \leq \Pr\left(Z \geq x\right) \leq \frac{\exp\left(-\frac{1}{2}x^2\right)}{x\sqrt{2\pi}}. \tag{8.4}$$

Suppose we take $x = (c \log n)^{1/2}$ in this formula, then we obtain that

$$\frac{(c \log n)^{1/2} n^{-c/2}}{(1 + c \log n)\sqrt{2\pi}} \leq \Pr\left(Z \geq (c \log n)^{1/2}\right) \leq \frac{n^{-c/2}}{(c \log n)^{1/2}\sqrt{2\pi}},$$

which is a little tighter than given by (8.3).

Chapter 9

Exercises and Complements

Exercise. Suppose that $S = \{a, b, c, d, e\}$ and let $\mathcal{B}$ consist of two sets $B_1 = \{a, b, c\}$ and $B_2 = \{c, d, e\}$. Find the sigma field $\mathcal{A}$ generated by $\mathcal{B}$.

Solution. We have

$$B_1^c = \{d, e\}, \quad B_2^c = \{a, b\}$$
$$B_1 \cup B_2 = S; \quad B_1 \cap B_2 = \{c\}$$

and so $\mathcal{A}$ contains these sets and the empty set. □

Exercise. The game of draw poker is played with 52 cards from a regular deck. Each person receives 5 cards face down. After some betting, which does not concern us, the winning hand is determined by the showdown, where each player reveals his cards. The possible winning hands are as follows [in approximate ranking – it has been a long time since I played]: A single pair, i.e., two cards of the same number; Two pairs; Three of a kind; Flush, i.e., five cards of the same suit; Straight, i.e., five cards in sequence; Full house, i.e., three of a kind and a pair; Four of a kind; Straight Flush, i.e., five cards in sequence and of the same suit. Calculate the odds of receiving each type of hand. Don't forget that each category defined above should contain the words "but nothing more".

Exercise. The Smiths have two children. At least one of them is a boy. What is the probability that both children are boys?

Exercise. Elvis Presley had a twin brother (Jesse Garon Presley) who died at birth. What is the probability that Elvis was an identical twin?

Solution. The hypotheses are: A: Elvis's birth event was an identical birth event; B: Elvis's birth event was a fraternal twin event. If identical twins are 8% of all twins, then identical birth events are 8% of all twin birth events, so the priors are

$$P(A) = 0.08 \text{ and } P(B) = 0.92$$

The evidence is E: Elvis's twin was male. The likelihoods are $P(E|A) = 1$ and $P(E|B) = 1/2$. Because identical twins are necessarily the same sex, but frater-

Probability, Statistics and Econometrics. http://dx.doi.org/10.1016/B978-0-12-810495-8.00010-5

nal twins are equally likely to be opposite sex by assumption. Hence,

$$P(A|E) = \frac{8}{54} = 0.15. \qquad \square$$

Exercise. You are in Las Vegas with $3 and you need $6 to pay off a debt. You consider two strategies: (a) bet all you have on Black; (b) bet $1 at a time on Black until you either go bankrupt or win $6. You can assume that the casino pays out twice the wager for a winning roll, and that the probability of Black is p, where $0 < p < 1$. Compare the two strategies and determine which has the larger probability q of succeeding (this depends on the value of p). [Hint: start with a simpler problem where your total capital is only $2, say, and you need $4, and then draw a tree to represent the evolution of your capital.]

Exercise. The game of craps is played with two six-sided dice. The rules are as follows. Only totals for the two dice count. The player throws the dice and wins at once if the total for the first throw is 7 or 11, loses at once if it is 2, 3, or 12. Any other throw is called his "point." If the first throw is a point, the player throws the dice repeatedly until he either wins by throwing his point again or loses by throwing 7. What is the probability of winning?

Exercise. What is the probability that an integer chosen at random is even? What is the probability that an integer chosen at random has 1 as its first digit?

Solution. We would like to say that the probability is 1/2 but the question is whether this can be made rigorous. One way of defining this is through limiting operations. That is we define the sequence of random variables X_n with support $S_n = \{1, \ldots, n\}$, and let each integer in S_n occur with probability $1/n$. Then we can define the probability that an integer chosen at random is even as

$$\lim_{n \to \infty} \Pr(X_n \text{ is even}) = \frac{1}{2}. \qquad \square$$

Exercise. Eighty individuals suffering from a given disease were randomly sampled from a population of sufferers. Event B – individuals took a particular drug; Event A – individual recovered. Verify that we have $\Pr(A|B) > \Pr(A|B^c)$ but both $\Pr(A|B, M) < \Pr(A|B^c, M)$ and $\Pr(A|B, F) < \Pr(A|B^c, F)$, where $\Pr(A|B, M)$, $\Pr(A|B, F)$ denote, respectively, the conditional probability of recovery for males (females). Discuss how this may happen.

	A	A^c	Totals
Combined			
B	20	20	40
B^c	16	24	40
Males			
B	18	12	30
B^c	7	3	10
Females			
B	2	8	10
B^c	9	21	30

Exercise. Consider the following functions and decide whether they are density functions.
(1) $f(x) = x^{-\alpha} 1(x > 0)$; (2) $f(x) = \sin(x) 1(0 < x < 2\pi)$.

Exercise. Prove that if F is a c.d.f., then for any continuous nondecreasing function $T : [0, 1] \to [0, 1]$, $T(F(x))$ is also a c.d.f.

Exercise. Suppose that Y, X are uniformly distributed on the circular region C defined by

$$X^2 + Y^2 \le \theta^2,$$

where θ is the radius of the circle and

$$f_{Y,X}(y, x) = \frac{1}{\pi \theta^2} 1((x, y) \in C),$$

where $1(a \in A) = 1$ if $a \in A$ and 0 else. Calculate
(i) The marginal densities of Y and X and the conditional density $Y|X$.
(ii) The regression function $E(Y|X = x)$.

Solution. *We have*

$$f_X(x) = \int_{-\sqrt{\theta^2 - x^2}}^{\sqrt{\theta^2 - x^2}} f_{Y,X}(y, x) dy = \frac{1}{\pi \theta^2} \int_{-\sqrt{\theta^2 - x^2}}^{\sqrt{\theta^2 - x^2}} dy$$

$$= \frac{2\sqrt{\theta^2 - x^2}}{\pi \theta^2} 1(-\theta \le x \le \theta)$$

and by symmetry

$$f_Y(y) = \frac{2\sqrt{\theta^2 - y^2}}{\pi \theta^2} 1(-\theta \le y \le \theta),$$

which is not uniform. It follows that

$$f_{Y|X}(y|x) = \frac{f_{Y,X}(y,x)}{f_X(x)} = \frac{\frac{1}{\pi\theta^2}1\,((x,y) \in C)}{\frac{2\sqrt{\theta^2-x^2}}{\pi\theta^2}1(-\theta \le x \le \theta)}$$

$$= \frac{1}{2\sqrt{\theta^2-x^2}}1(0 \le y^2 \le \theta^2 - x^2 \le \theta).$$

We have

$$E(Y|X=x) = \int \frac{1}{2\sqrt{\theta^2-x^2}}1(0 \le y^2 \le \theta^2 - x^2 \le \theta)y\,dy$$

$$= \frac{1}{2\sqrt{\theta^2-x^2}}\int_{-\sqrt{\theta^2-x^2}}^{\sqrt{\theta^2-x^2}} y\,dy$$

$$= 0.$$

We also have

$$E(Y^2|X=x) = \frac{1}{2\sqrt{\theta^2-x^2}}\int_{-\sqrt{\theta^2-x^2}}^{\sqrt{\theta^2-x^2}} y^2\,dy$$

$$= \frac{1}{3}\theta^2 - \frac{1}{3}x^2$$

$$= \mathrm{var}(Y|X=x) \qquad \square$$

Exercise. The Poisson Hotel. Consider a hotel with an infinite number of rooms numbered $\{0, 1, 2, \ldots\}$. Each room is occupied with probability $\frac{e^{-\lambda}\lambda^x}{x!} > 0$ so that we can't guarantee a room to any newcomer. How do you guarantee room for an infinite number of guests?

Solution. Consider the transformation $X \mapsto Y = 2^X$. The new hotel has an infinite number of empty rooms, as well as an infinite number of rooms with positive frequency of occupancy. $\qquad \square$

Exercise. Establish whether the following statements are True, False, or Indeterminate. Explain your reasoning.
(i) After a very fierce battle, 72% of soldiers have lost an eye, 85% have lost an arm, and 63% have lost a leg. Therefore, no less than 20% of them are missing an eye, an arm, and a leg.
(ii) Suppose that Y, X are continuous random variables with a joint density f and conditional densities generically denoted by $f(.|.)$. If for some y, x, $f(y|x) = 0$, then $f(y) = 0$.

Exercise. Show that for any X, Y with finite second moment

$$(\text{sd}(X) - \text{sd}(Y))^2 \le \text{var}(X \pm Y) \le (\text{sd}(X) + \text{sd}(Y))^2,$$

with equality if and only if $\rho_{XY} = \pm 1$. Similarly,

$$\text{var}(Y - X) = \text{var}(Y) - \text{var}(X)$$

if and only if $\rho_{XY} = \text{sd}(X)/\text{sd}(Y)$.

Example 9.1. Stock market again. Calculate $\text{cov}(X, Y)$.

Solution. In this case

$$E(XY) = \pi_{1,1} - \pi_{-1,1} - \pi_{1,-1} + \pi_{-1,-1} = 1 - 2\pi_{-1,1} - 2\pi_{1,-1}$$
$$E(X) = 2\pi_{1,-1} + 2\pi_{1,1} - 1$$
$$E(Y) = \pi_{1,1} + \pi_{-1,1} - \pi_{1,-1} - \pi_{-1,-1} = 2\pi_{1,1} + 2\pi_{-1,1} - 1$$
$$\text{cov}(X, Y) = 1 - 2\pi_{-1,1} - 2\pi_{1,-1} - \left(2\pi_{1,-1} + 2\pi_{1,1} - 1\right)\left(2\pi_{1,1} + 2\pi_{-1,1} - 1\right)$$
$$= -4\left(\pi_{-1,1}\pi_{1,-1} + (\pi_{-1,1} + \pi_{1,-1})\pi_{1,1} + \pi_{1,1}(1 - \pi_{1,1})\right)$$
$$\le 0. \qquad \square$$

Exercise. Consider the general case where F_X is not necessarily continuous or monotonic. Compare the following definitions of median

$$m_1 = \inf\{x : F_X(x) \ge 1/2\}$$
$$m_2 = \sup\{x : F_X(x) \le 1/2\}$$
$$m_3 = (m_1 + m_2)/2.$$

Prove that $m_2 \le m_3 \le m_1$. Under what circumstances are they all equal.

Solution. Consider the general case where F_X is not necessarily continuous or monotonic. Compare the following definitions of median. Let

$$U = \{x : F_X(x) > 1/2\}$$
$$L = \{x : F_X(x) < 1/2\}.$$

Then for any $x \in L, y \in U$, $F_X(x) < F_X(y)$ from which it follows that $x < y$ otherwise we violate the property that F_X is increasing. If I take inf and sup I may get weak inequality in the limit but can't reverse the inequality. $\qquad \square$

Exercise. Suppose that $X \ge 0$ is continuously distributed with strictly increasing c.d.f. Prove that for any $\theta > 0$

$$E(X^\theta) = \int_0^1 Q_X^\theta(\alpha)d\alpha.$$

Solution. Let $x = F_X^{-1}(\alpha) = Q_X(\alpha)$, whence $F_X(x) = \alpha$ and $f_X(x)dx = d\alpha$ so that

$$\int_0^\infty x^\theta f_X(x)dx = \int_0^1 Q_X^\theta(\alpha)d\alpha$$

as required. □

Exercise. Calculate the c.d.f. and p.d.f. of the random variable Y which is a piecewise linear combination of X, i.e.,

$$Y = \begin{cases} a_0 + b_0 X & X \le x_1 \\ a_1 + b_1 X & x_1 < X \le x_2 \\ \vdots \\ a_n + b_n X & x_n \le X \end{cases}$$

for constants (a_j, b_j), $j = 0, 1, \ldots, n$, where $\infty < x_1 < \cdots < x_n < \infty$.

Exercise. Suppose that $X = (U, V)$ and $Y = (V, W)$, where U, V, W are mutually independent continuous random variables with c.d.f.s F_j, $j = U, V, W$. Calculate the c.d.f. and p.d.f. of the random vector X, Y?

Solution. We have

$$F_{X,Y}(x, y) = \Pr(X \le x, Y \le y)$$
$$= \Pr(U \le x_1, V \le x_2, V \le y_1, W \le y_2)$$
$$= F_U(x_1)F_V(\min\{x_2, y_1\})F_W(y_2).$$

The random variable is degenerate on $\mathbb{R}^4$ meaning that $F_{X,Y}(x, y)$ is constant on the set $\{x, y : x_2 = y_1\}$. The Lebesgue density function is zero everywhere. □

Exercise. Suppose that u_1, u_2 are uniformly distributed random variables on $[0, 1]$ and let

$$X = \cos(2\pi u_1)\sqrt{2\ln(1/u_2)}$$
$$Y = \sin(2\pi u_1)\sqrt{2\ln(1/u_2)}.$$

Show that X, Y are mutually independent standard normal random variables.

Exercise. Consider the following function on $[0, 1] \times [0, 1]$

$$F(x, y) = \frac{x + y}{2}.$$

Is this a valid c.d.f.? Derive the marginal c.d.f.s and p.d.f.'s. Can you derive the joint p.d.f.?

Exercise. True, False, Explain: (a) If two random variables X and Y satisfy $E(X|Y) = 0$ and $E(Y|X) = 0$ almost surely, they are mutually independent; (b) Two events A and B with $P(A) = 1$ and $P(B) = 1$ must be mutually independent; (c) An empirical cumulative distribution function is discontinuous from the left.

Exercise. Suppose that there are three football teams: Internazionale, Manchester United, and Real Madrid. The teams are to play a "round-robin" tournament in which first Internazionale plays Manchester United, then Manchester United plays Real Madrid, then Real Madrid plays Internazionale and then Internazionale plays Manchester United again and so on. The tournament concludes only when one team has won two matches.

(i) Suppose that the teams are equally matched so that the probability of victory in any given game is equal to 1/2 (there are no draws allowed, result is decided by toss of the coin). Show that the probability of Real Madrid winning the tournament is only 1/4 compared with 6/16 for the two other teams.

(ii) Suppose that Real Madrid decides not to take part because the odds are against it, so that the tournament is now played just between Internazionale and Manchester United. The tournament organizers wanting to maximize revenue now allow draws between teams. Suppose that the probability of Internazionale beating Manchester United is π_1 in any one game, while the probability of Manchester United beating Internazionale in any one game is π_2. You are to calculate the probability that Internazionale wins the tournament, which is denoted by $p_{0,0}$. Proceed by the following steps.

(a) First, suppose that Manchester United has won one match and that Internazionale has won one match, and let $p_{1,1}$ be the probability that Internazionale wins the tournament from this point. Calculate $p_{1,1}$.

(b) Second, suppose that Internazionale has won one match and Manchester United has won none. Let the probability that Internazionale wins the tournament from this point be called $p_{1,0}$. Derive an expression for $p_{1,0}$.

(c) Complete the argument to obtain an expression for $p_{0,0}$.

Solution. *Note that since the are no ties, the max number of games to be played is four. IvM, MvR, RvI, and IvM. R does not play more than two of the four games, therefore for R to win it must win both games 2 and 3, and game 4 won't be played. In this case it also doesn't matter whether I or M wins game 1. Therefore,*

$$\Pr(R \text{ wins tournament}) = \frac{1}{2} \times \frac{1}{2} = \frac{1}{4}$$

Then by symmetry of M and I, they win each with prob 3/8. Second part. We have

$$p_{0,0} = \pi_1 p_{1,0} + \pi_2 p_{0,1} + (1 - \pi_1 - \pi_2) p_{0,0}$$
$$p_{1,0} = \pi_1 + \pi_2 p_{1,1} + (1 - \pi_1 - \pi_2) p_{1,0}$$
$$p_{0,1} = \pi_1 p_{1,1} + (1 - \pi_1 - \pi_2) p_{0,1}$$
$$p_{1,1} = \pi_1 + (1 - \pi_1 - \pi_2) p_{1,1}$$

Therefore,

$$p_{1,1} = \frac{\pi_1}{\pi_1 + \pi_2}$$

$$p_{1,0} = \frac{\pi_1 + \pi_2 p_{1,1}}{\pi_1 + \pi_2} = \frac{\pi_1 + \pi_2 \frac{\pi_1}{\pi_1 + \pi_2}}{\pi_1 + \pi_2} = \frac{\pi_1^2 + 2\pi_2 \pi_1}{(\pi_1 + \pi_2)^2}$$

$$p_{0,1} = \frac{\pi_1 p_{1,1}}{\pi_1 + \pi_2} = \frac{\pi_1 \frac{\pi_1}{\pi_1 + \pi_2}}{\pi_1 + \pi_2} = \frac{\pi_1^2}{(\pi_1 + \pi_2)^2}$$

$$p_{0,0} = \frac{1}{\pi_1 + \pi_2} \left(\pi_1 \frac{\pi_1^2 + 2\pi_2 \pi_1}{(\pi_1 + \pi_2)^2} + \pi_2 \frac{\pi_1^2}{(\pi_1 + \pi_2)^2} \right) = \frac{\pi_1^3 + 3\pi_2 \pi_1^2}{(\pi_1 + \pi_2)^3}.$$

If $\pi_1 = \pi_2$, $p_{0,0} = 1/2$ as you would expect by symmetry. □

Exercise. Suppose that the true ability of student is a random variable X and it is distributed as $N(\mu, \sigma^2)$ in the population, where μ, σ^2 are unknown parameters. Suppose however that the marking process records only Y, where

$$Y = X + u + v + w,$$

where u, v, w are i.i.d. mutually independent standard normal random variables representing the measurement errors introduced respectively by marker 1, marker 2, and marker 3.

(i) Derive an expression for the (population) best linear predictor of X given Y, which is denoted by $E_L(X|Y)$.

(ii) Suppose we have a sample of size n student scores $\{Y_i, i = 1, \ldots, n\}$ that have been marked by the three markers. The University has proposed to replace the raw score of student i, Y_i, by $E_L(X_i|Y_i)$, or at least some estimate of this quantity. Explain how we could make their policy operational, i.e., how could we estimate $E_L(X_i|Y_i)$ for student i. Which students would prefer this performance measure over Y_i?

(iii) How would we test the hypothesis that $\mu = 50$ versus the alternative hypothesis that $\mu < 50$.

Solution. *We have* $\text{var}(Y) = \sigma^2 + 3$ *and* $\text{cov}(X, Y) = \sigma^2$ *so that* $\beta = \sigma^2/(\sigma^2 + 3)$ *and* $\alpha = E(X) - \beta E(Y) = (1 - \beta)\mu = 3\mu/(\sigma^2 + 3)$. *Just need to estimate* μ *and* σ^2, *which can do straight from the Y data. In fact* $Y \sim N(\mu, \sigma^2 + 3)$. *We have to compare*

$$Y_i \text{ vs } \frac{3\mu}{\sigma^2 + 3} + \frac{\sigma^2}{\sigma^2 + 3} Y_i$$

Any student with $Y_i < \mu$ *would prefer the new scheme. This is a standard one-sided t-test.* $\square$

Exercise. Find the minimizers of

$$Q(\theta_1, \theta_2) = E\left[\{(X - \theta_1)^2 - \theta_2\}^2\right]$$

with respect to θ_1, θ_2.

Solution. We calculate the first order conditions. We write

$$Q(\theta_1, \theta_2) = E\left[\left\{X^2 - 2X\theta_1 + \theta_1^2 - \theta_2\right\}^2\right]$$

$$= E(X^4) - 4E(X^3)\theta_1 + 6E(X^2)\theta_1^2 - 2E(X^2)\theta_2 - 4E(X)\theta_1^3$$
$$+ 4E(X)\theta_1\theta_2 + \theta_1^4 - 2\theta_1^2\theta_2 + \theta_2^2$$
$$= E(X^4) + 6\theta_1^2 - 2\theta_2 + \theta_1^4 - 2\theta_1^2\theta_2 + \theta_2^2.$$

This way don't need to justify interchanging differentiation and expectation. Therefore,

$$\frac{\partial Q(\theta_1, \theta_2)}{\partial \theta_2} = -2 - 2\theta_1^2 + 2\theta_2$$

$$\frac{\partial Q(\theta_1, \theta_2)}{\partial \theta_1} = 12\theta_1 + 4\theta_1^3 - 4\theta_1\theta_2$$

It follows from the first equation that

$$\theta_2 = 1 + \theta_1^2$$

and substitute

$$12\theta_1 + 4\theta_1^3 - 4\theta_1\left(1 + \theta_1^2\right) = 8\theta_1$$

which has unique solution $\theta_1 = 0$ in which case the solution is $\theta_1 = 0$ and $\theta_2 = 1$, which is consistent with the population X. Should maybe check second order condition if you have time. When $EX^3 \neq 0$ we have

$$Q(\theta_1, \theta_2) = E(X^4) - 4E(X^3)\theta_1 - 6\theta_1^2 - 2\theta_2 + \theta_1^4 - 2\theta_1^2\theta_2 + \theta_2^2.$$

The first order condition for θ_2 does not change but the first order condition for θ_1 is

$$\frac{\partial Q(\theta_1, \theta_2)}{\partial \theta_1} = 12\theta_1 + 4\theta_1^3 - 4\theta_1\theta_2 - 4E(X^3).$$

Substituting in $\theta_2 = 1 + \theta_1^2$, we obtain

$$8\theta_1 - 4E(X^3) = 0,$$

which has solution $E(X^3)/2$. $\qquad\qquad\qquad\qquad\qquad\qquad\qquad\qquad\qquad$ □

Exercise. Find the minimizer of

$$Q(\theta) = -E\left[X \ln\theta + (1 - X)\ln(1 - \theta)\right],$$

with respect to $\theta \in [0, 1]$ when $X \in [0, 1]$.

Exercise. A, B, and C are to fight a three-cornered pistol duel. All know that A's chance of hitting his target is 0.3, C's is 0.5, and B never misses. They are to fire at their choice of target in succession in the order A, B, C until only one person is unhit. What should A's strategy be?

Exercise. Suppose that the joint probability density function of two random variables X, Y is

$$f_{XY}(x, y) = c + (x + y)/2, \quad 0 < x < 1, \ 0 < y < 1$$

and zero otherwise. Are X and Y independent? Find c. Find the expectation of X. Find the conditional expectation of Y given that $X = 1/2$.

Solution. We have

$$f_X(x) = \int_0^1 f_{XY}(x, y)dy = \int_0^1 (c + (x + y)/2)\,dy = c + \frac{x}{2} + \frac{1}{4}$$

$$f_Y(y) = \int_0^1 f_{XY}(x, y)dx = c + \frac{y}{2} + \frac{1}{4}.$$

Therefore,

$$\int_0^1 \int_0^1 f_{XY}(x, y)dxdy = \int_0^1 \left(c + \frac{y}{2} + \frac{1}{4}\right)dy = c + \frac{1}{2}$$

and so $c = 1/2$. Then

$$f_X(x)f_Y(y) = \left(\frac{x}{2} + \frac{3}{4}\right)\left(\frac{y}{2} + \frac{3}{4}\right) = \frac{3}{8}x + \frac{3}{8}y + \frac{1}{4}xy + \frac{9}{16} \neq \frac{1}{2} + \frac{1}{2}(x + y).$$

We have

$$E(X) = \int_0^1 \left(\frac{x}{2} + \frac{3}{4}\right)dx = 1.$$

$$E(Y|X = 1/2) = \int_0^1 y\frac{\frac{1}{2} + \frac{1}{2}\left(\frac{1}{2} + y\right)}{\left(\frac{1}{4} + \frac{3}{4}\right)}dy = \int_0^1 y\left(\frac{3}{4} + \frac{1}{2}y\right)dy = \frac{13}{24}. \quad \square$$

Exercise. Suppose that 1 percent of the population has a particular disease. A test has been developed with the following properties. If a person has the disease, the test comes out positive with probability 0.9 and negative with probability 0.1. If the person does not have the disease, the test comes out positive with probability 0.05 and negative with probability 0.95:

(a) What is the probability that a person randomly picked from the population has the disease if he tests positive?

(b) Suppose that in response to warnings about an epidemic 30 percent of the people who have the disease decide to have a test, and 15 percent of people who do not have the disease decide to have the test.

(c) What is the probability that someone who tests positive has the disease?

Solution. Define the events

$$X = \begin{cases} 1 & \text{if the person has the disease} \\ 0 & \text{if the person has not the disease} \end{cases}$$

$$Y = \begin{cases} 1 & \text{if the test comes out positive} \\ 0 & \text{if the test comes out negative} \end{cases}$$

The joint distribution is given below

	$Y = 1$	$Y = 0$
$X = 1$	$0.01 \times 0.9 = \frac{18}{2000}$	$0.01 \times 0.1 = \frac{2}{2000}$
$X = 0$	$0.99 \times 0.05 = \frac{99}{2000}$	$0.99 \times 0.95 = \frac{1881}{2000}$

Therefore, the probability of a randomly picked person having the disease given positive test result is

$$\Pr(X = 1|Y = 1) = \frac{18}{18 + 99} = \frac{2}{13}.$$

Define the random variable

$$Z = \begin{cases} 1 & \text{if the person decides to have the test} \\ 0 & \text{if the person decides not to have the test} \end{cases}$$

Then the joint distribution of X, Y conditional on $Z = 1$ is proportional to (such that the sum of all four elements sum to one)

	$Y = 1$	$Y = 0$
$X = 1$	$0.01 \times 0.3 \times 0.9 = \frac{108}{40000}$	$0.01 \times 0.3 \times 0.1 = \frac{12}{40000}$
$X = 0$	$0.99 \times 0.15 \times 0.05 = \frac{297}{40000}$	$0.99 \times 0.15 \times 0.95 = \frac{5643}{40000}$

Therefore, the probability of someone who tests positive having the disease is

$$\Pr(X = 1 | Y = 1, Z = 1) = \frac{108}{108 + 297} = \frac{4}{15}. \qquad \square$$

Exercise. Suppose that you throw a six sided die three times. What is the distribution of the maximum value m? There are 216 possible outcomes and

$$\Pr[m = 1] = \frac{1}{216}$$

$$\Pr[m = 2] = \frac{4 + 2 + 1}{216} = \frac{7}{216}$$

$$\Pr[m = 3] = \frac{9 + 6 + 4}{216} = \frac{19}{216}$$

$$\Pr[m = 4] = \frac{16 + 12 + 9}{216} = \frac{37}{216}$$

$$\Pr[m = 5] = \frac{25 + 20 + 16}{216} = \frac{61}{216}$$

$$\Pr[m = 6] = \frac{36 + 30 + 25}{216} = \frac{91}{216}.$$

Now suppose that this is done "without replacement", that is, if the first number drawn is x, then one chooses randomly from $\{1, 2, 3, 4, 5, 6\}/\{x\}$ and so on. In this case the total number of outcomes is $6 \times 5 \times 4 = 120$. Furthermore,

$$\Pr[m = 1] = 0$$

$$\Pr[m = 2] = 0$$

$$\Pr[m = 3] = \frac{2 + 2 + 2}{120} = \frac{6}{120}$$

$$\Pr[m = 4] = \frac{6 + 6 + 6}{120} = \frac{18}{120}$$

$$\Pr[m = 5] = \frac{12 + 12 + 12}{120} = \frac{36}{120}$$

$$\Pr[m = 6] = \frac{20 + 20 + 20}{120} = \frac{60}{120}.$$

Suppose that the die now has N sides.

Exercise. The legislatures of Utopia are trying to determine whether to impeach President Trumpet for an inappropriate hairstyle.

(1) The Congress meets first and can decide: (a) to impeach, (b) to pass the buck to the Senate (ask the Senate to make the decision), or (c) to end the process. If decision (b) is made, then the Senate gets to decide on essentially the same three options (in this case, (b) is to pass the buck back to the Congress). The probabilities of each decision are: p_a, p_b, and p_c for the Congress and q_a, q_b, and q_c for the Senate, where $p_c = 1 - p_a - p_b$ and $q_c = 1 - q_a - q_b$. What is the probability that the President is impeached? If each decision takes 1 month and $q_b = p_b$, what it the expected length of time before the process is terminated.

(2) A new system is brought in in which each house can only vote (a) to impeach or (b) to not impeach. Now however, the process only terminates when both houses arrive at the same decision (and they vote simultaneously). Let π_a be the probability of a vote to impeach in the Congress (at a given round of voting) and ρ_a be the probability of a vote to impeach in the Senate. What is the probability that the President is impeached in this system?

Solution. *We have*

$$p_I = p_a + p_b q_b p_a + p_b q_b p_b q_b p_a + \ldots + p_b q_a + p_b q_b p_b q_a + \ldots$$

$$= p_a \sum_{j=0}^{\infty} (p_b q_b)^j + p_b q_a \sum_{j=0}^{\infty} (p_b q_b)^j$$

$$= \frac{p_a + p_b q_a}{1 - p_b q_b}.$$

Here we summed the two geometric series. To calculate the expected length we see that it is

$$\underbrace{1 \times (p_a + p_c)}_{\text{terminates in one period}} + \underbrace{2 \times p_b \, (q_a + q_c)}_{\text{terminates in two periods}} + 3 \times \underbrace{p_b q_b \, (p_a + p_c)}_{\text{terminates in three periods}} + \ldots$$

$$= 1 \times (1 - p_b) + 2 \times p_b \, (1 - p_b) + 3 \times p_b^2 \, (1 - p_b) + \ldots$$

$$= (1 - p_b) \sum_{j=0}^{\infty} (j + 1) p_b^j.$$

We write for any p the function I

$$I(p) = \sum_{j=0}^{\infty} p^j = \frac{1}{1 - p}.$$

The right hand side has derivative $\left(\frac{1}{1-p} \right)^2$, *while*

$$\frac{dI(p)}{dp} = \sum_{j=0}^{\infty} \frac{d}{dp} p^j = \left(\frac{d}{dp} 1 + \frac{d}{dp} p + \frac{d}{dp} p^2 + \ldots \right)$$

$$= 1 + 2p + 3p^2 + \ldots$$

Therefore, expected length is $1/(1 - p_b)$.

Let p_I denote the probability of President being impeached. Just draw the one step tree, in which we have probability $\pi_a \rho_a$ they both vote for impeachment and probability $\pi_a (1 - \rho_a) + (1 - \pi_a)\rho_a$ that one of the houses votes not to impeach, in which case we return to square one. We have

$$p_I = \pi_a \rho_a + (\pi_a(1 - \rho_a) + (1 - \pi_a)\rho_a) \, p_I$$

and solving this equation we obtain

$$p_I = \frac{\pi_a \rho_a}{1 - (\pi_a(1 - \rho_a) + (1 - \pi_a)\rho_a)}. \qquad \square$$

Exercise. Suppose that a newsagent stocks N copies of a daily paper and wishes to choose N to maximize his profit. Let α be the profit on a paper that is sold, β is the loss on an unsold paper and γ is the loss if a customer who wishes to buy a paper is unable to do so because of insufficient stock. Suppose the newsagent has X customers on a given day, where X is a random variable with distribution function F. What is the optimal (or approximately optimal) choice of N? You may assume that N, X are continuous on $[0, \infty)$.

Solution. The net profit is

$$\pi(X, N) = \begin{cases} \alpha X + \beta(X - N) & X \le N \\ \alpha N + \gamma(N - X) & X > N. \end{cases}$$

The expected profit is

$$\begin{aligned} E\left[\pi(X, N)\right] &= E\left[(\alpha X + \beta(X - N))\, 1(X \le N)\right] \\ &\quad + E\left[(\alpha N + \gamma(N - X))\, 1(X > N)\right] \\ &= (\alpha + \beta)E[X1(X \le N)] - \beta N F(N) + (\alpha + \gamma)N(1 - F(N)) \\ &\quad - \gamma E[X(1 - 1(X \le N))] \\ &= (\alpha + \beta + \gamma)G(N) - (\alpha + \beta + \gamma)N F(N) + (\alpha + \gamma)N \\ &\quad - \gamma E(X), \end{aligned}$$

where $G(N) = E[X1(X \le N)]$. The first order condition is

$$(\alpha + \beta + \gamma)G'(N) - (\alpha + \beta + \gamma)F(N) - (\alpha + \beta + \gamma)N F'(N) + (\alpha + \gamma) = 0.$$

We have $G(N) = \int_0^N xf(x)dx$ so that $G'(N) = Nf(N)$ and the first order condition simplifies to

$$F(N) = \frac{\alpha + \gamma}{\alpha + \beta + \gamma}.$$

Therefore, $N_{opt} = F^{-1}((\alpha + \gamma)/(\alpha + \gamma + \beta))$. $\square$

Exercise. Suppose that a random variable X is the age (in years measured continuously) of a disabled individual and Y is the time (in years) since this person became disabled. Suppose that Y, X are uniformly distributed on the triangular region T defined by $X \in [0, \theta]$ and $Y \in [0, X]$, where θ is an unknown parameter, i.e.,

$$f_{Y,X}(y, x) = \frac{2}{\theta^2} 1((x, y) \in T),$$

where $1(a \in A) = 1$ if $a \in A$ and 0 else. Calculate
(i) The marginal densities of Y and X and the conditional density $Y|X$.
(ii) The regression function $E(Y|X = x)$.
(iv) Suppose you have a random sample $\{X_1, Y_1, \ldots, X_n, Y_n\}$ from the distribution described above. Derive the large sample properties of the ordinary least squares estimator of Y_i on a constant and X_i and provide a confidence interval for the slope coefficient.

Solution. *We have*

$$f_X(x) = \int_0^x f_{Y,X}(y,x)dy = \frac{2}{\theta^2}\int_0^x dy = \frac{2x}{\theta^2}1(0 \le x \le \theta)$$

and

$$f_Y(y) = \int_y^\theta f_{Y,X}(y,x)dx = \frac{2(\theta - y)}{\theta^2}1(0 \le y \le \theta),$$

which are not uniform. It follows that

$$f_{Y|X}(y|x) = \frac{f_{Y,X}(y,x)}{f_X(x)} = \frac{\frac{2}{\theta^2}1((x,y) \in T)}{\frac{2x}{\theta^2}1(0 \le x \le \theta)} = \frac{1}{x}1(0 \le y \le x \le \theta).$$

We have

$$E(Y|X = x) = \int \frac{y}{x}1(0 \le y \le x \le \theta)dy = \frac{1}{x}\int_0^x ydy = \frac{x}{2},$$

which is linear. We also have

$$E(Y^2|X = x) = \frac{1}{x}\int_0^x y^2dy = \frac{x^2}{3}$$

$$\mathrm{var}(Y|X = x) = \frac{x^2}{12}.$$

(iii) We have

$$E(X) = \frac{2}{\theta^2}\int_0^\theta x^2dx = \frac{2}{\theta^2}\frac{\theta^3}{3} = \frac{2}{3}\theta$$

$$E(Y) = \frac{2}{\theta^2}\int_0^\theta y(\theta - y)dy = \frac{1}{3}\theta$$

$$E(X^2) = \frac{2}{\theta^2}\int_0^\theta x^3dx = \frac{1}{2}\theta^2$$

$$E(Y^2) = \frac{2}{\theta^2}\int_0^\theta y^2(\theta - y)dy = \frac{1}{6}\theta^2$$

$$E(XY) = \frac{2}{\theta^2} \int_0^\theta x \int_0^x y \, dy \, dx = \frac{1}{4}\theta^2$$

$$\vdots$$

$$\text{var}(X) = \frac{1}{2}\theta^2 - \left(\frac{2}{3}\theta\right)^2 = \frac{1}{18}\theta^2$$

$$\text{var}(Y) = \frac{1}{6}\theta^2 - \left(\frac{1}{3}\theta\right)^2 = \frac{1}{18}\theta^2$$

$$\text{cov}(X,Y) = \frac{1}{4}\theta^2 - \frac{2}{9}\theta^2 = \frac{1}{36}\theta^2.$$

Therefore,

$$E_L(Y|X) = \frac{1}{2}X = E(Y|X)$$

Can apply standard theory for the OLS slope estimate except that we expect heteroskedasticity from the above arguments. Therefore we should estimate the standard errors by

$$\sqrt{\frac{\sum_{i=1}^n \left(X_i - \overline{X}\right)^2 \widehat{\varepsilon}_i^2}{\left(\sum_{i=1}^n \left(X_i - \overline{X}\right)^2\right)^2}}.$$ □

Exercise. Suppose that you play dice with your 4 your old son. To make it a happy ending game you decide to let him have two dice to your one. What is the probability that he wins? Now suppose that you throw n dice to his $2n$? In this case, you may use a central limit theorem.

Solution. Let X be his outcome (sum of two dice) and Y be your outcome. Then

$$(X,Y) \in \{2,3,\ldots,12\} \times \{1,2,\ldots,6\}.$$

We have to calculate $\Pr(X > Y)$. For example $(2,1)$ is consistent with the outcome of interest but $(2,3)$ is not. Since we assume that X, Y are independent random variables, the answer is given by

$$1 - \sum_{k=1}^6 \Pr(X \leq k)\Pr(Y = k) = 1 - \frac{1}{6}\sum_{k=2}^6 \Pr(X \leq k).$$

We have $\Pr(X = 2) = 1/36$, $\Pr(X = 3) = 2/36$, $\Pr(X = 4) = 3/36$, $\Pr(X = 5) = 4/36$, $\Pr(X = 6) = 5/36$, so that the required probability is

$$1 - \frac{1}{6}\frac{1}{36}(1 + 2 + 3 + 4 + 5) = 1 - \frac{15}{216} = \frac{201}{216}.$$

Suppose you throw n dice, then your total score is $\sum_{i=1}^{n} Y_i$ and we know that

$$\frac{1}{\sqrt{n}} \sum_{i=1}^{n} (Y_i - \mu) \Longrightarrow N(0, \sigma^2).$$

Likewise his outcome satisfies

$$\frac{1}{\sqrt{n}} \sum_{i=1}^{2n} (X_i - \mu) \Longrightarrow N(0, \frac{\sigma^2}{2})$$

and the two limiting random variables are independent. We have $\mu = 21/6$ and $\sigma^2 = 91/6 - (21/6)^2$. We have

$$\Pr\left(\sum_{i=1}^{n} Y_i \geq \sum_{i=1}^{2n} X_i\right) = \Pr\left(\frac{1}{2n} \sum_{i=1}^{n} Y_i \geq \frac{1}{2n} \sum_{i=1}^{2n} X_i\right) = \Pr\left(\overline{Y}_n/2 - \overline{X}_{2n} \geq 0\right)$$

By Chebychev's inequality, for $\eta > 0$

$$\Pr\left(\overline{Y}_n/2 - \overline{X}_{2n} \geq 0\right) \leq \Pr\left(\left|\overline{Y}_n/2 - \overline{X}_{2n} + \frac{\mu}{2}\right| \geq \eta\right)$$

$$\leq \frac{\mathrm{var}(\overline{Y}_n/2 - \overline{X}_{2n})}{\eta^2}$$

$$= \frac{3\sigma^2}{4n\eta^2} \to 0$$

as $n \to \infty$. CLT type of argument is ok. $\qquad\qquad\square$

Exercise. Suppose that $X \sim N(0, 1)$. Derive the density function of $Y = \cos(X)$ on $[-1, 1]$.

Solution. This can be done analytically but too hard, but might try to do it to see what the issues are. We have $X \sim N(0, 1)$

$$Y = \cos(X).$$

This function is not monotonic everywhere. The random variable Y has support $[-1, 1]$ and for any $y \in [-1, 1]$ we have to locate all the crossings of that by $\cos(x)$. We can apply the transformation formula from the notes after partitioning into regions where the transformation is monotonic. Specifically, we use the partition $[j\pi, (j+1)\pi]$, where: for $j = 0, \pm 2, \pm 4, \ldots$ in these regions the transformation is monotonic decreasing whereas in $j = \pm 1, \pm 3, \ldots$ the transformation is monotonic increasing. Therefore,

$$f_Y(y) = \sum_{j=-\infty}^{\infty} \phi(g_j^{-1}(y)) \left|\frac{d}{dy} g_j^{-1}(y)\right|$$

where ϕ is the normal density and $g(x) = \cos(x)$ with inverse g_j^{-1} on $[j\pi, (j + 1)\pi]$. When $x \in [j\pi, (j + 1)\pi]$ with j even

$$\cos(x) = \cos(x - j\pi)$$
$$g_j^{-1}(y) = ar\cos(y) + j\pi,$$

where $ar\cos(y)$ is the usual arcos defined on $[0, \pi]$. Similarly for the odd numbered parts except map into $[-\pi, 0]$. The Jacobian factor is $1/\sqrt{1 - y^2}$ for all j. In fact a pretty good approximation should be made by just restricting to $[-\pi, \pi]$ and following the scheme described in the notes for the quadratic function. Here is the code in GAUSS

```
(new;cls;n=100000;x=rndn(n,1);y=cos(x);library pgraph;hist(y,50))
```

and here is the histogram.

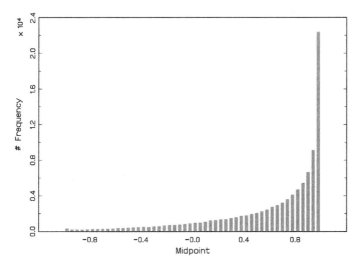

The density has a lot of value near $\cos = 1$, which is coming from the Jacobian part. □

Exercise. Sometimes you eat the bear and sometimes the bear eats you. Suppose that the outcome of a game is random and

$$X = \begin{cases} A & \text{with probability } 1/2 \\ \frac{1}{A} & \text{with probability } 1/2, \end{cases}$$

where $A > 0$. Show that $EX > 1$ but $E\log(X) = 0$. The game is played n times with each game being independent, and define the payoff to be $Y_n = X_1 \times X_2 \times \cdots \times X_n$, that is you bet everything you have each time. Calculate EY_n and

$E \log(Y_n)$. Show that for any ϵ with $0 < \epsilon < 1$:

$$\Pr(Y_n < \epsilon) \to \frac{1}{2}$$

$$\Pr\left(Y_n > \frac{1}{\epsilon}\right) \to \frac{1}{2}.$$

How much would you be willing to pay to play this game? Simulate the game using some computer program such as matlab or R and show the distribution of the payoffs after n periods with $n = 1, 10, 100$.

Solution. We have

$$EX = \frac{1}{2}A + \frac{1}{2}\frac{1}{A} = \frac{1}{2}\left(A + \frac{1}{A}\right) = \frac{1}{2}\frac{A^2 + 1}{A}.$$

We have

$$\frac{1}{2}\frac{A^2 + 1}{A} > 1$$

if and only if

$$A^2 - 2A + 1 > 0$$

but the lhs factors as $(A - 1)^2$, which is always strictly positive except when $A = 1$ (in which case it is zero and $E(X) = 1$ trivially). However,

$$E \log(X) = \frac{1}{2}\log(A) + \frac{1}{2}\log(\frac{1}{A}) = \frac{1}{2}\log(A) - \frac{1}{2}\log(A) = 0.$$

Now we have

$$EY_n = (EX)^n = \left(\frac{1}{2}\frac{A^2 + 1}{A}\right)^n \to \infty.$$

However, $E \log(Y_n) = 0$. In fact

$$\frac{1}{\sqrt{n}}\log Y_n = \frac{1}{\sqrt{n}}\sum_{i=1}^{n}\log(X_i) \Longrightarrow N(0, \sigma^2),$$

where $\sigma^2 = \text{var}(\log(X)) = \log(A)^2$. Risk neutral persons would like the bet, persons with log utility would be indifferent. Can also work out easily for general class of utility functions

$$U(y) = \frac{y^{1-\eta} - 1}{1 - \eta}.$$

Then

$$EU(Y_n) = \frac{E(X_1 \times \cdots \times X_n)^{1-\eta} - 1}{1 - \eta}$$

$$= \frac{E(X_1^{1-\eta})^n - 1}{1 - \eta}$$

$$= \frac{\frac{1}{2^n}\left(A^{1-\eta} + \frac{1}{A^{1-\eta}}\right)^n - 1}{1 - \eta}.$$

It depends on whether

$$\frac{1}{2}\left(A^{1-\eta} + \frac{1}{A^{1-\eta}}\right) > < = 1.$$

We have for any $\epsilon > 0$

$$\Pr(Y_n \leq \epsilon) = \Pr\left(\frac{1}{\sqrt{n}}\log Y_n \leq \frac{1}{\sqrt{n}}\log\epsilon\right) \to \Pr\left(N(0,\sigma^2) \leq 0\right) = 1/2. \quad \square$$

Part II

Statistics

Chapter 10

Introduction

10.1 SAMPLING THEORY

We suppose that there is a population random variable denoted X and we wish to learn something about this population on the basis of a sample of size n, $\{X_1, \ldots, X_n\}$ that has been drawn from the population. The leading case is the "random sampling" case where each draw is done "with replacement" (e.g., from an "infinite" population) and in the same way. In this case, each X_j is **independent and identically distributed** with the same distribution as the population.

In some applications it may be useful to be able to weaken the assumption that the population is the same for each observation, i.e., we may wish to allow reflecting **heterogeneous** individuals. In time series we might want to allow the sampled variables to possess **dependence**, e.g., X_j and X_k may be correlated.

In survey sampling one often has to consider a more complicated form of sampling called **stratified sampling**, in which one divides a population into groups, say men and women, and then constructs a random sample of men and a random sample of women. One reason for doing this arises when one of the subgroups is quite rare, in which case ordinary random sampling is quite likely to draw a sample that contains no members of that group. Stratified sampling should be combined with a reweighting procedure if one seeks to understand the original population.

A big issue with survey sampling is nonresponse, where a number of units do not respond. This may lead to **sample selection bias**, when the nonresponders are somehow different from the responders in a way that reflects the objective of the study.

Suppose that the population is actually finite, i.e., consists of $\{x_1, \ldots, x_N\}$. In this case, we may sample without **replacement**. That is, we draw $X_1, X_2, \ldots, X_n$ sequentially without returning the chosen values to the population, where $n \leq N$. This causes some heterogeneity and dependence, since if $X_1 = x_1$, then the distribution of X_2 must be affected, in particular its support has changed since it cannot take the value x_1. This setting is quite difficult to analyze, and in many cases, one may be willing to assume that N is very large, so as to ignore the issue.

Probability, Statistics and Econometrics. http://dx.doi.org/10.1016/B978-0-12-810495-8.00012-9

Nowadays, a big distinction is made between **observational** data and **experimental** data, where in the latter case one has some measure of control of the experimental settings that determined the data, whereas in the former case no control is possible.

10.2 SAMPLE STATISTICS

Data description is a common first step. A number of books emphasize the graphical approach, perhaps Tukey (1977) and Tufte (2001) are the best known. You should be familiar with graphical devices such as box plots, histograms and empirical distribution functions.

For discrete data, a common way of presentation is the **Contingency Table**, see below a (2×2) example:

	cancer	not
smokers	643	812
non-smokers	117	911

A statistic is any quantity we can write as a measurable function of the sample, i.e., $T(X_1, \ldots, X_n)$ for some function $T : \mathbb{R}^n \to \mathbb{R}$. For example, the following are important statistics:

$$\bar{X} = \frac{1}{n} \sum_{i=1}^{n} X_i$$

$$s^2 = \frac{1}{n} \sum_{i=1}^{n} (X_i - \bar{X})^2; \quad s_*^2 = \frac{1}{n-1} \sum_{i=1}^{n} (X_i - \bar{X})^2;$$

$$s_{XY} = \frac{1}{n-1} \sum_{i=1}^{n} (X_i - \bar{X})(Y_i - \bar{Y})$$

$$F_n(x) = \frac{1}{n} \sum_{i=1}^{n} 1(X_i \leq x),$$

called respectively the sample mean, sample variance, unbiased sample variance, sample covariance, and empirical distribution function. See Fig. 10.1.

The **Kernel Density Estimate** is formally an estimator of the density $f(x)$ of a random variable. See Fig. 10.2. It is defined as

$$\hat{f}(x) = \frac{1}{nh} \sum_{i=1}^{n} K\left(\frac{x - X_i}{h}\right),$$

where $K(\cdot)$ is a density function, e.g., normal $(0, 1)$, and h is a bandwidth. This gives a smooth curve compared with the lumpy histogram. The smoothness of

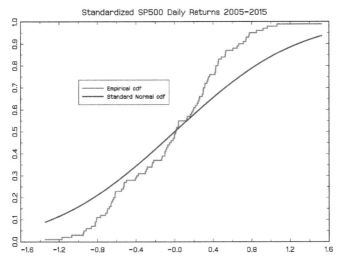

FIGURE 10.1   Shows the empirical c.d.f. of a subsample of the dataset of size 100

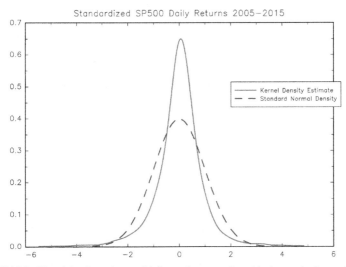

FIGURE 10.2   Kernel density estimate of daily stock returns alongside the standard normal density function

the curve is controlled by h: large h will make a smooth curve and small h will make a very wiggly curve, see Silverman (1986).

If stock returns were normally distributed $\Pr(X_t \leq -25) = 3 \times 10^{-138}$; If stock returns were logistic distributed $\Pr(X_t \leq -25) = 1 \times 10^{-11}$; If stock returns were Cauchy distributed $\Pr(X_t \leq -25) = 0.13$.

TABLE 10.1 Descriptive Statistics by Frequency

	Daily	Weekly	Monthly
Mean ($\times 100$)	0.029	0.141	0.606
St. Deviation ($\times 100$)	0.038	0.200	0.903
Skewness	−1.546	−0.375	−0.589
Excess Kurtosis	43.334	6.521	5.588
Minimum	−25.422	−6.577	−5.984
Maximum	9.623	6.534	3.450
Sample Size	11893	2475	568
Number zeros	81	15	3

Note: Descriptive statistics for the returns on the S&P500 index for the period 1955–2002 for three different data frequencies. Minimum and maximum are measured in standard deviations from the mean.

10.2.1 Properties of Descriptive Statistics

The descriptive statistics can all be analyzed straightforwardly in terms of their means and variances and large sample distribution, so we record them here (see Table 10.1).

Theorem 10.1. *Properties of Descriptive Statistics. Let $X_1, \ldots, X_n$ be random sample from a population with mean μ and variance σ^2 and kurtosis κ_4. Then, $E\bar{X} = \mu$ and $\mathrm{var}(\bar{X}) = \sigma^2/n$. Furthermore, as $n \to \infty$: $\bar{X} \overset{P}{\longrightarrow} \mu$ and $s^2 \overset{P}{\longrightarrow} \sigma^2$, and*

$$\sqrt{n} \left(\bar{X} - \mu \right) \overset{D}{\longrightarrow} N(0, \sigma^2)$$

$$\sqrt{n} \left(s^2 - \sigma^2 \right) \overset{D}{\longrightarrow} N(0, (\kappa_4 + 2)\sigma^4).$$

Proof. First, we have

$$E\bar{X} = E\frac{1}{n} \sum_{i=1}^{n} X_i$$

$$= \frac{1}{n} \sum_{i=1}^{n} E(X_i) \text{ (by the linearity of expectation)}$$

$$= \mu.$$

Furthermore,

$$\mathrm{var}(\bar{X}) = \mathrm{var} \left(\frac{1}{n} \sum_{i=1}^{n} X_i \right) = \frac{1}{n^2} \mathrm{var} \left(\sum_{i=1}^{n} X_i \right)$$

$$= \frac{1}{n^2} \sum_{i=1}^{n} \text{var}(X_i) \text{ (by independence)}$$

$$= \frac{\text{var}(X_i)}{n} = \frac{\sigma^2}{n} \text{ (by identical distribution)}$$

$$s^2 = \frac{1}{n} \sum_{i=1}^{n} (X_i - \bar{X})^2$$

$$= \frac{1}{n} \sum_{i=1}^{n} (X_i - \mu + \mu - \bar{X})^2$$

$$= \frac{1}{n} \sum_{i=1}^{n} (X_i - \mu)^2 + \frac{1}{n} \sum_{i=1}^{n} (\mu - \bar{X})^2 + 2\frac{1}{n} \sum_{i=1}^{n} (X_i - \mu)(\mu - \bar{X})$$

$$= \frac{1}{n} \sum_{i=1}^{n} (X_i - \mu)^2 - (\mu - \bar{X})^2.$$

We can calculate the exact mean and variance of s^2, but we defer this to later, and make do with a large sample theory. It follows by the Slutsky theorem that $s^2 \xrightarrow{P} \sigma^2$ since the second term converges to zero in probability, and the first term converges to σ^2 because $E[(X_i - \mu)^2] = \sigma^2$.

Furthermore,

$$\sqrt{n}\left(s^2 - \sigma^2\right) = \frac{1}{\sqrt{n}} \sum_{i=1}^{n} \left((X_i - \mu)^2 - \sigma^2\right) + R_n,$$

where $R_n = -\sqrt{n}(\mu - \bar{X})^2 \xrightarrow{P} 0$. It follows by the Lindeberg Levy CLT that with $Z_i = (X_i - \mu)^2 - \sigma^2$

$$\sqrt{n}\left(s^2 - \sigma^2\right) \xrightarrow{D} N(0, \text{var}(Z_i)).$$

We have

$$\text{var}(Z_i) = E\left[\left((X_i - \mu)^2 - \sigma^2\right)^2\right] = E\left[(X_i - \mu)^4\right] - \sigma^4$$

$$= \sigma^4 \left(\frac{E\left[(X_i - \mu)^4\right]}{\sigma^4} - 1\right) = \sigma^4 (\kappa_4 + 2).$$

This equals $2\sigma^4$ when $X_i \sim N(\mu, \sigma^2)$.

Finally, we note that

$$\text{cov}(\overline{X}, s^2) = \frac{1}{n} E\left[(X_i - \mu)^3\right]. \tag{10.1}$$

If $E[(X - \mu)^3] = 0$, then $\text{cov}(\overline{X}, s^2) = 0$. $\square$

10.2.2 Exact Properties Specific to the Normal Distribution

We consider some exact distributional results involving the sample mean and variance from a normal distribution. These will be useful below in carrying out hypothesis tests.

Theorem 10.2. *Suppose that* $X_i \sim N(\mu, \sigma^2)$. *Then we have the following results:*

(1) $\overline{X} \sim N(\mu, \sigma^2/n)$;

(2) $\overline{X}$ *and* s_*^2 *(or* s^2*) are independent;*

(3) $\frac{(n-1)s_*^2}{\sigma^2}$ *has a chi-squared distribution with* $(n-1)$ *degrees of freedom;*

(4) $\frac{\overline{X} - \mu}{s_*/\sqrt{n}}$ *has the* $t(n-1)$ *distribution;*

(5) Suppose that $X_i \sim N(\mu_X, \sigma_X^2)$ *and* $Y_i \sim N(\mu_Y, \sigma_Y^2)$ *with* X_i, Y_i *independent of each other. Then* $\frac{s_{*X}^2/s_{*Y}^2}{\sigma_X^2/\sigma_Y^2} \sim F(n, m)$.

Proof. Proof of (1) is by c.f. or m.g.f. argument. We have

$$\varphi_{\overline{X}}(t) = \varphi_X(t/n)^n.$$

For a normally distributed random variable the characteristic function and moment generating function are respectively:

$$\varphi_X(t) = e^{i\mu t - \frac{1}{2}\sigma^2 t^2} \quad ; \quad mgf_X(t) = e^{\mu t + \frac{1}{2}\sigma^2 t^2}.$$

Therefore,

$$\varphi_{\overline{X}}(t) = \left(e^{i\mu t/n - \frac{1}{2}\sigma^2 t^2/n^2}\right)^n = e^{i\mu t - \frac{1}{2}\sigma^2 t^2/n},$$

which is the c.f. of a normal random variable with mean μ and variance σ^2/n.

Proof of (2). Let $n = 2$, $X_1 \sim N(0, 1)$, $X_2 \sim N(0, 1)$, and

$$\overline{X} = \frac{X_1 + X_2}{2}$$

$$s_*^2 = \left(X_1 - \frac{X_1 + X_2}{2} \right)^2 + \left(X_2 - \frac{X_1 + X_2}{2} \right)^2$$

$$= \left(\frac{X_1 - X_2}{2} \right)^2 + \left(\frac{X_1 - X_2}{2} \right)^2 = \frac{(X_1 - X_2)^2}{2}$$

Claim that $Z_1 = X_1 + X_2$ and $Z_2 = X_1 - X_2$ are independent. Joint m.g.f. is

$$E(e^{t_1 Z_1 + t_2 Z_2}) = E e^{t_1 (X_1 + X_2) + t_2 (X_1 - X_2)}$$

$$= E e^{(t_1 + t_2) X_1 + (t_1 - t_2) X_2}$$

$$= E e^{(t_1 + t_2) X_1} E e^{(t_1 - t_2) X_2}$$

$$= e^{\frac{1}{2} (t_1 + t_2)^2} e^{\frac{1}{2} (t_1 - t_2)^2}$$

$$= e^{t_1^2 + t_2^2}$$

$$= E e^{t_1 Z_1} E e^{t_2 Z_2}.$$

But $E e^{t_1 Z_1} = e^{t_1^2}$ and $E e^{t_2 Z_2} = e^{t_2^2}$. A simpler way of seeing this is to note that Z_1 and Z_2 are normally distributed, since they are both a linear combination of the same normals, and are mutually uncorrelated, since

$$E[Z_1 Z_2] = E[(X_1 - X_2)(X_1 + X_2)] = E[(X_1^2 - X_2^2)] = 0.$$

For normal distributions, uncorrelatedness implies independence.

Finally, suppose for simplicity that $\mu = 0$ and $\sigma^2 = 1$. Then we claim that

$$\sum_{i=1}^{n} (X_i - \bar{X})^2 = \sum_{i=1}^{n} X_i^2 - n\bar{X}^2$$

is chi-squared with n degrees of freedom. We have

$$\sqrt{n}\bar{X} \sim N(0, 1) \Rightarrow n\bar{X}^2 \sim \chi^2(1),$$

while by independence of sample mean and variance

$$E e^{t \sum_{i=1}^{n} X_i^2} = E e^{t \sum_{i=1}^{n} (X_i - \bar{X})^2} E e^{tn\bar{X}^2}.$$

But

$$E e^{t \sum_{i=1}^{n} X_i^2} = \left(E e^{t X_i^2} \right)^n = \left(\frac{1}{1 - 2t} \right)^{n/2}$$

and

$$E^{tn\bar{X}^2} = \frac{1}{(1 - 2t)^{1/2}}.$$

Therefore,

$$Ee^{t\sum_{i=1}^{n}(X_i-\bar{X})^2} = \left(\frac{1}{1-2t}\right)^{\frac{n-1}{2}},$$

which is the m.g.f. of a $\chi^2(n-1)$ random variable.

The proofs of (4) and (5) are omitted, but they follow from the definition of t and F random variables and the properties already established. $\qquad\square$

We now move on to statistics which consists of a logical framework for analyzing data.

10.3 STATISTICAL PRINCIPLES

There are two general paradigms: **Frequentist** and **Bayesian**. In the Frequentist approach we have some model **P**, which is a collection of distributions or probability measures P. We obtain a sample $\mathcal{X}^n = \{X_1, \ldots, X_n\}$, which is obtained from some P, and we estimate various quantities $\theta(P)$, called **parameters**, by some function $\widehat{\theta}$ of the sample. The properties of $\widehat{\theta}$ are calculated treating this quantity as a random variable which arose as one realization of the sampling process. In the *classical parametric* approach, $\{P_\theta, \theta \in \Theta\}$, where $\Theta \subset \mathbb{R}^k$ is the parameter space and for each θ, P_θ is a probability measure [or equivalently density function when we are talking about continuous variables]. The objective is to learn about θ from the data. In this case, the entire distribution of the data is specified apart from the unknown parameters, i.e., correct specification assumes that $P \in \{P_\theta, \theta \in \Theta\}$.

Example 10.1. Suppose that X_i are i.i.d. with unknown distribution P. Let $\theta = E(X)$ be the parameter of interest.

In this case, very little is specified about P, whereas in the next example the entire distribution is specified apart from two unknown quantities.

Example 10.2. Suppose that $X \sim N(\mu, \sigma^2)$, where $\theta = (\mu, \sigma^2) \in \mathbb{R}^2$ are the parameters of interest.

The **likelihood function** plays an important role in parametric statistics; this is defined as

$$L(\theta|\mathcal{X}^n) = f(X_1, \ldots, X_n|\theta),$$

i.e., it is the density of the data under the parameter value θ, but treated as a function of θ for given data. When $X_1, \ldots, X_n$ are i.i.d. we may write the likelihood and log likelihood

$$L(\theta|\mathcal{X}^n) = \prod_{i=1}^{n} f(X_i|\theta)$$

$$\ell(\theta|\mathcal{X}^n) = \log L(\theta|\mathcal{X}^n) = \sum_{i=1}^{n} \log f(X_i|\theta) = \sum_{i=1}^{n} \ell_i(\theta|X_i),$$

where $\ell_i(\theta|X_i) = \log f(X_i|\theta)$.

The likelihood function is used to generate estimators and test statistics. The Maximum Likelihood Estimator $\widehat{\theta}_{MLE}$ maximizes $L(\theta|\mathcal{X}^n)$ with respect to θ or equivalently maximizes $\ell(\theta|\mathcal{X}^n)$ with respect to θ.

Example 10.3. Consider the Bernoulli population

$$X = \begin{cases} 1 & p \\ 0 & 1-p, \end{cases}$$

where $p \in [0, 1]$ is an unknown parameter. We observe a random sample $X_1, \ldots, X_n$ with k one's

$$L(p|\mathcal{X}_n) = \prod_{i=1}^{n} p^{X_i}(1-p)^{1-X_i} = \binom{n}{k} p^k(1-p)^{n-k}.$$

Example 10.4. Suppose that X_i are i.i.d. Normal with parameters μ, σ^2

$$L(\mu, \sigma^2|\mathcal{X}^n) = \prod_{i=1}^{n} \frac{1}{\sigma\sqrt{2\pi}} \exp\left(-\frac{1}{2}\left(\frac{X_i - \mu}{\sigma}\right)^2\right).$$

Identification is a key question in frequentist methods.

Definition 10.1. Two parameter points θ and θ' in a parameter set Θ are said to be observationally equivalent if for all $\mathcal{X}^n$

$$L(\theta|\mathcal{X}^n) = L(\theta'|\mathcal{X}^n). \tag{10.2}$$

Definition 10.2. A parameter point θ in Θ is said to be identifiable if there is no other $\theta' \in \Theta$ that is observationally equivalent to it. If there does not exist a single $\mathcal{X}^n$ for which the above holds for some $\theta' \neq \theta$, then the parameter is unidentified.

Example 10.5. Suppose that X_i are i.i.d. Normal with mean $\mu_1 + \mu_2$, where μ_1 and μ_2 are unknown, and variance one. Then for any μ'_1, μ'_2 with $\mu'_1 + \mu'_2 =$

$$\mu_1 + \mu_2$$

$$\ell(\mu_1, \mu_2 | \mathcal{X}^n) = -\frac{n}{2} \log 2\pi - \frac{1}{2} \sum_{i=1}^{n} (X_i - \mu_1 - \mu_2)^2 = \ell(\mu_1', \mu_2' | \mathcal{X}^n)$$

One might conclude that the model is badly specified, or that there are too many unknown parameters. In the next example, identification also fails even though there is only one unknown quantity.

Example 10.6. Suppose that X_i are i.i.d. Normal with mean $\sin(\theta)$, and variance one. Then for any θ' with $\theta' = \theta + 2\pi$

$$\ell(\theta | \mathcal{X}^n) = -\frac{n}{2} \log 2\pi - \frac{1}{2} \sum_{i=1}^{n} (X_i - \sin(\theta))^2 = \ell(\theta' | \mathcal{X}^n).$$

Although identification fails in both the previous examples, in the second case the failure is less problematic because observationally equivalent points are separated by a distance 2π. This is called a failure of **global identification** but not **local identification**. It can be resolved by defining a parameter space that is of width less than 2π, whereas no such fix is available in the former example.

In the **nonparametric** approach, **P** is an even larger family of probability measures. For example, **P** could consist of all twice differentiable density functions. In this case, the objective is to estimate the true density $f \in \mathbf{P}$ based on the data. The likelihood function is less central in this approach. Questions we will address later:

- How to compute the maximum likelihood estimator $\widehat{\theta}_{MLE}$?
- What are the properties of $\widehat{\theta}_{MLE}$?
- Is $\widehat{\theta}_{MLE}$ the best estimator of θ?
- How to test hypotheses about and construct confidence intervals for θ?

10.3.1   Some Important Concepts

10.3.1.1   Sufficiency

Let T(data) be some statistic computed from the data. If the conditional distribution of the sample given the value of T(data) does not depend on θ, then we say that T is a sufficient statistic for θ. That is, given T, there is nothing left in the data. The **sufficiency principle** is that any inference about θ should only depend on T not on the sample space $\mathcal{S}$ as well. Obviously, the data itself has this property so we are looking for a reduction of this to a small number of statistics.

Theorem 10.3. *(Factorization) T is a sufficient statistic for θ, i.e., $f(\mathcal{X}^n|T)$ does not depend on θ, if and only if*

$$\frac{f(\mathcal{X}^n|\theta)}{f(T|\theta)}$$

does not depend on θ. Here, f is generic notation for density function.

The proof of this theorem involves the change of variables arguments that we learned already.

Example 10.7. Suppose that $X_1, \ldots, X_n \sim N(\mu, 1)$. Then

$$f(\mathcal{X}^n|\mu) = \prod_{i=1}^{n} \frac{1}{(2\pi)^{n/2}} \exp\left(-\frac{1}{2}(X_i - \mu)^2\right)$$

$$= \frac{1}{(2\pi)^{n/2}} \exp\left(-\frac{1}{2}\sum_{i=1}^{n}(X_i - \mu)^2\right)$$

$$= \frac{1}{(2\pi)^{n/2}} \exp\left(-\frac{1}{2}[\sum_{i=1}^{n}(X_i - \bar{X})^2 + n(\bar{X} - \mu)^2]\right).$$

Note that $\bar{X} \sim N\left(\mu, \frac{1}{n}\right)$ has density

$$f(\overline{X}|\mu) = \sqrt{\frac{n}{2\pi}} \exp\left(-\frac{n}{2}(\bar{X} - \mu)^2\right).$$

Therefore

$$\frac{f(\mathcal{X}^n|\mu)}{f(\overline{X}|\mu)} = \frac{1}{(2\pi)^{(n-1)/2}} \exp\left(-\frac{1}{2}\sum_{i=1}^{n}(X_i - \bar{X})^2\right),$$

which does not depend on θ.

More generally if (X, Y) are bivariate normal, the **minimal sufficient statistics** are: $\bar{X}$, $\bar{Y}$, s_X^2, s_Y^2, s_{XY}. This means that regarding bivariate normal data, we may just confine our attention to functions of these five sample quantities without any loss of generality.

10.3.1.2 Ancillarity

You have two imperfect, e.g., time *measuring devices*, one based in New York and one in LA. The one in LA is much more accurate. However, for political reasons, which one is used is determined by the flip of a coin. The process is illustrated below

$$LA \quad N(\mu, 0.01)$$

$$
\begin{array}{c}
.5H \nearrow \\
\bullet \\
.5T \searrow
\end{array}
\qquad\qquad
\begin{array}{c}
\searrow \\
X \\
\nearrow
\end{array}
$$

$$NY \quad N(\mu, 0.1)$$

The coin is flipped with outcome the random variable Z. It turns out that it comes out heads and LA does its thing, call it X. The question is: how do we evaluate the uncertainty about X? A blind approach would be to say that

$$\mathrm{var}(X) = 0.5 \times 0.01 + 0.5 \times 0.1 = 0.055$$

But surely, we would agree that we should use $\mathrm{var}(X|Z = LA) = 0.01$. Furthermore, if we are interested in learning about μ, we might as well work with the conditional distribution of $X|Z$ rather than the joint distribution of X, Z.[1] This is an example of conditioning on an ancillary statistic — the coin tossing contains no information about μ. A more substantive example is provided by regression: suppose that (y_i, x_i) are i.i.d. with $E(y_i|x_i) = \beta x_i$. If the marginal distribution of x_i does not depend on β, then we can say that $x_1, \ldots, x_n$ are ancillary and that any inference statement in this case should be made in the conditional distribution $f(\cdot|x_1, \ldots, x_n)$, i.e., we should really think of the covariates as being fixed in repeated samples. This concept has been considerably elaborated in time series, where it goes under the name of exogeneity. See Engle et al. (1983) for ideology on this.

10.3.2 Bayesian Methods

Bayesians have a comprehensive approach to inference that is different from the Frequentist approach that I am more comfortable with. In the Bayesian approach, parameters are also random variables. There is a prior density function, denoted by $\pi(\theta)$, which reflects our knowledge about θ before seeing the sample. The objective is to update the prior using the sample data as represented by the likelihood and obtain the posterior by Bayes' Theorem. We use the notation $\pi(\theta|\mathcal{X}^n)$ to denote the posterior density of the parameter given the data. This is obtained by the formula

$$\underbrace{\pi(\theta|\mathcal{X}^n)}_{\text{posterior}} \propto \underbrace{L(\theta|\mathcal{X}^n)}_{\text{likelihood}} \times \underbrace{\pi(\theta)}_{\text{prior}} = f(\mathcal{X}^n|\theta) \times \pi(\theta), \qquad (10.3)$$

---

1. An example where this is not true. Suppose that the probability of heads is p and that the two conditional distributions are $N(\mu(p), 0.01)$ and $N(\mu(p), 0.1)$. In this case, if we want to learn about p, the outcome of Z is valuable information and we should not just consider the distribution of $X|Z$.

where we are using both the notation we used in the frequentist session for the likelihood $L(\theta|\mathcal{X}^n)$ and to make it clearer how this is just a rewrite of Bayes theorem we also use $f(\mathcal{X}^n|\theta)$ for the conditional density of the data given θ, so that $f(\mathcal{X}^n|\theta) = L(\theta|\mathcal{X}^n)$. Here, the proportional sign means that the right hand side does not necessarily integrate to one and one should normalize the prior so obtained to satisfy this requirement, that is, divide by the marginal density, which we may denote by $f(\mathcal{X}^n) = \int f(\mathcal{X}^n|\theta)\pi(\theta)d\theta$. To summarize, what you know about θ after the data arrive is what you knew before (the prior) and what the data told you (likelihood). Once one has the posterior density the plan is to report various features of it like its mean, its median or its mode as 'the estimator of θ.' The mode of the posterior is the natural analogue of the MLE since it maximizes the posterior.

Example 10.8. Suppose that X is the outcome of a coin toss, whose bias is unknown, i.e., $X = 1$ with probability $p \in (0, 1)$ and $X = 0$ with probability $1 - p$. Suppose that one tosses the coin n times and find k heads and $n - k$ tails. The likelihood of the sample (distribution of the data) is

$$f(\mathcal{X}^n|p) = \binom{n}{k} p^k (1 - p)^{n-k}.$$

Suppose that the prior distribution on p, $\pi(p)$, is uniform over $[0, 1]$, that is, it places equal probability on different values of p within this interval. In this case, the posterior density of p is

$$\pi(p|\mathcal{X}^n) = \frac{f(\mathcal{X}^n|p)\pi(p)}{\int f(\mathcal{X}^n|p)\pi(p)dp} = \frac{p^k(1-p)^{n-k}}{\int_0^1 p^k(1-p)^{n-k}dp}$$
$$= \frac{(n+1)!}{k!(n-k)!} p^k(1-p)^{n-k}.$$

In fact, this is the distribution of a $Beta(k + 1, n - k + 1)$ random variable. The posterior mean is $(k + 1)/(n + 2)$.

Example 10.9. Suppose that we observe a single data point $X \sim N(\mu_x, \sigma_x^2)$, where σ_x^2 is assumed to be known and not of interest. The prior for the parameter μ_x is the density of $\mu_x \sim N(\mu, \sigma^2)$, where μ and σ^2 are known and fixed. Then the posterior density of μ_x is given by (see Theorem 7.16)

$$\mu_x|X \sim N(m, v)$$

$$\overbrace{\phantom{\frac{\sigma_x^2}{\sigma^2+\sigma_x^2}\mu}}^{\text{contribution of prior}} \quad \overbrace{\phantom{\frac{\sigma^2}{\sigma^2+\sigma_x^2}X}}^{\text{contribution of data}}$$
$$m = \frac{\sigma_x^2}{\sigma^2 + \sigma_x^2}\mu + \frac{\sigma^2}{\sigma^2 + \sigma_x^2}X$$

$$v = \frac{\sigma_x^2 \sigma^2}{\sigma^2 + \sigma_x^2} = \left(\frac{1}{\sigma^2} + \frac{1}{\sigma_x^2} \right)^{-1}.$$

The posterior mean is a weighted average of the prior mean and the data mean, while the posterior variance is the harmonic average of the variance of the prior and the data.

Example 10.10. Suppose now we observe n observations $\mathcal{X}^n$. In this case we have $\overline{X} \sim N(\mu_x, \sigma_x^2/n)$. We can show that the posterior density becomes

$$\mu_x | \mathcal{X}^n \sim N(m_n, v_n)$$

with m_n, v_n as defined above except that $\sigma_x^2 \mapsto \sigma_x^2/n$. That is, the posterior mean is

$$m_n = \frac{\sigma_x^2/n}{\sigma^2 + \sigma_x^2/n} \mu + \frac{\sigma^2}{\sigma^2 + \sigma_x^2/n} \overline{X}$$

$$v_n = \left(\frac{1}{\sigma^2} + \frac{n}{\sigma_x^2} \right)^{-1}$$

When $n \to \infty$, $m_n \overset{P}{\longrightarrow} \mu_x$. Bayesians also have a **law of small numbers**, that is, when $n \to 0$, we have $m_n \overset{P}{\longrightarrow} \mu$.

In this case, it is as if we had two independent measurements of μ_x, one from the distribution $N(\mu_x, \sigma_x^2/n)$ and the other from the distribution $N(\mu, \sigma^2)$ and we combined the two measurements in an equal fashion.

The prior in the above example is **informative**, and it puts most weight close to the point μ, with a degree of certainty expressed by σ^2. When σ^2 is very small, the prior information is very precise. An alternative class of prior distributions are called **ignorance priors**, in which effectively $\sigma^2 \to \infty$. Formally, we take the prior measure (not probability measure) to be Lebesgue measure on $\mathbb{R}$, that is μ is essentially equally likely to be in any interval of the real line. This is called an **improper prior**, because it is not a probability measure. Nevertheless, Bayes theorem works in this case, since the normalization enforces that the posterior is a proper density (integrates to one). In that case, the posterior density of $\mu_x | X$ is $N(X, \sigma_x^2)$ consistent with the above arguments, and the posterior density of $\mu_x | \mathcal{X}^n$ is $N(\overline{X}, \sigma_x^2/n)$. Do we need a prior for the prior? In the above example how come μ and σ^2 are known?

In general, calculating posterior densities analytically can be too difficult. However, it is easy to do it by simulation methods such as **Markov Chain Monte Carlo** (MCMC). We shall not have anything explicit to say about these methods.

Some Bayesians talk a lot about coherence and rationality. Others talk about flexibility and applicability. They often say words to the effect that: "Let me through, I am a Bayesian, I have the solution to the problem that you Frequentists have messed up". Efron (1986) and Cox (2005) compare the Frequentist and Bayesian approaches. The Bayesian approach generically imposes much more structure, such as the prior distribution, which may not be warranted. However, it can deliver reasonable answers in some complex cases where the frequentist approach fails. Both approaches have merit and ultimately it may be a matter of taste, as to which approach you prefer. There is even a term that signifies possession of both tastes simultaneously, **Empirical Bayes**, where the prior is replaced by preexisting estimated distributions.

Chapter 11

Estimation Theory

11.1 ESTIMATION METHODS

Estimation is a formal process of using sample information to calculate population quantities, parameters. We discuss two general strategies for obtaining estimators of population parameters of interest from samples of data:

1. The Analogy principle or Method of Moments
2. Maximum Likelihood

There are other ways of organizing the material, but this approach gets to the main issues.

11.1.1 The Original Method of Moments or Analogy Principle

In many cases, parameters of interest can be expressed as functionals of the probability distribution or c.d.f., that is, we can write $\theta(F_X)$, formally a mapping from the set of c.d.f.s to the real line. For example: moments, quantiles, density functions can be expressed in this way:

$$\mu = E(X) = \int x \, dF_X \quad ; \quad \sigma^2 = \mathrm{var}(X) = E(X^2) - E^2(X)$$

$$\kappa_3 = \frac{E\left[(X - E(X))^3\right]}{\mathrm{var}(X)^{3/2}},$$

where F_X is the c.d.f. of X. Suppose that we have a sample $X_1, \ldots, X_n$ from the population. Why not just substitute population moments by sample moments, e.g. $E(X)$ by $\overline{X}$, and $\mathrm{var}(X)$ by s^2, and κ_3 by

$$\widehat{\kappa}_3 = \frac{\frac{1}{n}\sum_{i=1}^{n}(X_i - \overline{X})^3}{\left[\frac{1}{n}\sum_{i=1}^{n}(X_i - \overline{X})^2\right]^{3/2}} = g\left(\frac{1}{n}\sum_{i=1}^{n}X_i, \frac{1}{n}\sum_{i=1}^{n}X_i^2, \frac{1}{n}\sum_{i=1}^{n}X_i^3\right).$$

This function g is quite complicated but it is continuous and differentiable in its three arguments (at almost all points of $\mathbb{R}^3$). The analogy principle can be made explicit by noting that we may for example write $\overline{X} = \int x \, dF_n$, where F_n is the empirical distribution, which is the natural analogue of the population distribution function. Likewise for any other moment or cumulant. But what

Probability, Statistics and Econometrics. http://dx.doi.org/10.1016/B978-0-12-810495-8.00013-0

151

about sample quantiles? In the population we have defined the median M as the middle of the population distribution. We could estimate M by the middle of the empirical distribution. The idea is to order the sample information and take the middle value. Define the **order statistics**

$$X_{(1)} \leq \ldots \leq X_{(n)}$$

and then define the sample median as $\widehat{M} = X_{[n/2]}$, where $[n/2]$ denotes the largest integer less than or equal to $n/2$. An alternative way of looking at this is to recall that the population median is the unique value that solves the equation $F_X(M) = 0.5$ when F_X is continuous and strictly increasing. Therefore, look for the value $\widehat{M}$ that solves the equation

$$F_n(\widehat{M}) = \frac{1}{2}.$$

However, the empirical distribution function is not strictly increasing everywhere, and so it may not be possible to uniquely define the median from this equation. Therefore, we have to use the generalized inverse. That is, we define the α sample quantile

$$\widehat{Q}_X(\alpha) = \inf\{x : F_n(x) \geq \alpha\}, \tag{11.1}$$

with the sample median being the case with $\alpha = 1/2$. This is an implicit equation for the sample quantile.

We may generalize the analogue notion further. Another population relation we may make use of is the argument that $E(X)$ is the unique minimizer of $E((X - \theta)^2) = \int (x - \theta)^2 dF_X$ with respect to θ. Therefore, we can define an estimator of $E(X)$ as the minimizer of the sample objective function

$$\int (x - \theta)^2 dF_n = \frac{1}{n} \sum_{i=1}^{n} (X_i - \theta)^2.$$

It is easy to see that $\overline{X}$ is the unique minimizer of this objective function. This principle also carries over to the median case. Recall that M is the unique minimizer of $E(|X - \theta|) = \int |x - \theta| dF_X$ with respect to θ. The analogy principle suggests that we find $\widehat{M}$ as the minimizer of

$$\int |x - \theta| dF_n = \frac{1}{n} \sum_{i=1}^{n} |X_i - \theta|. \tag{11.2}$$

This objective function will not generally have a unique minimizer, and we should choose one of the minimizers. However, the solution is essentially the sample median, modulo the way we impose uniqueness. Finally, we may recall that the population median M satisfies $E(\text{sign}(X - M)) = 0$, and define $\widehat{M}$ as the solution to the sample equation

$$\int \text{sign}(x - \theta)dF_n = \frac{1}{n}\sum_{i=1}^{n}\text{sign}(X_i - \theta) = 0. \tag{11.3}$$

In this approach the empirical distribution function is of central importance; knowing its behaviour allows one to derive the behaviour of the analogue defined estimators.

The special case of the analogue principle that is to do with moments is called the Method of Moments (MoM), and goes back to the early 20th century. In this case, we use the moments to define estimators of parameters in a parametric model $\{P_\theta, \theta \in \Theta\}$.

Example 11.1. The standard t-distribution $f(x|v) \propto (1 + x^2/v)^{-(v+1)/2}$, where v is the degrees of freedom. In this case, we have

$$\text{var}(X) = \frac{v}{v - 2} \implies v = \frac{2\text{var}(X)}{\text{var}(X) - 1}$$

whenever $v > 2$. We can thus estimate the parameter v by

$$\widehat{v} = \frac{2s^2}{s^2 - 1}.$$

This is a very simple to compute estimator, whereas, the Maximum Likelihood estimator below is more complicated (although it also works for $v \leq 2$).

Example 11.2. The unit Pareto distribution $f(x|\theta) = \theta x^{-(\theta+1)}$, $x \geq 1$. We have, provided $\theta > 1$,

$$E(X) = \frac{\theta}{\theta - 1}$$

and so

$$\theta = \frac{E(X)}{E(X) - 1}.$$

Therefore, we may let

$$\widehat{\theta} = \frac{\overline{X}}{\overline{X} - 1}.$$

Alternatively, we have

$$Q_X(\alpha|\theta) = \left(\frac{1}{1 - \alpha}\right)^{1/\theta}.$$

Therefore, we may write

$$\tilde{\alpha} = \frac{\log(2)}{\log(M)},$$

where M is the sample median. This estimator is defined for all $\theta > 0$.

We can define this principle more generally, i.e., where there are multiple unknown parameters of interest. Suppose that $\theta_1, \ldots, \theta_k$ are the parameters of interest, and suppose that

$$\mu_1 = g_1(\theta_1, \ldots, \theta_k), \ldots, \mu_k = g_k(\theta_1, \ldots, \theta_k), \tag{11.4}$$

for some functions $g_1, \ldots, g_k$, where μ_j are some population quantities, for example $\mu_j = E(X^j)$, $j = 1, \ldots, k$. Now suppose that we can solve the system of equations (11.4) to write

$$\theta_1 = f_1(\mu_1, \ldots, \mu_k), \ldots, \theta_k = f_k(\mu_1, \ldots, \mu_k)$$

for some functions $f_1, \ldots, f_k$. This may not be explicit, i.e., we may be able to prove the existence of unique functions f_j but may not be able to write them down. We will deal with this issue more concretely in a later chapter. Then we estimate θ_j by

$$\hat{\theta}_j = f_j(\widehat{m}_1, \ldots, \widehat{m}_k),$$

where $\widehat{m}_j$ are sample analogues or estimators of μ_j.

Example 11.3. The Gamma(α, β) distribution $f(x|\alpha, \beta) \propto x^{\alpha-1} \exp(-x/\beta)$. In this case, we have

$$E(X) = \alpha\beta, \ \operatorname{var}(X) = \alpha\beta^2,$$

which leads to the exact solution:

$$\frac{E^2(X)}{\operatorname{var}(X)} \doteq \alpha \quad ; \quad \frac{E(X)}{\alpha} = \beta.$$

Therefore, let $\widehat{\alpha} = \overline{X}^2/s^2$ and $\widehat{\beta} = \overline{X}/\widehat{\alpha}$.

Example 11.4. The Beta(α, β) distribution $f(x|\alpha, \beta) \propto x^{\alpha-1}(1-x)^{\beta-1}$. In this case, we have

$$EX = \frac{\alpha}{\alpha + \beta}, \ \operatorname{var}(X) = \frac{\alpha\beta}{(\alpha + \beta)^2(\alpha + \beta + 1)}$$

In this case there are no explicit solutions. Then, define $\hat{\alpha}$, $\hat{\beta}$ to solve the equations

$$\bar{X} = \frac{\hat{\alpha}}{\hat{\alpha} + \hat{\beta}}, \quad s^2 = \frac{\hat{\alpha}\hat{\beta}}{(\hat{\alpha} + \hat{\beta})^2(\hat{\alpha} + \hat{\beta} + 1)}.$$

Example 11.5. Suppose that you want to measure the sides of a table, i.e., length (L) and width (W). However, your research assistant reports to you only the area (A). Luckily, she was trained at Oxford and so makes an error in each measurement. Specifically,

$$L_i = L + \varepsilon_i \quad ; \quad W_i = W + \eta_i,$$

where ε_i, η_i are mutually independent standard normal random variables. The RA reports $\{A_i\}_{i=1}^n$, where $A_i = L_i W_i$. In this case

$$E A_i = L \times W$$
$$E(A_i^2) = L^2 W^2 + L^2 + W^2 + 1.$$

These two equations can be solved explicitly for the unknown quantities L, W in terms of $E(A_i)$ and $E(A_i^2)$.

11.1.2 Maximum Likelihood

The method of maximum likelihood was apparently invented by R.A. Fisher in 1912 when he was 22 years old and an undergraduate at Cambridge, Aldrich (1997). It is widely used in many fields of science. For fully specified parametric models with a finite number of parameters and certain other regularity conditions, it is the best procedure according to the widely accepted criterion of asymptotic variance. There is a school of thought that argues that in any problem all one has to do is to specify a parametric model, derive the likelihood, and compute the Maximum Likelihood Estimator (MLE) and other related quantities. The context is a **parametric model** $\{P_\theta, \theta \in \Theta\}$, where Θ contains all the possible values of θ.

As we have seen, the likelihood function for an i.i.d. sample $\mathcal{X}^n = \{X_1, \dots, X_n\}$ is

$$L(\theta | \mathcal{X}^n) = \prod_{i=1}^n f(X_i | \theta).$$

The MLE $\hat{\theta} = \hat{\theta}(\mathcal{X}^n)$ maximizes $L(\theta | \mathcal{X}^n)$, or equivalently $\ell(\theta | \mathcal{X}^n) = \log L(\theta | \mathcal{X}^n)$, with respect to $\theta \in \Theta \subset \mathbb{R}^k$. There are two issues.

Existence: Does there exist a maximum? If $\theta \mapsto \ell(\theta|\mathcal{X}^n)$ is *continuous* and the parameter set Θ is a *compact*, i.e., a closed and bounded, subset of $\mathbb{R}^k$, then there exists such a maximum. More generally, if $\hat{\theta}$ comes 'close' [this can happen in certain microeconometric models that have discontinuities in θ] to maximizing ℓ over Θ, then this is usually close enough for theoretical and practical purposes. There are some cases where the maximum does not exist because the likelihood function is unbounded in θ, such as mixture models.

Uniqueness: Is the set of maximizing values: a singleton, a finite set, or an uncountable set, e.g., an interval? If $\ell(\theta|\mathcal{X}^n)$ is **globally concave**, then $\hat{\theta}$ is unique. Otherwise, we can select some element of the set of maximizers so this is usually no problem. However, it may point to a more fundamental problem, which is whether the model is identified. Let us consider the concept of in sample identification.

Definition 11.1. A parameter point θ in Θ is said to be not uniquely identified in sample if for the sample $\mathcal{X}^n$, there exists $\theta' \in \Theta$ such that

$$L(\theta|\mathcal{X}^n) = L(\theta'|\mathcal{X}^n).$$

According to this we are unable to distinguish between θ and θ' given the data available to us.

Example 11.6. Suppose that X_i are i.i.d. with Laplace density $\exp(-|x - \theta|)$. Then

$$\ell(\theta|\mathcal{X}^n) = -\sum_{i=1}^{n} |X_i - \theta|.$$

We show in Fig. 11.1 a case (from some particular $\mathcal{X}^n$) where $n = 2, 4, 6, 8, 10$, and 100 with θ varying over $[0, 1]$.

Note that if a maximum exists it could be on the boundary of the parameter space or it could be in the interior. If the maximum is in the interior of the parameter space, then we can usually find it by calculus. Provided the log likelihood is twice differentiable at θ we can define the **score function** and **Hessian**:

$$s(\theta|\mathcal{X}^n) = \frac{\partial \ell}{\partial \theta}(\theta|\mathcal{X}^n) \tag{11.5}$$

$$h(\theta|\mathcal{X}^n) = \frac{\partial^2 \ell}{\partial \theta^2}(\theta|\mathcal{X}^n). \tag{11.6}$$

It then follows that the maximizing value $\widehat{\theta}$ should satisfy

$$s(\widehat{\theta}|\mathcal{X}^n) = 0. \tag{11.7}$$

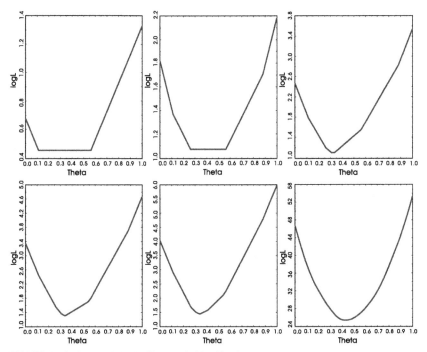

FIGURE 11.1 Shows the lack of in sample identification

In the multivariate case this is a vector of k (possibly nonlinear) equations in k unknowns. This is a necessary condition for an interior maximum of the likelihood function being reached. A sufficient condition in the scalar case for an *interior local maximum* is that the second derivative at $\widehat{\theta}$ is negative, i.e.,

$$h(\widehat{\theta}|\mathcal{X}^n) < 0.$$

For a global maximum it suffices to have the second derivative be negative for all θ. In the multivariate case, this condition has a natural extension using the language of matrices.

Example 11.7. The Binomial case where $X_i = 1$ with probability p and $X_i = 0$ with probability $1 - p$. In this case the natural parameter set is $\Theta = [0, 1]$ and the likelihood, score, and Hessian are:

$$\ell(p|\mathcal{X}^n) = \sum_{i=1}^n X_i \log p + (1 - X_i) \log(1 - p)$$

$$s(p|\mathcal{X}^n) = \sum_{i=1}^n \left(\frac{X_i}{p} - \frac{1 - X_i}{1 - p} \right) = \sum_{i=1}^n \frac{X_i - p}{p(1 - p)}$$

$$h(p|\mathcal{X}^n) = \sum_{i=1}^{n}\left(-\frac{X_i}{p^2} + \frac{1-X_i}{(1-p)^2}\right) = -\sum_{i=1}^{n}\frac{(X_i-p)^2}{p^2(1-p)^2} + \sum_{i=1}^{n}\frac{(X_i-p)}{p(1-p)}.$$

From this we see that

$$\widehat{p}_{MLE} = \frac{1}{n}\sum_{i=1}^{n}X_i = \frac{k}{n},$$

where k is the number of ones in the sample. Then

$$h(\widehat{p}_{MLE}|\mathcal{X}^n) = -\sum_{i=1}^{n}\frac{(X_i - \widehat{p}_{MLE})^2}{\widehat{p}_{MLE}^2(1 - \widehat{p}_{MLE})^2} < 0$$

as required. If $X_i = 1$ for all i, then $\ell(p|\mathcal{X}^n) = n\log p$ so that $\widehat{p}_{MLE} = 1$. In this case, the first order condition method is not useful since the likelihood is not differentiable at the boundary (not defined for $p > 1$ or $p < 0$).

Example 11.8. The Poisson case with unknown parameter λ has natural parameter space $\Theta = \mathbb{R}_+$ and the likelihood, score, and Hessian are:

$$\ell(\lambda|\mathcal{X}^n) = \sum_{i=1}^{n}X_i\log\lambda - n\lambda - \sum_{i=1}^{n}\log X_i$$

$$s(\lambda|\mathcal{X}^n) = \sum_{i=1}^{n}\frac{X_i}{\lambda} - n \quad ; \quad h(\lambda|\mathcal{X}^n) = -\sum_{i=1}^{n}\frac{X_i}{\lambda^2}.$$

Therefore,

$$\widehat{\lambda}_{MLE} = \frac{1}{n}\sum_{i=1}^{n}X_i.$$

Example 11.9. The Uniform distribution $U(0,\theta)$ has likelihood

$$L(\theta|\mathcal{X}^n) = \prod_{i=1}^{n}\frac{1}{\theta}1(0 \le X_i \le \theta) = \begin{cases} \frac{1}{\theta^n} & \text{if } \max X_i \le \theta \\ 0 & \text{otherwise.} \end{cases}$$

The natural parameter space here is $\Theta = \mathbb{R}_+$. In this case, L is differentiable with respect to θ for all $\theta \ge \max X_i$ but discontinuous at exactly this point. The maximum of L is at $\hat{\theta} = \max X_i$, and so does not satisfy a first order condition.

Fig. 11.2 shows the likelihood function for a sample of uniform data with true parameter $\theta = 1$ and sample size $n = 1000$.

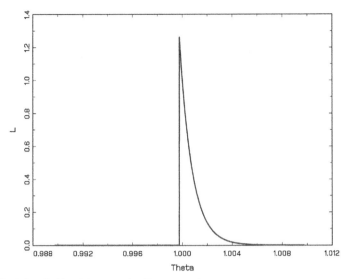

FIGURE 11.2 Likelihood function of uniform example

Example 11.10. The normal distribution $X \sim N(\mu, \sigma^2)$. Here, there are two parameters $\theta = (\mu, \sigma^2)$ with natural parameter set $\Theta = \mathbb{R} \times \mathbb{R}_+$. We have

$$L(\theta | \mathcal{X}^n) = \prod_{i=1}^{n} \frac{1}{\sigma (2\pi)^{1/2}} \exp\left(-\frac{1}{2} \left(\frac{X_i - \mu}{\sigma} \right)^2 \right)$$

$$\ell(\theta | \mathcal{X}^n) = -\frac{n}{2} \log 2\pi - \frac{n}{2} \log \sigma^2 - \frac{1}{2\sigma^2} \sum_{i=1}^{n} (X_i - \mu)^2.$$

The first order conditions are:

$$s_\mu(\theta | \mathcal{X}^n) = \frac{\partial \ell}{\partial \mu}(\theta | \mathcal{X}^n) = +\frac{1}{\sigma^2} \sum_{i=1}^{n} (X_i - \mu)$$

$$s_{\sigma^2}(\theta | \mathcal{X}^n) = \frac{\partial \ell}{\partial \sigma^2}(\theta | \mathcal{X}^n) = -\frac{n}{2\sigma^2} + \frac{1}{2\sigma^4} \sum_{i=1}^{n} (X_i - \mu)^2.$$

Setting these equations to zero we have two equations in two unknowns. In fact the first equation can be solved directly by itself

$$\sum_{i=1}^{n} (X_i - \hat{\mu}_{MLE}) = 0 \Leftrightarrow \hat{\mu}_{MLE} = \frac{1}{n} \sum_{i=1}^{n} X_i.$$

The second equation can be solved exactly conditional on $\hat{\mu}_{MLE}$ to give

$$\hat{\sigma}^2_{MLE} = \frac{1}{n} \sum_{i=1}^{n} (X_i - \hat{\mu}_{MLE})^2.$$

To check the second order conditions here we need to derive the second derivatives.

These are all examples where the solutions are in closed form, i.e., one can explicitly write

$$\hat{\theta}_{MLE} = g(\mathcal{X}^n)$$

for some known function g. More generally, the MLE is not explicitly defined. For example, consider the Cauchy distribution:

$$f(x|\theta) = \frac{1}{\pi} \frac{1}{1 + (x - \theta)^2},$$

for which the log likelihood function and its score function are:

$$\ell(\theta|\mathcal{X}^n) = -\log n\pi - \sum_{i=1}^{n} \log[1 + (X_i - \theta)^2]$$

$$s(\theta|\mathcal{X}^n) = 2 \sum_{i=1}^{n} \frac{(X_i - \theta)}{1 + (X_i - \theta)^2}.$$

This gives a nonlinear equation in θ

$$g(\hat{\theta}, \mathcal{X}^n) = 0.$$

How do we solve this? By numerical methods.

Example 11.11. Cauchy data with $\theta = 0$ and sample size $n = 1000$. See Fig. 11.3.

11.1.3 Computation

Many software languages such as MATLAB and R have modules that will maximize any given function in a number of different ways, all you need to do is to program in the criterion function and deal with input and output. Many programs will compute MLE's for standard models such as probit, logit, censored regression, for example STATA, SAS, BMDP, and SPSS.

Methods can be divided according to whether they use derivatives (and then whether first or second) or not. Grid search (works well for scalar parameters),

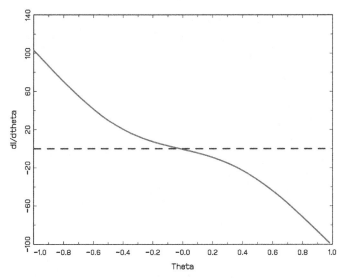

FIGURE 11.3   Score function of the Cauchy MLE

this just involves computing $\ell(\theta|\mathcal{X}^n)$ at a fine grid of points and then choosing the best value in terms of the height of the likelihood. In multiparameter problems, this can perform poorly because a very large grid is required to achieve good accuracy. In this case, derivative based methods are widely applied. These are typically variants of the classical Newton Raphson method for finding the zero of a function that you learnt in high school. Perhaps the variable step algorithm is the most commonly used derivative method. Given starting values θ_1 one iteratively computes ($r = 2, 3, \ldots$)

$$\theta_{r+1} = \theta_r + \lambda_{opt} H_r^{-1} s_r \tag{11.8}$$

where $s_r = \sum_{i=1}^n \frac{\partial \ell_i}{\partial \theta}(\theta_r|X_i)$, and ℓ_i is the contribution of the i'th observation to the log-likelihood, while $H_r = \sum_{i=1}^n \left(\frac{\partial \ell_i}{\partial \theta}(\theta_r|X_i) \right)^2$ or $H_r = -\partial^2 \ell(\theta_r|\mathcal{X}^n)/\partial \theta^2$. The step length λ_{opt} is chosen to maximize the criterion $\ell(\theta_{r+1}(\lambda)|\mathcal{X}^n)$ at each iteration. This can be done by a simple grid search since λ is a scalar (this method is usually applied in the context where θ is multivariate, but we have written this down just in the univariate case). The iterations are terminated when the outcome doesn't change much as measured by either $|\theta_{r+1} - \theta_r|$ or $|\ell(\theta_{r+1}|\mathcal{X}^n) - \ell(\theta_r|\mathcal{X}^n)|$. In some cases, computation of derivatives is very difficult and one may substitute analytic derivatives by **numerical derivatives**, which for example replace the functions $f'(x)$ and $f''(x)$ by respectively

$$f'_\epsilon(x) = \frac{f(x+\epsilon) - f(x-\epsilon)}{2\epsilon} \quad ; \quad f''_\epsilon(x) = \frac{f(x+\epsilon) - 2f(x) + f(x-\epsilon)}{\epsilon^2},$$
(11.9)

where ϵ is a small number, say $\epsilon = 10^{-8}$. This only requires the evaluation of the function f and the choice of ϵ.

In some problems, one can divide the parameters into groups that can be treated differently. For example, there may be a simple way of obtaining good estimators for a subset of the parameters. **Two-step Estimator.** Suppose that $\theta = (\theta_1, \theta_2)$ and that $\tilde{\theta}_2$ is a preliminary estimate. Let

$$\widehat{\theta}_1 = \arg \max_{\theta_1 \in \Theta_1} \ell(\theta_1, \tilde{\theta}_2 | \mathcal{X}^n).$$

A leading example here is Heckman's two-step estimator in **sample selection** models, and more generally the generated regressor problem. An important question here is whether the two-step estimator is fully efficient; this will depend on the quality of the preliminary estimate and the structure of the likelihood. A second approach is called **Concentrated/Profiled Likelihood.** Suppose that $\widehat{\theta}_1(\theta_2)$ is the MLE of θ_1 when θ_2 is fixed. Then define the profile or concentrated likelihood

$$\ell^p(\theta_2 | \mathcal{X}^n) = \ell\left(\widehat{\theta}_1(\theta_2), \theta_2 | \mathcal{X}^n\right),$$

which is a function of θ_2 only. In many respects one can treat $\ell^p(\theta_2 | \mathcal{X}^n)$ as a proper likelihood. Maximizing $\ell^p(\theta_2 | \mathcal{X}^n)$ with respect to θ_2 to obtain $\widehat{\theta}_2$ and $\widehat{\theta}_1(\widehat{\theta}_2)$ gives the same answer as jointly maximizing $\ell(\theta | \mathcal{X}^n)$ with respect to θ. This construction is useful when θ_2 is one-dimensional and $\widehat{\theta}_1(\theta_2)$ is high-dimensional but easy to obtain. For example in the transformation model, if the scalar λ were known, then the MLE of β is obtained from the least squares regression of $\tau(y_i; \lambda)$ on X_i. One can then plot out the profile likelihood to aid in the computation of the more difficult maximization problem. There are many other varieties of likelihood including marginal likelihood, conditional likelihood, partial likelihood, and pseudo likelihood.

Invariance Property of MLE

Consider the function $\tau(\theta): \mathbb{R} \to \mathbb{R}$. What is the maximum likelihood estimator of τ? For example, if $\theta = \sigma^2$ is the variance parameter, we may be interested in the standard deviation $\sigma = \tau_1(\sigma^2) = \sqrt{\sigma^2}$ or the logarithm of σ^2, i.e., $\tau_2(\sigma^2) = \log \sigma^2$, or "the precision" $\tau_3(\sigma^2) = 1/\sigma^2$. Let

$$L^*(\tau | \mathcal{X}^n) = \sup_{\{\theta : \tau(\theta) = \tau\}} L(\theta | \mathcal{X}^n)$$

be the induced likelihood function. When τ is one to one, this is $L^*(\tau | \mathcal{X}^n) = L(\tau^{-1}(\theta)|\mathcal{X}^n)$. We have

$$
\begin{aligned}
L^*(\widehat{\tau}|\mathcal{X}^n) &= \sup_{\{\theta : \tau(\theta) = \widehat{\tau}\}} L(\theta|\mathcal{X}^n) \\
&\leq \sup_{\theta \in \Theta} L(\theta|\mathcal{X}^n) = L(\widehat{\theta}|\mathcal{X}^n) \\
&= \sup_{\{\theta : \tau(\theta) = \tau(\widehat{\theta})\}} L(\theta|\mathcal{X}^n) \\
&= L^*(\tau(\widehat{\theta})|\mathcal{X}^n).
\end{aligned}
$$

Therefore, we can say that $\widehat{\tau}_{mle} = \tau(\widehat{\theta}_{mle})$. We can view this as a reparameterization from $\theta \mapsto \tau$.

Example 11.12. The Pareto distribution $f(x|\alpha) = \alpha x^{-(\alpha+1)}$, $x \geq 1$. We have, provided $\alpha > 1$, that $\alpha = \mu/(1 + \mu)$, where $\mu = E(X)$, and so we can write the log likelihood in terms of μ as

$$
\ell(\mu|\mathcal{X}^n) = n \log \mu - n \log(1 + \mu) - \frac{1 + 2\mu}{1 + \mu} \sum_{i=1}^{n} \log X_i,
$$

from which we can directly compute the MLE for μ.

What if the function τ is not one to one, e.g., $\tau(\theta) = \text{sign}(\theta)$?

11.2 COMPARISON OF ESTIMATORS AND OPTIMALITY

We now discuss the statistical properties of estimators $\hat{\theta}$ of a scalar parameter θ. These can be divided into: finite sample properties and large sample (asymptotic) properties. The estimator $\hat{\theta}$ is a random variable with a distribution, say P_{n,θ_0}, that depends on the true value of θ, sometimes distinguished by the zero subscript, and on the sample size n. It may have a finite mean and variance. Supposing that these quantities exist, we define

$$
E(\hat{\theta}) = \mathcal{E}(\theta) ; \quad \text{var}(\hat{\theta}) = \mathcal{V}(\theta).
$$

Both quantities depend on θ, which we do not know. We say that

$$
b(\theta) = \mathcal{E}(\theta) - \theta
$$

is the bias of $\hat{\theta}$. An ideal estimator would have

$$
b(\theta) = 0 \text{ and } \mathcal{V}(\theta) = 0 \text{ for all } \theta \in \Theta.
$$

Unfortunately, this is impossible unless Θ is trivial. Both bias and variance can be considered to be undesirable properties. A more general notion of estimator performance is the **mean squared error**.

Definition 11.2. Mean squared error (MSE). Suppose that the parameter estimator $\widehat{\theta}$ has finite variance. Then define the MSE

$$MSE(\widehat{\theta}, \theta_0) = E[(\widehat{\theta} - \theta_0)^2],$$

where the expectation is taken using the distribution P_{n,θ_0}. For convenience sometimes we replace θ_0 by θ. Note that $MSE(\widehat{\theta}, \theta_0)$ may depend on other unknown quantities.

This is a widely agreed on criterion for measuring estimator performance. An alternative measure the Mean Absolute Error is defined as $E[|\widehat{\theta} - \theta_0|]$; this is harder to work with analytically and we shall most just work with the MSE. In general the MSE depends on $\widehat{\theta}$, θ_0, and on the sample size n. An ideal estimator would have zero MSE whatever the truth is. Unfortunately, this is impossible unless the problem is trivial. One can always construct an estimator with zero MSE at a single point. For example, consider the estimator $\hat{\theta} = 0$. This estimator has

$$MSE(\widehat{\theta}, \theta) = \theta^2 \geq 0,$$

which is equal to zero if and only if $\theta = 0$.

We want an estimator that does well over a range of θ, since we do not know what the truth is.

Theorem 11.1. *Let $\widehat{\theta}$ be an estimator of a parameter θ whose true value is θ_0. Then we have*

$$MSE(\widehat{\theta}, \theta_0) = \overbrace{E[\{\widehat{\theta} - E(\widehat{\theta})\}^2]}^{variance} + \overbrace{\{E(\widehat{\theta}) - \theta)\}^2}^{bias} = \operatorname{var}(\hat{\theta}) + bias^2(\theta).$$

The mean squared error allows a trade-off between bias and variance. Big bias could be offset by small variance and vice versa.

Example 11.13. Suppose that $X \sim N(\mu, \sigma^2)$, where $\theta = (\mu, \sigma^2)$. Then, $E(\bar{X}) = \mu$ and $\operatorname{var}(\bar{X}) = \sigma^2/n$, so that bias $\equiv 0$, and

$$MSE(\bar{X}, \mu) = \sigma^2/n,$$

for all μ.

Now consider estimators of σ^2 in the same setup

$$s_*^2 = \frac{1}{n-1} \sum_{i=1}^n (X_i - \bar{X})^2 \quad ; \quad s^2 = \frac{1}{n} \sum_{i=1}^n (X_i - \bar{X})^2.$$

Theorem 11.2. *Suppose that $X \sim N(\mu, \sigma^2)$. Then we have:*

$$E(s_*^2) = \sigma^2 \quad ; \quad \text{var}(s_*^2) = \frac{2\sigma^4}{n-1},$$

$$E(s^2) = \frac{n-1}{n}\sigma^2 \quad ; \quad \text{var}(s^2) = \frac{2\sigma^4(n-1)}{n^2}.$$

Therefore,

$$MSE(s^2, \sigma^2) = \frac{\sigma^4}{n^2} + \frac{2\sigma^4(n-1)}{n^2} = \frac{(2n-1)\sigma^4}{n^2} \leq \frac{2\sigma^4}{n-1} = MSE(s_*^2, \sigma^2),$$

$$(11.10)$$

i.e., the maximum likelihood estimator is better according to mean squared error no matter what σ^2 is.

Proof. Write

$$s_*^2 = \frac{1}{n-1} \left\{ \sum_{i=1}^n (X_i - \mu)^2 - n(\bar{X} - \mu)^2 \right\}.$$

Then, by the properties of variance

$$\text{var}\,[(n-1)s_*^2] = \text{var}[\sum_{i=1}^n (X_i - \mu)^2] + n^2 \text{var}[(\bar{X} - \mu)^2]$$

$$- 2n \times \text{cov}[\sum_{i=1}^n (X_i - \mu)^2, (\bar{X} - \mu)^2].$$

We have under the normality assumption

$$\text{var}[\sum_{i=1}^n (X_i - \mu)^2] = n\text{var}[(X_i - \mu)^2] = E[(X_i - \mu)^4] - E^2[(X_i - \mu)^2]$$

$$= 2n\sigma^4$$

$$(\bar{X} - \mu)^2 = \left[\frac{1}{n}\sum_{i=1}^{n}(X_i - \mu)\right]^2$$

$$= \frac{1}{n^2}\sum_{i=1}^{n}(X_i - \mu)^2 + \frac{1}{n^2}\sum_{i=1}^{n}\sum_{\substack{j=1 \\ i \neq j}}^{n}(X_i - \mu)(X_j - \mu)$$

and so it follows that

$$\mathrm{cov}\left(\sum_{i=1}^{n}(X_i - \mu)^2, (\bar{X} - \mu)^2\right) = \sum_{i=1}^{n}\mathrm{cov}\left((X_i - \mu)^2, (\bar{X} - \mu)^2\right) \quad (11.11)$$

$$= \sum_{i=1}^{n}\mathrm{cov}\left((X_i - \mu)^2, \frac{1}{n^2}\sum_{i=1}^{n}(X_i - \mu)^2\right) \quad (11.12)$$

$$= \sum_{i=1}^{n}\mathrm{cov}\left((X_i - \mu)^2, \frac{1}{n^2}(X_i - \mu)^2\right) \quad (11.13)$$

$$= \frac{1}{n^2}\mathrm{var}[\sum_{i=1}^{n}(X_i - \mu)^2]$$

$$= \frac{2\sigma^4}{n}.$$

where in (11.11) and (11.13) we use the fact that $\mathrm{cov}(A + B, C) = \mathrm{cov}(A, C) + \mathrm{cov}(B, C)$ for any random variables A, B, C for which the moments are defined and in (11.12) we use the fact that $\mathrm{cov}((X_i - \mu)^2, (X_j - \mu)(X_k - \mu)) = 0$ for $j \neq k$.

Furthermore, $E[(\bar{X} - \mu)^2] = \mathrm{var}(\bar{X}) = \sigma^2/n$, while

$$E[(\bar{X} - \mu)^4] = \frac{1}{n^4}\sum_{i=1}^{n}E[(X_i - \mu)^4] + \frac{3}{n^4}\sum\sum_{i \neq j}E[(X_i - \mu)^2]E[(X_j - \mu)^2]$$

$$= \frac{3\sigma^4}{n^3} + \frac{3(n-1)\sigma^4}{n^3}.$$

Therefore, $\mathrm{var}[(\bar{X} - \mu)^2] = \frac{2\sigma^4}{n^2}$, so that

$$MSE(s_*^2, \sigma^2) = \frac{1}{(n-1)^2}\left[2n\sigma^4 + 2\sigma^4 - 4\sigma^4\right] = \frac{2\sigma^4}{n-1}.$$

Now consider the MLE $s^2 = (n-1)s_*^2/n$. We have

$$Es^2 = \frac{n-1}{n}\sigma^2$$

$$\mathrm{var}\, s^2 = \frac{2\sigma^4}{n-1}\left(\frac{n-1}{n}\right)^2 = \frac{2\sigma^4(n-1)}{n^2}.$$

Therefore,

$$\mathrm{MSE}(s^2, \sigma^2) = \frac{\sigma^4}{n^2} + \frac{2\sigma^4(n-1)}{n^2} = \frac{(2n-1)\sigma^4}{n^2}.$$

The result follows. ☐

Mean squared error provides an unambiguous way to rank estimators for a given parameter value, at least in the scalar case. In general, there are many different estimators of a parameter θ. In particular cases we can calculate MSE and rank estimators. We would like a general result that describes the best procedure to use for whatever parameter is true. Unfortunately, requiring a best MSE estimator uniformly over θ is not possible, or rather not useful, because at any given point $\theta = \theta_0$ the estimator $\hat{\theta} = \theta_0$ is best since it has $MSE = 0$ there. We can resolve this in a number of ways.

1. Take some representative values of the parameter space. For example, the minimax approach considers the following criterion

$$\max_{\theta \in \Theta} MSE(\theta; \hat{\theta}),$$

which amounts to the worst case scenario. One should find the estimator that minimizes this worst case MSE. You then get a logically consistent theory; but hard to work out in general. Also, it is rather pessimistic. In most cases, we don't expect nature to be playing against us.
2. Restrict the class of estimators. For example suppose that $\hat{\theta}$ is unbiased, i.e.,

$$b(\theta) \equiv 0, \text{ for all } \theta \in \Theta.$$

In that case, the Gauss–Markov Theorem says that the sample mean is the BLUE (Best Linear Unbiased).
3. If we have large sample sizes, then many estimators are asymptotically normal with mean zero and variance V. In this case, we can rank estimators that are asymptotically normal unambiguously by their asymptotic variance.

An estimator is said to be UMVUE [**Uniformly Minimum Variance Unbiased Estimator**] if has the property claimed in its title. An alternative acronym here is BUE [**Best Unbiased Estimator**]. We have an extensive theory of optimality about Unbiased Estimators. Specifically, the Cramér–Rao Theorem.

Theorem 11.3. CRAMÉR–RAO. *Let $\tilde{\theta}$ be any unbiased estimator of $\theta \in \mathbb{R}$. Then, under regularity conditions [We assume that the support of X does not depend on θ and that all "limit" operations can be interchanged], we have*

$$\text{var}(\tilde{\theta}) \geq \left[E\left(s(\theta_0 | \mathcal{X}^n) \right)^2 \right]^{-1} = \left[\text{var}\left(s(\theta | \mathcal{X}^n) \right) \right]^{-1} = \mathcal{I}^{-1}(\theta), \qquad (11.14)$$

which is known as the information inequality.

Proof. For any unbiased estimator $\tilde{\theta}$

$$E(\tilde{\theta}) = \int \tilde{\theta}(\mathcal{X}^n) L(\theta | \mathcal{X}^n) dX_1, \ldots, dX_n = \theta.$$

Differentiating both sides of this equation with respect to θ, we obtain

$$
\begin{aligned}
1 &= \int \tilde{\theta}(\mathcal{X}^n) \frac{\partial L}{\partial \theta}(\theta | \mathcal{X}^n) dX_1 \cdots dX_n \\
&= \int \tilde{\theta}(\mathcal{X}^n) \frac{\partial L}{\partial \theta}(\theta | \mathcal{X}^n) \frac{1}{L(\theta | \mathcal{X}^n)} \cdot L(\theta | \mathcal{X}^n) dX_1 \cdots dX_n \\
&= \int \tilde{\theta}(\mathcal{X}^n) \frac{\partial \ell}{\partial \theta}(\theta | \mathcal{X}^n) L(\theta | \mathcal{X}^n) dX_1 \cdots dX_n = E\left[\tilde{\theta}(\mathcal{X}^n) s(\theta | \mathcal{X}^n) \right]. \quad (11.15)
\end{aligned}
$$

Furthermore, for all θ,

$$\int L(\theta | \mathcal{X}^n) dX_1 \cdots dX_n = 1,$$

which implies that

$$
\begin{aligned}
0 &= \int \frac{\partial L}{\partial \theta}(\theta | \mathcal{X}^n) dX_1 \cdots dX_n = \int \frac{\partial \ell}{\partial \theta}(\theta | \mathcal{X}^n) L(\theta | \mathcal{X}^n) dX_1 \cdots dX_n \\
&= E\left[s(\theta | \mathcal{X}^n) \right]. \qquad (11.16)
\end{aligned}
$$

Combining these two results we have obtained

$$\int (\tilde{\theta}(\mathcal{X}^n) - \theta) s(\theta | \mathcal{X}^n) L(\theta | \mathcal{X}^n) dX_1 \cdots dX_n = \text{cov}\left(\tilde{\theta}, s(\theta | \mathcal{X}^n) \right) = 1.$$

We now use the Cauchy–Schwarz inequality [taking $f = (\tilde{\theta}(\mathcal{X}^n) - \theta) \times L^{1/2}(\theta | \mathcal{X}^n)$ and $g = \frac{\partial \ell}{\partial \theta}(\theta | \mathcal{X}^n) L^{1/2}(\theta | \mathcal{X}^n)$], to obtain that

$$
\left\{ \int (\tilde{\theta}(\mathcal{X}^n) - \theta)^2 L(\theta | \mathcal{X}^n) dX_1 \cdots dX_n \right\}
$$
$$
\times \left\{ \int \left(s(\theta | \mathcal{X}^n) \right)^2 L(\theta | \mathcal{X}^n) dX_1 \cdots dX_n \right\} \geq 1,
$$

i.e.,

$$\int (\tilde{\theta}(\mathcal{X}^n) - \theta)^2 L(\theta|\mathcal{X}^n) dX_1 \cdots dX_n \geq \frac{1}{\int (s(\theta|\mathcal{X}^n))^2 L(\theta|\mathcal{X}^n) dX_1 \cdots dX_n}$$

as required. □

Remarks. 1. Differentiating (11.16) with respect to θ yields the **information equality**

$$\mathcal{I}(\theta) = E\left[\left(s(\theta|\mathcal{X}^n)\right)^2\right] = -E\left[h(\theta|\mathcal{X}^n)\right], \qquad (11.17)$$

which relates the variance of the score function to the mean of the **Hessian**. This says that the information $\mathcal{I}(\theta)$ can be expressed as minus the expected value of the Hessian. As shown in Rothenberg (1971), a parameter θ is locally identifiable at θ_0 if and only if $\mathcal{I}(\theta)$ is nonzero in a neighbourhood of θ_0. This is because heuristically in a neighbourhood of the true parameter value the expected log likelihood is a quadratic function of θ

$$E\ell(\theta|\mathcal{X}^n) \simeq E\ell(\theta_0|\mathcal{X}^n) + E\frac{\partial}{\partial\theta}\ell(\theta_0|\mathcal{X}^n)(\theta - \theta_0)$$

$$+ \frac{1}{2}E\frac{\partial^2}{\partial\theta^2}\ell(\theta_0|\mathcal{X}^n)(\theta - \theta_0)^2$$

$$\simeq E\ell(\theta_0|\mathcal{X}^n) - \frac{1}{2}\mathcal{I}(\theta_0)(\theta - \theta_0)^2.$$

Provided $\mathcal{I}(\theta_0) > 0$, this shows that $E\ell(\theta|\mathcal{X}^n)$ is uniquely maximized at $\theta = \theta_0$.

2. The CR result does not apply to distributions like the uniform whose support depends on θ. Does not apply to non-differentiable densities (for example $f(x) = \exp(-|x - \theta|)$) either.

3. This result only outlines the possible, in the sense of the best achievable variance. It does not say what happens in a particular case. In finite samples, the information bound may not be achieved by any estimator. But when the MLE is the sample mean, it typically is achieved, because the MLE is unbiased, specifically

$$X \sim N(\mu, 1) \quad \hat{\mu}_{MLE} = \bar{X} \quad \mathcal{I}_n^{-1} = \frac{1}{n}$$

$$X \sim B(n, p) \quad \widehat{p}_{MLE} = \bar{X} \quad \mathcal{I}_n^{-1} = \frac{p(1-p)}{n}$$

$$X \sim P(\lambda) \quad \hat{\lambda}_{MLE} = \bar{X} \quad \mathcal{I}_n^{-1} = \frac{\lambda}{n}.$$

In this case, the MLE is BUE.

4. The matrix extension of (11.14) is straightforward, but requires matrix inversion, which we will treat later.

Example 11.14. Let $X \sim N(\mu, \sigma^2)$. Then,

$$-E\left(\frac{\partial^2 \ell}{\partial \mu^2}(\mu, \sigma^2)\right) = \frac{n}{\sigma^2}$$

$$-E\left(\frac{\partial^2 \ell}{\partial (\sigma^2)^2}(\mu, \sigma^2)\right) = \frac{n}{2\sigma^4}$$

$$E\left(\frac{\partial^2 \ell}{\partial \mu \partial \sigma^2}(\mu, \sigma^2)\right) = 0.$$

Suppose that σ^2 is known. Then for any unbiased estimators of μ, we have

$$\text{var}(\hat{\mu}) \geq \frac{\sigma^2}{n}.$$

In this case, the MLE $\bar{X}$ has variance σ^2/n, so it is UMVUE in this case. In fact, it remains the UMVUE even when σ^2 is unknown since its variance is unaffected by this issue.

Example 11.15. Suppose that μ is known, then for any unbiased estimator of σ^2 we have

$$\text{var}(\hat{\sigma}^2) \geq \frac{2\sigma^4}{n}.$$

In this case, the MLE is

$$\frac{1}{n}\sum_{i=1}^{n}(X_i - \mu)^2$$

and is unbiased with variance $2\sigma^4/n$, so it is UMVUE in this case.

Example 11.16. Suppose that both μ, σ^2 are unknown. Then, the MLE s^2 is biased, and the unbiased estimator s_*^2 has variance

$$\frac{2\sigma^4}{n-1} > \frac{2\sigma^4}{n}.$$

In this case, the Cramér–Rao lower bound for σ^2 is *unattainable* in any finite sample.

11.2.1 Asymptotic Properties

In many cases calculating exactly the MSE is difficult and we may just work with an approximation to it called Asymptotic Mean Squared Error, which arises by taking $n \to \infty$; this will be a valid approximation provided the sample size is large.

Definition 11.3. An estimator is consistent if for all $\theta \in \Theta$

$$\widehat{\theta} \xrightarrow{P} \theta.$$

It is sufficient (but not necessary) for consistency that: (1) $\widehat{\theta}$ is asymptotically unbiased, i.e., $E\widehat{\theta} \to \theta$, and (2) var$(\widehat{\theta}) \to 0$.

Definition 11.4. An estimator is asymptotically normal if for all θ, there is a positive, finite quantity $V(\theta)$ such that

$$\sqrt{n}\left(\widehat{\theta} - \theta\right) \xrightarrow{D} N(0, V(\theta)). \tag{11.18}$$

This says essentially that the asymptotic MSE of $\widehat{\theta}$ is equal to $V(\theta)/n$, where V depends on θ and on $\widehat{\theta}$. It follows that we may rank estimators according to the V in their limiting distribution.

Definition 11.5. Suppose that $\widehat{\theta}_1$ and $\widehat{\theta}_2$ are two estimators of θ that both satisfy (11.18) with asymptotic variance $V_1(\theta)$ and $V_2(\theta)$, respectively. Suppose that

$$V_1(\theta) \leq V_2(\theta) \tag{11.19}$$

for all $\theta \in \Theta$. Then we say that $\widehat{\theta}_1$ is more asymptotically efficient than $\widehat{\theta}_2$.

Example 11.17. Suppose that $X \sim N(\mu, \sigma^2)$ and let

$$\widehat{\mu} = \frac{1}{n} \sum_{i=1}^{n} X_i.$$

Then, $E(\widehat{\mu}) = \mu$ and var$(\widehat{\mu}) = \sigma^2/n$, so that bias $\equiv 0$, and MSE $= \sigma^2/n$, for all μ. In addition

$$\widehat{\mu} \xrightarrow{P} \mu \quad ; \quad \sqrt{n}\left(\widehat{\mu} - \mu\right) \xrightarrow{D} N(0, \sigma^2).$$

Example 11.18. An alternative estimator would be based on the average of every even observation

$$\widehat{\mu}_E = \frac{2}{n} \sum_{i=1}^{n/2} X_{2i}.$$

This is unbiased but has variance (and hence MSE) equal to $2\sigma^2/n$, which is inferior to that of $\widehat{\mu}$. Furthermore,

$$\widehat{\mu}_E \xrightarrow{P} \mu \quad ; \quad \sqrt{n}\left(\widehat{\mu}_E - \mu\right) \xrightarrow{D} N(0, 2\sigma^2).$$

It is asymptotically inefficient.

Example 11.19. Suppose that $X \sim N(\mu, \sigma^2)$, and consider the following estimators of σ^2:

$$s_*^2 = \frac{1}{n-1} \sum_{i=1}^{n} (X_i - \bar{X})^2 \quad ; \quad s^2 = \frac{1}{n} \sum_{i=1}^{n} (X_i - \bar{X})^2.$$

We showed above that in finite samples $\text{MSE}(s^2, \sigma^2) \leq \text{MSE}(s_*^2, \sigma^2)$ for all parameter values. Note that as $n \to \infty$, the difference between s_*^2 and s^2 disappears, i.e.,

$$\sqrt{n}\left(s^2 - \sigma^2\right) \xrightarrow{D} N(0, 2\sigma^4)$$
$$\sqrt{n}\left(s_*^2 - \sigma^2\right) \xrightarrow{D} N(0, 2\sigma^4),$$

so they are equally asymptotically efficient. In fact, if μ were known, the estimator $s_\mu^2 = \sum_{i=1}^{n} (X_i - \mu)^2 / n$ also satisfies $\sqrt{n}\left(s_\mu^2 - \sigma^2\right) \xrightarrow{D} N(0, 2\sigma^4)$.

Theorem 11.4. *Asymptotic CR bound. Under quite general conditions, it can be shown that as $n \to \infty$*

$$\sqrt{n}(\hat{\theta}_{MLE} - \theta) \xrightarrow{D} N(0, \mathcal{I}_\infty^{-1}(\theta)),$$
$$\mathcal{I}_\infty(\theta) = \lim_{n \to \infty} \frac{1}{n} \mathcal{I}_n(\theta).$$

Let $\tilde{\theta}$ be any other estimator with

$$\sqrt{n}(\tilde{\theta} - \theta) \xrightarrow{D} N(0, V(\theta)).$$

Then

$$V(\theta) \geq \mathcal{I}_\infty^{-1}(\theta).$$

This implies that in large samples the MLE is efficient, because it is asymptotically unbiased.

11.3 ROBUSTNESS AND OTHER ISSUES WITH THE MLE

We have shown how the MLE is the most efficient method when the sample size is large. This was predicated on a complete and correct specification of the data distribution, that is, the true P satisfies $P \in \{P_\theta, \theta \in \Theta\}$. An alternative question to ask about any given statistical method is: how well it works when not all the assumptions made are correct? Frequently, misspecification causes inconsistency, although in some cases only an increase in variance. A leading example here is estimation of the population mean by the sample mean. The sample mean can be interpreted as the MLE for normally distributed data. If the data are heavy tailed such as a t distribution, then the sample mean suffers loss of precision relative to the best attainable method (which is then the t-MLE). In fact, the normal based MLE is often highly susceptible to fat tailed distributions suffering great losses in variance (and even inconsistency when for example the distribution is Cauchy). By contrast, the sample median estimator does close to optimally in a much bigger range of circumstances (and is consistent even for the Cauchy distribution). We compare three different procedures for estimating the centre of location (mean or median) in terms of their performances in three different scenarios. The estimators we consider are: the sample median (the MLE for double exponential distribution); the sample mean = (the MLE for Gaussian distribution); and the Cauchy MLE. We consider three (symmetric) distributions for P: Normal $N(0, 1)$; Double exponential $f(x) = \frac{1}{2}e^{-|x|}$; and Cauchy $f(x) = \frac{1}{\pi(1+x^2)}$. Below we give the asymptotic variances of the three estimation procedures under the three different data distributions

	Mean	Median	Cauchy MLE
Norm	1.00	1.57	1.32
Exp	1.40	1.00	1.18
Cauchy	∞	2.47	2.00

This shows the range of outcomes that are obtained depending on the estimation procedure and the true distribution.

One form of misspecification that has received a lot of attention is the **gross error model**, where the typist occasionally hits the wrong key and you get some extra zeros on the end. In this case, the normal-based likelihood procedures can be wildly inaccurate. They have what is known as **unbounded influence functions**, and can be arbitrarily messed up by such errors as under the Cauchy distribution. The median has a bounded influence function as does the trimmed mean (i.e., throw away the 5% largest and smallest observations). As estimators of a population centre of symmetry these are robust. In conclusion, sometimes the MLE is robust, but sometimes it is not. In practice, one has to recognize the frequent arbitrariness of the model and accept that it will only provide an approximation to the data distribution. A literature has developed that treats the consequences of misspecified likelihood estimation, see White (1982). Some authors use the adjectives "quasi" or "pseudo" before likelihood in order to emphasize their belief that the model is only an approximation. As we have argued, in some cases this misspecification still permits consistent (but inefficient) estimation of quantities of interest, whereas in other cases it does not.[1]

There are some further areas of criticism of maximum likelihood.

Firstly, the MLE can be computationally intensive and in practice may not be worth the additional cost involved in their computation relative to simpler methods like the Method of Moments.

Secondly, there are even some models for which the MLE is not best. These situations violate the regularity conditions that go along with the distribution and optimality theory. For example, the fixed effect panel data regression model has parameters increasing in number with sample size.

Finally, the Bayesian school argues that one should treat the parameters as random variables about which there is some knowledge expressed through a prior probability distribution $\pi(\theta)$. See Leamer (1978) for further discussion. These methods are enjoying a revival due in part to advances in computational methodology that has made it possible to actually carry out the Bayesian procedures for reasonable models.

---

1. In the same vein, economic models often do not make predictions about entire distributions but do impose restrictions in the form of conditional moments, e.g. Euler equations from dynamic optimization. This is why the Generalized Method of Moments (GMM) is so widely used in some analyses. Going even further, non and semiparametric methods are targeted to do well over a large class of models.

Chapter 12

Hypothesis Testing

12.1 HYPOTHESES

In addition to point estimation we often want to know how good our estimator is and whether it is compatible with certain preconceived 'hypotheses' about the data. Suppose that we observe certain data, and there is a true data distribution denoted by f, which is known to lie in a family of models $\mathcal{F}$. The purpose is to evaluate whether the data are compatible with certain preconceived 'hypotheses'. The context is a parametric model $\{P_\theta, \theta \in \Theta\}$, where Θ contains all the possible values of θ.

Definition 12.1. We suppose there is a further reduction of Θ called a **Null hypothesis** H_0 ($\Theta_0 \subseteq \Theta$). The **Alternative hypothesis** H_1 ($\Theta_1 \subseteq \Theta$) is the complement of the null hypothesis in Θ, i.e.,

$$\Theta_0 \cap \Theta_1 = \phi \text{ and } \Theta_0 \cup \Theta_1 = \Theta.$$

For example, H_0 could be:

1. The prediction of a scientific theory. For example, the interest elasticity of demand for money is zero; the gravitational constant is 9.
2. The absence of some structure, e.g., independence of an error term over time, homoskedasticity etc.
3. A simplification of an otherwise complicated model

Example 12.1. A female colleague of the famous statistician R.A. Fisher claimed to be able to tell whether the tea or the milk was added first to a cup. Fisher proposed to give her eight cups, four of each variety, in random order. One could then ask what the probability was for her getting the number she got correct, but just by chance. The null hypothesis was that the Lady had no such ability. The test statistic was a simple count of the number of successes in selecting the 4 cups. The critical region was the single case of 4 successes of 4 possible based on a conventional probability criterion ($<5\%$; 1 of 70 $\simeq$ 1.4%). The lady correctly identified every cup, which would be considered a statistically significant result.

Our purpose here is to provide a method for interpreting what the data say about the hypothesis. We distinguish between a **Simple hypothesis** (under H_0,

Probability, Statistics and Econometrics. http://dx.doi.org/10.1016/B978-0-12-810495-8.00014-2
175

the data distribution is completely specified) and a **Composite hypothesis** (in which case, H_0 does not completely determine the distribution, i.e., there are 'nuisance' parameters not specified by H_0). We also distinguish between **Single** and **Multiple** hypotheses (one or more restriction on parameters of f). We shall also distinguish between **one-sided** and **two-sided** alternatives; when we have a single real-valued parameter, this is an easy notion to comprehend.

Example 12.2. Suppose that $X \sim N(\mu, 1)$. $H_0 : \mu = \mu_0$ **simple single** null hypothesis. $H_A : \mu \neq \mu_0$ **composite** alternative (**two-sided**). One sided alternative $H_A : \mu > \mu_0$ composite alternative (**one-sided**).

Example 12.3. Suppose that $X \sim N(\mu, \sigma^2)$. $H_0 : \mu = \mu_0$ composite null because σ^2 is not restricted. $H_A : \mu \neq \mu_0$ composite alternative (two-sided); $H_A : \mu > \mu_0$ composite alternative (one-sided)

Example 12.4. Suppose that $X \sim N(\mu, \sigma^2)$. $H_0 : \mu = \mu_0$, $\sigma^2 = \sigma_0^2$ simple null, **multiple** hypotheses

One may observe that apparently for the one-sided alternative hypothesis, $\Theta_0 \cup \Theta_1 \neq \Theta$. We may understand this in two ways. First, write the null hypothesis as $H_0 : \mu \leq \mu_0$ in which case $\Theta_0 \cup \Theta_1 = \Theta = \mathbb{R}$; in this case, μ_0 is called the **least favourable case** (of the null hypothesis). Second, we may redefine $\Theta = \mathbb{R}_+ = \{\theta : \theta \geq 0\}$ so that $\Theta_0 \cup \Theta_1 = \Theta$.

12.2 TEST PROCEDURE

A hypothesis test is a procedure that allows one to carry out the simple decision rule:

$$\varphi : \mathcal{X}^n \to \{ \overset{\textit{Accept}}{1} , \overset{\textit{Reject}}{0} \}.$$

It is like a criminal trial, which also has two outcomes (in most places): Guilty or not Guilty.

Essentially, we need to partition the data into two regions. There are many ways to do this. A common intermediate step is to calculate a scalar **Test statistic** $T(\mathcal{X}^n, \theta) \in \mathbb{R}$ that can measure the consistency of the data with H_0. The logic of the test is to design this such that large values of T are incompatible with the null hypothesis but small values of T are compatible with null.

So how big should T be before I reject? Define the following quantities: **Significance level** $\alpha \in (0, 1)$, **Critical region** R_α, and **Acceptance region** $C_\alpha = R_\alpha^c$. Usually, C_α is an interval such as $[\underline{c_\alpha}, \overline{c_\alpha}]$ with the limits being called **critical values**.

The test is carried out such that: if $T \in C_\alpha$, then accept the null hypothesis; if $T \in R_\alpha$, then reject the null hypothesis. The usual approach is to choose the partition such that

$$\textbf{Exact} \qquad \Pr(T \in R_\alpha | H_0 \text{ is true}) = \alpha \qquad (12.1)$$

$$\textbf{Approximate} \qquad \lim_{n \to \infty} \Pr(T \in R_\alpha | H_0 \text{ is true}) = \alpha. \qquad (12.2)$$

When the null hypothesis is true, the rule yields reject decision α proportion of times (or approximately α proportion of times) so that were this test applied to many such data sets generated by H_0, you would indeed reject α proportion of times. Note that accepting the null hypothesis does not mean we can conclude that it is true, only that there is insufficient evidence from this test that it is false. This is an example of a **transposed conditional**.

How to choose α? This is about measuring the standard of evidence against the null hypothesis that leads you to reject it. Lawyers use "**beyond reasonable doubt**" as the standard of evidence in criminal trials, and "**the balance of probabilities**" in civil trials. In statistics, these are quantitatively expressed through α. Values such as $\alpha = 0.05$ and $\alpha = 0.01$ are common standards in social sciences and medical research.

The main issue is how to choose T and R_α. This involves calculating $\Pr(T \in R_\alpha | H_0)$ or finding an approximation to it. In some special cases (normality) we can find a T whose distribution under H_0 whose distribution is known exactly or approximately in large samples. This is called the **pivotal case**. In other cases, the distribution of T under H_0 may depend (even in large samples) on unknown quantities that have to be estimated.

Example 12.5. Suppose that $X_1 \ldots, X_n$ are i.i.d. $N(\mu, \sigma^2)$, where σ^2 is known. Suppose that $H_0 : \mu = \mu_0$. Then

$$T = \frac{(\bar{X} - \mu_0)}{\sigma/\sqrt{n}} \sim N(0, 1) \text{ under } H_0.$$

Let $R_\alpha = \{x : |x| \geq z_{\alpha/2}\}$. The rule is to reject if $|T| \geq z_{\alpha/2}$, where $\Phi(z_\alpha) = 1 - \alpha$. Critical values $\pm z_{\alpha/2}$. If the alternative is one-sided, then reject if $T > z_\alpha$, i.e., critical value is z_α. Suppose now that σ^2 is unknown, in which case the null is composite with the value of σ^2 unrestricted. In this case, we use the celebrated **t-test**

$$T = \frac{\bar{X} - \mu_0}{s_*/\sqrt{n}} \sim t(n - 1) \text{ under } H_0.$$

Reject if $|T| > t_{\alpha/2}(n - 1)$ or $T > t_\alpha(n - 1)$.

Typical critical values are shown in the table below:

α	0.05	0.025	0.005
z_α	1.645	1.96	2.81
$t_\alpha(9)$	1.83	2.26	3.25
$t_\alpha(4)$	2.13	2.78	4.60

In some fields of science it is more common to talk about a 5 sigma standard, that is $c_\alpha = 5$. This corresponds to a significance level α of 2.9×10^{-7} under the normal distribution.

Note that as $n \to \infty$,

$$t_\alpha(n) \to z_\alpha$$

for all α. In practice when $n > 30$ the two critical values are the same to two decimal places.

In the previous example, when the **nuisance parameter** σ^2 was unknown and we had a composite null hypothesis, we still obtained (12.1). That is, for all $\sigma^2 \in \mathbb{R}_+$, we have

$$\Pr(T \in R_\alpha | \mu = \mu_0, \sigma^2) = \alpha.$$

However, in other composite cases, this may not be exactly true.

Example 12.6. Suppose that $X_1 \ldots, X_n$ are i.i.d. $N(\mu, \sigma^2)$, where σ^2 is known. Suppose that $H_0 : \mu \le \mu_0$. Then

$$T = \frac{(\bar{X} - \mu_0)}{\sigma/\sqrt{n}} \sim N(\mu - \mu_0, 1) \text{ under } H_0.$$

Let $R_\alpha = \{x : x \ge z_\alpha\}$. The rule is to reject if $T \ge z_\alpha$. In this case, we have for all $\mu \le \mu_0$

$$\Pr(T \in R_\alpha | \mu) \le \alpha$$

with equality only when $\mu = \mu_0$.

In general, we only may obtain

$$\textbf{Exact} \qquad \sup_{\theta \in \Theta_0} \Pr(T \in R_\alpha | \theta) \le \alpha \qquad (12.3)$$

$$\textbf{Approximate} \qquad \lim_{n \to \infty} \sup_{\theta \in \Theta_0} \Pr(T \in R_\alpha | \theta) \le \alpha, \qquad (12.4)$$

and in such cases where the inequality may be strict over some subset of the null hypothesis we say that the test is **conservative**. If there is a value $\theta_0 \in \Theta_0$ such that $\Pr(T \in R_\alpha | \theta_0) = \alpha$ or $\lim_{n \to \infty} \Pr(T \in R_\alpha | \theta_0) = \alpha$, this value is called the **least favourable** case. By themselves the objectives (12.3) and (12.4) are not hard to achieve: one can always just use a random number generator to achieve the right rejection probability. However, as we will see below, it may not be possible to achieve these objectives in some cases if one simultaneously wants to reject false hypotheses frequently.

Sachs (1999) used rather complete data records from Switzerland to analyze the relationships between the signs of the Zodiac and (1) who purchases literature on astrology, (2) marriages, (3) divorces, (4) who lives single, (5) choice of university major, (6) profession, (7) cause of death, (8) suicide, (9) criminal convictions, (10) driving record, and (11) who plays football. For example, for his analyses of who marries whom, Sachs used the records of weddings in Switzerland from 1987 through 1994. In all 11 behaviour domains, Sachs found numerous significant associations between the signs of the Zodiac and behaviour.[1]

Example 12.7. We want to test whether Zodiac sign has any influence on success measured by income at age 40. We have a sample of individuals from each Zodiac sign and assume that their (log of) income $X_j \sim N(\mu_j, \sigma_0^2)$, $j = 1, 2 \ldots, 12$, where σ_0^2 is known but μ_j are not. In this case the null hypothesis is that $H_0 : \mu_1 = \mu_2 = \cdots = \mu_{12} = \mu_0$, where μ_0 is a known number, versus the alternative that the μ_j are not all the same. These are multiple restrictions, which may better be described as

$$\mu_1 = \mu_0, \ldots, \mu_{12} = \mu_0. \tag{12.5}$$

Suppose we have independent samples of size n_j, $j = 1, \ldots, 12$ from each Zodiac sign. A simple test statistic

$$\tau = \sum_{j=1}^{12} \left(\frac{\overline{X}_j - \mu_0}{\sigma_0/\sqrt{n_j}} \right)^2 = \sum_{j=1}^{12} n_j \left(\frac{\overline{X}_j - \mu_0}{\sigma_0} \right)^2 \sim \chi^2(12). \tag{12.6}$$

We reject the null hypothesis when $\tau > \chi_\alpha^2(12)$. See Fig. 12.1.

For large sample tests, the logic is based on LLN, CLT, and Slutsky theorems.

Example 12.8. Suppose that X is i.i.d. with $E(X) = \mu$ and $\text{var}(X) = \sigma^2$, where σ^2 is unknown. We test the hypothesis that $\mu = \mu_0$. In this case, under the null hypothesis

$$T = \frac{\sqrt{n}(\bar{X} - \mu_0)}{s} \xrightarrow{D} N(0, 1).$$

Reject the null if $|T| > z_{\alpha/2}$ or $T > z_\alpha$. The test is asymptotically valid.

---

1. Unfortunately, perhaps, NASA (2016) has recently decided that there are actually thirteen Zodiac signs not twelve as was previously the case because the earth's axis has shifted.

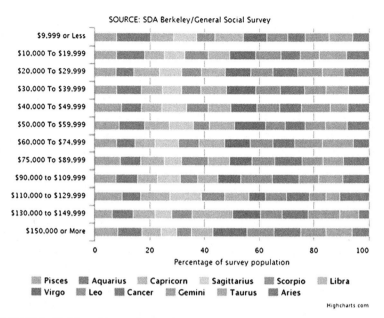

SOURCE: SDA Berkeley/General Social Survey

FIGURE 12.1 Variation of income by star sign

Example 12.9. In the Zodiac example, suppose that we just assume that their (log of) income is i.i.d. with mean μ_j, $j = 1, 2 \ldots, 12$ and known variance σ^2. Then asymptotically

$$\tau = \sum_{j=1}^{12} \left(\frac{\overline{X}_j - \mu_0}{\sigma_0/\sqrt{n_j}} \right)^2 \xrightarrow{D} \chi^2(12)$$

We reject the null hypothesis when $\tau > \chi^2_\alpha(12)$. The test is asymptotically valid.

We next consider the multiple testing issue, which is currently a major field of research in statistics. Consider the Zodiac example and compute for $j = 1, \ldots, 12$

$$\tau_j = \frac{\overline{X}_j - \mu_0}{\sigma_0/\sqrt{n_j}} \sim N(0, 1) \qquad ; \qquad C_j = \left\{ \mathcal{X}^n : |\tau_j| \le z_{\alpha/2} \right\}.$$

Why not just carry out 12 tests using τ_j, i.e., reject if any one of them rejects? This is called the **finite induced test**. We calculate the rejection probability under the null:

$$\Pr[C_1 \cap \ldots \cap C_{12}] = \Pr\left[|\tau_1| \le z_{\alpha/2}, \ldots, |\tau_{12}| \le z_{\alpha/2}\right]$$
$$= \Pr\left[|\tau_1| \le z_{\alpha/2}\right] \times \cdots \times \Pr\left[|\tau_{12}| \le z_{\alpha/2}\right]$$
$$= (1-\alpha)^{12} < 1 - \alpha.$$

This says that if use the critical value $z_{\alpha/2}$ we will over reject the null hypothesis (**liberal test**). Instead, if we use the critical value $z_{\gamma/2}$ with γ such that $(1-\gamma)^{12} = 1 - \alpha$, then the resulting test of the multiple null will have significance level α. So it is a perfectly valid test after this adjustment. The critical region of this test is a cuboid rather than a spheroid. These two different tests have overlapping critical regions, i.e., one may reject both tests, reject neither test, or reject one but not the other test. The calculation above requires heavily on the independence of τ_j otherwise the exact critical value for this procedure is harder to obtain.

Example 12.10. Suppose we want to predict future stock returns Y and I have a database of quadrillions of different predictors, X_j. The semistrong Efficient Markets Hypothesis, or EMH, (with constant risk premium) says that $\rho_j = \text{cov}(X_j, Y) = 0$. Suppose that everything has mean zero and variance one and is mutually independent, and I observe a sample of size n on all variables. For each predictor I compute

$$\widehat{\rho}_j = \frac{1}{n} \sum_{i=1}^{n} X_{ji} Y_i$$

Under EMH, the CLT says that

$$\sqrt{n}\widehat{\rho}_j \xrightarrow{D} N(0, 1).$$

Reject if $|\sqrt{n}\widehat{\rho}_j| \ge z_{\alpha/2}$. Bright idea: Suppose I just did all the possible tests and take the predictor with the maximum test statistic? This can be thought of as an application of the Infinite monkey theorem. The significance level of this procedure is $1 - (1 - \alpha)^{\text{quadrillions}} \simeq 1$.

12.3 LIKELIHOOD TESTS

Suppose we have the null $\theta \in \Theta_0$ and the alternative $\theta \in \Theta_1 = \Theta_0^c$. The likelihood ratio statistic is

$$\lambda(\mathcal{X}^n) = \frac{\max_{\theta \in \Theta} L(\theta|\mathcal{X}^n)}{\max_{\theta \in \Theta_0} L(\theta|\mathcal{X}^n)} = \frac{L(\widehat{\theta}_{MLE}|\mathcal{X}^n)}{L(\widehat{\theta}_{RMLE}|\mathcal{X}^n)},$$

where $\widehat{\theta}_{MLE}$ is MLE (max over Θ) and the $\widehat{\theta}_{RMLE}$ is the "restricted MLE" over Θ_0. Note that some authors define the likelihood ratio as $1/\lambda$, and in some cases it is defined as $\max_{\theta \in \Theta_1} L(\theta | \mathcal{X}^n) / \max_{\theta \in \Theta_0} L(\theta | \mathcal{X}^n)$. There are two other well known tests that are related to the LR test, the Wald test and the Score test (or LM test). Suppose that we can express the restrictions imposed by the null hypothesis in the form $g(\theta_0) = 0$ for some differentiable function g such that $G(\theta_0) = g'(\theta_0) \neq 0$. That is, the null is simple. The Wald statistic and Score test for this case are

$$W = \frac{ng(\widehat{\theta})^2}{G(\widehat{\theta})^2 \mathcal{I}(\widehat{\theta})} \quad ; \quad LM = \frac{ns(\widehat{\theta}_{RMLE})^2}{\mathcal{I}(\widehat{\theta}_{RMLE})}.$$

Logic: Note that $\lambda(\mathcal{X}^n) \geq 1$ and small values of λ would point to the veracity of the null hypothesis, while large values would go against it. The logic of the Wald test is that under the null hypothesis $g(\widehat{\theta})$ should be close to zero. The logic of the score test is that under the null hypothesis $s(\widehat{\theta}_{RMLE})$ should be close to zero, while under the alternative hypothesis it will not be.

We continue this discussion for the LRT. A LRT is any test that rejects when $\lambda(\mathcal{X}^n) \geq c$ for some $c \geq 1$, i.e., we have a rejection region

$$R_\alpha(\lambda) = \{\lambda : \lambda \geq c\}.$$

The key issue is to find c to control the significance level.

Example 12.11. $X \sim N(\mu, 1)$. $H_0 : \mu = \mu_0$ vs. $H_A : \mu \neq \mu_0$. In this case the denominator is

$$L(\mu_0 | \mathcal{X}^n) = \frac{1}{(2\pi)^{n/2}} \exp\left(-\frac{1}{2} \sum_{i=1}^n (X_i - \mu_0)^2\right).$$

The MLE is $\hat{\mu}_{MLE} = \bar{X}$, so

$$\lambda(\mathcal{X}^n) = \frac{(2\pi)^{-n/2} \exp\left(-\frac{1}{2} \sum_{i=1}^n (X_i - \bar{X})^2\right)}{(2\pi)^{-n/2} \exp\left(-\frac{1}{2} \sum_{i=1}^n (X_i - \mu_0)^2\right)} = \exp\left(\frac{n}{2}(\bar{X} - \mu_0)^2\right)$$

$$\log \lambda(\mathcal{X}^n) = \frac{n}{2}(\bar{X} - \mu_0)^2.$$

So that in this case the LRT rejects if

$$\lambda(\mathcal{X}^n) \geq c \Leftrightarrow \sqrt{n}|\bar{X} - \mu_0| \geq \sqrt{-2 \log c}$$

for any c. Therefore, we take c that solves $z_{\alpha/2} = \sqrt{2 \log c}$, which says that $c = \exp\left(\frac{1}{2} z_{\alpha/2}^2\right)$ works.

Example 12.12. Zodiac. In this case we may show

$$\log \lambda(\mathcal{X}^n) = \frac{1}{2\sigma_0^2} \sum_{j=1}^{12} \sum_{i=1}^{n_j} (X_{ji} - \mu_0)^2 + \frac{1}{2\sigma^2} \sum_{j=1}^{12} \sum_{i=1}^{n_j} (X_{ji} - \overline{X}_j)^2$$

$$= \frac{1}{2\sigma_0^2} \sum_{j=1}^{12} \sum_{i=1}^{n_j} \left\{ (X_{ji} - \mu_0)^2 - (X_{ji} - \overline{X}_j)^2 \right\}$$

$$= \frac{1}{2} \sum_{j=1}^{12} n_j \frac{(\overline{X}_j - \mu_0)^2}{\sigma_0^2}$$

The test we used earlier is equivalent to LRT.

Example 12.13. The Binomial case where $X_i = 1$ with probability p and $X_i = 0$ with probability $1 - p$ and we observe X_i, $i = 1, \ldots, n$. Suppose the null hypothesis is that $p \le p_0$ versus $p > p_0$. The likelihood ratio is

$$\lambda(\mathcal{X}^n) = \frac{\widehat{p}^k(1 - \widehat{p})^{n-k}}{p_0^k(1 - p_0)^{n-k}} = \left(\frac{k}{np_0} \right)^k \left(\frac{l}{nq_0} \right)^l,$$

where $q_0 = 1 - p_0$ and $l = n - k$. This is a discrete random variable since k takes the values $0, 1, \ldots, n$. Can see that any rejection region $R_\alpha(\lambda) = \{\lambda : \lambda \ge c\}$ is equivalent to a rejection region $\{k : k \ge c'\}$ for some $c' \in \{0, 1, \ldots, n\}$. We can calculate exactly the probability

$$\Pr(k \ge c') = \sum_{j \ge c'} \binom{n}{j} p_0^j (1 - p_0)^{n-j}$$

for any c', but we may not be able to find $c' \in \{0, 1, \ldots, n\}$ such that $\Pr(k \ge c') = \alpha$, because of the discreteness issue. Typically therefore we will have a conservative test with $\Pr(T \in R_\alpha | \theta) < \alpha$.

We can define the LRT for any setting where we have a likelihood and clearly defined null and alternative hypothesis. However, it is often hard to get exact tests. Instead we may work with approximate tests based on large samples.

Theorem 12.1. *Under some regularity conditions, under* H_0

$$2 \log \lambda(\mathcal{X}^n), W, LM \xrightarrow{D} \chi^2(1). \tag{12.7}$$

We will discuss the theory more in detail later.

Example 12.14. The Binomial case. In this case the log likelihood ratio is

$$LR = n\left(\widehat{p}\log\left(\frac{\widehat{p}}{p_0}\right) + (1 - \widehat{p})\log\left(\frac{1 - \widehat{p}}{1 - p_0}\right)\right) = n\phi(\widehat{p}).$$

We have under the null hypothesis $\sqrt{n}(\widehat{p} - p_0) \xrightarrow{D} N(0, p_0(1 - p_0))$. The function ϕ is twice differentiable with

$$\phi'(p) = \log\left(\frac{p}{1 - p}\right) - \log\left(\frac{p_0}{1 - p_0}\right)$$

$$\phi''(p) = \frac{1}{p(1 - p)}$$

and $\phi'(p_0) = 0$ but $\phi''(p_0) \neq 0$. Applying the delta method corollary we obtain (12.7). The Wald statistic and Score test are

$$W = \frac{n(\widehat{p} - p_0)^2}{\widehat{p}(1 - \widehat{p})} \quad ; \quad LM = \frac{n(\widehat{p} - p_0)^2}{p_0(1 - p_0)}.$$

By even simpler arguments we also obtain the chi-squared limiting distribution for W, LM under the null hypothesis.

12.4 POWER OF TESTS

We next define the power of a test. Hypothesis testing, like criminal trials, makes two types of errors.

Definition 12.2. Type I error: Reject H_0 when H_0 is true; **Type II error**: accept H_0 when it is false. Let

$$\alpha = \Pr(\text{Type I error}) = \Pr(\text{Reject } H_0 | H_0 \text{ is true})$$
$$\beta = \Pr(\text{Type II error}) = \Pr(\text{Accept } H_0 | H_A \text{ is true}).$$

If the hypotheses are composite then α, β may depend on the particular value of θ. There is generally a trade-off between α and β. α is called the **size** of the test or the **significance level**, while $\pi = 1 - \beta$ is called the **power** of the test. We want a test with high power or low error rate of type II. Power will depend on the particular alternative value and on the sample size.

Example 12.15. Suppose that $X \sim N(\mu, 1)$ and $H_0 : \mu = \mu_0$ versus $H_0 : \mu > \mu_0$. We have for all $\mu \in \mathbb{R}$,

$$T = \sqrt{n}\left(\overline{X} - \mu_0\right) = \sqrt{n}\left(\overline{X} - \mu\right) + \sqrt{n}\left(\mu - \mu_0\right) \sim N(\overbrace{\sqrt{n}(\mu - \mu_0)}^{\delta_n(\mu)}, 1).$$

Suppose that we reject the null hypothesis if $T > z_\alpha$. It follows that

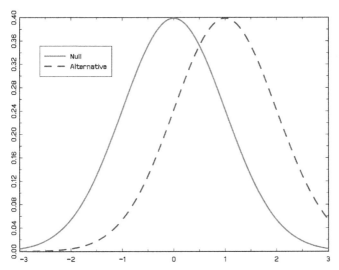

FIGURE 12.2   Comparison of distribution of test statistic under the null hypothesis and under an alternative hypothesis

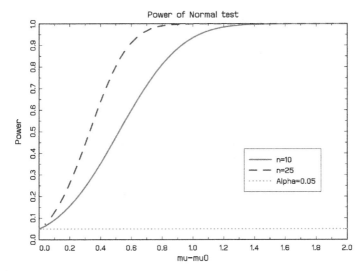

FIGURE 12.3   Power of the test

$$\pi_n(\mu) = \Pr\left(T \geq z_\alpha | \mu\right) = \Pr(N(0, 1) + \delta_n(\mu) \geq z_\alpha) = 1 - \Phi(z_\alpha - \delta_n(\mu)).$$

When $\mu > \mu_0$, $\delta_n(\mu) > 0$, and $\pi_n(\mu) > \alpha$. The larger is $\delta_n(\mu)$, the larger is the power. As $\mu \to \infty$, we find $\pi_n(\mu) \to 1$. On the other hand, as $\mu \to \mu_0$ we have $\pi_n(\mu) \to \alpha$, that is, the type II error converges to $1 - \alpha$. See Figs 12.2 and 12.3.

This shows that the power of the test is larger as: the alternative is further from the null hypothesis and as the sample size is larger. Likewise, the power of the test decreases as the alternative gets closer to the null. In general, we find that $\inf_{\theta \in \Theta_1} \pi_n(\theta) \leq \alpha$. A test for which $\inf_{\theta \in \Theta_1} \pi_n(\theta) = \alpha$ is said to be **unbiased**, meaning the rejection frequency is at least as big under the alternative as under the null. This would seem like a pretty reasonable requirement; it is easy to establish in simple cases like we show here but harder to show in more complicated cases. Indeed, one often finds that in complicated multiple testing environments there are alternatives against which a test has zero power.

Example 12.16. Zodiac. Suppose that we consider the test statistic

$$T = \frac{1}{\sqrt{12}} \sum_{j=1}^{12} \frac{(\overline{X}_j - \mu_0)}{\sigma_0/\sqrt{n_j}} \sim N(0, 1) \text{ under } H_0.$$

Large values of T are generally incompatible with null hypothesis and makes a valid test. However, we have zero power against some alternatives. Suppose that $n_j = n/12$. If $(\mu_1, \ldots, \mu_{12})$ is such that

$$\frac{1}{12} \sum_{j=1}^{12} \mu_j = \mu_0$$

we have $\delta_n(\mu) = 0$ and $T \sim N(0, 1)$ under these members of H_A, that is, the test has zero power against these alternatives. In some sense, made precise below, the set $\{(\mu_1, \ldots, \mu_{12}) : \frac{1}{12} \sum_{j=1}^{12} \mu_j = \mu_0\}$ is much larger than the set $\{(\mu_1, \ldots, \mu_{12}) : \frac{1}{12} \sum_{j=1}^{12} \mu_j \neq \mu_0\}$.

12.4.1 Neyman Pearson Optimal Testing

We would like to simultaneously minimize α and maximize π, i.e., to set type I and type II errors to zero, but these objectives are generally in conflict. We instead first specify and control α, and then find a test with the best π for the given α.

We now consider the class of all tests with size α for $0 \leq \alpha \leq 1$. Want to find the test for which $\pi(\theta)$ is uniformly maximized over Θ_1. If such a test exists, it is said to be **Uniformly Most Powerful** (UMP). Not possible in general.

We now give the Neyman–Pearson lemma which applies to the special case of a simple null and a simple alternative, that is,

$$\Theta_0 = \{\theta_0\}, \ \Theta_1 = \{\theta_1\}$$

i.e., $H_0 : \theta = \theta_0$ and $H_A : \theta = \theta_1$. In this case, with $n = 1$, we define the likelihood ratio as

$$\lambda(x) = \frac{f(x|\theta_0)}{f(x|\theta_1)} = \frac{f_0(x)}{f_1(x)}.$$

Theorem 12.2. *(Neyman–Pearson) Let R be any critical region with*

$$\Pr(X \in R|\theta_0) \leq \alpha$$

Suppose there exists a critical region R_λ of the form

$$R_\lambda = \left\{ x : \frac{f(x|\theta_1)}{f(x|\theta_0)} \geq k \right\} \text{ such that } \Pr(X \in R_\lambda|\theta_0) = \alpha.$$

Then,

$$\Pr(X \in R_\lambda|\theta_1) \geq \Pr(X \in R|\theta_1),$$

i.e., a test based on the likelihood ratio has better power.[2]

Proof. We show the proof for continuous data only. Writing $R_\lambda = (R_\lambda \cap R) \cup (R_\lambda \cap R^c)$ and $R = (R_\lambda \cap R) \cup (R_\lambda^c \cap R)$ we obtain that

$$\Pr(X \in R_\lambda|\theta_1) - \Pr(X \in R|\theta_1) = \int_{R_\lambda \cap R^c} f_1(x)dx - \int_{R_\lambda^c \cap R} f_1(x)dx.$$

On $R_\lambda \cap R^c \subseteq R_\lambda$, we have

$$f_1(x) \geq kf_0(x),$$

so that

$$\int_{R_\lambda \cap R^c} f_1(x)dx \geq k \int_{R_\lambda \cap R^c} f_0(x)dx.$$

On $R_\lambda^c \cap R \subseteq R_\lambda^c$, we have

$$\int_{R_\lambda^c \cap R} f_1(x)dx < k \int_{R_\lambda^c \cap R} f_0(x)dx.$$

---

2. Note that the critical region is here defined in terms of $1/\lambda \geq k$ which is equivalent to $\lambda \leq c = 1/k$.

Therefore,

$$\Pr(X \in R_\lambda | \theta_1) - \Pr(X \in R | \theta_1) \geq k \left[\int_{R_\lambda \cap R^c} f_0(x)dx - \int_{R_\lambda^c \cap R} f_0(x)dx \right]$$

$$= k \left[\int_{R_\lambda} f_0(x)dx - \int_R f_0(x)dx \right]$$

$$= k[\Pr(X \in R_\lambda | \theta_0) - \Pr(X \in R | \theta_0)]$$

$$\geq 0,$$

since $k \geq 0$ and $\Pr(X \in R_\lambda | \theta_0) = \alpha$ and $\Pr(X \in R | \theta_0) \leq \alpha$. □

Remarks. 1. When X is discrete it may not be possible to find R_λ for all such α. For example, suppose that X is the number of successes in three independent trials and that $\theta_0 = 1/4$ or $\theta_1 = 3/4$. We have to find k such that

$$\Pr \left[X : \frac{f_1(X)}{f_0(X)} \geq k \right] = 0.05,$$

which is equivalent to finding k' such that

$$\Pr \left[X \geq k' \right] = 0.05.$$

Since X can only be $0, 1, 2, 3$ this can not be done exactly. One way out of this is just to work with those specific α for which an exact likelihood ratio critical region can be found. An alternative is to use randomization.

2. The extension to one-sided composite hypotheses

$$H_0 : \theta \leq \theta_0, \quad H_A : \theta > \theta_0. \tag{12.8}$$

The **Karlin–Rubin** theorem says that the LR test is UMP provided there is a sufficient statistic $T(X)$ that has the monotone likelihood ratio (MLR) property: for all $\theta_1 > \theta_0$, $\frac{f(x|\theta_1)}{f(x|\theta_0)}$ is a nondecreasing function of x on (joint support) $\{x : f(x|\theta_1) > 0 \text{ and } f(x|\theta_0) > 0\}$. Reason is that every pair of parameter values θ_1, θ_2 with $\theta_1 < \theta_2$ establishes the same preference ordering over the sample points. Examples: One parameter exponential families, e.g., Normal, Poisson, and Binomial.

3. In general, testing against two-sided alternatives, UMP's do not exist. For example, suppose that $X \sim N(\mu, 1)$; $H_0 : \mu = 0$ vs. $\mu > 0$. In this case, the best critical region is $\{\mathcal{X}^n : \bar{X} > z_\alpha/\sqrt{n}\}$. For any $\mu > 0$, this test is most powerful for testing the hypothesis $\mu = 0$ against the point alternative μ. The critical region is independent of μ. In the two-sided test, the test with rejection region

$$\left\{ \mathcal{X}^n : |\bar{X}| > \frac{z_{\alpha/2}}{\sqrt{n}} \right\}$$

is less powerful than the test with rejection region

$$\left\{ \mathcal{X}^n : \bar{X} > \frac{z_\alpha}{\sqrt{n}} \right\}$$

when $\mu > 0$, and less powerful than the test with rejection region

$$\left\{ \mathcal{X}^n : \bar{X} < \frac{z_\alpha}{\sqrt{n}} \right\}$$

when $\mu < 0$.

4. So in many cases optimal tests do not exist. In this case we turn to restricted classes to obtain optimality results, for example, Unbiased and Invariant Tests. An unbiased test satisfies

$$\pi(\theta) \geq \alpha \text{ for all } \theta \in \Theta_1.$$

The one-sided test is biased (against all alternatives) because when $\mu < 0$ the power is zero. The above two-sided normal test is UMP unbiased. Alternatively, one can eliminate some tests by requiring invariance under a group of transformations.

5. Although we may only be able to obtain optimal tests in limited circumstances using the Neyman–Pearson theory, we can use the theory to define the **power envelope**, that is, compute the optimal power that could be achieved against a specific point alternative, and then change the alternative value and again compute the optimal power under Neyman–Pearson rules. The curve that traces out the optimal power as a function of the alternative values is the power envelope. This gives a benchmark against which to compare tests that are designed against the composite alternative.

12.4.2 Consistency of Tests and Local Power

In many cases it is hard if not impossible to derive the exact distribution of a test statistic under the null hypothesis, instead we may work with large sample approximation. In this case, we try to achieve **asymptotic size** control by working with a limiting distribution. We next consider how a test performs under the alternative hypothesis when the sample size is large.

Definition 12.3. A test with power function $\pi_n(\theta)$ is consistent if $\lim_{n \to \infty} \pi_n(\theta) = 1$ for all $\theta \in \Theta_1$.

This is a desirable property. Many tests that we have considered are consistent under some conditions, including the general class of Likelihood Ratio tests.

Example 12.17. Suppose that $X \sim N(\mu, 1)$ and $H_0 : \mu = \mu_0$ versus $H_1 : \mu > \mu_0$. We have for all $\mu > \mu_0$ that $\sqrt{n}(\mu - \mu_0) \to \infty$ and so for $T = \sqrt{n}\left(\overline{X} - \mu_0\right)$

$$
\begin{aligned}
\pi_n(\mu) &= \Pr\left(T \geq z_\alpha \,|\, \mu\right) \\
&= 1 - \Phi(z_\alpha - \sqrt{n}(\mu - \mu_0)) \\
&\to 1.
\end{aligned}
$$

This test is consistent against all alternatives $\mu > \mu_0$.

Consistency says that for fixed alternatives, the power goes to one (the Type II error probability goes to zero). This property can be established for many tests based on consistent estimators, so it is a minimal requirement for a good testing procedure. How do we discriminate between tests that are consistent?

The approach we consider here is to consider alternatives that are close to the null hypothesis. Suppose that the true parameter θ is actually a function of sample size so that

$$
\theta_n = \theta_0 + \delta_n(c), \tag{12.9}
$$

where $\delta_n(c) \to 0$ as $n \to \infty$ and $c \in C$. If $\delta_n(c) = c/\sqrt{n}$ for $c \in \mathbb{R}_+$, we have the so-called **Pitman alternatives**, and we typically obtain

$$
\pi_n(\theta_n) \to \pi_L(c; \alpha) \in [\alpha, 1].
$$

That is, we may show (for a large class of testing problems) that under a sequence of local alternatives, the power function converges to a function bounded between the size and one, so that the test has some power against these alternatives. We hope that $\pi_L(c; \alpha) \geq \alpha$ for all $c \neq 0$ because otherwise the test is not able to detect departures from the null hypothesis at this scale. The function $\pi_L(c; \alpha)$ is called the **local power function**. There is an elaborate theory of optimal large sample testing that compares tests according to their power against Pitman alternatives.

Definition 12.4. Suppose that test statistic T has local power function $\pi_L(c; \alpha)$ and test statistic T^* has local power function $\pi_L^*(c; \alpha)$. The test T is more powerful than T^* if

$$
\pi_L(c; \alpha) \geq \pi_L^*(c; \alpha) \tag{12.10}
$$

for all c in the (local) alternative set C.

It turns out that in many cases Likelihood Ratio tests cannot be beaten over all local alternatives according to this criterion, i.e., they are essentially asymptotically optimal. Generally speaking, efficient estimators produce efficient tests.

Example 12.18. Suppose that $X \sim N(\mu, 1)$ and $H_0 : \mu = \mu_0$ versus $H_1 : \mu > \mu_0$. We compare the two statistics

$$T = \sqrt{n}(\widehat{\mu} - \mu_0), \quad \widehat{\mu} = \frac{1}{n} \sum_{i=1}^{n} X_i.$$

$$T_E = \frac{\sqrt{n}(\widehat{\mu}_E - \mu_0)}{\sqrt{2}}, \quad \widehat{\mu}_E = \frac{2}{n} \sum_{i=1}^{n/2} X_{2i}.$$

Both T and T_E are consistent against all fixed alternatives. The local power function of T and T_E are respectively

$$\pi_L(c; \alpha) = 1 - \Phi(z_\alpha - c) \quad ; \quad \pi_L^E(c; \alpha) = 1 - \Phi\left(z_\alpha - \frac{c}{\sqrt{2}}\right),$$

and clearly $\pi_L(c; \alpha) \geq \pi_L^E(c; \alpha)$ for all $c, \alpha > 0$.

Example 12.19. The Binomial case. Suppose that

$$p_n = p_0 + \frac{c}{\sqrt{n}}$$

Then writing $\widehat{p} - p_0 = \widehat{p} - p_n + p_n - p_0$ we obtain (by the triangular array CLT)

$$\sqrt{n}(\widehat{p} - p_0) \xrightarrow{D} N(c, p_0(1 - p_0)),$$

from which it follows that the Likelihood tests all converge in distribution to the same random variable $Z(\delta)^2$, where $Z(\delta) \sim N(\delta, 1)$ and $\delta = c/\sqrt{p_0(1 - p_0)}$. This is called a non-central chi-squared distribution.

Example 12.20. Zodiac. Suppose that for $j = 1, 2, \ldots, 12$

$$\mu_{nj} = \mu_0 + \frac{c_j}{\sqrt{n}}.$$

Then writing $\overline{X}_j - \mu_0 = \overline{X}_j - \mu_{nj} + \mu_{nj} - \mu_0$ we obtain that

$$\sqrt{n_j}\left(\frac{\overline{X}_j - \mu_{nj}}{\sigma_0}\right) \xrightarrow{D} Z_j(c_j/\sigma_0) \sim N(c_j, 1),$$

from which it follows that

$$\sum_{j=1}^{12} n_j \left(\frac{\overline{X}_j - \mu_0}{\sigma_0}\right)^2 \xrightarrow{D} \sum_{j=1}^{12} Z_j (c_j/\sigma_0)^2.$$

Note that the mean of the limiting distribution is $12 + \sum_{j=1}^{12} c_j^2/\sigma_0^2$ and provided $\sum_{j=1}^{12} c_j^2 \neq 0$ the local power will be greater than the size, that is, it suffices that only one of the $c_j \neq 0$.

If the alternatives are even further from the null hypothesis, i.e., $\sqrt{n}\delta_n(c) \to \infty$ as $n \to \infty$ (or equivalently $c = c_n \to \infty$), then many tests can achieve power approaching one, as for the case with a fixed alternative. On the other hand, if the alternatives are too close to the null hypothesis then as we have seen the power tends in the best case to α, that is,

$$\lim_{n \to \infty} \inf_{\theta \in \Theta_1} \pi_n(\theta) = \alpha. \tag{12.11}$$

Example 12.21. Suppose that $X \sim N(\mu, 1)$ and $H_0 : \mu = \mu_0$ versus $H_1 : \mu > \mu_0$. If we take the sequence $\mu_n = \mu_0 + n^{-1} \in H_1$, then

$$\pi(\mu_n) = 1 - \Phi(z_\alpha - (1/\sqrt{n})) \to 1 - \Phi(z_\alpha) = \alpha.$$

We can't generally make tests that are uniformly consistent except when the alternative is separated from the null as in the simple case of Neyman–Pearson. Another way of expressing this is to consider a sequence $\theta_m \to \theta_0$ as $m \to \infty$, we have

$$\alpha = \lim_{n \to \infty} \lim_{m \to \infty} \pi_n(\theta_m) \neq \lim_{m \to \infty} \lim_{n \to \infty} \pi_n(\theta_m) = 1.$$

We have predicated our arguments so far on the case where α is fixed, i.e., the Type I error stays bounded away from zero, and have shown that the Type II error goes to zero with large sample size. We next show that actually one can make both Type I and Type II error go to zero simultaneously. That is, we construct a test for which $\alpha_n(\theta) \to 0$ for all $\theta \in \Theta_0$ and $\beta_n(\theta) \to 0$ for all $\theta \in \Theta_1$.

Example 12.22. Suppose that $X \sim N(\mu, 1)$ and null hypothesis is $\mu = 0$ versus $\mu > 0$. Usually, we reject if $\sqrt{n}\overline{X} \geq z_\alpha$ for some fixed α, but now we allow $z_\alpha \to \infty$. We have rejection probability of $\Pr(Z \geq z_\alpha - \sqrt{n}\mu) \to 1$ if and only if $z_\alpha - \sqrt{n}\mu \to -\infty$, where $Z \sim N(0, 1)$. Therefore, provided $z_\alpha \to \infty$ such that $z_\alpha/\sqrt{n} \to 0$, the test will have zero Type I and Type II errors for fixed μ, asymptotically. There are many such values of z_α (and corresponding α) that satisfy this.

12.4.3   Nonparametric Testing

So far we have mostly focussed on the parametric case where a correctly specified model has been assumed. We now consider the nonparametric case where we do not specify the null or the alternative to be parametric.

Example 12.23. Suppose that X_i are i.i.d. with distribution F such that $E(X^2) < \infty$. We wish to test the hypothesis that $\mu(F) = E(X) = 0$ versus the alternative that $\mu(F) > 0$. The test statistic we consider is

$$T = \frac{\sqrt{n}\bar{X}}{s},$$

which converges to a standard normal under the null hypothesis. Therefore, we can obtain

$$\lim_{n \to \infty} \Pr(T \geq z_\alpha | H_0) = \alpha.$$

Furthermore, can show that

$$\Pr(T \geq z_\alpha) \to 1 \tag{12.12}$$

for any F such that $\mu(F) > 0$ and we may also derive the local power function for the test. Let $\mu_n = \mu + cn^{-1/2}$, then the local power function is

$$\pi_L(c; \alpha) = 1 - \Phi(z_\alpha - c/\sigma),$$

where $\sigma^2(F) = \text{var}(X)$.

We next consider an example of a **specification test**, where the null hypothesis is well defined but the alternative hypothesis is very general.

Example 12.24. Suppose that X_i are i.i.d. discrete random variables with some discrete distribution F_X such that $EX^4 < \infty$ with $\mu = E(X)$, $\sigma^2 = \text{var}(X)$. We wish to test whether X is Poisson distributed for some parameter $\lambda \in \mathbb{R}_+$. The alternative is that is not Poisson distributed. This is outside of the Likelihood framework because the alternative hypothesis here is any distribution excluding the Poisson. Both the null and the alternative are highly composite. A simple test can be based on comparison of the mean with the variance. Let

$$T = \frac{\sqrt{n}\left(\bar{X} - s^2\right)}{\sqrt{\hat{v}}}, \tag{12.13}$$

where $\widehat{v}$ is an estimate of the (asymptotic) variance v of $\sqrt{n}\left(\overline{X} - s^2\right)$. In fact

$$
\text{var}\left[\sqrt{n}\left(\overline{X} - s^2\right)\right] = \text{var}\left[\frac{1}{\sqrt{n}}\sum_{i=1}^{n}\left\{X_i - \left(X_i - \overline{X}\right)^2\right\}\right]
$$
$$
= n\text{var}\left(\overline{X}\right) + n\text{var}\left(s^2\right) - 2n\text{cov}\left(\overline{X}, s^2\right)
$$
$$
\longrightarrow \sigma^2 + \sigma^4\left(\kappa_4 + 2\right) - 2\kappa_3\sigma^3,
$$

where κ_3 and κ_4 are the skewness and kurtosis of X. The last line is an asymptotic approximation. If X were Poisson λ, then $\mu = \sigma^2 = \lambda$, $\kappa_3 = \lambda^{-1/2}$, and $\kappa_4 = \lambda^{-1}$, so that $v = \lambda + \lambda^2(2 + \lambda^{-1}) - 2\lambda^{3/2}\lambda^{-1/2} = 2\lambda^2$. We may consider several candidates for $\widehat{v}$

$$
\widehat{v}_1 = 2\overline{X}^2 \quad ; \quad \widehat{v}_2 = 2s^4 \quad ; \quad \widehat{v}_3 = \frac{1}{n}\sum_{i=1}^{n}\left\{X_i - \left(X_i - \overline{X}\right)^2\right\}^2,
$$

where the first two exploit knowledge of the null distribution whereas the last just exploits the i.i.d. property. For any value λ of the null hypothesis we have that $T \xrightarrow{D} N(0, 1)$. This follows from some arguments we already gave for the sample mean and variance, namely

$$
\frac{1}{\sqrt{n}}\sum_{i=1}^{n}\left\{X_i - \left(X_i - \overline{X}\right)^2\right\} = \frac{1}{\sqrt{n}}\sum_{i=1}^{n}\left\{X_i - \left(X_i - \mu\right)^2\right\} - \sqrt{n}\left(\overline{X} - \mu\right)^2,
$$

and applying the CLT to the standardized sum of $Z_i = X_i - (X_i - \mu)^2$. The power of this test only depends to first order on the difference between the mean and the variance of X. The test will have zero power against distributions that are not Poisson but for which $\mu = \sigma^2$, so it is not a consistent test if we do not restrict the class of alternatives further. We consider local power. Suppose that we have a sequence of distributions such that $EX^4 \leq C$ and

$$
\lim_{n\to\infty}\sqrt{n}(\mu - \sigma^2) = c.
$$

Then for the test defined in (12.13), we have

$$
T \xrightarrow{D} N(m, w)
$$
$$
m = \frac{c}{\sqrt{v_\infty}} \quad ; \quad w = \frac{v}{v_\infty}
$$

where $v_\infty = p \lim_{n\to\infty} \widehat{v}$. The derivation is left as an exercise. Note that

$$p \lim_{n\to\infty} \widehat{v}_1 = 2\mu^2 = p \lim_{n\to\infty} \widehat{v}_2 = 2\sigma^4$$
$$p \lim_{n\to\infty} \widehat{v}_3 = \sigma^2 + \sigma^4 (\kappa_4 + 2) - 2\kappa_3\sigma^3.$$

In the case where $\kappa_3 = \kappa_4 = 0$, we have $p \lim_{n\to\infty} \widehat{v}_3 = \sigma^2 + 2\sigma^4$, and in that case the local power function of $\widehat{v}_1, \widehat{v}_2$ dominates that of $\widehat{v}_3$. Note that if we consider a sequence of local alternatives where all moments converge to the corresponding Poisson ones, then the three normalizations yield the same local power function.

So far so good. The bad news is that in 1956, Bahadur and Savage proved that, in a nonparametric setting, it is impossible to construct a test about the value of the mean of a distribution that has size α and has power greater than α for even one distribution. Consider the example above where we test $\mu(F) = 0$ versus $\mu(F) > 0$. Let $\mathcal{F}_0 = \{F : \mu(F) = 0 \text{ and } \sigma^2(F) < \infty\}$ denote the set of distributions consistent with the null hypothesis. Correct size control here requires that we satisfy

$$\lim_{n\to\infty} \sup_{F\in\mathcal{F}_0} \Pr(T \geq z_\alpha) \leq \alpha. \tag{12.14}$$

This is easy to accomplish if one doesn't care about power – just use a random number generator for your test. However, if one wants to simultaneously achieve power $> \alpha$ and even (12.12) for the test, then, as Bahadur and Savage (1956) show, this is not possible. The issue is that $\mathcal{F}_0 = \{F : \mu(F) = 0 \text{ and } \sigma^2(F) < \infty\}$ is a very big set that contains many distributions for which the CLT provides a poor approximation; indeed, one can find sequences $\{F_m\}_{m=1}^\infty \subset \mathcal{F}_0$ such that the CLT breaks down either because $\sigma^2(F_m)$ gets too big or too small. Romano (2004) shows that the t-test achieves (12.14) and (12.12) when a restricted subset of $\mathcal{F}_0$ is considered. For example

$$\mathcal{F}_{C,\delta} = \{F : \mu(F) = 0, \ \sigma^2(F) < \infty, \text{ and } E\left(\left|\frac{X - \mu(F)}{\sigma(F)}\right|^{2+\delta}\right) \leq C\}$$

for $\delta > 0$ and $C < \infty$ is such a class. **Uniform size control** requires us to be very pessimistic about the type of distributions we might face, as if nature is playing against us. Even the class of distributions $\mathcal{F}_{C,\delta}$ is very big and contains distributions that we don't think are reasonable distributions for the data we have.

12.5 CRITICISMS OF THE STANDARD HYPOTHESIS TESTING APPROACH

We have taken the standard approach to hypothesis testing as given, but it is fair to say that it is one of the most controversial parts of the statistical canon.

1. It is very primitive decision-making. The outcome is only one of two things and doesn't take account of the potentially different losses associated with the outcomes.
2. There is an asymmetric way in which the null hypothesis is treated versus the alternative. In some cases, such as testing the Efficient Markets Hypothesis we may feel comfortable with not specifying clearly what the alternative is and paying special attention to the null hypothesis, whereas in other contexts such as comparing the efficacy of alternative policies we may find this straightjacket uncomfortable.
3. Failure to reject the null hypothesis does not mean that it is true or even close to true. It may be that the test does not have power against the particular true hypothesis.
4. The significance level α is arbitrary. Some argue that α should be made a function of sample size, because in practice as n gets large almost any hypothesis is rejected. In reality hypotheses are neighbourhoods not points. One can extend the usual theory to allow Θ_0 to be an interval around some point θ_0, although it may be hard apriori to specify which interval.
5. A related criticism is that in many contexts we care about the **economic significance** of the departure from the null hypothesis. If the income difference between two groups is £10 per year, even if it is statistically significant based on large samples, then it is not so important. On the other hand if the difference were £100000 per year, even if the difference were not statistically significant, we would be paying attention to it.
6. In practice asymptotic approximations are often used and it may not be possible to control the size of the test.

An approach that gives more information than the straight yes/no of a formal hypothesis test is to report the p-value. This scans through all the α and finds the marginal level for rejection.

Definition 12.5. Suppose that T is a given test statistic. Then define the (one-sided) p-value

$$p_{\text{obs}} = \Pr\left(T \geq T_{\text{obs}} | H_0\right).$$

In the two-sided case, we use the same definition with $T \mapsto |T|$ and $T_{\text{obs}} \mapsto |T_{\text{obs}}|$.

Low p_{obs} is evidence against the null hypothesis. More information is conveyed by this approach – the reader can decide on his or her own α and carry out the test. This just gives more information, but does not solve the conceptual issues around hypothesis testing. Apparently, p-values are widely abused and misused, Trafimow and Marks (2015). The American Statistical Association (2016) recently felt compelled to issue an edict on the matter in which they list six principles to guide empirical researchers:

1.   P-values can indicate how incompatible the data are with a specified statistical model.

2.   P-values do not measure the probability that the studied hypothesis is true, or the probability that the data were produced by random chance alone.

3.   Scientific conclusions and business or policy decisions should not be based only on whether a p-value passes a specific threshold.

4.   Proper inference requires full reporting and transparency

5.   A p-value, or statistical significance, does not measure the size of an effect or the importance of a result.

6.   By itself, a p-value does not provide a good measure of evidence regarding a model or hypothesis.

This seems like a good place to stop.

Chapter 13

Confidence Intervals and Sets

13.1 DEFINITIONS

Confidence sets are a way of summarizing information about the precision of an estimator $\hat{\theta}$ of a parameter θ. A confidence set $\mathcal{C}_\alpha(\mathcal{X}^n) \subseteq \Theta \subseteq \mathbb{R}^p$ is chosen such that

Exact $\Pr[\theta \in \mathcal{C}_\alpha(\mathcal{X}^n)] = 1 - \alpha$

Approximate $\lim_{n\to\infty} \Pr[\theta \in \mathcal{C}_\alpha(\mathcal{X}^n)] = 1 - \alpha.$

We say that the **coverage** of this set is $1 - \alpha$ (or approximate coverage), e.g., if $\alpha \sim 0.05$, the set has 95% coverage. Note that $\mathcal{C}_\alpha(\mathcal{X}^n)$ is a **random set**, designed to vary from sample to sample to achieve the stated coverage.

For a univariate parameter, $\mathcal{C}_\alpha(\mathcal{X}^n)$ will usually be an interval

$$[L(\mathcal{X}^n), U(\mathcal{X}^n)] \subset \Theta \subset \mathbb{R}.$$

The smaller the interval the more confidence we have in the estimate

Example 13.1. The opinion poll might say that of all voters 45% ± 3% would vote for President Trump. Here, 45% is an estimate derived from a sample of voters and 3% is the 'margin of error.' This says that if we were to draw a large number of similar samples and form the interval from them, then the true value (parameter) lies in these intervals with the stated probability, usually 95%. What is the probability that he wins the election?

A general method for constructing confidence intervals can be based on a statistic $T(\mathcal{X}^n, \theta)$ whose distribution is known exactly or approximately. We let

$$\mathcal{C}_\alpha(\mathcal{X}^n) = \{\theta : L \leq T(\mathcal{X}^n, \theta) \leq U\},$$

where

Exact $\Pr(L \leq T(\mathcal{X}^n, \theta) \leq U) = 1 - \alpha,$

Approximate $\lim_{n\to\infty} \Pr(L \leq T(\mathcal{X}^n, \theta) \leq U) = 1 - \alpha,$

and the probability is calculated under θ. The confidence interval is basically the set of non-rejectable null hypotheses about θ.

Probability, Statistics and Econometrics. http://dx.doi.org/10.1016/B978-0-12-810495-8.00015-4

Example 13.2. Suppose that $X \sim N(\mu, \sigma^2)$ with σ^2 known. Then

$$T = \frac{\overline{X} - \mu}{\sigma/\sqrt{n}} \sim N(0, 1).$$

It follows that a two-sided coverage $1 - \alpha$ confidence interval for μ is given by

$$\mathcal{C}_\alpha(\mathcal{X}^n) = \{\mu : -z_{\alpha/2} \le T \le z_{\alpha/2}\} = \left\{ \mu : -z_{\alpha/2} \le \frac{\overline{X} - \mu}{\sigma/\sqrt{n}} \le z_{\alpha/2} \right\}.$$

We may rewrite this interval as

$$\mathcal{C}_\alpha(\mathcal{X}^n) = \left[\bar{X} - \frac{\sigma z_{\alpha/2}}{\sqrt{n}}, \ \bar{X} + \frac{\sigma z_{\alpha/2}}{\sqrt{n}} \right] = \bar{X} \pm \frac{\sigma z_{\alpha/2}}{\sqrt{n}}.$$

The acceptance region of the test of the null hypothesis that $\mu = \mu_0$ (against two-sided alternative) using

$$T = \frac{\overline{X} - \mu_0}{\sigma/\sqrt{n}}$$

is $\left\{ T : -z_{\alpha/2} \le T \le z_{\alpha/2} \right\}$, which can be rewritten for $\overline{X}$ as

$$C_\alpha(\mu_0) = \left\{ x : x \in \left[\mu_0 - \frac{\sigma z_{\alpha/2}}{\sqrt{n}}, \mu_0 + \frac{\sigma z_{\alpha/2}}{\sqrt{n}} \right] \right\} = \mu_0 \pm \frac{\sigma z_{\alpha/2}}{\sqrt{n}}.$$

We accept the null hypothesis when $\overline{X} \in C_\alpha(\mu_0)$. We have for any $\mu_0 \in \mathcal{C}_\alpha(\mathcal{X}^n)$ that $\overline{X} \in C_\alpha(\mu_0)$.

A confidence interval is a region of parameter space determined by the data that contains the true parameter with given probability. An acceptance region is a region of the data (test statistic) determined by the null hypothesis that contains the test statistic with given probability.

Example 13.3. Suppose that $X \sim N(\mu, \sigma^2)$ with σ^2 unknown. Then, a two-sided coverage $1 - \alpha$ confidence interval for μ is given by

$$\mathcal{C}_\alpha(\mathcal{X}^n) = \left[\bar{X} - \frac{s_* t_{\alpha/2}(n-1)}{\sqrt{n}}, \ \bar{X} + \frac{s_* t_{\alpha/2}(n-1)}{\sqrt{n}} \right] = \bar{X} \pm \frac{s_* t_{\alpha/2}(n-1)}{\sqrt{n}}$$

The acceptance region for the test of $\mu = \mu_0$ is the set where $\overline{X}$ lies in

$$C_\alpha = \mu_0 \pm \frac{s_* t_{\alpha/2}(n-1)}{\sqrt{n}}$$

Example 13.4. A two-sided asymptotic coverage $1 - \alpha$ confidence interval for μ is given by

$$\mathcal{C}_\alpha(\mathcal{X}^n) = \left[\bar{X} - \frac{s z_{\alpha/2}}{\sqrt{n}}, \ \bar{X} + \frac{s z_{\alpha/2}}{\sqrt{n}} \right] = \bar{X} \pm \frac{s z_{\alpha/2}}{\sqrt{n}}.$$

Example 13.5. Suppose that $X \sim N(0, \sigma^2)$ with σ^2 unknown. We make use of the fact that in this case

$$\frac{ns^2}{\sigma^2} \sim \chi^2(n) \tag{13.1}$$

so that

$$\Pr\left(\chi^2_{\alpha/2}(n) < \frac{ns^2}{\sigma^2} < \chi^2_{1-\alpha/2}(n) \right) = 1 - \alpha.$$

Then, a two-sided coverage $1 - \alpha$ confidence interval for σ^2 is given by

$$\mathcal{C}_\alpha(\mathcal{X}^n) = \left[\frac{ns^2}{\chi^2_{1-\alpha/2}(n)}, \ \frac{ns^2}{\chi^2_{\alpha/2}(n)} \right].$$

This confidence interval is not symmetric because the chi-squared distribution is not symmetric. Note that with probability one $\mathcal{C}_\alpha(\mathcal{X}^n) \subset (0, \infty)$, i.e., it respects that fact that $\sigma^2 > 0$.

13.1.1 General Large Sample Setting

Suppose that

$$T_n = \sqrt{n}\left(\widehat{\theta} - \theta \right) \overset{D}{\longrightarrow} N(0, V(\theta, \phi)),$$

where $V(\theta, \phi)$ is a known unknown (i.e., a known function of the unknown parameters θ, ϕ). Then provided V is continuous in θ, ϕ and we have a consistent estimator $\widehat{\phi} \overset{P}{\longrightarrow} \phi$, we have

$$\frac{\sqrt{n}\left(\widehat{\theta} - \theta \right)}{\sqrt{V(\widehat{\theta}, \widehat{\phi})}} \overset{D}{\longrightarrow} N(0, 1).$$

Therefore, we may take the confidence interval

$$\mathcal{C}_\alpha(\mathcal{X}^n) = \widehat{\theta} \pm \frac{z_{\alpha/2}\sqrt{V(\widehat{\theta}, \widehat{\phi})}}{\sqrt{n}}.$$

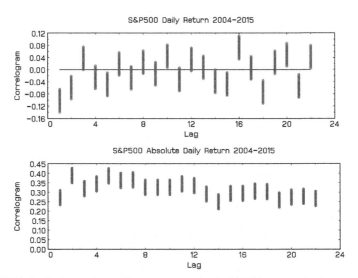

FIGURE 13.1 Confidence interval for correlogram of daily S&P500 return series

A good confidence interval shrinks with sample size, that is, as $n \to \infty$ we have $\mathcal{C}_\alpha(\mathcal{X}^n) \to \{\theta\}$ in some sense, because $\widehat{\theta} \to \theta$ and $V(\widehat{\theta}, \widehat{\phi})/n \to 0$.

Example 13.6. Suppose I want to predict future stock returns Y and I have a predictor, X. Suppose that $E(X) = E(Y) = 0$ and $E(XY) = \rho$. Furthermore, define $\text{var}(XY) = v = E(X^2 Y^2) - E^2(XY)$. Suppose that we observe a random sample $\{X_1, Y_1, \ldots, X_n, Y_n\}$. Let

$$\widehat{\rho} = \frac{1}{n} \sum_{i=1}^{n} X_i Y_i$$

The CLT says that

$$\sqrt{n}(\widehat{\rho} - \rho) = \frac{1}{\sqrt{n}} \sum_{i=1}^{n} (X_i Y_i - E(X_i Y_i)) \xrightarrow{D} N(0, v).$$

The confidence interval is

$$\widehat{\rho} \pm z_{\alpha/2} \sqrt{\frac{\widehat{v}}{n}} \quad ; \quad \widehat{v} = \frac{1}{n} \sum_{i=1}^{n} X_i^2 Y_i^2 - \left(\frac{1}{n} \sum_{i=1}^{n} X_i Y_i \right)^2.$$

$Y_i = r_i$ and $X_i = r_{i-j}$; and $Y_i = |r_i|$ and $X_i = |r_{i-j}|$. See Figs 13.1, 13.2 and 13.3.

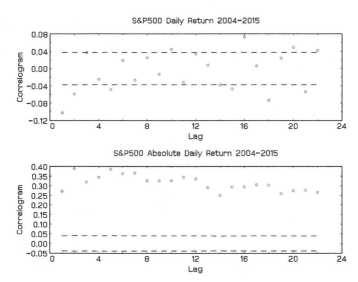

FIGURE 13.2   Correlogram of daily return series with Bartlett confidence bands

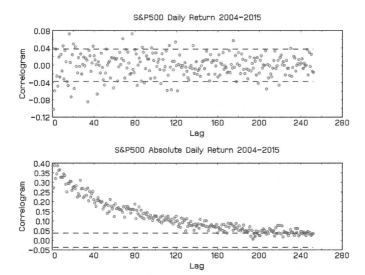

FIGURE 13.3   Correlogram and confidence bands for absolute value of daily return series

13.2   LIKELIHOOD RATIO CONFIDENCE INTERVAL

The likelihood ratio statistic for the simple null of $\theta = \theta_0$ is

$$\lambda(\mathcal{X}^n; \theta_0) = \frac{\max_{\theta \in \Theta} L(\theta|\mathcal{X}^n)}{L(\theta_0|\mathcal{X}^n)}.$$

An LRT is any test that accepts when $\lambda(\mathcal{X}^n; \theta_0) \leq c_\alpha$ for some determined c_α. An LR confidence interval is of the form

$$C_\alpha(\mathcal{X}^n) = \left\{ \theta_0 : \lambda(\mathcal{X}^n; \theta_0) \leq c_\alpha \right\}.$$

Example 13.7. $X \sim N(\mu, 1)$. $H_0 : \mu = \mu_0$ vs. $H_A : \mu \neq \mu_0$. In this case

$$\log \lambda(\mathcal{X}^n) = \frac{n}{2}(\bar{X} - \mu_0)^2$$

The distribution of $2 \log \lambda(\mathcal{X}^n)$ is $\chi^2(1)$. Therefore, we have

$$\left\{ \mu_0 : n(\bar{X} - \mu_0)^2 \leq \chi_\alpha^2(1) \right\} = \left\{ \mu_0 : -\sqrt{\frac{\chi_\alpha^2(1)}{n}} \leq \bar{X} - \mu_0 \leq +\sqrt{\frac{\chi_\alpha^2(1)}{n}} \right\}$$

$$= \left\{ \mu_0 : \bar{X} - \sqrt{\frac{\chi_\alpha^2(1)}{n}} \leq \mu_0 \leq \bar{X} + \sqrt{\frac{\chi_\alpha^2(1)}{n}} \right\}$$

$$= \left\{ \mu_0 : \bar{X} - \frac{z_{\alpha/2}}{\sqrt{n}} \leq \mu_0 \leq \bar{X} + \frac{z_{\alpha/2}}{\sqrt{n}} \right\}.$$

In general, the method is to obtain the critical value from the large sample distribution of LRT.

Example 13.8. Consider the Exponential distribution with $f(x|\theta) = \frac{1}{\theta} e^{-x/\theta}$, $0 \leq x < \infty$, $\theta > 0$. $H_0 : \theta = \theta_0$

$$\ell(\theta|\mathcal{X}_n) = -n \log \theta - \frac{1}{\theta} \sum_{i=1}^{n} X_i,$$

which implies that $\hat{\theta}_{MLE} = \frac{1}{n} \sum_{i=1}^{n} X_i$. Therefore,

$$\lambda = \exp(\ell_n(\theta_0) - \ell_n(\hat{\theta}_{MLE})) = \frac{\frac{1}{\theta_0^n} \exp(-\sum_{i=1}^{n} X_i/\theta_0)}{\frac{1}{(\sum_{i=1}^{n} X_i/n)^n} e^{-n}}$$

$$= \left(\frac{\sum_{i=1}^{n} X_i}{\theta_0} \right)^n e^n e^{-\sum_{i=1}^{n} X_i/\theta_0}$$

$$A(\theta_0) = \left\{ \mathcal{X}^n : \left(\frac{\sum_{i=1}^{n} X_i}{\theta_0} \right)^n e^{-\frac{\sum_{i=1}^{n} X_i}{\theta_0}} \geq c_\alpha \right\},$$

where c_α satisfied $\Pr(\mathcal{X}^n \in A(\theta_0)) = 1 - \alpha$. The confidence set is

$$C_\alpha(\mathcal{X}^n) = \left\{ \theta : \left(\frac{\sum_{i=1}^{n} X_i}{\theta} \right)^n e^{-\sum_{i=1}^{n} X_i/\theta} \geq c_\alpha \right\},$$

which is a nonlinear equation in θ. Note that this set is determined only by $\sum_{i=1}^{n} X_i$ and n. Therefore, we can express this set equivalently as

$$\mathcal{C}_\alpha(\mathcal{X}^n) = \{\theta : a_n \cdot \sum_{i=1}^{n} X_i \leq \theta \leq b_n \cdot \sum_{i=1}^{n} X_i\},$$

where a_n, b_n are chosen to satisfy coverage $1 - \alpha$. Note these are not the usual symmetric intervals we have in normal theory because the parameter space is restricted, and $X > 0$ and has a skewed distribution. However, in large samples the confidence interval is going to approach the usual interval $\overline{X} \pm z_{\alpha/2}\sigma/\sqrt{n}$ because of the asymptotic normality of $\sum_{i=1}^{n} X_i$ after standardization.

Example 13.9. Suppose that $X \sim U(0, \theta)$, and consider the hypothesis $\theta = \theta_0$. We have

$$\hat{\theta} = \max\{X_1, \ldots, X_n\}$$

$$L(\theta | \mathcal{X}^n) = \frac{1}{\theta^n} 1(\max_{1 \leq i \leq n} X_i \leq \theta)$$

$$\lambda(\mathcal{X}^n) = \left(\frac{\hat{\theta}}{\theta_0}\right)^n 1(\max_{1 \leq i \leq n} X_i \leq \theta_0).$$

If $\theta_0 < \max_{1 \leq i \leq n} X_i$ you clearly reject, but under the null this never happens. Reject if $\lambda(\mathcal{X}^n) \leq c_\alpha$. The confidence interval is

$$\mathcal{C}_\alpha(\mathcal{X}^n) = \left\{\theta_0 : \left(\frac{\hat{\theta}}{\theta_0}\right)^n 1(\max_{1 \leq i \leq n} X_i \leq \theta_0) \geq c_\alpha\right\}$$

It is going to be of the form (c_α is going to be less than 1)

$$\left[\hat{\theta}, \frac{\hat{\theta}}{c_\alpha^{1/n}}\right].$$

In this case, $\hat{\theta}$ is not asymptotically normal; in fact it converges at rate n to an extreme value distribution. The confidence set is naturally one-sided. The asymptotic interval can be obtained from the limiting distribution of $\hat{\theta}$, which is extreme value.

Example 13.10. Suppose that $X \sim Be(p)$ want an interval for the binary proportion p. Recall that

$$\Pr\left(\sum_{i=1}^{n} X_i \leq k\right) = \sum_{j=0}^{k} \binom{n}{j} p^j (1 - p)^{n-j}$$

Therefore, an exact interval $[p_L, p_U]$ could be obtained by solving the two equations

$$\sum_{j=0}^{\sum_{i=1}^{n} X_i} \binom{n}{j} p_U^j (1 - p_U)^{n-j} = 1 - \frac{\alpha}{2}$$

$$\sum_{j=0}^{\sum_{i=1}^{n} X_i} \binom{n}{j} p_L^j (1 - p_L)^{n-j} = \frac{\alpha}{2}.$$

This can only be solved for certain values of α, depending on n. Blyth (1986) showed that for those α

$$\frac{1}{1 + \frac{n-x+1}{x} F_{\alpha/2}(2(n-x+1), 2x)} \leq p \leq \frac{\frac{x+1}{n-x} F_{\alpha/2}(2(x+1), 2(n-x))}{1 + \frac{n-x+1}{x} F_{\alpha/2}(2(x+1), 2(n-x))}$$

forms an exact interval.

Example 13.11. We next consider large sample confidence intervals. Try the (Wald) test statistic for $H_0 : p = p_0$, $H_A : p \neq p_0$

$$T = \frac{\sqrt{n}(\widehat{p} - p_0)}{\sqrt{\widehat{p}(1 - \widehat{p})}} \quad ; \quad \widehat{p} = \frac{1}{n} \sum_{i=1}^{n} X_i = \frac{k}{n}.$$

We know that under H_0

$$T \xrightarrow{D} N(0, 1).$$

It follows that a two-sided coverage $1 - \alpha$ confidence interval for p is given by

$$\mathcal{C}_\alpha(\mathcal{X}^n) = \{p : -z_{\alpha/2} \leq T \leq z_{\alpha/2}\},$$

which can be rewritten as

$$\widehat{p} \pm \frac{\sqrt{\widehat{p}(1 - \widehat{p})}}{\sqrt{n}} z_{\alpha/2}.$$

Take $n = 60$, $\alpha = 0.05$, $\widehat{p} \pm 0.253\sqrt{\widehat{p}(1 - \widehat{p})}$.

This is fine except when either $\widehat{p} = 0$ or $\widehat{p} = 1$, which can happen when the sample size is small and p_0 is close to 0 or 1.

Consider an alternative (LM) test statistic

$$T^* = \frac{\sqrt{n}(\widehat{p} - p_0)}{\sqrt{p_0(1 - p_0)}}, \tag{13.2}$$

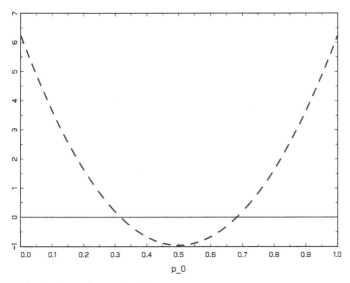

FIGURE 13.4   Confidence interval for binary parameter

which is also asymptotically standard normal under the null hypothesis. The corresponding confidence interval is

$$C_\alpha(\mathcal{X}^n) = \left\{ p_0 : -z_{\alpha/2} \le T^* \le z_{\alpha/2} \right\}. \tag{13.3}$$

What is this set? We have

$$\left\{ p_0 : \frac{n(\widehat{p} - p_0)^2}{p_0(1 - p_0)} \le z_{\alpha/2}^2 \right\}$$
$$= \left\{ p_0 : n(\widehat{p} - p_0)^2 \le z_{\alpha/2}^2 p_0(1 - p_0) \right\}$$
$$= \left\{ p_0 : n\widehat{p}^2 - 2n\widehat{p}p_0 + np_0^2 - z_{\alpha/2}^2 p_0 + z_{\alpha/2}^2 p_0^2 \le 0 \right\}$$
$$= \left\{ p_0 : (n + z_{\alpha/2}^2) p_0^2 - (2n\widehat{p} + z_{\alpha/2}^2) p_0 + n\widehat{p}^2 \le 0 \right\}.$$

The set consists of all points between the two roots of the quadratic equation, i.e.

$$\frac{(2n\widehat{p} + z_{\alpha/2}^2) \pm \sqrt{(2n\widehat{p} + z_{\alpha/2}^2)^2 - 4(n + z_{\alpha/2}^2)n\widehat{p}^2}}{2(n + z_{\alpha/2}^2)}.$$

We show in Fig. 13.4 the case $n = 25$, $\widehat{p} = 0.5$.

This works also when $\widehat{p} \in \{0, 1\}$. For example, suppose that $\widehat{p} = 0$. Then

$$
C_\alpha(\mathcal{X}^n) = \left\{ p_0 : p_0 \leq \frac{z_{\alpha/2}^2}{n + z_{\alpha/2}^2} \right\}.
$$

For $\alpha = 0.05$ and $n = 10$, we get $[0, 0.28]$. For $n = 100$, we get $[0, 0.037]$.

13.2.1 A Bayesian Interval

We consider how to construct a Bayesian confidence interval. We will work with the specific Binomial case for simplicity. Suppose that one observes k values of $X = 1$ and $n - k$ values of $X = 0$, and suppose that the prior distribution on p, $\pi(p)$, is uniform over $[0, 1]$. In this case, we have seen that the posterior density of p is

$$
\pi(p|\mathcal{X}^n) = \frac{(n+1)!}{k!\,(n-k)!} p^k (1-p)^{n-k}.
$$

In fact, this is the distribution of a $Beta(k+1, n-k+1)$ random variable.

A Bayesian interval $[L, U]$ satisfies

$$
\int_L^U \pi(p|\mathcal{X}^n)dp = 1 - \alpha.
$$

In general there are many solutions to this equation. The simplest approach is to take equal tail probabilities, that is, $\int_0^L \pi(p|\mathcal{X}^n)dp = \int_U^1 \pi(p|\mathcal{X}^n)dp = \alpha/2$. An alternative approach is called Highest Posterior Density (HPD), which selects L, U subject to the criterion that $\pi(p|\mathcal{X}^n) \geq c$ for some constant c (to be determined). That is, we find L, U such that $\pi(p|\mathcal{X}^n)$ is maximized. May find simulation methods convenient to calculate the integral.

Consider the special case that $k = 0$ so that $\widehat{p} = 0$, in which case we have to solve

$$
(n+1)\int_0^U (1-p)^n dp = 1 - \alpha = \left(1 - (1-U)^{n+1}\right).
$$

Therefore, $U = 1 - \alpha^{1/(n+1)}$. When taking the significance level $\alpha = 0.05$ and $n = 10$, one obtains $U = 0.238$, which means that with 95% confidence we may assert that the random set $[0, 0.238]$ contains p. When $n = 100$ we obtain $[0, 0.029]$.

Example 13.12. Suppose that the population probability in favour of Remain is $p \in [0, 1]$ and we sample $n = 100$ individuals and find that $k = 55$ of them are in favour of Remain. What is the probability that $p > 1/2$? We suppose again the ignorance prior, whence

$$\frac{101!}{55!45!} \int_{0.5}^{1} p^{55}(1-p)^{45} dp = 0.840\,14.$$

13.3 METHODS OF EVALUATING INTERVALS

1. Intrinsic beauty of $\mathcal{C}_\alpha(\mathcal{X}^n)$, or rather convenience and plausibility. One might prefer intervals and connected sets in general to sets with holes in. One might also wish that the confidence interval respects the parameter space, such as in the case of a variance parameter.

2. We generally want as small a confidence set as possible as this is most revealing. Formally, since the set is random, we consider the expected length (or volume) of $\mathcal{C}_\alpha(\mathcal{X}^n)$. The interval for the normal mean

$$\bar{X} \pm \frac{s_*}{\sqrt{n}} t_{\alpha/2}$$

has length $\frac{2s_*}{\sqrt{n}} z_{\alpha/2}$, and expected squared length $\frac{4\sigma^2}{n} t_{\alpha/2}^2$. Any other interval has longer length, which we next show. Consider the interval

$$\mathcal{C}_\alpha(\mathcal{X}^n) = \left[\bar{X} - \frac{s_* t_{\alpha_1}(n-1)}{\sqrt{n}}, \ \bar{X} + \frac{s_* t_{\alpha_2}(n-1)}{\sqrt{n}} \right],$$

where $\alpha_1 + \alpha_2 = \alpha$. Let $\alpha_2 = \theta$ and then $\alpha_1 = \alpha - \theta$, so we consider minimizing the length of the interval which is equivalent to

$$\min_{\theta \in [0,\alpha]} Q(\theta) = \min_{\theta \in [0,\alpha]} F^{-1}(1-\theta) - F^{-1}(\alpha - \theta), \qquad (13.4)$$

where F is the c.d.f. of the t-distribution, which is symmetric about zero. The first order condition is

$$Q'(\theta) = \frac{-1}{f(F^{-1}(1-\theta))} + \frac{1}{f(F^{-1}(\alpha - \theta))} = 0,$$

where f is the density. When $\theta = \alpha/2$, $F^{-1}(1-\alpha/2) = F^{-1}(\alpha/2)$ by symmetry. Therefore, the result follows (check the second order condition!).

3. A Uniformly Most Accurate (UMA) confidence interval minimizes the probability of **False Coverage**

$$\Pr\left(\theta' \in \mathcal{C}_\alpha(\mathcal{X}^n) | \theta \right)$$

uniformly over $\theta' \in \Theta$ with $\theta' \neq \theta$. This is perhaps a more sensible notion of the length of the interval than the Lebesgue measure discussed above. This corresponds to the notion in testing theory of UMP tests. Such an interval is only available in the same special cases [i.e., one sided intervals].

4. One can restrict the optimality criterion by requiring that the confidence interval be unbiased, i.e.,

$$\Pr(\theta' \in \mathcal{C}_\alpha(\mathcal{X}^n)|\theta) \leq 1 - \alpha \quad \text{for all } \theta' \neq \theta.$$

We then have a theory of UMAU intervals which applies to two sided intervals. This parallels the theory of similar tests.

Chapter 14

Asymptotic Tests and the Bootstrap

14.1 SIMULATION METHODS

Suppose that X_i is i.i.d. from some distribution say $F(.|\theta)$ and want to calculate the distribution of some statistic $T(\mathcal{X}^n, \theta)$, which is complicated. That is, we seek

$$H_n(x; \theta) = \Pr\left[T(\mathcal{X}^n, \theta) \le x\right].$$

And suppose that n is small, say $n = 2$, so we can't rely on large samples. What do we do?

Suppose that θ is known. Then

1. Generate a sample of data $\mathcal{X}^{n*} = \{X_1^*, \ldots, X_n^*\}$ from $F(.|\theta)$
2. Compute $T(\mathcal{X}^{n*}, \theta)$
3. Repeat S times and let T_s^* denote the value of $T(\mathcal{X}^{n*}, \theta)$ for the sth sample
4. Calculate the (empirical) distribution of $\{T_1^*, \ldots, T_S^*\}$ and use this distribution in place of $H_n(x; \theta)$, i.e.,

$$\widehat{H}(x; \theta) = \widehat{H}_S(x; \theta) = \frac{1}{S}\sum_{s=1}^{S} 1\left(T_s^* \le x\right).$$

By the LLN as $S \to \infty$ we have

$$\widehat{H}_S(x; \theta) \xrightarrow{P} H_n(x; \theta)$$

for every n and every x.

For example, suppose that X_i are i.i.d. $N(0, 1)$ and $T(\mathcal{X}^n, \theta) = \frac{1}{n}\sum_{i=1}^{n}\cos(X_i)$ with $n = 2$. The distribution of T is hard to obtain analytically, but very easy to describe by simulation methods. See Fig. 14.1.

Now suppose that we don't know θ, how do we proceed.

1. Estimate θ from the data by $\widehat{\theta}$
2. Generate a sample of data $\mathcal{X}^{n*} = \{X_1^*, \ldots, X_n^*\}$ from $F(.|\widehat{\theta})$
3. Compute $T(\mathcal{X}^{n*}, \widehat{\theta})$
4. Repeat S times and let T_s^* denote the value of $T(\mathcal{X}^{n*}, \widehat{\theta})$ for the sth sample

Probability, Statistics and Econometrics. http://dx.doi.org/10.1016/B978-0-12-810495-8.00016-6

211

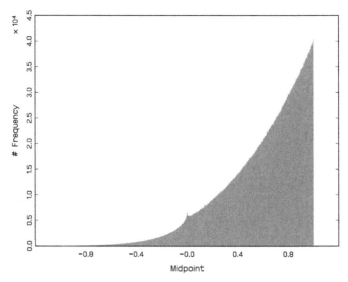

FIGURE 14.1   Results of simulation

5. Calculate the (empirical) distribution of $\{T_1^*, \ldots, T_S^*\}$ and use this distribution

Does it work? Under general conditions we expect that

$$\sup_{x \in \mathbb{R}} \left| F(x|\widehat{\theta}) - F(x|\theta_0) \right| \overset{P}{\longrightarrow} 0,$$

see below, and so we expect that the estimated distribution is close to the true one.

For example X_i are i.i.d. $N(\mu, 1)$ (with $\mu = 0$) but we estimate μ by $\overline{X}$.

14.2   BOOTSTRAP

We next consider a more general setting where that $X_1, \ldots, X_n$ are i.i.d. with distribution function F that is unknown. We have a statistic $T(\theta; \mathcal{X}^n)$, which is a function of the data $X_1, \ldots, X_n$ and a parameter value θ that is estimated by $\widehat{\theta}(\mathcal{X}^n)$. As before we seek

$$H_n(x; \theta) = \Pr\left[T(\mathcal{X}^n, \theta) \le x \right],$$

but now we can't simulate from the distribution F or can we?

The Bootstrap principle is to treat the empirical distribution F_n as the population and then to sample from the new population, which we know. This is called **The Russian Doll Principle**, and like the actual dolls, it can be iterated many times, although we only consider the basic method.

The **Bootstrap** is a very popular method for obtaining confidence intervals or performing hypothesis tests. It is related to the **Jacknife** and to **Permutation** tests, which historically precede it. There can be computational reasons why this method is preferred to the usual approach based on estimating the unknown quantities of the asymptotic distribution. There can also be statistical reasons why the bootstrap is better than the asymptotic plug-in approach. The bootstrap has been shown to work in a large variety of situations; we are just going to look at the simplest i.i.d. cases.

Bootstrap Algorithm

1. Generate a sample of data $\mathcal{X}^{n*} = \{X_1^*, \ldots, X_n^*\}$ from the empirical distribution F_n, that is, drawn with replacement from $\{X_1, \ldots, X_n\}$
2. Compute $T(\mathcal{X}^{n*}, \widehat{\theta})$, where $\widehat{\theta}$ is the sample estimate
3. Repeat S times and let T_s^* denote the value of $T(\mathcal{X}^{n*}, \widehat{\theta})$ for the sth sample
4. Calculate the (empirical) distribution of $\{T_1^*, \ldots, T_S^*\}$ and use this distribution in place of $H_n(x; \theta)$, i.e.,

$$\widehat{H}_B(x; \widehat{\theta}) = \frac{1}{S} \sum_{s=1}^{S} 1\left(T_s^* \leq x\right). \tag{14.1}$$

For example a critical value can be calculated as quantiles of this distribution e.g., $\widehat{H}_B^{-1}(\alpha; \widehat{\theta})$. Does it work? We first consider how this works for a small sample where it is possible to write out all the outcomes.

Example 14.1. Suppose that $n = 2$ and the sample is X_1, X_2. Then the bootstrap samples of size $n = 2$ are

$$\{\{X_1, X_1\}, \{X_2, X_2\}, \{X_1, X_2\}, \{X_2, X_1\}\},$$

each of which are equally likely with probability $1/4$. The bootstrap distribution of

$$T_s^* = \frac{1}{2}\left(\cos(X_1^*) + \cos(X_2^*)\right) = \begin{cases} \frac{1}{2}\left(\cos(X_1) + \cos(X_1)\right) & \text{prob } \frac{1}{4} \\ \frac{1}{2}\left(\cos(X_1) + \cos(X_2)\right) & \text{prob } \frac{1}{2} \\ \frac{1}{2}\left(\cos(X_2) + \cos(X_2)\right) & \text{prob } \frac{1}{4}. \end{cases}$$

In this case not enough n to make a good approximation.

However, when the sample size n increases, this discreteness issue disappears. Consider now the case where $n = 10$. The distribution of T is shown in Fig. 14.2, it is quite smooth and almost bell-shaped.

The distribution of T^* is shown in Fig. 14.3.

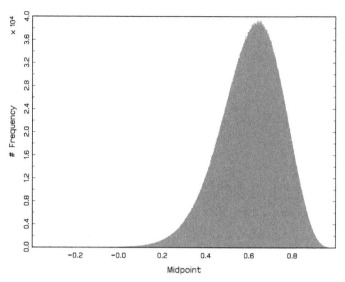

FIGURE 14.2   Distribution of statistic

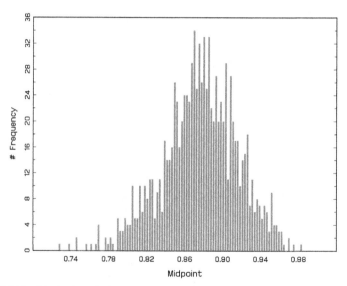

FIGURE 14.3   Distribution of T^*

It is better but no cigar: the shape is about right, but the mean and variance seem off, i.e., they don't match those of T. So what is wrong? We next give some analysis.

Suppose that X_i are i.i.d. with distribution F and take $T = \overline{X}$ to be the statistic of interest. We calculate the first two (conditional moments) of

$$T_s^* = \overline{X}^*.$$

First notice that X_i^* are drawn independently from

$$X^* = \begin{cases} X_1 & \text{prob } \frac{1}{n} \\ \vdots \\ X_n & \text{prob } \frac{1}{n}. \end{cases}$$

Conditioning on the sample, this is just a generalized multinomial distribution whose mean and variance are easy to obtain. In particular

$$E\left(X^* | \mathcal{X}^n\right) = \overline{X}$$

$$\text{var}\left(X^* | \mathcal{X}^n\right) = \frac{1}{n} \sum_{i=1}^{n} \left(X_i - \overline{X}\right)^2$$

$$\kappa_3\left(X^* | \mathcal{X}^n\right) = \frac{1}{n} \sum_{i=1}^{n} \left(X_i - \overline{X}\right)^3$$

etc.

It follows that:

$$E\left(\bar{X}^* | \mathcal{X}^n\right) = \frac{1}{n} \sum_{i=1}^{n} E\left(X_i^* | \mathcal{X}^n\right)$$

$$= E\left(X_i^* | \mathcal{X}^n\right) = \overline{X},$$

$$\text{var}\left(\bar{X}^* | \mathcal{X}^n\right) = \frac{1}{n^2} \sum_{i=1}^{n} \text{var}\left(X_i^* | \mathcal{X}^n\right)$$

$$= \frac{1}{n} \text{var}\left(X_i^* | \mathcal{X}^n\right)$$

$$= \frac{1}{n^2} \sum_{i=1}^{n} \left(X_i - \overline{X}\right)^2 = \frac{1}{n} s^2.$$

This says that the random variable

$$T^* = \sqrt{n}\left(\bar{X}^* - \overline{X}\right)$$

has conditional mean zero and conditional variance given by the sample variance of the original data. When n is large, s^2 converges to the population variance

σ^2, and we furthermore can show that T_n^* is asymptotically normal (conditional on the sample it is a sum of i.i.d. random variables with mean zero and finite variance) and has the same distribution as

$$T = \sqrt{n}\left(\overline{X} - \mu\right) \overset{D}{\longrightarrow} N(0, \sigma^2)$$

i.e.,

$$T^* = \sqrt{n}\left(\bar{X}^* - \overline{X}\right) \overset{D}{\longrightarrow} N(0, \sigma^2).$$

Theorem 14.1. *(Bickel and Freedman, 1981) Suppose that $X_1, \ldots, X_n$ are i.i.d. with finite mean μ and positive variance σ^2. Then, along almost all sample sequences $\{X_1, \ldots, X_n\}$, as $n, m \to \infty$*

$$\Pr\left(T^* \le x \mid X_1, \ldots, X_n\right) \longrightarrow \Pr\left(U \le x\right),$$

where $U \sim N(0, \sigma^2)$.

Therefore, we can show that for large n that

$$T_n = \frac{1}{\sqrt{n}} \sum_{i=1}^{n} \{\cos(X_i) - E\left[\cos(X_i)\right]\}$$

$$T_n^* = \frac{1}{\sqrt{n}} \sum_{i=1}^{n} \{\cos(X_i^*) - \cos(X_i)\}$$

have the same distribution. We don't know $E\left[\cos(X_i)\right]$, so that we can't translate this theory back to our original example – this doesn't say that the distributions of

$$\frac{1}{n} \sum_{i=1}^{n} \cos(X_i) \text{ and } \frac{1}{n} \sum_{i=1}^{n} \cos(X_i^*)$$

are the same.

Instead let's work with $\sin(X_i)$, which we know to have mean zero. The theory predicts that the following have the same distribution

$$T_n = \frac{1}{\sqrt{n}} \sum_{i=1}^{n} \sin(X_i)$$

$$T_n^* = \frac{1}{\sqrt{n}} \sum_{i=1}^{n} \{\sin(X_i^*) - \sin(X_i)\}.$$

In fact, the approximation is quite good. See Fig. 14.4.

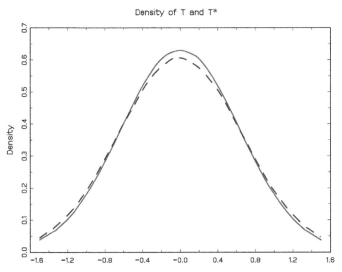

FIGURE 14.4   Comparison of density of T and T^*

General principle of bootstrap. *It needs to be applied to a statistic that is asymptotically normal. If so, then gives good approximation when sample size is large.*

This idea can be used to obtain confidence intervals or to obtain critical values for tests. Recall that the asymptotic approach calculates the confidence interval as follows. For a one-sided interval of coverage $1 - \alpha$

$$\mathcal{C}_\alpha(\mathcal{X}^n) = \{t : T(\mathcal{X}^n; t) \le \widehat{H}_A^{-1}(1 - \alpha)\}.$$

This then ensures that $\Pr(\theta \in \mathcal{C}_\alpha(\mathcal{X}^n)) \to 1 - \alpha$. For the Bootstrap, we just replace the asymptotic critical value $\widehat{H}_A^{-1}(\alpha)$ by the bootstrap critical value $\widehat{H}_B^{-1}(\alpha; \widehat{\theta})$ obtained from the bootstrap samples of T^*, i.e.,

$$\mathcal{C}_\alpha^*(\mathcal{X}^n) = \{t : T(\mathcal{X}^n; t) \le \widehat{H}_B^{-1}(1 - \alpha; \widehat{\theta})\}.$$

Then also $\Pr(\theta \in \mathcal{C}_\alpha^*(\mathcal{X}^n)) \to 1 - \alpha$.

For a two-sided interval of coverage $1 - \alpha$

$$\mathcal{C}_\alpha(\mathcal{X}^n) = \{t : \widehat{H}_A^{-1}(\alpha/2) \le T(\mathcal{X}^n; t) \le \widehat{H}_A^{-1}(1 - \alpha/2)\}.$$

Usually, $\widehat{H}_A(\cdot)$ is symmetric about zero and $\widehat{H}_A^{-1}(\alpha/2) = -\widehat{H}_A^{-1}(1 - \alpha/2)$. For the Bootstrap, we take

$$\mathcal{C}_\alpha^*(\mathcal{X}^n) = \{t : \widehat{H}_B^{-1}(\alpha/2; \widehat{\theta}) \le T(\mathcal{X}^n; t) \le \widehat{H}_B^{-1}(1 - \alpha/2; \widehat{\theta})\}.$$

In this case, there is no reason to expect $\widehat{H}_B(\cdot; \widehat{\theta})$ to be exactly symmetric about zero and so one typically calculates the two separate critical values.

To carry out a test of the hypothesis that $\theta = \theta_0$: reject if $\theta_0 \notin C_\alpha^*(\mathcal{X}^n)$ or $C_\alpha(\mathcal{X}^n)$.

In some cases $H(x, F)$ does not depend on F, in which cases T is called a **pivot** or an **asymptotic pivot**.

Example 14.2. Suppose that X_i is i.i.d. with mean μ and variance σ^2. The usual t test statistic satisfies

$$T = \frac{\sqrt{n}(\bar{X} - \mu)}{s} \xrightarrow{D} N(0, 1).$$

In that case $\widehat{H}_A(x) = \Phi(x)$ is a known quantity and we can test the hypothesis that $\mu = \mu_0$ using the standard normal critical values which are defined as $z_\alpha = \Phi^{-1}(1 - \alpha)$. The bootstrap confidence interval can be based on $\widehat{H}_B^{-1}(\alpha; \widehat{\theta})$ from any of the following statistics:

$$T^* = \sqrt{n}(\bar{X}^* - \bar{X})$$

$$T^{**} = \frac{\sqrt{n}(\bar{X}^* - \bar{X})}{s}$$

$$T^{***} = \frac{\sqrt{n}(\bar{X}^* - \bar{X})}{s^*}.$$

The bootstrap can be a useful alternative to conduct inference in settings where the large sample theory is complicated or just tedious to carry out.

Example 14.3. Test of skewness. Suppose that X_i is i.i.d. with $EX_i^6 < \infty$ and consider the problem of testing whether $\kappa_3 = \theta$ versus the two sided alternative for some specific $\theta \in \mathbb{R}$. The sample skewness

$$\widehat{\kappa}_3 = \frac{\frac{1}{n}\sum_{i=1}^n (X_i - \overline{X})^3}{\left[\frac{1}{n}\sum_{i=1}^n (X_i - \overline{X})^2\right]^{3/2}}$$

can be shown to be asymptotically normal but the asymptotic variance is very complicated to write down. Let

$$T = \sqrt{n}(\widehat{\kappa}_3 - \theta) \quad ; \quad T^* = \sqrt{n}\left(\widehat{\kappa}_3^* - \widehat{\kappa}_3\right),$$

where

$$\widehat{\kappa}_3^* = \frac{\frac{1}{n}\sum_{i=1}^n (X_i^* - \overline{X}^*)^3}{\left[\frac{1}{n}\sum_{i=1}^n (X_i^* - \overline{X}^*)^2\right]^{3/2}}.$$

To approximate the distribution of T we use the distribution of T^*, which does not require any analytical effort.

To calculate the distribution $\widehat{H}_B$ in practice we use simulations. How to choose the number of simulations? In practice it is not necessary to take $S = \infty$. Take $\alpha(S + 1)$ to be an integer, so that the relevant quantiles of the bootstrap distribution are uniquely defined. For example take $S = 199$, which works for $\alpha = 0.01$ and $\alpha = 0.05$ etc.

14.2.1 Subsampling

Subsampling is an alternative resampling type idea that achieves similar objectives to the bootstrap. Let b be an integer with $1 < b < n$. Then let

$$\mathcal{X}_i^b = \{X_{i+1}, \dots, X_{i+b}\}.$$

This is a subsample of the original dataset of size b starting at i. There are $n - b + 1$ such subsamples: $\mathcal{X}_1^b, \dots, \mathcal{X}_{n-b+1}^b$. We may construct estimators and test statistics based on each subsample and then learn about their distribution by the cross subsample variation. For example, let

$$\overline{X}_{i,b} = \frac{1}{b} \sum_{j=1}^{b} X_{i+j}$$

for each $i = 1, \dots, n - b + 1$. We argue that we can estimate

$$G_n(t) = \Pr\left(\sqrt{n}\left(\overline{X} - \mu\right) \leq t\right)$$

by the empirical distribution of $\overline{X}_{i,b}$ across the samples $i = 1, \dots, n - b + 1$, that is

$$\widehat{G}_{n,b}(t) = \frac{1}{N - b + 1} \sum_{i=1}^{N-b+1} 1\left(\sqrt{b}\left(\overline{X}_{i,b} - \mu\right) \leq t\right).$$

By the CLT we know that as $b \to \infty$

$$\sqrt{b}\left(\overline{X}_{i,b} - \mu\right) \xrightarrow{D} N(0, \sigma^2),$$

so this idea seems plausible. In fact one can work with overlapping blocks or nonoverlapping blocks; generally, overlapping blocks are more efficient.

Chapter 15

Exercises and Complements

Exercise. Suppose that X has the Bernoulli distribution with parameter p_X. Furthermore, suppose that conditional on $X = 1$, Y is Bernoulli with parameter p_{Y1}, but that conditional on $X = 0$, Y is Bernoulli with parameter p_{Y0}.
(a). What is the marginal distribution of Y?
(b). What is the joint distribution of X, Y?
(c). Suppose you have a random sample $\{(X_1, Y_1), \ldots, (X_n, Y_n)\}$ from the joint distribution. Let

$$\widehat{p}_X = \frac{1}{n} \sum_{i=1}^n 1(X_i = 1) \text{ and } \widehat{p}_Y = \frac{1}{n} \sum_{i=1}^n 1(Y_i = 1).$$

What are the statistical properties of $\widehat{p}_X$ and $\widehat{p}_Y$?

Solution. We use the formula $f_{X,Y} = f_{Y|X} f_X$, so that

$$(X, Y) = \begin{cases} (1, 1) & \text{with prob } p_X p_{Y1} \\ (1, 0) & \text{with prob } p_X (1 - p_{Y1}) \\ (0, 1) & \text{with prob } (1 - p_X) p_{Y0} \\ (0, 0) & \text{with prob } (1 - p_X)(1 - p_{Y0}) \end{cases}$$

Marginal distribution of Y

$$Y = \begin{cases} 1 & \text{with prob } p_X p_{Y1} + (1 - p_X) p_{Y0} \\ 0 & \text{with prob } p_X (1 - p_{Y1}) + (1 - p_X)(1 - p_{Y0}) \end{cases}$$

The Likelihood function is just the p.m.f. function under the parameter values. Let n_i, $i = 1, 2, 3, 4$ denote the cell counts with $\sum_{i=1}^4 n_i = n$. Then

$$L = (p_X p_{Y1})^{n_1} (p_X (1 - p_{Y1}))^{n_2} ((1 - p_X) p_{Y0})^{n_3} ((1 - p_X)(1 - p_{Y0}))^{n_4}$$

$$\ell = n_1 \log (p_X p_{Y1}) + n_2 \log (p_X (1 - p_{Y1})) + n_3 \log ((1 - p_X) p_{Y0})$$

$$+ n_4 \log ((1 - p_X)(1 - p_{Y0})).$$

Probability, Statistics and Econometrics. http://dx.doi.org/10.1016/B978-0-12-810495-8.00017-8

Suppose you have a random sample $\{(X_1, Y_1), \ldots, (X_n, Y_n)\}$ from the joint distribution. Let

$$\widehat{p}_X = \frac{1}{n} \sum_{i=1}^{n} 1(X_i = 1) \quad ; \quad \widehat{p}_Y = \frac{1}{n} \sum_{i=1}^{n} 1(Y_i = 1).$$

They are both unbiased for p_X and $p_Y = p_X p_{Y1} + (1 - p_X) p_{Y0}$ respectively. Consistent and asymptotically normal as $n \to \infty$. Can't estimate p_{Y1}, p_{Y0} from just the marginal information. With

$$\widehat{p}_{11} = \frac{1}{n} \sum_{i=1}^{n} 1(X_i = 1, Y_i = 1) = \frac{n_1}{n}$$

we can just use

$$\widehat{p}_{Y1} = \frac{\widehat{p}_{11}}{\widehat{p}_X} \quad ; \quad \widehat{p}_{Y0} = \frac{\widehat{p}_Y - \widehat{p}_{11}}{1 - \widehat{p}_X}. \qquad \square$$

Exercise. The random variable X has the following distribution

$$X = \begin{cases} 0 & \text{with probability} \quad 1 - p \\ \theta & \text{with probability} \quad p \end{cases}$$

for some unknown θ with $0 < \theta < 1$ and some small known p. Suppose that observations $X_1, X_2, \ldots$ are to be drawn sequentially. Consider the following strategy for determining θ. Sample until the first occasion on which $X_n = \theta$. Thus n is a random variable $n \in \{1, 2, \ldots\}$. Calculate the distribution of the number of observations n and its expected value. In what sense is this method consistent?

Exercise. Suppose that X, Y are two random variables with

$$\text{cov}(X, Y) = \sigma_{XY}.$$

Suppose you have a random sample $\{(X_1, Y_1), \ldots, (X_n, Y_n)\}$ and let

$$\overline{X} = \frac{1}{n} \sum_{i=1}^{n} X_i \quad ; \quad \overline{Y} = \frac{1}{n} \sum_{i=1}^{n} Y_i$$

$$\widehat{\sigma}_{XY} = \frac{1}{n} \sum_{i=1}^{n} (X_i - \overline{X})(Y_i - \overline{Y}).$$

Show that $\widehat{\sigma}_{XY}$ is biased. Use (7.10) to show how to construct an unbiased estimator of σ_{XY}.

Exercise. Write down the likelihood function for the parameter θ based on the random sample $\{X_1, \ldots, X_n\}$ and describe the maximum likelihood estimator(s) $\widehat{\theta}$ of θ, when the population random variable X has the following distributions:

(a) A normal distribution $N[0, \theta^2]$;
(b) A uniform distribution $U[0, \exp(\theta)]$;
(c) A uniform distribution $U[\theta - 1, \theta + 1]$;
(d) A uniform distribution $U[\theta, 2\theta]$.

Exercise. Suppose that $X \sim N(\theta, \sigma^2 I_2)$, where I_2 is the 2×2 identity matrix and $X = (X_1, X_2)^\mathsf{T}$, while σ^2 and $\theta = (\theta_1, \theta_2)^\mathsf{T}$ are unknown parameters. We have samples $\{X_{11}, \ldots, X_{1n}\}$ and $\{X_{21}, \ldots, X_{2m}\}$, for large m and n. Let $\widehat{\theta}_1 = n^{-1} \sum_{i=1}^{n} X_{1i}, \widehat{\theta}_2 = m^{-1} \sum_{i=1}^{m} X_{2i}, \widehat{\sigma}_1^2 = (n-1)^{-1} \sum_{i=1}^{n} (X_{1i} - \widehat{\theta}_1)^2$, and $\widehat{\sigma}_2^2 = (m-1)^{-1} \sum_{i=1}^{m} (X_{2i} - \widehat{\theta}_2)^2$. You may assume that $m, n \to \infty$ such that $m/n \to \pi \in (0, \infty)$.

a). What are the asymptotic properties of $\widehat{\sigma}_1^2$ and $\widehat{\sigma}_2^2$ as $m, n \to \infty$, i.e., what are the probability limits and the asymptotic distributions?
b). Now consider the class of random variables $\widehat{\sigma}^2(\omega) = \omega \widehat{\sigma}_1^2 + (1 - \omega) \widehat{\sigma}_2^2$, where $\omega \in [0, 1]$. Show that $E(\widehat{\sigma}^2(\omega)) = \sigma^2$ for all ω.
c). Which member of this class has (asymptotically) the smallest variance.

Exercise. Suppose that $X \sim N(0, \sigma^2)$. Describe how to carry out a likelihood ratio test of:

(a) $H_0 : \sigma^2 = 1$ versus the alternative $H_A : \sigma^2 = 2$;
(b) $H_0 : \sigma^2 = 1$ versus the alternative $H_A : \sigma^2 > 1$;
(c) $H_0 : \sigma^2 = 1$ versus the alternative $H_A : \sigma^2 \neq 1$;
(d) Which of the above tests are UMP? Which of the above tests are unbiased?

Exercise. Suppose that $X_i \sim N(\mu, \sigma^2), i = 1, \ldots, n$. Consider the null hypothesis

$$H_0 : \mu = \sigma^2 = \theta. \qquad (15.1)$$

First of all, describe how to estimate the common parameter θ under the null hypothesis. You should write down the constrained likelihood function and explain how in practice you would find the estimator $\widehat{\theta}_{MLE}$. Next give the asymptotic distribution of $\widehat{\theta}_{MLE}$ under the null hypothesis. Next, describe the three methods [Wald, Lagrange Multiplier, and Likelihood Ratio] of obtaining tests of this null hypothesis against the two-sided alternative that $\mu \neq \sigma^2$. Finally, describe the corresponding confidence intervals.

Exercise. Suppose that $X_i \sim N(\theta, \theta), i = 1, \ldots, n$ as in question (2). Let $\widehat{\theta}_1 = \overline{X}$ and $\widehat{\theta}_2 = s^2$ be estimators of θ. Calculate the joint asymptotic distribution of the vector $(\widehat{\theta}_1, \widehat{\theta}_2)$. Consider the family of estimators

$$\widehat{\theta}(\alpha) = \alpha \widehat{\theta}_1 + (1 - \alpha) \widehat{\theta}_2,$$

and derive the asymptotic distribution of $\widehat{\theta}(\alpha)$ for each α. What is the optimal [according to asymptotic variance] choice of α? Suppose that $\widehat{\theta}_3$ is the maximum likelihood estimator developed in question 2 and let now

$$\widehat{\theta}(\alpha) = \alpha\widehat{\theta}_1 + \gamma\widehat{\theta}_2 + (1 - \alpha - \gamma)\widehat{\theta}_3.$$

What is the optimal choice of α, γ?

Solution. We have

$$\sqrt{n}\left(\widehat{\theta}(\alpha) - \theta\right) = \alpha\sqrt{n}\left(\overline{X} - \theta\right) + (1 - \alpha)\sqrt{n}\left(s^2 - \theta\right)$$

$$= \frac{1}{\sqrt{n}}\sum_{i=1}^{n}\alpha(X_i - \theta) + (1 - \alpha)\left[(X_i - \theta)^2 - \theta\right] + R_n,$$

where $R_n \xrightarrow{P} 0$. Let $Z_i(\alpha) = \alpha(X_i - \theta) + (1 - \alpha)\left[(X_i - \theta)^2 - \theta\right]$. Then $EZ_i(\alpha) = 0$ and

$$\text{var}(Z_i) = E\left[\left(\alpha(X_i - \theta) + (1 - \alpha)\left[(X_i - \theta)^2 - \theta\right]\right)^2\right]$$

$$= \alpha^2 E\left[(X_i - \theta)^2\right] + (1 - \alpha)^2 E\left[\left[(X_i - \theta)^2 - \theta\right]^2\right]$$

$$+ 2\alpha(1 - \alpha)E\left[(X_i - \theta)\left[(X_i - \theta)^2 - \theta\right]^2\right]$$

$$= \alpha^2 E\left[(X_i - \theta)^2\right] + (1 - \alpha)^2 E\left[\left[(X_i - \theta)^2 - \theta\right]^2\right]$$

$$= \alpha^2\theta + 2(1 - \alpha)^2\theta^2 = V(\alpha)$$

using the result for the sample variance of a normal distribution. Furthermore

$$\frac{1}{\sqrt{n}}\sum_{i=1}^{n}Z_i(\alpha) \xrightarrow{D} N(0, V(\alpha))$$

so that

$$\sqrt{n}\left(\widehat{\theta}(\alpha) - \theta\right) \xrightarrow{D} N(0, V(\alpha)).$$

Optimal choice of α minimizes $V(\alpha)$ with respect to α – the first order condition is

$$2\alpha\theta = 4(1 - \alpha)\theta^2$$

so that

$$\widehat{\alpha} = \frac{2\theta}{1 + 2\theta}. \qquad \square$$

Exercise. You have captured k enemy tanks from a population of unknown size N, and you observe the "serial number" of each tank. That is, the enemy tanks are $\{1, 2, \ldots, N\}$, where N is unknown, and you observe a sample $X_1, \ldots, X_k$ from this distribution. Given this data propose an unbiased estimate of the population size, i.e., how many of the blighters are there?

Solution. The outcomes are (i, j) with $i \neq j$, i.e., the sampling is without replacement. The maximum value seems like a good place to start $Y = \max(X_1, X_2)$. $Y = 2$ when $X_1 = 1$ and $X_2 = 2$ or $X_1 = 2$ and $X_2 = 1$, and each of these events occurs with probability $1/N(N - 1)$. In general Y takes values $2, 3, \ldots, N$ with

$$\Pr(Y = 2) = \frac{2}{N(N - 1)}$$

$$\Pr(Y = 3) = \frac{4}{N(N - 1)}$$

$$\vdots$$

$$\Pr(Y = N) = \frac{2(N - 1)}{N(N - 1)}.$$

Check these numbers add up to one. Then

$$E(Y) = \frac{2}{N(N - 1)} \sum_{i=1}^{N} i(i - 1) = \frac{2}{3} N + \frac{2}{3}.$$

Therefore, take

$$\widehat{N} = \frac{3}{2} Y - 1,$$

which is unbiased. □

Exercise. Suppose that $X_i, i = 1, 2, \ldots, n$ are i.i.d. Uniform $U(0, \theta)$. Show that the sample maximum

$$\hat{\theta} = \max_{1 \leq i \leq n} X_i$$

is consistent.

Exercise. Suppose I have one observation X from a Uniform on $[\theta_0, \theta_1]$. Suppose that $\theta_0 = 0$ and $\theta_1 = 1$. Is the parameter identified?

Solution. According to the above definition these parameter values are identified because for any $\theta \in (0, 1)$

$$\Pr\{L(\theta, \theta + 1 | X) \neq L(0, 1 | X)\} = \theta > 0.$$

That is, for any alternative parameter values with the same range there is a set of data that would reject those parameter values. If I take any $[a, b]$ for which $b - a \neq 1$, then

$$L(a, b|X) = \frac{1}{b - a} 1(X \in [a, b])$$

and same argument holds. Maybe you think the answer is unreasonable in this case. We have for any $\theta \in [0, X]$

$$L(0, 1|X) = 1(X \in [0, 1]) = 1(X \in [\theta, \theta + 1]) = L(\theta, \theta + 1|X).$$

Therefore, in sample there is a lack of identification. In this case, the issue is really "micronumerosity", since as the number of observations increases this issue is resolved. Specifically, we have for any $\theta \in (0, 1)$

$$
\begin{aligned}
p \lim_{n \to \infty} \frac{1}{n} \sum_{i=1}^{n} L(\theta, \theta + 1|\mathcal{X}^n) &= \int L(\theta, \theta + 1|X) f(X) dX \\
&= E\left[L(\theta, \theta + 1|X)\right] \\
&= E 1(X \in [\theta, \theta + 1]) \\
&= 1 - \theta \\
&\neq E\left[L(0, 1|X)\right] = 1. \qquad \square
\end{aligned}
$$

Exercise. A set of numbers is said to satisfy Benford's law if the leading digit D ($d \in \{1, \ldots, 9\}$) occurs with probability

$$P(d) = \log_{10}(d + 1) - \log_{10}(d)$$

Numerically, the leading digits have the following distribution in **Benford's law**, where d is the leading digit and $P(d)$ the probability. Show that

$$\Pr(D \leq d) = \log_{10}(d + 1).$$

Investigate whether some real dataset obeys this law.

Solution. Calculate $\widehat{P}(d)$, $d = 1, \ldots, 9$. Suppose i.i.d. sampling. We have

$$\sqrt{n}\left(\widehat{P}(d) - P(d)\right) \xrightarrow{D} N\left(0, P(d)(1 - P(d))\right)$$

and $\widehat{P}(d)$, $\widehat{P}(d')$ are asymptotically correlated so

$$\text{cov}\left(\sqrt{n}\widehat{P}(d), \sqrt{n}\widehat{P}(d')\right) = -P(d)P(d').$$

Could use t-statistics or Wald test. $\qquad \square$

Exercise. Suppose that $X_i \sim N(\mu_X, 1)$ and $Y_i \sim N(\mu_Y, 1), i = 1, \ldots, n$, where X_i and Y_i are mutually independent. Explain how to carry out a test of the hypothesis that $\mu_X = 0$. Now we want to test the hypothesis that $\mu_X = \mu_Y = 0$. Propose a method for testing this hypothesis based on t-statistics from the first part.

Solution. We have

$$\frac{\sqrt{n}\overline{X}}{s_X} \sim t(n-1)$$

$$\frac{\sqrt{n}\overline{Y}}{s_Y} \sim t(n-1).$$

For the joint hypothesis we may consider the square critical region $\pm t_{\theta/2}(n-1) \times \pm t_{\theta/2}(n-1)$. Then the rejection probability is $1 - (1-\theta)^2$. Take θ such that $1 - (1-\theta)^2 = \alpha$. Alternatively do an F-test. □

Exercise. According to the British Parachute Association, between 1996–2015 there were a total of 43 fatalities from skydiving out of a total of 5116806 jumps. Provide a confidence interval for the true risk of mortality from such an activity. You may use either Binomial distribution or Poisson distribution.

Exercise. Suppose that $X_1, \ldots, X_n$ are independent and identically distributed with mean μ and variance σ^2. The coefficient of variation may be defined as $cv = \sigma/\mu$. Propose a bootstrap method for approximating the distribution of

$$\sqrt{n}(\widehat{cv} - cv)$$

$$\widehat{cv} = \frac{s}{\overline{X}},$$

where $\overline{X} = \sum_{i=1}^n X_i/n$ and $s^2 = \sum_{i=1}^n (X_i - \overline{X})^2/n$. How can you obtain a confidence interval for the parameter cv?

Solution. Let $X_1^*, \ldots, X_n^*$ be drawn without replacement from the sample $X_1, \ldots, X_n$. Then compute

$$\overline{X}^* = \frac{1}{n}\sum_{i=1}^n X_i^*$$

$$s^* = \sqrt{\frac{1}{n}\sum_{i=1}^n \left(X_i^* - \overline{X}^*\right)}$$

$$\widehat{cv}^* = \frac{s^*}{\overline{X}^*}$$

Then we calculate the distribution of

$$T^* = \sqrt{n}(\widehat{cv}^* - \widehat{cv})$$

across the bootstrap samples. Let $c_{\alpha/2}$ and $c_{1-\alpha/2}$ be the corresponding quantiles of this distribution. Then by the bootstrap theory we have

$$\Pr\left[\sqrt{n}(\widehat{cv} - cv) \leq c_{\alpha/2}\right] \simeq \frac{\alpha}{2}$$
$$\Pr\left[\sqrt{n}(\widehat{cv} - cv) \geq c_{1-\alpha/2}\right] \simeq \frac{\alpha}{2}$$

Therefore, the interval we need is

$$\left[\widehat{cv} - \frac{c_{\alpha/2}}{\sqrt{n}}, \widehat{cv} + \frac{c_{1-\alpha/2}}{\sqrt{n}}\right]. \qquad \Box$$

Part III

Econometrics

Chapter 16

Linear Algebra

16.1 MATRICES

Define the $n \times 1$ column vector

$$x = \begin{pmatrix} x_1 \\ \vdots \\ x_n \end{pmatrix}$$

and the $n \times K$ matrix

$$A = \begin{pmatrix} a_{11} & \cdots & a_{1K} \\ \vdots & & \vdots \\ a_{n1} & & a_{nK} \end{pmatrix} = (a_{ij})_{i,j} \; ;$$

The transpose of a matrix $A = (a_{ij})$ is the matrix $A^\mathsf{T} = (a_{ji})$. For example

$$\begin{pmatrix} 1 & 2 & 3 \\ 4 & 5 & 6 \end{pmatrix}^\mathsf{T} = \begin{pmatrix} 1 & 4 \\ 2 & 5 \\ 3 & 6 \end{pmatrix}.$$

Matrices can be added in an obvious way, provided they are **conformable** meaning they have the same (row and column) dimensions

$$A + B = \begin{pmatrix} a_{11} + b_{11} & \cdots & a_{1K} + b_{1K} \\ \vdots & & \vdots \\ a_{1n} + b_{1n} & & a_{nK} + b_{nK} \end{pmatrix}.$$

Multiplication is a little more complicated and requires that the number of columns of A be equal to the number of rows of B. Suppose that A is $n \times K$ and B is $K \times m$, then

$$AB = \begin{pmatrix} \sum_{j=1}^{K} a_{1j} b_{j1} & \cdots & \sum_{j=1}^{K} a_{1j} b_{jm} \\ \vdots & & \vdots \\ \sum_{j=1}^{K} a_{nj} b_{j1} & & \sum_{j=1}^{K} a_{nj} b_{jm} \end{pmatrix}$$

Probability, Statistics and Econometrics. http://dx.doi.org/10.1016/B978-0-12-810495-8.00019-1

231

is an $n \times m$ matrix. If $n = K$, the matrix A is square. If $m = n$, then we can define both AB and BA, which are both $n \times n$ matrices. Matrix multiplication is distributive, meaning that $(AB)C = A(BC)$. Note however that in general matrices do not **commute** so that $AB \neq BA$ (in general, when $m \neq n$, AB and BA may not even have the same dimensions).

For vectors $x, y \in \mathbb{R}^n$, we define the **inner product**

$$x^\mathsf{T} y = \sum_{i=1}^{n} x_i y_i \in \mathbb{R}.$$

Two vectors are orthogonal if $x^\mathsf{T} y = 0$. The Euclidean **norm** of a vector is denoted

$$\|x\| = \left(x^\mathsf{T} x\right)^{1/2} = \left(\sum_{i=1}^{n} x_i^2\right)^{1/2} \in \mathbb{R}_+.$$

This measures the length of the vector. We have the triangle inequality for two vectors x, y

$$\|x + y\| \leq \|x\| + \|y\|.$$

This says that the length of the sum is less than or equal to the sum of the lengths.

The identity matrix is a special kind of square matrix

$$I_n = \begin{pmatrix} 1 & \cdots & 0 \\ \vdots & & \vdots \\ 0 & & 1 \end{pmatrix},$$

and satisfies $AI = IA = A$ for all square conformable matrices. The zero matrix $\mathbf{0}$ consists of zeros, and satisfies $A + \mathbf{0} = \mathbf{0} + A = \mathbf{0}$ for any conformable A.

A square matrix B such that $AB = BA = I$ is called the **inverse** of A; not all square matrices have an inverse, but if they do then it is unique, i.e., if B^* also satisfies $AB^* = B^*A = I$, then $B = B^*$. This is left as an exercise. If the matrix A has an inverse it is called nonsingular otherwise it is called **singular**.

For example, a diagonal matrix

$$D = \begin{pmatrix} d_1 & \cdots & 0 \\ \vdots & & \vdots \\ 0 & & d_n \end{pmatrix}$$

has inverse

$$D^{-1} = \begin{pmatrix} d_1^{-1} & \cdots & 0 \\ \vdots & & \vdots \\ 0 & & d_n^{-1} \end{pmatrix}.$$

Diagonal matrices are quite important. They are automatically symmetric and they have the special feature that when pre and postmultiplying an $n \times n$ matrix A by a diagonal D one gets

$$D^{-1}AD^{-1} = \begin{pmatrix} d_1 & \cdots & 0 \\ \vdots & & \vdots \\ 0 & & d_n \end{pmatrix}^{-1} \begin{pmatrix} a_{11} & \cdots & a_{1n} \\ \vdots & & \vdots \\ a_{n1} & & a_{nn} \end{pmatrix} \begin{pmatrix} d_1 & \cdots & 0 \\ \vdots & & \vdots \\ 0 & & d_n \end{pmatrix}^{-1}$$

$$= \begin{pmatrix} \frac{a_{11}}{d_1^2} & \cdots & \frac{a_{1n}}{d_1 d_n} \\ \vdots & & \vdots \\ \frac{a_{n1}}{d_1 d_n} & & \frac{a_{nn}}{d_n^2} \end{pmatrix}$$

$$= \left(a_{ij}/d_i d_j \right)_{i,j}.$$

Example 16.1. Derive the inverse of the reverse diagonal matrix

$$R = \begin{pmatrix} 0 & \cdots & d_1 \\ \vdots & \ddots & \vdots \\ d_n & & 0 \end{pmatrix}$$

Diagonal matrices are examples of **sparse matrices**, that is, they have many zeros relative to the non-zero elements.

We next consider the relationship between different vectors.

Definition 16.1. A set of vectors $\{x_1, \ldots, x_K\}$ with $x_i \in \mathbb{R}^n$ is called **linearly dependent** if there exist scalars $\alpha_1, \ldots, \alpha_K$ not all zero such that

$$\alpha_1 x_1 + \ldots + \alpha_K x_K = 0.$$

Suppose that $\alpha_i \neq 0$, then we can write

$$x_i = \frac{-1}{\alpha_i} \sum_{j \neq i} \alpha_j x_j$$

so that x_i is a linear combination of the other vectors.

Example 16.2. The two vectors

$$x_1 = \begin{pmatrix} 1 \\ 1 \end{pmatrix} \quad ; \quad x_2 = \begin{pmatrix} -3 \\ -3 \end{pmatrix}$$

are linearly dependent because

$$3x_1 + x_2 = 0.$$

Definition 16.2. A set of vectors $\{x_1, \ldots, x_K\}$ with $x_i \in \mathbb{R}^n$ is **linearly independent** if whenever for some scalars $\alpha_1, \ldots, \alpha_K$

$$\alpha_1 x_1 + \ldots + \alpha_K x_K = 0,$$

then necessarily $\alpha_1 = 0, \ldots, \alpha_K = 0$. If $X\alpha = 0$, where X is the matrix $X = (x_1, \ldots, x_K)$, then $\alpha = 0$ where $\alpha = (\alpha_1, \ldots, \alpha_K)^\mathsf{T}$.

Definition 16.3. The column rank of an $n \times K$ matrix A is the dimension of the column space of A, which is equal to the number of linearly independent columns, while the row rank of A is the dimension of the row space of A. The column rank and the row rank are always equal. This number is simply called the **rank** of A. A square matrix of full rank is invertible.

The rank of an $n \times K$ matrix can be: $0, 1, \ldots$, or $\min\{n, K\}$. A full rank square matrix has rank $n = K$, and is nonsingular. The zero matrix is of rank zero by convention, otherwise the rank has to be greater than or equal to one. The matrix

$$A = \begin{pmatrix} 1 & 1 & \ldots & 1 \\ & 1 & \ldots & \\ & & \ddots & \vdots \\ 1 & & & 1 \end{pmatrix} = ii^\mathsf{T},$$

where $i = (1, \ldots, 1)^\mathsf{T}$, is of rank one because the column vector i is technically linearly independent in the sense that $\alpha i = 0$ if and only if $\alpha = 0$. In fact, suppose that v is any $n \times 1$ column vector. Then

$$A = vv^\mathsf{T} = \begin{pmatrix} v_1^2 & v_1 v_2 & \ldots & v_1 v_n \\ & v_2^2 & \ldots & v_2 v_n \\ & & \ddots & \vdots \\ & & & v_n^2 \end{pmatrix} = (a_1, \ldots, a_n)$$

is a rank one matrix. This can be seen by the following argument. Suppose that for some α_j we have

$$\sum_{j=1}^{n} \alpha_j a_j = 0.$$

Then

$$\sum_{j=1}^{n} \alpha_j v_j \times v = 0,$$

which is possible whenever $\sum_{j=1}^{n} \alpha_j v_j = 0$. But there are many candidates for this.

Let V be an $n \times K$ full rank matrix with $K \leq n$. Then the $n \times n$ matrix VV^T is of rank K, while the $K \times K$ matrix $V^\mathsf{T}V$ is of rank K and hence invertible.

The **Trace** of a square matrix A, denoted $\mathrm{tr}(A)$, is defined as the sum of the diagonal elements. For conformable matrices

$$\mathrm{tr}(A + B) = \mathrm{tr}(A) + \mathrm{tr}(B)$$

$$\sum_{i=1}^{n} \left(\sum_{j=1}^{n} a_{ij} b_{ji} \right) = \mathrm{tr}(AB) = \mathrm{tr}(BA) = \sum_{i=1}^{n} \left(\sum_{j=1}^{n} b_{ij} a_{ji} \right)$$

This is true even if $AB \neq BA$. For example, when V is $n \times K$ matrix $\mathrm{tr}(VV^\mathsf{T}) = \mathrm{tr}(V^\mathsf{T}V)$. For example for column vector x and conformable square matrix A, we have

$$x^\mathsf{T}Ax = \mathrm{tr}(x^\mathsf{T}Ax) = \mathrm{tr}(xx^\mathsf{T}A)$$

The **determinant** of square matrix is defined recursively. For 2×2 matrices

$$\det(A) = \det \begin{pmatrix} a_{11} & a_{12} \\ a_{21} & a_{22} \end{pmatrix} = a_{11}a_{22} - a_{12}a_{21}.$$

For a 3×3 matrix

$$A = \begin{pmatrix} a_{11} & a_{12} & a_{13} \\ a_{21} & a_{22} & a_{23} \\ a_{31} & a_{32} & a_{33} \end{pmatrix}$$

we have

$$\det(A) = a_{11} \det(A_{11}) - a_{12} \det(A_{12}) + a_{13} \det(A_{13}),$$

where the matrices A_{ij} are defined as the original matrix with the ith row and jth column deleted

$$A_{11} = \begin{pmatrix} a_{22} & a_{23} \\ a_{32} & a_{33} \end{pmatrix} \ ; \ A_{12} = \begin{pmatrix} a_{21} & a_{23} \\ a_{31} & a_{33} \end{pmatrix} \ ; \ A_{13} = \begin{pmatrix} a_{21} & a_{22} \\ a_{31} & a_{32} \end{pmatrix}.$$

In general we have

$$\det(A) = \sum_{j=1}^{n} (-1)^{j-1} \det(A_{1j}),$$

where A_{ij} is the $n - 1 \times n - 1$ matrix with the ith row and the jth column removed so that for example

$$A_{11} = \begin{pmatrix} a_{22} & \cdots & a_{2n} \\ \vdots & & \\ a_{n2} & \cdots & a_{nn} \end{pmatrix}.$$

For conformable matrices

$$\mathrm{tr}(AB) = \mathrm{tr}(BA) \ ; \ \det(AB) = \det(BA).$$

This is true even if $AB \neq BA$.

A **symmetric matrix**, necessarily square, is one in which $a_{ij} = a_{ji}$ for all $i, j = 1, \ldots, n$. For example,

$$A = \begin{bmatrix} a_{11} & a_{12} & a_{13} \\ a_{12} & a_{22} & a_{23} \\ a_{13} & a_{23} & a_{33} \end{bmatrix} = A^{\mathsf{T}}.$$

In general, an $n \times n$ symmetric matrix contains $n(n + 1)/2$ unique elements.

Matrices can be viewed as linear transformations. Suppose that A is $n \times K$ and of full rank, and u, v are $K \times 1$ vectors. Then we have $Au \in \mathbb{R}^n$, so that $A : \mathbb{R}^K \to \mathbb{R}^n$. They are linear because for $c \in \mathbb{R}$

$$A(cu) = cAu$$
$$A(u + v) = Au + Av.$$

16.1.1 Linear Spaces

Definition 16.4. The Euclidean space $\mathbb{R}^n$ is a vector space (linear space) since it has addition and scalar multiplication defined. A subset $\mathbb{L}$ is a subspace if, for any $x, z \in \mathbb{L} \subset \mathbb{R}^n$ and any $\alpha, \beta \in \mathbb{R}$ we have

$$\alpha x + \beta z \in \mathbb{L}$$

For example,

$$\mathbb{L} = \left\{ x : \sum_{j=1}^{n} x_j = 0 \right\}$$

is a proper subspace of $\mathbb{R}^n$ of **dimension** $n-1$. Show this.

Definition 16.5. A set of vectors $x_1, \ldots, x_K \in \mathbb{R}^n$ generate a subspace of $\mathbb{R}^n$ called the span of $x_1, \ldots, x_K$

$$\mathcal{C}(x_1, \ldots, x_K) = \{\alpha_1 x_1 + \ldots + \alpha_K x_K : \alpha_1, \ldots, \alpha_K \in \mathbb{R}\} = \{X\alpha, \quad \alpha \in \mathbb{R}^K\}.$$

Definition 16.6. The null space of $x_1, \ldots, x_K$

$$\mathcal{N}(x_1, \ldots, x_K) = \{\alpha_1 x_1 + \ldots + \alpha_K x_K = 0 : \alpha_1, \ldots, \alpha_K \in \mathbb{R}\}$$

is a subspace of $\mathbb{R}^n$. This is also denoted by $\mathcal{C}^{\perp}(X)$ and called the orthocomplement of $\mathcal{C}(X)$.

Definition 16.7. A basis for a space $\mathbb{L}$ is a set of linearly independent vectors $x_1, \ldots, x_K \in \mathbb{R}^n$ such that for any $x \in \mathbb{L}$, there exist scalars $\alpha_1, \ldots, \alpha_K$ such that

$$x = \alpha_1 x_1 + \ldots + \alpha_K x_K$$

The dimension of the space $\mathbb{L}$ is K.

If the vectors $x_1, \ldots, x_K$ are linearly independent then the dimension of $\mathcal{C}(x_1, \ldots, x_K)$ is K and the dimension of $\mathcal{N}(x_1, \ldots, x_K)$ is $n - K$. A basis is not unique.

Definition 16.8. Let $x_1, \ldots, x_K \in \mathbb{R}^n$ be a basis for the space $\mathbb{L}$. Suppose that $x_i^\mathsf{T} x_j = 0$ for $i \neq j$ and $x_i^\mathsf{T} x_i = 1$. Then the basis is orthonormal and there is only one such orthonormal basis.

Example 16.3. For example $\mathbb{R}_n$ has orthonormal basis $e_1 = (1, 0, \ldots, 0)^\mathsf{T}, \ldots, e_n = (0, 0, \ldots, 0, 1)^\mathsf{T}$.

16.1.2   Eigenvectors and Eigenvalues

We next define the concept of **Eigenvectors** and **Eigenvalues**.

Definition 16.9. For a real matrix A with dimensions $n \times n$, a vector $u \in \mathbb{R}^n$ with $u \neq 0$ and scalar $\lambda \in \mathbb{R}$ are called an eigenvector and eigenvalue respectively of the matrix A if

$$Au = \lambda u. \tag{16.1}$$

Clearly, $u = 0$ trivially satisfies Eq. (16.1) for any λ, which is why we don't consider it. The interpretation of eigenvector is a direction that is invariant under the transformation A. Most vectors u will have their "direction" changed by a given transformation A, the eigenvectors are the special ones that are unchanged in direction and just scaled according to λ by the transformation. For an identity matrix $A = I_n$, the eigenvectors are any vectors $u \in \mathbb{R}^n$ and the eigenvalues are all $\lambda = 1$ because $Iu = u$ for all $u \in \mathbb{R}^n$, the identity transformation does not change anything. Do eigenvalues/eigenvectors always exist, and how many of them are there?

We can write Eq. (16.1) as

$$(A - \lambda I)u = 0, \tag{16.2}$$

where 0 is a vector of zeros. If $u \neq 0$, then $A - \lambda I$ must be singular otherwise we would have a contradiction. Therefore,

$$\det(A - \lambda I) = 0,$$

which gives one way of finding the eigenvalues. The left hand side of the equation is an nth order polynomial in λ, denoted $p_n(\lambda)$, called the **characteristic polynomial**. We know from the mathematical analysis of polynomial equations that $p_n(\lambda) = 0$ will always have at least one solution, although some of them may be complex valued. In general, there may be one solution, two solutions, or even as many as n distinct solutions, but no more than that, that is, we can write

$$p_n(\lambda) = (\lambda_1 - \lambda)^{k_1} \times \cdots \times (\lambda_p - \lambda)^{k_p},$$

where λ_j, $j = 1, \ldots, p$ are distinct solutions and k_j are called the multiplicity of the solution, where $p \leq n$ and $\sum_{j=1}^{p} k_j = n$. For example, $k_j = 1$ for all j is the case where there are n distinct solutions $\lambda_1, \ldots, \lambda_n$. The **Cayley Hamilton Theorem** says that the matrix A satisfies its own characteristic polynomial, i.e. $p_n(A) = 0$. The eigenvectors are then found by finding the vectors $u \in \mathbb{R}^n$ that solve (16.2).

For real symmetric matrices A the eigenvalues are all real valued because in that case the polynomial coefficients satisfy the conditions to guarantee real solutions. A proof of this result is simple but requires complex numbers.

Example 16.4. In the 2×2 case we may use this to find explicitly the eigenvalues and hence the eigenvectors. Suppose that

$$A = \begin{pmatrix} a & b \\ c & d \end{pmatrix}.$$

Then we must solve the quadratic equation

$$\det(A - \lambda I) = (a - \lambda)(d - \lambda) - bc = \lambda^2 - (a + d)\lambda + ad - bc = 0$$

for λ. There will always be a solution in the complex plane (fundamental theorem of algebra); the solution will be real provided

$$\Delta = (a + d)^2 - 4(ad - bc) \geq 0.$$

The general solutions are $\frac{1}{2}(a + d + \sqrt{\Delta})$ and $\frac{1}{2}(a + d - \sqrt{\Delta})$. In the special case that $c = b = 0$ it is clear that $\lambda = a$ and $\lambda = d$ are the solutions. In the special case that $a = d = 1$ and $b = c = \rho$, the eigenvalues are $1 + \rho$ and $1 - \rho$. How to find the eigenvectors? We look for solutions to

$$\begin{pmatrix} -\rho & \rho \\ \rho & -\rho \end{pmatrix} \begin{pmatrix} u \\ v \end{pmatrix} = \begin{pmatrix} 0 \\ 0 \end{pmatrix}.$$

That is $v = u$, which implies that any multiple of $(1, 1)$ is a candidate eigenvector. For the other eigenvector we have to solve

$$\begin{pmatrix} \rho & \rho \\ \rho & \rho \end{pmatrix} \begin{pmatrix} u \\ v \end{pmatrix} = \begin{pmatrix} 0 \\ 0 \end{pmatrix}$$

so that $u = -v$, and any multiple of $(1, -1)$ is a candidate.

If there are n distinct eigenvalues, then eigenvectors are unique upto a scaling factor. Note that if $Au = \lambda u$, then $Au' = \lambda u'$, where $u' = ku$ for any scalar k.

Theorem 16.1. *Eigenvectors corresponding to distinct eigenvalues are **orthogonal**.*

Proof. Suppose that $Au = \lambda u$ and $Av = \mu v$. Then $v^T Au = \lambda v^T u$ and $u^T Av = \mu u^T v$. Therefore,

$$0 = v^T Au - u^T Av = \lambda v^T u - \mu u^T v = (\lambda - \mu)v^T u,$$

which means that $v^T u = 0$. □

Let λ^* be such that $p_n(\lambda^*) = 0$ and suppose that $u_1, \ldots, u_m$ are vectors such that $(A - \lambda^* I) u_i = \mathbf{0}$, then for any $v = \sum_{i=1}^{m} \alpha_i u_i$ with $\alpha_i \in \mathbb{R}$, we have

$$(A - \lambda^* I) v = \mathbf{0}.$$

Some matrices have repeated eigenvalues, in which case the corresponding eigenvectors form a vector space of the same dimensions as the cardinality of multiplicity.

Example 16.5. Consider the real symmetric matrix

$$A = \begin{pmatrix} 1 & \rho & \rho \\ \rho & 1 & \rho \\ \rho & \rho & 1 \end{pmatrix}.$$

We have two distinct eigenvalues $\lambda = 1 - \rho$ and $\mu = 1 + 2\rho$. Define the vectors:

$$u_1 = \begin{pmatrix} -1 \\ 1 \\ 0 \end{pmatrix} \quad ; \quad u_2 = \begin{pmatrix} -1 \\ 0 \\ 1 \end{pmatrix} \quad ; \quad u_3 = \begin{pmatrix} 1 \\ 1 \\ 1 \end{pmatrix}.$$

Then check that u_1 and u_2 are distinct eigenvectors associated with the eigenvalue λ, while u_3 is the eigenvector associated with μ. We have $u_1^{\mathsf{T}} u_3 = u_2^{\mathsf{T}} u_3 = 0$ but $u_1^{\mathsf{T}} u_2 = 1 \neq 0$. Define the space

$$\mathbb{L} = \{ \alpha u_1 + \beta u_2 : \alpha, \beta \in \mathbb{R} \}.$$

This space has dimensions two since u_1, u_2 are linearly independent. Define $e_1 = u_1$, $e_2 = u_1 - 2u_2$, and $e_3 = u_3$. Then $\{e_1, e_2\}$ is an orthogonal basis for $\mathbb{L}$. Note also that e_1, e_2 are eigenvectors associated with λ. Finally, we may scale the vectors e_j to have unit length; for example let $e_3^* = e_3 / \sqrt{3}$.

Theorem 16.2. *Suppose that A is a real symmetric matrix, then it possesses an **Eigendecomposition**, whereby it can be written as*

$$A = Q \Lambda Q^{-1}$$

$$\Lambda = \begin{pmatrix} \lambda_1 & 0 & \cdots \\ 0 & & \vdots \\ \vdots & & \lambda_n \end{pmatrix},$$

where $Q = (q_1, \ldots, q_n)$ are linearly independent eigenvectors of A associated with the eigenvalues in Λ. By convention we organize the eigenvalues in decreasing order so that $\lambda_1 \geq \lambda_2 \geq \cdots \geq \lambda_n$. Moreover, there exists a unique orthonormal matrix U

$$A = U \Lambda U^{\mathsf{T}} = \sum_{i=1}^{n} \lambda_i u_i u_i^{\mathsf{T}} \tag{16.3}$$

$$U U^{\mathsf{T}} = \left(u_i^{\mathsf{T}} u_j \right)_{i,j} = I_n = U^{\mathsf{T}} U$$

where u_i, λ_i, $i = 1, \ldots, n$ are the real eigenvectors and real valued eigenvalues (not necessarily distinct) of the matrix A. The matrix U is orthonormal and *satisfies $AU = \Lambda U$. We may equivalently write*

$$U^\mathsf{T} A U = \Lambda \tag{16.4}$$

In general finding eigenvectors requires we solve the equation $Bu = \mathbf{0}$ for a singular matrix $B = A - \lambda I$. There are many methods for doing this but they are quite involved to describe, so we refer the reader to elsewhere. In low dimensional cases as we have seen it is easy to see how to find the solutions.

It follows from this theorem that

$$\mathrm{tr}(A) = \mathrm{tr}(U \Lambda U^\mathsf{T}) = \mathrm{tr}(U^\mathsf{T} U \Lambda) = \sum_{i=1}^{n} \lambda_i \; ;$$

$$\det(A) = \det(U \Lambda U^\mathsf{T}) = \det(U^\mathsf{T} U \Lambda) = \prod_{i=1}^{n} \lambda_i .$$

It also follows that if $c \in \mathbb{R}$, the eigenvalues of $A + c I_n$ are $\lambda_1 + c, \ldots, \lambda_n + c$ and the eigenvectors of $A + c I_n$ are the same as the eigenvectors of A since for eigenvalue, eigenvector pair λ, u we have

$$(A + c I_n) u = Au + cu = (\lambda + c)u.$$

Corollary 16.1. *(Singular Value Decomposition) Suppose that A is an $n \times K$ real matrix. Then there exists a factorization, called a singular value decomposition of A of the form*

$$A = U S V^\mathsf{T},$$

where U is an $n \times n$ orthonormal matrix, V is a $K \times K$ orthonormal matrix, and S is an $n \times K$ matrix with non-negative real numbers on the diagonal, of the form

$$S = \begin{bmatrix} s_1 & & \\ & \ddots & \\ & & s_K \\ 0 & \cdots & 0 \\ \vdots & & \vdots \end{bmatrix} = \mathrm{diag}\{s_1, \ldots, s_K\} | 0_{n-K \times K} .$$

It follows that for any matrix A we obtain $A^\mathsf{T} A = V S^2 V^\mathsf{T} = V \Lambda V^\mathsf{T}$, where Λ is the matrix of eigenvalues.

Definition 16.10. A **positive (semi)definite** matrix (psd) A satisfies

$$x^\mathsf{T} A x = \sum_{i=1}^{n} \sum_{j=1}^{n} a_{ij} x_i x_j \geq 0$$

for all vectors x. A strictly positive definite matrix (pd) is one for which $x^\mathsf{T} A x > 0$ for all x.

A negative semi-definite matrix satisfies $x^\mathsf{T} A x \leq 0$ for all vectors x. A matrix may be indefinite, i.e., $x^\mathsf{T} A x > 0$ for some x and $x^\mathsf{T} A x < 0$ for other x. The definiteness question can be answered for a real symmetric matrix from its eigenvalues. From the eigendecomposition we see that for any vector x

$$x^\mathsf{T} A x = x^\mathsf{T} U \Lambda U^\mathsf{T} x = y^\mathsf{T} \Lambda y = \sum_{j=1}^{n} \lambda_j y_j^2,$$

where $y = U^\mathsf{T} x$ and $x = U y$ are in one to one correspondence. A real symmetric matrix is psd if all its eigenvalues are nonnegative.

Example 16.6. Consider the matrix

$$A = \begin{bmatrix} 1 & \rho \\ \rho & 1 \end{bmatrix}.$$

Then, for any $x = (x_1, x_2)^\mathsf{T}$ we have

$$x^\mathsf{T} A x = x_1^2 + x_2^2 + 2 x_1 x_2 \rho.$$

The eigenvalues of A are $1 - \rho, \rho + 1$. Therefore, it is psd if and only if $\rho \in [-1, 1]$.

Definition 16.11. A matrix $A \geq B$ if and only if $A - B$ is psd.

The matrix order is only a partial order, meaning not all matrices can be compared, as the following example illustrates.

Example 16.7.

$$A = \begin{bmatrix} 1 & 0 \\ 0 & 1 \end{bmatrix}, \quad B = \begin{bmatrix} 2 & 0 \\ 0 & 1/4 \end{bmatrix}$$

$$A - B = \begin{bmatrix} -1 & 0 \\ 0 & 3/4 \end{bmatrix}$$

Scalar functions of a matrix give a total order, but different scalar functions yield different rankings

$$2 = \text{tr}(A) \le \text{tr}(B) = 9/4$$
$$1 = \det(A) \ge \det(B) = 1/2.$$

Theorem 16.3. *Let A be a real symmetric matrix. Then, the largest eigenvalue of A denoted* λ_1 *or* $\lambda_{\max}(A)$, *is the value of the optimized criterion in the constrained optimization problem*

$$\max_{x:\, x^\mathsf{T} x = 1} x^\mathsf{T} A x$$

and the optimizing choice of x is the corresponding eigenvector.

Proof. For every eigenvalue λ there is x such that $Ax = \lambda x$, which implies that

$$x^\mathsf{T} A x = \lambda x^\mathsf{T} x = \lambda$$

so just take the largest such. □

Likewise the smallest eigenvalue is defined through a minimization problem. That is,

$$\lambda_{\min}(A) = \min_{x:\, x^\mathsf{T} x = 1} x^\mathsf{T} A x.$$

The eigendecomposition can be used to define functions of matrices. For example, the square root of a symmetric positive definite matrix is

$$X = A^{1/2} = U \Lambda^{1/2} U^\mathsf{T} = U \begin{pmatrix} \lambda_1^{1/2} & 0 & \cdots \\ 0 & & \vdots \\ \vdots & & \lambda_n^{1/2} \end{pmatrix} U^\mathsf{T}.$$

We have $XX = U \Lambda^{1/2} U^\mathsf{T} U \Lambda^{1/2} U^\mathsf{T} = U \Lambda^{1/2} \Lambda^{1/2} U^\mathsf{T} = U \Lambda U^\mathsf{T}$. One may define exponentials and logarithms of matrices in this way.

The eigendecomposition is also useful in establish bounds on quadratic forms.

Theorem 16.4. *Suppose that the* $n \times K$ *matrix A has full rank with* $K \le n$. *Then for some* $C > 0$ *we have for all* $x \in \mathbb{R}^K$

$$C \|x\| \le \|Ax\| \le \frac{1}{C} \|x\|.$$

Proof. The matrix A is not necessarily symmetric or even square, but $A^\mathsf{T} A$ and $A A^\mathsf{T}$ are symmetric. Because A is of full rank, so is $A^\mathsf{T} A$. Therefore, we have

$$\lambda_{\min}(A^\mathsf{T} A) = \inf_x (x/\|x\|) A^\mathsf{T} A (x/\|x\|) \geq C > 0,$$

which implies that for any x,

$$x^\mathsf{T} A^\mathsf{T} A \, x \geq C \|x\|^2$$

as required. Similarly for the upper bound. $\qquad\square$

16.1.3 Applications

Definition 16.12. Suppose that $X \in \mathbb{R}^d$ is a random variable. The covariance matrix of the random vector X is defined as

$$\mathrm{cov}(X) = E\left[(X - \mu)(X - \mu)^\mathsf{T}\right] = E\left[XX^\mathsf{T}\right] - \mu\mu^\mathsf{T} = \Sigma$$

$$= \begin{pmatrix} \sigma_{11} & \cdots & \sigma_{1d} \\ & & \\ \sigma_{1d} & & \sigma_{dd} \end{pmatrix},$$

where $\mu = E(X)$ and $\sigma_{ij} = \mathrm{cov}(X_i, X_j)$.

Because Σ is a covariance matrix this means that it is symmetric (check this) and positive semi-definite, because for any vector $w \in \mathbb{R}^d$

$$0 \leq \mathrm{var}(w^\mathsf{T} X) = E\left[w^\mathsf{T}(X - \mu)(X - \mu)^\mathsf{T} w\right] = w^\mathsf{T} \Sigma w.$$

Because it is real and symmetric we may define the inverse and the square root of Σ, provided it is strictly positive definite. In fact, the matrix $\Sigma^{-1/2}$ can be defined from the eigendecomposition, as explained above. This is the matrix equivalent of "one over the standard deviation" and it allows us to "standardize" vector random variables.

Theorem 16.5. *Let* $Z = \Sigma^{-1/2}(X - \mu)$. *Then* $EZ = 0$ *and* $\mathrm{cov}(Z) = I_d$.

Proof. We have

$$\begin{aligned} E(ZZ^\mathsf{T}) &= E\left[\Sigma^{-1/2}(X - \mu)(X - \mu)^\mathsf{T} \Sigma^{-1/2}\right] \\ &= \Sigma^{-1/2} E\left[(X - \mu)(X - \mu)^\mathsf{T}\right] \Sigma^{-1/2} \\ &= \Sigma^{-1/2} \Sigma \Sigma^{-1/2} \\ &= I_d. \end{aligned}$$

$\qquad\square$

Example 16.8. MULTIVARIATE NORMAL. We say that $X = (X_1, \ldots, X_k) \sim MVN_k(\mu, \Sigma)$, when

$$f_X(x|\mu, \Sigma) = \frac{1}{(2\pi)^{k/2} \det(\Sigma)^{1/2}} \exp\left(-\frac{1}{2}(x - \mu)^\mathsf{T} \Sigma^{-1}(x - \mu)\right),$$

where Σ is a $k \times k$ covariance matrix

$$\Sigma = \begin{pmatrix} \sigma_{11} & \sigma_{12} & \cdots & \sigma_{1k} \\ & \ddots & & \vdots \\ & & & \sigma_{kk} \end{pmatrix},$$

and $\det(\Sigma)$ is the determinant of Σ. The characteristic function of X is

$$E\left[\exp(it^\mathsf{T} X)\right] = \varphi_X(t|\mu, \Sigma) = \exp\left(-t^\mathsf{T}\mu + \frac{1}{2}t^\mathsf{T}\Sigma t\right)$$

for any $t \in \mathbb{R}^k$.

Theorem 16.6. *Suppose that we partition $X = (X_a^\mathsf{T}, X_b^\mathsf{T})^\mathsf{T}$ and*

$$\mu = \begin{pmatrix} \mu_a \\ \mu_b \end{pmatrix} \quad ; \quad \Sigma = \begin{pmatrix} \Sigma_{aa} & \Sigma_{ab} \\ \Sigma_{ba} & \Sigma_{bb} \end{pmatrix}.$$

(a) If $X \sim MVN_k(\mu, \Sigma)$ then $X_a \sim N(\mu_a, \Sigma_{aa})$. This is shown by integration of the joint density with respect to the other variables.
(b) The conditional distributions of X are Gaussian too, i.e.,

$$f_{X_a|X_b}(X_a) \sim N(\mu_{X_a|X_b}, \Sigma_{X_a|X_b}),$$

where the conditional mean vector and conditional covariance matrix are given by

$$\mu_{X_a|X_b} = E(X_a|X_b) = \mu_a + \Sigma_{ab}\Sigma_{bb}^{-1}(X_b - \mu_b)$$
$$\Sigma_{X_a|X_b} = \Sigma_{aa} - \Sigma_{ab}\Sigma_{bb}^{-1}\Sigma_{ba}.$$

(c) Iff Σ is diagonal, then $X_1, \ldots, X_k$ are mutually independent. In this case

$$\det(\Sigma) = \sigma_{11} \times \ldots \times \sigma_{kk}$$

$$-\frac{1}{2}(x - \mu)^\mathsf{T}\Sigma^{-1}(x - \mu) = -\frac{1}{2}\sum_{\ell=1}^{k} \frac{(x_\ell - \mu_\ell)^2}{\sigma_{\ell\ell}},$$

so that

$$f_X(x|\mu, \Sigma) = \frac{1}{\sigma_{11}^{1/2}\sqrt{2\pi}} \exp\left(-\frac{1}{2}\left(\frac{x_1 - \mu_1}{\sigma_{11}}\right)^2\right) \cdots$$
$$\times \frac{1}{\sigma_{kk}^{1/2}\sqrt{2\pi}} \exp\left(-\frac{1}{2}\left(\frac{x_k - \mu_k}{\sigma_{kk}}\right)^2\right)$$

Example 16.9. Suppose that $X \in \mathbb{R}^d$ and $X \sim N(\mu, \Sigma)$. We have the eigende-composition where $\lambda_1 \geq \lambda_2 \geq \cdots \geq 0$

$$\Sigma = \sum_{i=1}^{d} \lambda_i u_i u_i^\mathsf{T}.$$

The first **Principal Component** of the random vector X is the scalar combination $u^\mathsf{T}X$ such that

$$\mathrm{var}(u^\mathsf{T}X) = E\left[u^\mathsf{T}(X - \mu)(X - \mu)^\mathsf{T}u\right] = u^\mathsf{T}\Sigma u$$

is maximized subject to $u^\mathsf{T}u = 1$, i.e., u is the eigenvector of Σ corresponding to the largest eigenvalue of Σ: u_1. The largest eigenvalue $\lambda_1 = \mathrm{var}(u_1^\mathsf{T}X)$. Can define

$$u_1^\mathsf{T}X, \ldots, u_d^\mathsf{T}X$$

as the Principal components of X in decreasing order of importance. The field of Principal Components Analysis originates with Pearson (1901) and is now very widely applied to understand multivariate statistics. See Fig. 16.1.

Example 16.10. Suppose that $X \in \mathbb{R}^d$ and

$$X \sim N(\mu, \Sigma).$$

The parameters θ contain all the elements of $\mu = (\mu_1 \ldots, \mu_d)$ and the unique elements of the covariance matrix

$$\Sigma = \begin{pmatrix} \sigma_{11} & \cdots & \sigma_{1d} \\ & & \\ \sigma_{1d} & & \sigma_{dd} \end{pmatrix}.$$

Suppose we have a sample $X_1, \ldots, X_n$. The log likelihood is

$$\ell(\theta|\mathcal{X}^n) = -\frac{nd}{2}\log 2\pi - \frac{n}{2}\log\det(\Sigma) - \frac{1}{2}\sum_{i=1}^{n}(X_i - \mu)^\mathsf{T}\Sigma^{-1}(X_i - \mu)$$

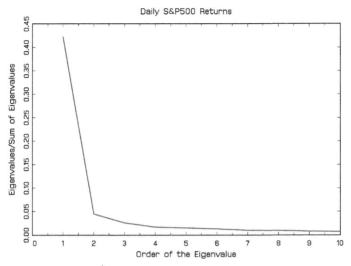

FIGURE 16.1 Shows $\lambda_i / \sum_{i=1}^{d} \lambda_i$, which is the percentage of total variance explained: 0.422, 0.044, 0.026, etc. $d = 441$ stocks, $n = 2700$ sample observations

$$= -\frac{nd}{2} \log 2\pi - \frac{n}{2} \log \det(\Sigma) - \frac{1}{2} \sum_{i=1}^{n} \operatorname{tr} \left((X_i - \mu)(X_i - \mu)^\mathsf{T} \Sigma^{-1} \right)$$

$$= -\frac{nd}{2} \log 2\pi - \frac{n}{2} \log \det(\Sigma) - \frac{1}{2} \sum_{i=1}^{n} \operatorname{tr} \left((X_i - \mu)(X_i - \mu)^\mathsf{T} \Sigma^{-1} \right)$$

$$= -\frac{nd}{2} \log 2\pi - \frac{n}{2} \log \det(\Sigma) - \frac{n}{2} \operatorname{tr} \left(S\Sigma^{-1} \right)$$
$$- \frac{n}{2} (\overline{X} - \mu)^\mathsf{T} \Sigma^{-1} (\overline{X} - \mu),$$

where the sample mean and sample covariance matrix respectively are:

$$\overline{X} = \frac{1}{n} \sum_{i=1}^{n} X_i \quad ; \quad S = \frac{1}{n} \sum_{i=1}^{n} (X_i - \overline{X})(X_i - \overline{X})^\mathsf{T}.$$

This follows because

$$\sum_{i=1}^{n} (X_i - \mu)(X_i - \mu)^\mathsf{T} = \sum_{i=1}^{n} (X_i - \overline{X})(X_i - \overline{X})^\mathsf{T} + n(\overline{X} - \mu)(\overline{X} - \mu)^\mathsf{T}$$

It can be shown that $\overline{X}$ is the MLE of μ (this is easy) and S is the MLE of Σ (this is hard).

Example 16.11. The motivating idea behind the search engine Google is that you want the first items returned by a search to be the most important items. One way is to count the number of sites that contain a link to a given site, and the site that is linked to the most is then the most important site. This has the drawback that all links are treated as equal. If your site is referenced from the home page of Justin Bieber, it counts no more than if it's referenced by an unknown person with no fan base. The Page rank method takes account of the importance of each website in terms of its links. Suppose there are N web sites, the page rank vector r satisfies

$$r = \frac{1-d}{N} i + d\mathbf{A}r,$$

where i is a vector of ones, while $\mathbf{A} = (A_{ij})$ is the **Adjacency matrix** with $A_{ij} = 0$ if page j does not link to page i, and normalized such that, for each j, $\sum_{i=1}^{n} A_{ij} = 1$. Here, $d \leq 1$ is a dampening factor. When $d = 1$ we have

$$\mathbf{A}r = r$$

so that r is the eigenvector of A corresponding to unit eigenvalue.

Example 16.12. Input output analysis. Suppose that the economy has n sectors. Each sector produces x_i units of a single homogeneous good. Assume that the jth sector, in order to produce 1 unit, must use a_{ij} units from sector i. Furthermore, assume that each sector sells some of its output to other sectors (intermediate output) and some of its output to consumers (final output, or final demand). Call final demand in the ith sector d_i. Then we might write

$$x - Ax = d$$

where $A = (a_{ij})$. We can solve this equation by

$$x = (I - A)^{-1} d$$

provided the inverse exists.

Theorem 16.7. *Let A be an $n \times m$ matrix of real numbers. Either there exists $\pi \in \mathbb{R}^m$ such that $A\pi \geq 0$ for all elements, or there exists $\alpha \in \mathbb{R}^n$ such that $A^\mathsf{T}\alpha < 0$ for all elements.*

Example 16.13. Dirty Harry offers the following odds on the Premiership title: Arsenal 2 to 1, Manchester City 3 to 1, Chelsea 4 to 1 and Manchester United 5 to 1. You may assume that there are only 4 teams with positive probability of winning. Is it possible to find a combination of bets at these odds that you will surely win no matter who wins the Premiership? We can represent the payoff matrix for the bettor as

$$A = \begin{pmatrix} 3 & -1 & -1 & -1 \\ -1 & 4 & -1 & -1 \\ -1 & -1 & 5 & -1 \\ -1 & -1 & -1 & 6 \end{pmatrix}.$$

This matrix is positive definite and has eigenvalues 1.1961136, 4.4922513, 5.6077247, 6.7039104 with first eigenvector

$$u = \begin{pmatrix} 0.687 \\ 0.507 \\ 0.401 \\ 0.332 \end{pmatrix},$$

that is $Au = \lambda u \geq 0$. This says that you should bet in proportion to $u_i / \sum_{i=1}^{4} u_i$, i.e., 0.357 on Arsenal, 0.263 on Manchester City, 0.208 on Chelsea, and 0.172 on Manchester United. No matter what you will make 1.196.

16.2 SYSTEMS OF LINEAR EQUATIONS AND PROJECTION

We next consider linear equations and their solution. Consider the system of equations

$$Ax = y, \tag{16.5}$$

where A is $n \times K$ and y is $n \times 1$, and both are given. We seek the $K \times 1$ solution vector x. In general, there may be no solution to these equations, many solutions, or a unique solution. We suppose that A is of full rank. There are several cases.

1. Suppose that $n = K$. Then, since A is nonsingular we may write the unique solution

$$x = A^{-1} y$$

2. Second, suppose that $n < K$. In this case, there are multiple solutions. Suppose that $y = 0$. Then for any $K \times 1$ vector w

$$x = \left(I_K - A^\mathsf{T} (AA^\mathsf{T})^{-1} A \right) w$$

is a solution to (16.5). The set of solutions $\mathcal{N} = \{x \in \mathbb{R}^K : Ax = 0\}$ is a subspace of $\mathbb{R}^K$ because $0 \in \mathcal{N}$ and if $x_1, x_2 \in \mathcal{N}$ then $\alpha_1 x_1 + \alpha_2 x_2 \in \mathcal{N}$. In fact, $\mathcal{N}$ is of dimension $K - n$. Now consider the general case with $y \neq 0$.

Then for any $K \times 1$ vector w the vector

$$x = \left(I_p - A^\mathsf{T}(AA^\mathsf{T})^{-1}A\right)w + A^\mathsf{T}(AA^\mathsf{T})^{-1}y$$

is a solution to (16.5).

3. Suppose that $n > K$. In this case, the are no solutions to (16.5) except in trivial cases. In that case, the best we can hope for is to find a vector x that minimizes the error, i.e.,

$$x = \arg\min_{x \in \mathbb{R}^K} \|Ax - y\| = \arg\min_{x \in \mathbb{R}^K} (Ax - y)^\mathsf{T}(Ax - y). \qquad (16.6)$$

The Projection theorem is a famous result of convex analysis that gives the conditions under which there is a unique solution to (16.6) and characterizes the solution.

Theorem 16.8. *Let $x \in \mathbb{R}^n$ and let $\mathbb{L}$ be a subspace of $\mathbb{R}^n$. Then there exists a unique point $\widehat{y} \in \mathbb{L}$ for which Euclidean distance*

$$\|x - y\|^2 = \sum_{i=1}^{n}(x_i - y_i)^2$$

is minimized over $\mathbb{L}$. In that case, a necessary and sufficient condition for $\widehat{y}$ is that the vector $x - \widehat{y}$ be orthogonal to $\mathbb{L}$, meaning for any $y \in \mathbb{L}$

$$\langle y, x - \widehat{y}\rangle = y^\mathsf{T}(x - \widehat{y}) = \sum_{i=1}^{n} y_i(x_i - \widehat{y}_i) = 0$$

Example 16.14. Let $n = 3$ and

$$X = \begin{pmatrix} 1 & 0 \\ 0 & 1 \\ 0 & 0 \end{pmatrix} \quad ; \quad y = \begin{pmatrix} 1 \\ 1 \\ 1 \end{pmatrix}.$$

Then $\mathcal{C}(X)$ is the set of all vectors in $\mathbb{R}^3$ with third component zero. What is the closest point in $\mathcal{C}(X)$ to y? This is

$$(1, 1, 0)^\mathsf{T} = \widehat{y}, \quad y - \widehat{y} = (0, 0, 1)^\mathsf{T}$$

In fact $y - \widehat{y}$ is orthogonal to $\mathcal{C}(X)$ (i.e., to X and any linear combination thereof), i.e., $y - \widehat{y} \in \mathcal{C}^\perp(X) = \{(0, 0, \alpha)^\mathsf{T}, \alpha \in \mathbb{R}\}$.

Chapter 17

The Least Squares Procedure

17.1 PROJECTION APPROACH

We observe the following data

$$y = \begin{pmatrix} y_1 \\ \vdots \\ y_n \end{pmatrix} \in \mathbb{R}^n \quad ; \quad X = \begin{pmatrix} x_{11} & \cdots & x_{1K} \\ \vdots & & \vdots \\ x_{n1} & & x_{nK} \end{pmatrix} = (x_1, \ldots, x_K).$$

We would like to find β such that $y = X\beta$ but when $n > K$ this is not possible, so we do next best thing, which is to find the best linear (in X) approximation to y.

Definition 17.1. The (Ordinary) Least Squares (OLS) procedure chooses $\widehat{\beta}$ to minimize the quadratic form

$$S(\beta) = (y - X\beta)^\mathsf{T}(y - X\beta) = \|y - X\beta\|^2$$

with respect to $\beta \in \mathbb{R}^K$.

The data: $y, x_1, \ldots, x_K$, can all be viewed as elements of the vector space $\mathbb{R}^n$. Define the column span of X,

$$\mathcal{C}(X) = \{\alpha_1 x_1 + \cdots + \alpha_K x_K\} = \{X\alpha : \alpha \in \mathbb{R}^K\} \subseteq \mathbb{R}^n.$$

Then, $\mathcal{C}(X)$ is a linear subspace of $\mathbb{R}^n$. The projection theorem says that there is a unique solution to the minimization problem, call it $\widehat{y}$, which is characterized by the fact that $y - \widehat{y} = \widehat{\varepsilon}$ is orthogonal to the space $\mathcal{C}(X)$. That is, we can write uniquely

$$y = \widehat{y} + \widehat{\varepsilon},$$

where (the "fitted value") $\widehat{y} \in \mathcal{C}(X)$ and (the "residual") $\widehat{\varepsilon} \in \mathcal{C}^\perp(X)$. This means that

$$\widehat{y} = X\widehat{\beta}, \text{ some } \widehat{\beta} \in \mathbb{R}^K \text{ and } X^\mathsf{T}\widehat{\varepsilon} = 0.$$

Probability, Statistics and Econometrics. http://dx.doi.org/10.1016/B978-0-12-810495-8.00020-8

The orthogonality conditions can be written out explicitly

$$\sum_{i=1}^{n} x_{1i}\widehat{\varepsilon}_i = 0$$

$$\sum_{i=1}^{n} x_{2i}\widehat{\varepsilon}_i = 0$$

$$\vdots$$

$$\sum_{i=1}^{n} x_{Ki}\widehat{\varepsilon}_i = 0.$$

Note that if, as usual $X_{1i} = 1$, then, we have $\sum_i = 1^n \widehat{\varepsilon}_i = 0$.

The vector $\widehat{y}$ is interpreted as the best linear fit to the vector y, which establishes a connection with the regression material of Chapter 7, although we have not yet specified any random structure generating the data, the results are data specific.

We may write $\widehat{\varepsilon} = y - X\widehat{\beta}$ so that the orthogonality conditions may be rewritten as

$$X^{\mathsf{T}}(y - X\widehat{\beta}) = 0. \tag{17.1}$$

We can rewrite this equation as the so-called **normal equations**

$$X^{\mathsf{T}}X\widehat{\beta} = X^{\mathsf{T}}y \tag{17.2}$$

$$X^{\mathsf{T}}X = \begin{pmatrix} \sum_{i=1}^{n} x_{1i}^2 & & \sum_{i=1}^{n} x_{1i}x_{Ki} \\ & \ddots & \\ & & \sum_{i=1}^{n} x_{Ki}^2 \end{pmatrix} \quad ; \quad X^{\mathsf{T}}y = \begin{pmatrix} \sum_{i=1}^{n} x_{1i}y_i \\ \vdots \\ \sum_{i=1}^{n} x_{Ki}y_i \end{pmatrix}.$$

There always exists some $\widehat{\beta}$ such that $S(\widehat{\beta})$ is minimal, but it may not be unique. When $\text{rank}(X) = K$, then $X^{\mathsf{T}}X$ is of full rank and hence invertible. Then $\widehat{\beta}$ is uniquely defined for any y, i.e.,

$$\widehat{\beta} = (X^{\mathsf{T}}X)^{-1}X^{\mathsf{T}}y.$$

How do we find $\widehat{y}$ and $\widehat{\varepsilon}$?

Definition 17.2. When X is of full rank define the $n \times n$ Projector matrices

$$P_X = X(X^{\mathsf{T}}X)^{-1}X^{\mathsf{T}} \quad ; \quad M_X = I - X(X^{\mathsf{T}}X)^{-1}X^{\mathsf{T}}$$

which project onto $C(X)$ and onto the orthogonal complement of $C(X)$, denoted $C^\perp(X)$. For any y, we can uniquely write

$$y = \widehat{y} + \widehat{\varepsilon} = P_X y + M_X y.$$

We have $P_X X = X$ and $M_X X = 0$. The matrices P_X and M_X are symmetric and **idempotent**, i.e.,

$$P_X = P_X^\mathsf{T} \quad ; \quad P_X^2 = P_X.$$

After applying P_X once you are ready in $C(X)$. This means that they have eigenvalues either 0 or 1 using the eigendecomposition. Let $P_X = U \Lambda U^\mathsf{T}$ for orthonormal U and diagonal Λ. Then

$$(P_X)^2 = \left(U \Lambda U^\mathsf{T}\right)\left(U \Lambda U^\mathsf{T}\right) = \left(U \Lambda^2 U^\mathsf{T}\right)$$

so if $P_X^2 = P_X$, then $\Lambda^2 = \Lambda$, and eigenvalues have to be in $\{0, 1\}$. P_X is of rank K and has K eigenvalues equal to 1 and $n - K$ eigenvalues equal to 0, with the reverse for M_X.

Theorem 17.1. *The space $C(X)$ is invariant to nonsingular linear transforms. That is for $A_{K \times K}$ with $\det A \neq 0$, we have*

$$C(XA) = C(X).$$

Proof. Let $v \in C(X)$. Then there exists an $\alpha \in \mathbb{R}^K$ such that $v = X\alpha$. Therefore,

$$v = X A A^{-1} \alpha = X A \gamma,$$

where $\gamma = A^{-1}\alpha \in \mathbb{R}^K$. Likewise for any $v = X A \gamma$, we can write $v = X\alpha$ for $\alpha = A^{-1}\gamma$. That is, $X \in C(XA)$ and so $C(X) = C(XA)$. □

Since $C(X)$ is invariant to linear transformations, so are $\widehat{y}$ and $\widehat{\varepsilon}$ (but not $\widehat{\beta}$). For example, rescaling of the components of X does not affect the values of $\widehat{y}$ and $\widehat{\varepsilon}$.

$$y \text{ on } (x_1, x_2, x_3) \tag{17.3}$$
$$y \text{ on } (x_1 + x_2, 2x_2 - x_3, 3x_1 - 2x_2 + 5x_3) \tag{17.4}$$

in which case the transformation is

$$A = \begin{pmatrix} 1 & 0 & 3 \\ 1 & 2 & -2 \\ 0 & -1 & 5 \end{pmatrix},$$

which is of full rank. Therefore, (17.3) and (17.4) yield the same $\widehat{y}, \widehat{\varepsilon}$.

Example 17.1. Dummy variables. Suppose that $x_{ji} = 1$ if $j \in I_\ell$ and $x_{ji} = 0$ if $j \notin I_\ell$, where $\{I_\ell\}$ forms a partition of $\{1, \ldots, n\}$. Specifically,

$$I_\ell \cap I_{\ell'} = \varnothing, \; \ell \neq \ell' \; ; \quad \cup_{\ell=1}^L I_\ell = \{1, \ldots, n\}.$$

For example, day of the week dummies. In this case $L = 5$

$$X = \begin{pmatrix} 1 & 0 & 0 & 0 & 0 \\ 0 & 1 & 0 & 0 & 0 \\ \vdots & 0 & 1 & 0 & 0 \\ \vdots & & 0 & 1 & 0 \\ \vdots & & & 0 & 1 \\ & & & \vdots & \vdots \end{pmatrix}.$$

We have a diagonal **hat matrix**

$$X^\mathsf{T}X = \begin{pmatrix} n_1 & 0 & & & 0 \\ & n_2 & 0 & & \\ & & n_3 & & \\ & & & n_4 & \\ & & & & n_5 \end{pmatrix}.$$

Emphasizing $\mathcal{C}(X)$ rather than X itself is called the **coordinate free** approach. Some aspects of model/estimate are properties of $\mathcal{C}(X)$, the choice of coordinates is irrelevant.

When X is not of full rank, the space $\mathcal{C}(X)$ is still well defined, as is the projection from y onto $\mathcal{C}(X)$. The fitted value $\widehat{y}$ and residual $\widehat{\varepsilon}$ are uniquely defined in this case, but there is no unique coefficient vector $\widehat{\beta}$. This case is often called multicollinearity in econometrics, although it also arises in big data where the number of covariates is large relative to the number of observations. Suppose that X is of deficient rank $J < K$. The singular value decomposition of X is

$$X = USV^\mathsf{T},$$

where $S = \mathrm{diag}\{s_1, s_2, \ldots, s_J, 0, \ldots, 0\}|0_{n-K \times K}$. Then we may write for $\lambda_j > 0$

$$X^\mathsf{T}X = U\Lambda U^\mathsf{T}, \quad U^\mathsf{T}X^\mathsf{T}XU = \Lambda$$

$$\Lambda = \begin{bmatrix} \lambda_1 & & & 0 \\ & \ddots & & \\ & & \lambda_J & \\ 0 & & & 0 \end{bmatrix}.$$

Then the normal equations (17.2) can be rewritten

$$U \Lambda U^\mathsf{T} \widehat{\beta} = V S^\mathsf{T} U y.$$

Premultiplying by U^T we obtain J equations in J unknowns

$$\lambda_j u_j^\mathsf{T} \widehat{\beta} = u_j^\mathsf{T} V S^\mathsf{T} U y.$$

We may solve for $u_j^\mathsf{T} \widehat{\beta} = u_j^\mathsf{T} V S^\mathsf{T} U y / \lambda_j$, $j = 1, \dots, J$. Let U_J denote the $K \times J$ matrix of eigenvectors of X corresponding to the non-zero eigenvalues. Then we may write

$$X\beta = X U_J U_J^\mathsf{T} \beta = \widetilde{X} \widetilde{\beta}_J$$

with $\widetilde{\beta}_J$ being $J \times 1$ vector of unknown quantities. Then $\widehat{\widetilde{\beta}}_J = (\widetilde{X}^\mathsf{T} \widetilde{X})^{-1} \widetilde{X}^\mathsf{T} y = (U_J^\mathsf{T} X^\mathsf{T} X U_J)^{-1} U_J^\mathsf{T} X^\mathsf{T} y$ and $\widehat{y} = P_{\widetilde{X}} y$.

17.2 PARTITIONED REGRESSION

We next consider an important application of the projection idea. Partition

$$X = (X_{1n \times K_1}, X_{2n \times K_2}), \quad K_1 + K_2 = K,$$

and suppose we are interested only in $\widehat{\beta}_1$ in the **long regression**.

We are going to show a formula for $\widehat{\beta}_1$ that does not involve computing all of $\widehat{\beta}$ and reading off the subvector $\widehat{\beta}_1$. This will be called the **Frisch–Waugh–Lovell Theorem**. A key property of projection is given below.

Theorem 17.2. *Suppose that X_1 and X_2 are orthogonal, i.e., $X_1^\mathsf{T} X_2 = 0$. Then*

$$P_X = P_{X_1} + P_{X_2}.$$

This can be verified algebraically, but also should be obvious geometrically. We return to the general case. We have

$$\widehat{y} = X\widehat{\beta} = P_X y = P_{X_1} y + P_{X_2} y = X_1 \widehat{\beta}_1 + X_2 \widehat{\beta}_2.$$

This just says that if X_1 and X_2 were orthogonal, then we could get $\widehat{\beta}_1$ by regressing y on X_1 only, and $\widehat{\beta}_2$ by regressing y on X_2 only.

$$\begin{pmatrix} \widehat{\beta}_1 \\ \widehat{\beta}_2 \end{pmatrix} = \begin{bmatrix} X_1^\mathsf{T} X_1 & 0 \\ 0 & X_2^\mathsf{T} X_2 \end{bmatrix}^{-1} \begin{pmatrix} X_1^\mathsf{T} y \\ X_2^\mathsf{T} y \end{pmatrix} = \begin{pmatrix} (X_1^\mathsf{T} X_1)^{-1} X_1^\mathsf{T} y \\ (X_2^\mathsf{T} X_2)^{-1} X_2^\mathsf{T} y \end{pmatrix}.$$

It is rare that design matrices X_1 and X_2 are orthogonal, but we can construct equivalent regressors that are orthogonal. Suppose we have general X_1 and X_2, whose dimensions satisfy $K_1 + K_2 = K$. We make the following observations:

1. (X_1, X_2) and $(M_2 X_1, X_2)$ span the same space. This follows because $X_1 = M_2 X_1 + P_2 X_1$, where $\mathcal{C}(P_2 X_1) \subset \mathcal{C}(X_2)$. Therefore, $\mathcal{C}(M_2 X_1, X_2) = \mathcal{C}(X_1, X_2)$.
2. $M_2 X_1$ and X_2 are orthogonal.

This says that if we regress y on (X_1, X_2) or y on $(M_2 X_1, X_2)$ we get the same $\widehat{y}$ and $\widehat{\varepsilon}$, and that if we wanted the coefficients on $M_2 X_1$ from the second regression we could in fact just regress y on $M_2 X_1$ only.

What are the coefficients on $M_2 X_1$? Recall that

$$\begin{aligned} \widehat{y} &= X_1 \widehat{\beta}_1 + X_2 \widehat{\beta}_2 \\ &= (M_2 + P_2) X_1 \widehat{\beta}_1 + X_2 \widehat{\beta}_2 \\ &= M_2 X_1 \widehat{\beta}_1 + X_2 [\widehat{\beta}_2 + (X_2^\mathsf{T} X_2)^{-1} X_2^\mathsf{T} X_1 \widehat{\beta}_1] \\ &= M_2 X_1 \widehat{\beta}_1 + X_2 \widehat{C}, \end{aligned}$$

where $\widehat{C} = \widehat{\beta}_2 + (X_2^\mathsf{T} X_2)^{-1} X_2^\mathsf{T} X_1 \widehat{\beta}_1$. So the coefficient on $M_2 X_1$ is the original $\widehat{\beta}_1$, while that on X_2 is some combination of $\widehat{\beta}_1$ and $\widehat{\beta}_2$. Note that $M_2 X_1$ are the residuals from a regression of X_1 on X_2.

Theorem 17.3. *Frisch–Waugh–Lovell. The coefficient on $M_{X_2} X_1$ is the original $\widehat{\beta}_1$, i.e.,*

$$\begin{aligned} \widehat{\beta}_1 &= (X_1^\mathsf{T} M_{X_2} X_1)^{-1} X_1^\mathsf{T} M_{X_2} y = ((X_1^\mathsf{T} M_{X_2}) \overbrace{(M_{X_2} X_1)}^{\widetilde{X}_1})^{-1} (X_1^\mathsf{T} M_{X_2}) \overbrace{M_{X_2} y}^{\widetilde{y}} \\ &= (\widetilde{X}_1^\mathsf{T} \widetilde{X}_1)^{-1} \widetilde{X}_1^\mathsf{T} \widetilde{y} \end{aligned}$$

PRACTICAL IMPLICATION. If K is large and we are primarily interested in first K_1 variables, then we can get $\widehat{\beta}_1$ by regressing y [or $M_2 y$ equivalently] on $M_2 X_1$ only, i.e.,

$$\widehat{\beta}_1 = (X_1^\mathsf{T} M_2 X_1)^{-1} X_1^\mathsf{T} M_2 y = (X_1^\mathsf{T} M_2 M_2 X_1)^{-1} X_1^\mathsf{T} M_2 M_2 y.$$

This involves inversion of only $K_1 \times K_1$ and $K_2 \times K_2$ matrices, which involves less computing time than inverting $K \times K$ matrices, especially when K is large [this computation can be as bad as $O(K^3)$].

Example 17.2. Suppose that $X_2 = (1, 1, \ldots, 1)^{\mathsf{T}} = i$ and $X_1 = x_1$, then

$$M_{X_2} = I_n - i(i^{\mathsf{T}}i)^{-1}i^{\mathsf{T}} = I_n - \frac{ii^{\mathsf{T}}}{n}$$

$$M_{X_2}x_1 = x_1 - \frac{1}{n}\sum_{i=1}^{n} x_{ji} \begin{pmatrix} 1 \\ \vdots \\ 1 \end{pmatrix} = \begin{pmatrix} x_{11} - \overline{x}_1 \\ \vdots \\ x_{1n} - \overline{x}_1 \end{pmatrix}$$

$$\widehat{\beta}_1 = \frac{\sum_{i=1}^{n} (x_{1i} - \overline{x}_1)(y_i - \overline{y})}{\sum_{i=1}^{n} (x_{1i} - \overline{x}_1)^2}$$

When regression includes an intercept, can first demean the X variables (and the y's) then do regression on the demeaned variables.

Other examples include seasonal components (dummy variables), trends, etc. Common practice is to deseasonalize data or detrend data before analyzing effect of interest. This argument shows it is justified.

17.3 RESTRICTED LEAST SQUARES

Suppose we have q linear restrictions on β, i.e.,

$$\begin{bmatrix} R_{11} & \cdots & R_{1K} \\ & & \\ R_{q1} & \cdots & R_{qK} \end{bmatrix} \begin{pmatrix} \beta_1 \\ \vdots \\ \beta_K \end{pmatrix} = R\beta = r = \begin{pmatrix} r_1 \\ \vdots \\ r_q \end{pmatrix} \qquad (17.5)$$

where R is $q \times K$ with $q < K$ and R is of rank q.

Example 17.3. Suppose that $\beta_1 + \cdots + \beta_K = 1$ (constant returns to scale). Then substituting in $\beta_K = 1 - \beta_1 - \cdots - \beta_{K-1}$, we obtain

$$X\beta = \sum_{j=1}^{K} x_j\beta_j = \sum_{j=1}^{K-1} x_j\beta_j + x_K(1 - \beta_1 - \cdots - \beta_{K-1})$$

$$= \sum_{j=1}^{K-1} (x_j - x_K)\beta_j + x_K.$$

This depends on only $\beta_1, \ldots, \beta_{K-1}$.

We want to minimize the quadratic form

$$S(\beta) = (y - X\beta)^{\mathsf{T}}(y - X\beta)$$

subject to the restrictions. Let $\widetilde{\beta}$ denote the solution.

Partition X, β, and R

$$X = (\underset{n \times (K-q)}{X_1}, \underset{n \times q}{X_2}) \quad ; \quad R = (\underset{q \times (K-q)}{R_1}, \underset{q \times q}{R_2}) \quad ; \quad \beta = \begin{pmatrix} \beta_1 \\ {}^{(K-q) \times 1} \\ \beta_2 \\ {}_{q \times 1} \end{pmatrix},$$

$$X_1 \beta_1 + X_2 \beta_2 = X\beta \quad ; \quad R_1 \beta_1 + R_2 \beta_2 = r,$$

where R_2 is of full rank q and invertible. This may require some reordering. We can write

$$\beta_2 = R_2^{-1}(r - R_1 \beta_1)$$

Therefore,

$$X\beta = X_1 \beta_1 + X_2[R_2^{-1}(r - R_1 \beta_1)] = (X_1 - X_2 R_2^{-1} R_1)\beta_1 + X_2 R_2^{-1} r.$$

In other words, we can find $\widehat{\beta}_1$ by minimizing

$$(y^* - X_1^* \beta_1)^\mathsf{T} (y^* - X_1^* \beta_1)$$

with respect to β_1, where $y^* = y - X_2 R_2^{-1} r$ and $X_1^* = X_1 - X_2 R_2^{-1} R_1$ to get

$$\widetilde{\beta}_1 = \left(X_1^{*\mathsf{T}} X_1^* \right)^{-1} X_1^{*\mathsf{T}} y^*$$
$$\widetilde{\beta}_2 = R_2^{-1}(r - R_1 \widetilde{\beta}_1).$$

In fact there are other more convenient expressions for this.

Theorem 17.4. *Iterated Projection.* *Suppose that* $X = (X_1, X_2)$, *and let* $\mathcal{C}(X_1)$ *be the columns span of* X_1 *so that* $\mathcal{C}(X_1)$ *is a subspace of* $\mathcal{C}(X)$. *Then*

$$P_{X_1} = P_{X_1} P_X.$$

This says that one can first project onto the bigger space and then onto the smaller space

Proof. Using the orthogonal representation of $\mathcal{C}(X)$ we have

$$P_X y = X_1 \widetilde{\beta}_1 + M_{X_1} X_2 \widetilde{\beta}_2$$

where $\widetilde{\beta}_1 = (X_1^\mathsf{T} X_1)^{-1} X_1^\mathsf{T} y$, and

$$P_{X_1} P_X y = P_{X_1} X_1 \widehat{\beta}_1 + P_{X_1} M_{X_1} X_2 \widehat{\beta}_2 = X_1 \widehat{\beta}_1 \qquad \square$$

Theorem 17.5. *Consider the special case of (17.5) where* $r = 0$. *Then*

$$\widetilde{\beta} = \widehat{\beta} - (X^\mathsf{T} X)^{-1} R^\mathsf{T} \left[R(X^\mathsf{T} X)^{-1} R^\mathsf{T} \right]^{-1} R\widehat{\beta}$$

$$= \left(I_K - (X^\mathsf{T} X)^{-1} R^\mathsf{T} \left[R(X^\mathsf{T} X)^{-1} R^\mathsf{T} \right]^{-1} R \right) \widehat{\beta}$$

Proof. Define

$$\mathcal{S} = \left\{ z \in \mathbb{R}^n : z = X\beta,\ R\beta = 0 \right\}.$$

This is a subspace of $\mathcal{C}(X)$, because if $z_1, z_2 \in \mathcal{S}$, we have $\alpha_1 z_1 + \alpha_2 z_2 \in \mathcal{S}$ for any scalars α_1, α_2. This is because there exist β_1, β_2 such that $z_1 = X\beta_1, z_2 = X\beta_2$ with $R\beta_1 = 0$, $R\beta_2 = 0$. Therefore,

$$\alpha_1 z_1 + \alpha_2 z_2 = \alpha_1 X\beta_1 + \alpha_2 X\beta_2 = X(\alpha_1\beta_1 + \alpha_2\beta_2)$$
$$R(\alpha_1\beta_1 + \alpha_2\beta_2) = \alpha_1 R\beta_1 + \alpha_2 R\beta_2 = 0.$$

Therefore, find the restricted least squares estimator using the principle of iterated projection – find $y \in \mathcal{S}$ to minimize

$$(\widehat{y} - y)^\mathsf{T} (\widehat{y} - y) = \left(X\widehat{\beta} - X\beta \right)^\mathsf{T} \left(X\widehat{\beta} - X\beta \right) = \left(\widehat{\beta} - \beta \right)^\mathsf{T} X^\mathsf{T} X \left(\widehat{\beta} - \beta \right).$$

The projection operator onto $\mathcal{S}$ is

$$M_W = I_n - W(W^\mathsf{T} W)^{-1} W^\mathsf{T} \quad ; \quad W = X(X^\mathsf{T} X)^{-1} R^\mathsf{T}$$

Hence $M_W X\widehat{\beta} = X\widetilde{\beta}$ and the result follows. $\qquad\square$

17.3.1 Backfitting in Linear Regression

We next consider an iterative approach to computing OLS estimators. Suppose that we have $y, x_1, \ldots, x_K$ vectors in $\mathbb{R}^n$. Define the projection operators $P_j = x_j(x_j^\mathsf{T} x_j)^{-1} x_j^\mathsf{T}$, $P_X = X(X^\mathsf{T} X)^{-1} X^\mathsf{T}$, $M_j = I_n - P_j$, and $M_X = I_n - P_X$, where $X = (x_1, \ldots, x_K)$. Thus

$$y = P_X y + M_X y = \widehat{y} + \widehat{\varepsilon}. \tag{17.6}$$

Suppose that one proceeds as follows

Backfitting Algorithm

1. First regresses y on x_1 and get the residuals $M_1 y$.
2. Then regress $M_1 y$ on x_2 to get residuals $M_2 M_1 y$.
3. Continue doing one dimension regressions in the order x_1 then x_2 etc. until the process converges.

The residual after K cycles of the backfitting algorithm is

$$\widehat{\varepsilon}^K = T^K y \quad ; \quad T = M_K M_{K-1} \cdots M_1,$$

where $T : \mathbb{R}^n \to \mathbb{R}^n$.

Theorem 17.6. *Suppose that X is of full rank. Then, we have as $K \to \infty$*

$$T^K y \to M_X y = \widehat{\varepsilon}.$$

Proof. We prove that T is a strict contraction mapping for $z \in \mathcal{C}(X)$, that is $\|Tz\| < \|z\|$ for any $z \in \mathcal{C}(X)$. This means that T shrinks any such vectors. First, for any vector z write $Tz = M_K M_{K-1} \cdots M_1 z = M_K v$ for $v = M_{K-1} \cdots M_1 z$. Then

$$
\begin{aligned}
\|Tz\|^2 &= z^\mathsf{T} T^2 z \\
&= v^\mathsf{T} M_K v \\
&\leq \frac{v^\mathsf{T} M_K v}{v^\mathsf{T} v} v^\mathsf{T} v \\
&\leq \lambda_{\max}(M_K) \|M_{K-1} \cdots M_1 z\|^2 \\
&\leq \|M_{K-1} \cdots M_1 z\|^2 \\
&\leq \|z\|^2
\end{aligned}
$$

since $\lambda_{\max}(M_j) = 1$ (M_j are symmetric idempotent). Therefore, T is a weak contraction. Furthermore, if $\|Tz\| = \|z\|$ then $\|M_1 z\| = \|z\|$ from the above argument. This implies that z is orthogonal to the space spanned by x_1, i.e., $z \in \mathcal{C}(x_1)^\perp$. Similarly one obtains that $z \in \mathcal{C}(x_j)^\perp$, $j = 2, \ldots, K$. In other words, if $\|Tz\| = \|z\|$, then $z \in \mathcal{C}(X)^\perp$. Therefore, if $z \in \mathcal{C}(X)$, it must be that

$$\|Tz\| < \|z\| \leq (1 - \epsilon) \|z\|$$

for some $0 < \epsilon \leq 1$. Also, if $z \in \mathcal{C}(X)$, then $Tz \in \mathcal{C}(X)$. Hence

$$\left\| T^K z \right\| \leq (1 - \epsilon) \left\| T^{K-1} z \right\| \leq (1 - \epsilon)^K \|z\|.$$

Then combine with (17.6) we obtain the result. $\qquad\square$

This says that one can compute the regression of y on $x_1, \ldots, x_K$ by computing a sequence of linear one dimensional regressions. This method is of interest when the number of covariates is large, since it avoids directly inverting the full design matrix.

17.3.2 Goodness of Fit

We may decompose the total sum of squares as follows using the orthogonality

$$y^\mathsf{T} y = \widehat{y}^\mathsf{T} \widehat{y} + \widehat{\varepsilon}^\mathsf{T} \widehat{\varepsilon} \qquad (17.7)$$

This is valid for any set of $X = (x_1, \ldots, x_K)$. It follows that

$$\widehat{y}^\mathsf{T} \widehat{y} \le y^\mathsf{T} y, \qquad (17.8)$$

i.e., the Euclidean norm of the projected vector is smaller than the norm of the original series. The notion of fit is widely used in practice. It captures the idea of how much of the variation in the data is explained by the covariates, i.e., by how much $\widehat{y}^\mathsf{T} \widehat{y} \le y^\mathsf{T} y$. One possibility is to measure the fit by the residual sum of squares

$$S(\widehat{\beta}) = RSS = \sum_{i=1}^{n} (y_i - \widehat{y}_i)^2 = \| y - \widehat{y} \|^2 = \widehat{\varepsilon}^\mathsf{T} \widehat{\varepsilon} = y^\mathsf{T} M_X y = y^\mathsf{T} y - \widehat{y}^\mathsf{T} \widehat{y},$$

which captures the Euclidean distance of the sample from the "fitted value". In general, the smaller the RSS the better. However, the numerical value of RSS depends on the units used to measure y in so that one cannot compare across different X's.

The idea is to compare the RSS from a given X with the RSS of the X that contains only ones. When $X = i$ ($i = (1, \ldots, 1)^\mathsf{T}$), that is, we just calculate the mean of y, we have

$$y^\mathsf{T} y = \overline{y}^2 i^\mathsf{T} i + \overline{\varepsilon}^\mathsf{T} \overline{\varepsilon},$$

where $\overline{\varepsilon} = y - \overline{y} i$.

Definition 17.3. For a general $X = (x_1, \ldots, x_K)$, we define

$$R^2 = 1 - \frac{\widehat{\varepsilon}^\mathsf{T} \widehat{\varepsilon}}{\overline{\varepsilon}^\mathsf{T} \overline{\varepsilon}}.$$

Remarks. 1. When X contains a column vector of ones, $0 \le R^2 \le 1$. If X does not contain a column vector of ones, R^2 could be less than zero.
2. In the bivariate case, R^2 is the squared sample correlation between y and x.
3. R^2 is invariant to some changes of units. If $y \mapsto ay + b$ for any constants a, b, then $\widehat{y}_i \mapsto a\widehat{y}_i + b$ and $\overline{y} \mapsto a\overline{y} + b$, so R^2 is the same in this case. Clearly, if $X \mapsto XA$ for a nonsingular matrix A, then $\widehat{y}$ is unchanged, as is y and $\overline{y}$.
4. R^2 always increases with the addition of variables. With $K = n$ we can make $R^2 = 1$.
5. R^2 can't be used to compare across different y.

Chapter 18

Linear Model

18.1 INTRODUCTION

The linear model is the basis for most of econometrics. We will discuss here some probabilistic assumptions that underly this and that allow us to understand the properties of the OLS "estimator" defined above.

18.2 THE MODEL

We next specify a model of how our data

$$y, X \in \mathbb{R}^{n(K+1)}$$

were generated. We suppose that there is a random mechanism which is behind everything – the data we have is one realization of an infinity of such potential outcomes. In fact, we will specify a model for how y responds to X and do not specify much about X itself except that we suppose throughout that

$$\text{rank}(X) = K < n. \tag{18.1}$$

Note that this is an assumption, but it is immediately verifiable from the data in contrast to some other assumptions we will make.

We shall make the following assumptions regarding the way the data $y, X \in \mathbb{R}^{n(K+1)}$ were generated:

Assumption A. 1. *There exists a vector $\beta \in \mathbb{R}^K$ such that with probability one*

$$E(y|X) = X\beta$$

2. *There exists a positive definite finite $n \times n$ matrix $\Sigma(X)$ such that with probability one*

$$\text{var}(y|X) = \Sigma(X)$$

3. *Conditional on X we have with probability one*

$$y \sim N(X\beta, \ \Sigma(X))$$

Probability, Statistics and Econometrics. http://dx.doi.org/10.1016/B978-0-12-810495-8.00021-X

4. *Conditional on X, we have with probability one*

$$y \sim N(X\beta, \sigma^2 I).$$

For the most part we shall just require assumptions A1 and A2, which just specify the first two conditional moments of the $n \times 1$ vector y with regard to the $n \times K$ matrix X.

We write the regression model in the more familiar form. Define

$$\varepsilon = y - X\beta = \begin{pmatrix} \varepsilon_1 \\ \vdots \\ \varepsilon_n \end{pmatrix}.$$

Then

$$y = X\beta + \varepsilon,$$

where Assumptions A1 and A2 are equivalent to

$$E(\varepsilon|X) = 0 \tag{18.2}$$

$$E(\varepsilon\varepsilon^\mathsf{T}|X) = \Sigma(X) \tag{18.3}$$

with probability one. The linear regression model is more commonly stated like this with statistical assumptions made about the unobservable ε rather than directly on the observable y. The assumptions about the vector ε are very weak (and incomplete since we only specify some moments).

Assumption A1 $[E(\varepsilon|X) = 0]$ can be expressed as (local notation change alert)

$$E\left(\varepsilon_i | \overbrace{x_1, \ldots, x_n}^{\text{future and past}} \right) = 0 \quad ; \quad x_i = \begin{pmatrix} x_{i1} \\ \vdots \\ x_{iK} \end{pmatrix} \in \mathbb{R}^K$$

with probability one. This is consistent with the design being fixed in repeated samples (such as $x_i = i$) and it is also consistent with the case where (x_i, ε_i) are i.i.d. In a time series settings this would be called **strong exogeneity**, and it would rule out for example a lagged dependent variables in X.

The condition (18.3) is very general, essentially all that is being assumed here is that the conditional variance is finite with probability one. In particular, the $n \times n$ covariance matrix $\Sigma(X)$ can depend on the covariates, and can allow correlation between the error terms. A special case of substantial interest is where

$$\Sigma(X) = \sigma^2 I_n, \tag{18.4}$$

which is called the **homoskedastic** (and uncorrelated) case. The heteroskedastic case has

$$
\Sigma(X) = \begin{bmatrix} \sigma_1^2 & & 0 \\ & \ddots & \\ 0 & & \sigma_n^2 \end{bmatrix},
$$

where σ_i^2 may all be distinct. Another case of interest is the so-called **clustered** or **block-diagonal** case, where

$$
\Sigma(X) = \begin{bmatrix} B_1 & & 0 \\ & \ddots & \\ 0 & & B_p \end{bmatrix},
$$

where B_j are non-zero blocks with dimensions $n_j \times n_j$, $j = 1, \ldots, p$, such that $\sum_{j=1}^{p} n_j$, and the off-diagonal elements are non-zero. Finally, in time series problems, $\Sigma(X)$ may have all entries non-zero but have the property that entries get smaller and smaller the further they are away from the diagonal.

Chapter 19

Statistical Properties of the OLS Estimator

19.1 PROPERTIES OF OLS

We now investigate the statistical properties of the OLS estimator of β. Specifically, we calculate its exact mean and variance and compare it with other possible estimators under the assumptions A1 and A2. We shall examine later what happens when the sample size increases.

Definition 19.1. The estimator $\widehat{\beta}$ is linear in y, i.e., there exists a matrix C not depending on y such that

$$\widehat{\beta} = (X^\mathsf{T} X)^{-1} X^\mathsf{T} y = Cy.$$

This property makes a lot of calculations simple. In a time series context where X may contain lagged values of y this property is not so meaningful.

We want to evaluate how $\widehat{\beta}$ varies across hypothetical repeated samples under Assumption A.

Theorem 19.1. *Suppose that assumption A1 holds. Then, we have*

$$E(\widehat{\beta}|X) = (X^\mathsf{T} X)^{-1} X^\mathsf{T} E(y|X) = (X^\mathsf{T} X)^{-1} X^\mathsf{T} X\beta = \beta,$$

where this equality holds for all β. We say that $\widehat{\beta}$ is conditionally unbiased. It follows that it is unconditionally unbiased using the Law of Iterated Expectation.

Furthermore, we shall calculate the $K \times K$ conditional covariance matrix of $\widehat{\beta}$,

$$\text{var}(\widehat{\beta}|X) = E\left[(\widehat{\beta} - E(\widehat{\beta}|X))(\widehat{\beta} - E(\widehat{\beta}|X))^\mathsf{T}|X\right] = E\left[(\widehat{\beta} - \beta)(\widehat{\beta} - \beta)^\mathsf{T}|X\right].$$

This has diagonal elements $\text{var}(\widehat{\beta}_j|X)$ and off-diagonals $\text{cov}(\widehat{\beta}_j, \widehat{\beta}_k|X)$.

Theorem 19.2. *Suppose that assumptions A1 and A2 hold. Then*

$$\text{var}(\widehat{\beta}|X) = (X^\mathsf{T} X)^{-1} X^\mathsf{T} E(\varepsilon\varepsilon^\mathsf{T}|X)X(X^\mathsf{T} X)^{-1}$$
$$= (X^\mathsf{T} X)^{-1} X^\mathsf{T} \Sigma(X)X(X^\mathsf{T} X)^{-1}.$$

Probability, Statistics and Econometrics. http://dx.doi.org/10.1016/B978-0-12-810495-8.00022-1
267

In the homoskedastic special case, $\Sigma(X) = \sigma^2 I_n$, this simplifies to

$$\text{var}(\widehat{\beta}|X) = \sigma^2 (X^\mathsf{T} X)^{-1}. \tag{19.1}$$

The matrix $X^\mathsf{T} X$ is generally not diagonal, except in special cases such as dummy variables.

We next consider the unconditional variance, which follows also from the law of iterated expectation

$$\text{var}(\widehat{\beta}) = E\text{var}(\widehat{\beta}|X) = E\left[(X^\mathsf{T} X)^{-1} X^\mathsf{T} \Sigma(X) X (X^\mathsf{T} X)^{-1}\right]$$
$$= \sigma^2 E\left[(X^\mathsf{T} X)^{-1}\right] \text{ in the homoskedastic case,}$$

provided the moment exists. Under the assumption that X is full rank with probability one we may always define $(X^\mathsf{T} X)^{-1}$. However, this is not sufficient to guarantee the existence of the expectation of its inverse.

Example 19.1. Suppose that $n = K = 1$ and $x_1 \sim N(0, 1)$, then $\Pr(x_1^2 = 0) = 0$ but $E(x_1^{-2}) = \infty$. However, when $n \geq 2$ this problem goes away because we have $E((\sum_{i=1}^n x_i^2)^{-1}) < \infty$.

However, according to the ancillarity principle we should really just consider the conditional distribution.

The properties of an individual coefficient can be obtained from the partitioned regression formula $\widehat{\beta}_1 = (X_1^\mathsf{T} M_2 X_1)^{-1} X_1^\mathsf{T} M_2 y$. In general we have

$$\text{var}[\widehat{\beta}_1|X] = (X_1^\mathsf{T} M_2 X_1)^{-1} X_1^\mathsf{T} M_2 E\left(\varepsilon\varepsilon^\mathsf{T}|X\right) M_2 X_1 (X_1^\mathsf{T} M_2 X_1)^{-1}$$
$$= (X_1^\mathsf{T} M_2 X_1)^{-1} X_1^\mathsf{T} M_2 \Sigma(X) M_2 X_1 (X_1^\mathsf{T} M_2 X_1)^{-1}$$
$$= \sigma^2 (X_1^\mathsf{T} M_2 X_1)^{-1} \text{ in the homoskedastic case.}$$

In the special case that $X_2 = (1, \ldots, 1)^\mathsf{T}$, we have

$$\text{var}(\widehat{\beta}_1|X) = \frac{\sigma^2}{\sum_{i=1}^n (x_i - \overline{x})^2}.$$

This is the well known variance of the least squares estimator in the single regressor plus intercept regression.

We now turn to the distribution of $\widehat{\beta}$. This will be important when we want to conduct hypothesis tests and construct confidence intervals. In order to get the *exact* distribution we will need to make the additional assumption, A3.

Theorem 19.3. *Suppose that condition A3 holds. Then, the distribution of $\widehat{\beta}$ conditional on X is the multivariate normal distribution*

$$\widehat{\beta} \sim N(\beta, V(X)), \quad V(X) = (X^\mathsf{T} X)^{-1} X^\mathsf{T} \Sigma(X) X (X^\mathsf{T} X)^{-1}.$$

This follows because $\widehat{\beta} = \sum_{i=1}^{n} c_i y_i$, where c_i depends only on the covariates, i.e., $\widehat{\beta}$ is a linear combination of independent normals, and hence it is normal, conditionally. The unconditional distribution of $\widehat{\beta}$ will not be normal – in fact, it will be a scale mixture of normals. However, it follows that

$$V(X)^{-1/2}\left(\widehat{\beta} - \beta\right) \sim N(0, I_K)$$

conditional on X, and because the right hand side distribution does not depend on X, this result is unconditional too. Hence, the quadratic form

$$\tau = \left(\widehat{\beta} - \beta\right)^{\mathsf{T}} V(X)^{-1} \left(\widehat{\beta} - \beta\right) \sim \chi^2(K) \tag{19.2}$$

conditionally and unconditionally. The distribution of τ does not depend on unknown quantities, which will be helpful later when constructing hypothesis tests and confidence intervals.

We are also interested in estimation of $m = E(y|X) = X\beta \in \mathbb{R}^n$ and in the estimation of the function $m(x) = E(y_i|x_i = x)$ for any $x \in \mathbb{R}^K$. Let $\widehat{m} = X\widehat{\beta}$ and $\widehat{m}(x) = x^{\mathsf{T}}\widehat{\beta}$.

Theorem 19.4. *Suppose that assumptions A1 and A2 hold. Then $\widehat{m}$ is unbiased, i.e., $E(\widehat{m}|X) = m$, with*

$$\mathrm{var}(\widehat{m}|X) = X(X^{\mathsf{T}}X)^{-1}X^{\mathsf{T}}\Sigma(X)X(X^{\mathsf{T}}X)^{-1})X^{\mathsf{T}}.$$

Likewise, $\widehat{m}(x)$ is unbiased, i.e., $E(\widehat{m}(x)|X) = m(x)$, with

$$\mathrm{var}(\widehat{m}(x)|X) = x(X^{\mathsf{T}}X)^{-1}X^{\mathsf{T}}\Sigma(X)X(X^{\mathsf{T}}X)^{-1})x^{\mathsf{T}}.$$

Furthermore, if assumption A3 holds, then conditionally on X,

$$\widehat{m} \sim N(m, X(X^{\mathsf{T}}X)^{-1}X^{\mathsf{T}}\Sigma(X)X(X^{\mathsf{T}}X)^{-1}X^{\mathsf{T}}).$$

Note however, that $\mathrm{var}(\widehat{m}|X)$ is of rank $K < n$.

In the homoskedastic special case A4 we have conditionally

$$\widehat{\beta} \sim N(\beta, \sigma^2(X^{\mathsf{T}}X)^{-1})$$
$$\widehat{m} \sim N(m, \sigma^2 X(X^{\mathsf{T}}X)^{-1}X^{\mathsf{T}}).$$

Suppose we assume condition A4, which is a complete specification of the conditional distribution of y. Then the density function of the vector y [conditional on X] is

$$f_{y|X}(y) = \frac{1}{(2\pi\sigma^2)^{n/2}} \exp\left(-\frac{1}{2\sigma^2}(y - X\beta)^{\mathsf{T}}(y - X\beta)\right). \tag{19.3}$$

The density function depends on the unknown parameters β, σ^2. The log likelihood function for the observed data is

$$\ell(b, \omega^2 | y, X) = -\frac{n}{2} \log 2\pi - \frac{n}{2} \log \omega^2 - \frac{1}{2\omega^2}(y - Xb)^{\mathsf{T}}(y - Xb), \quad (19.4)$$

where b and ω are unknown parameters. Perhaps we are being overly pedantic here by emphasizing the difference between the true values β, σ^2 and the arguments b and ω of ℓ, and we shall not do this again. The maximum likelihood estimator $\widehat{\beta}_{mle}, \widehat{\sigma}^2_{mle}$ maximizes $\ell(b, \omega^2)$ with respect to b and ω^2. It is easy to see that

$$\widehat{\beta}_{mle} = \widehat{\beta} \quad ; \quad \widehat{\sigma}^2_{mle} = \frac{1}{n}(y - X\widehat{\beta}_{mle})^{\mathsf{T}}(y - X\widehat{\beta}_{mle}).$$

Basically, the criterion function (19.4) is the least squares criterion apart from an affine transformation involving only ω. Note however, that if we had a different assumption about the errors than normality, e.g., they were from a t-distribution, then we would have a different likelihood and a different estimator than $\widehat{\beta}$. In particular, the estimator may not be explicitly defined and may be a nonlinear function of y.

We next consider two widely used estimates of σ^2

$$\widehat{\sigma}^2_{mle} = \frac{\widehat{\varepsilon}^{\mathsf{T}}\widehat{\varepsilon}}{n}$$

$$s^2_* = \frac{\widehat{\varepsilon}^{\mathsf{T}}\widehat{\varepsilon}}{n - K}$$

The first estimate is the maximum likelihood estimator of σ^2. The second estimate is a modification of the MLE, which we can show is unbiased.

Theorem 19.5. *Suppose that A1, A2 hold and that* $\Sigma(X) = \sigma^2 I$. *Then*

$$E(s^2_*) = \sigma^2.$$

Proof. We have

$$\widehat{\varepsilon} = M_X y = M_X X\beta + M_X \varepsilon = M_X \varepsilon$$

so that $\widehat{\varepsilon}^{\mathsf{T}}\widehat{\varepsilon}$ is a quadratic form in normal random variables

$$\widehat{\varepsilon}^{\mathsf{T}}\widehat{\varepsilon} = y^{\mathsf{T}} M_X M_X y = \varepsilon^{\mathsf{T}} M_X M_X \varepsilon = \varepsilon^{\mathsf{T}} M_X \varepsilon$$

Therefore, under A2

$$E\left[\widehat{\varepsilon}^{\mathsf{T}}\widehat{\varepsilon} | X\right] = E\left[\operatorname{tr}\left(\varepsilon^{\mathsf{T}} M_X \varepsilon\right) | X\right] = E\left[\operatorname{tr}\left(\varepsilon\varepsilon^{\mathsf{T}} M_X\right) | X\right]$$
$$= \operatorname{tr}\left(E\left(\varepsilon\varepsilon^{\mathsf{T}} | X\right) M_X\right) = \operatorname{tr}\left(\Sigma(X) M_X\right).$$

If $\Sigma(X) = \sigma^2 I$, then

$$\text{tr}\,(\Sigma(X)M_X) = \sigma^2 \text{tr}\,(M_X) = \sigma^2(n - K).\qquad\square$$

19.1.1 Alternative Estimators

There are many possible alternative estimators to OLS that have been developed over the years. A major alternative is called the **Least Absolute Deviations** (LAD) procedure that minimizes the L_1 norm of the error term

$$\|y - Xb\|_1,$$

where $\|u\|_1 = \sum_{i=1}^{n} |u_i|$. This procedure goes back to Laplace in the 18th century but was put on a firm footing by Koenker and Bassett (1978). The resulting estimator denoted $\widehat{\beta}_{LAD}$ is a regression analogue of the sample median and has certain desirable properties in the face of outliers in the covariates. We discuss this procedure in more detail below.

Consider the scalar regression $y_i = \beta x_i + \varepsilon_i$. The OLS estimator is $\widehat{\beta} = \sum_{i=1}^{n} x_i y_i / \sum_{i=1}^{n} x_i^2$. Also plausible are $\widetilde{\beta} = \overline{y}/\overline{x}$ and $\overline{\beta} = \sum_{i=1}^{n} y_i / x_i$. Another example that arises from accounting practice, is the so-called high-low method for determining average cost. The corresponding estimator is

$$\beta_{H-L} = \frac{y_H - y_L}{x_H - x_L},$$

where x_H, x_L are the highest and lowest values achieved by the covariate respectively, and y_H, y_L are the "concomitants", that is, the corresponding values of the outcome variable. This estimator is also linear and unbiased under Assumption A.

A major class of estimators goes by the name of **Instrumental variables**. These are designed to outflank issues arising from endogeneity, which is of central importance in applied work. These are of the general form

$$\widehat{\beta} = (Z^\mathsf{T} X)^{-1} Z^\mathsf{T} y,$$

where Z is a full rank $n \times K$ matrix of instruments. We will discuss this class of estimators somewhat more in the final chapter, as they are included as a special case of the Generalized Method of Moments.

19.2 OPTIMALITY

There are many estimators of β. How do we choose between estimators? Computational convenience is an important issue, but the above estimators are all similar in their computational requirements. We now investigate statistical optimality.

Definition 19.2. The mean squared error (hereafter MSE) matrix of a generic estimator $\widehat{\theta}$ of a parameter $\theta \in \mathbb{R}^p$ is

$$
\begin{aligned}
\mathcal{M}(\widehat{\theta}, \theta) &= E[(\widehat{\theta} - \theta)(\widehat{\theta} - \theta)^\mathsf{T}] \\
&= E[(\widehat{\theta} - E(\widehat{\theta}) + E(\widehat{\theta}) - \theta)(\widehat{\theta} - E(\widehat{\theta}) + E(\widehat{\theta}) - \theta)^\mathsf{T}] \\
&= \underbrace{E[(\widehat{\theta} - E(\widehat{\theta}))(\widehat{\theta} - E(\widehat{\theta}))^\mathsf{T}]}_{\text{variance}} + \underbrace{[E(\widehat{\theta}) - \theta][E(\widehat{\theta}) - \theta]^\mathsf{T}}_{\text{squared bias}}.
\end{aligned}
$$

The expectation here can be conditional on X or unconditional. The MSE matrix is generally a function of the true parameter θ. We would like a method that does well for all θ, not just a subset of parameter values – the estimator $\widehat{\theta} = 0$ is an example of a procedure that will have MSE equal to zero at $\theta = 0$, and hence will do well at this point, but as θ moves away, the MSE increases quadratically without limit. Note that no estimator can dominate uniformly across θ according to MSE because it would have to beat all constant estimators which have zero MSE at a single point. This is impossible unless there is no randomness. This is the same issue we discussed in the scalar case in an earlier chapter.

In the multivariate case, an additional issue arises even when comparing two estimators at a single point of the parameter space. MSE defines a complete ordering when $p = 1$, i.e., one can always rank any two estimators according to MSE. When $p > 1$, this is not so. In the general case we say that $\widehat{\theta}$ is better (according to MSE) than $\widetilde{\theta}$ (at some fixed point θ) if $B \geq A$ (i.e., $B - A$ is a positive semidefinite matrix), where B is the MSE matrix of $\widetilde{\theta}$ and A is the MSE of $\widehat{\theta}$. For example, suppose that

$$
A = \begin{bmatrix} 1 & 0 \\ 0 & 1 \end{bmatrix}, \quad B = \begin{bmatrix} 2 & 0 \\ 0 & 1/4 \end{bmatrix}.
$$

In this case, we can not rank the estimators. The problem is due to the multivariate nature of the optimality criterion. One solution is to take a scalar function of MSE such as the trace or determinant, which will result in a complete ordering. For example, for positive definite Q let

$$
\text{tr}\left(E[(\widehat{\theta} - \theta)^\mathsf{T} Q(\widehat{\theta} - \theta)] \right) = \text{tr}(\mathcal{M}Q).
$$

For example, consider linear combinations of the parameter $c^\mathsf{T}\theta$. In this case, the MSE of $c^\mathsf{T}(\widehat{\theta} - \theta)$ is scalar and can be considered as the trace MSE with the particular $Q = cc^\mathsf{T}$. However, different scalar functions will rank estimators differently, e.g., what is good for some c may be bad for some other c'.

Example 19.2. For example, the estimation of $m = X\beta$ by $\widehat{m} = X\widehat{\beta}$, yields

$$\text{tr}\left(E[(\widehat{m} - m)^\mathsf{T} Q(\widehat{m} - m)]\right) = \text{tr}\left(X(X^\mathsf{T}X)^{-1}X^\mathsf{T}\Sigma(X)X(X^\mathsf{T}X)^{-1}X^\mathsf{T}Q\right).$$

Under homoskedasticity and with $Q = I_n$, this equals $\sigma^2 K$. For other Q we obtain a different result.

The OLS estimator is **admissible** in the scalar case, meaning that no estimator uniformly dominates it according to mean squared error. However, in the multivariate case when the rank of Q is greater than or equal to 3 Stein (shrinkage) estimators, which are biased, improve on least squares according to MSE.

An alternative approach is to consider the minimax approach. For example, we might take the performance measure of the estimator $\widehat{\theta}$ to be

$$\mathcal{R}(\widehat{\theta}) = \max_{\theta \in \Theta} \text{tr}(\mathcal{M}(\widehat{\theta}, \theta)),$$

which takes the most pessimistic view. In this case, we might try and find the estimator that minimizes this criterion – this would be called a minimax estimator. The theory for this class of estimators is very complicated, and in any case it is not such a desirable criterion because it is so pessimistic about nature trying to do the worst to us.

Instead, we might reduce the class of allowable estimators. If we restrict attention to unbiased estimators then this rules out estimators like $\widehat{\theta} = 0$ because they will be biased. In this case there is some hope of an optimality theory for the class of unbiased estimators. We will now return to the linear regression model and make the further restriction that the estimators we consider are linear in y. That is, we suppose that we have the set of all estimators $\widetilde{\beta}$ that satisfy

$$\widetilde{\beta} = Ay$$

for some fixed matrix A such that with probability one

$$E(\widetilde{\beta}|X) = \beta, \quad \forall \beta.$$

This latter condition implies that $(AX - I)\beta = 0$ for all β, which is equivalent to $AX = I$.

Theorem 19.6. *Gauss Markov Suppose that assumptions A1 and A2 hold and that $\Sigma(X) = \sigma^2 I_n$. Then the OLS estimator $\widehat{\beta}$ is Best Linear Unbiased (BLUE), i.e., with probability one*

$$\text{var}(\widehat{\beta}|X) \le \text{var}(\widetilde{\beta}|X)$$

for any other LUE.

Proof. $\text{var}(\widehat{\beta}|X) = \sigma^2 (X^\mathsf{T} X)^{-1}$; $\text{var}(\widetilde{\beta}|X) = \sigma^2 A A^\mathsf{T}$

$$
\begin{aligned}
\text{var}(\widetilde{\beta}|X) - \text{var}(\widehat{\beta}|X) &= \sigma^2 [A A^\mathsf{T} - (X^\mathsf{T} X)^{-1}] \\
&= \sigma^2 [A A^\mathsf{T} - A X (X^\mathsf{T} X)^{-1} X^\mathsf{T} A^\mathsf{T}] \\
&= \sigma^2 A [I - X (X^\mathsf{T} X)^{-1} X^\mathsf{T}] A^\mathsf{T} \\
&= \sigma^2 A M_X A^\mathsf{T} \\
&\geq 0. \qquad\qquad\qquad\qquad \square
\end{aligned}
$$

Remarks. 1. No assumption is made about the distribution of the errors; it only assumes 0 mean and $\sigma^2 I$ variance.

2. Result only compares *linear* estimators; it says nothing about for example $\sum_{i=1}^{n} |y_i - \beta x_i|$.

3. Result only compares *unbiased* estimators [biased estimators can have 0 variances].

4. There are extensions to consider affine estimators $\widetilde{\beta} = a + A y$ for vectors a. There are also equivalent results for the invariant quantity $\widehat{y}$.

5. This says that for any linear combination $c^\mathsf{T} \beta$, the OLS is BLUE when X is of full rank. When X is not of full rank, one can show that for an estimable linear combination $c^\mathsf{T} \beta$, the OLS is BLUE.

If we dispense with the unbiasedness assumption and add the model assumption of error normality we get the well-known result.

Theorem 19.7. *Cramér–Rao* Suppose that Assumption A4 holds. Then, $\widehat{\beta}$ is Best Unbiased.

By making the stronger assumption A4, we get a much stronger conclusion. This allows us to compare say LAD estimation with OLS. The log-likelihood is given in (19.3), and it can be shown that the information matrix is

$$
\mathcal{I}(\beta, \sigma^2) = \begin{bmatrix} \frac{1}{\sigma^2} X^\mathsf{T} X & 0 \\ 0 & \frac{n}{2\sigma^4} \end{bmatrix}. \tag{19.5}
$$

This structure is block diagonal, which has some statistical implications. The inverse information is also block diagonal

$$
\mathcal{I}(\beta, \sigma^2)^{-1} = \begin{bmatrix} \sigma^2 (X^\mathsf{T} X)^{-1} & 0 \\ 0 & \frac{2\sigma^4}{n} \end{bmatrix}
$$

and represents the lower bound for the variance of unbiased estimators. The MLE of β is unbiased and achieves the bound, whereas the MLE of σ^2 is biased and does not achieve the bound in finite samples. Suppose that the parameter β were known, the information with regard to the unknown parameter σ^2 is $n/2\sigma^4$. On the other hand suppose that the parameter σ^2 is known, the information matrix with regard to the unknown parameter vector β is $X^\mathsf{T}X/\sigma^2$. This says that knowledge of the other parameter provides no additional information about the unknown parameter.

Chapter 20

Hypothesis Testing for Linear Regression

20.1 HYPOTHESES OF INTEREST

We shall work with the classical assumption A4 that (conditional on X)

$$y \sim N(X\beta, \sigma^2 I), \qquad (20.1)$$

which allows the derivation of exact tests. In a later chapter we will relax this assumption and consider asymptotic approximations. We are interested in

1. Single (Linear) Hypothesis: $c^\mathsf{T}\beta = \gamma_{\text{scalar}}$, e.g., $\beta_2 = 0$ (t-test).
2. Multiple (Linear) Hypothesis: $R_{q \times K}\beta_{K \times 1} = r_{q \times 1}$, $q \leq K$, e.g., $\beta_2 = \beta_3 = \cdots = \beta_K = 0$.
3. Single Non-linear Hypothesis: $\beta_1^2 + \beta_2^2 + \cdots + \beta_K^2 = 1$.

Note that these are all composite hypotheses, i.e., there are nuisance parameters like σ^2 that are not specified by the null hypothesis. We first present some examples

Example 20.1. (a) The theoretical model is the Cobb–Douglas production function $Q = AK^\alpha L^\beta$. Empirical version: take logs and add an error term to give a linear regression

$$q = a + \alpha k + \beta \ell + \varepsilon.$$

It is often of interest whether constant returns to scale operate, i.e., would like to test whether $\alpha + \beta = 1$ is true. We may specify the alternative as $\alpha + \beta < 1$, because we can rule out increasing returns to scale.

Example 20.2. (b) Market efficiency

$$r_t = \mu + \gamma^\mathsf{T} I_{t-1} + \varepsilon_t,$$

where r_t are *returns* on some asset held between period $t - 1$ and t, while I_t is *public information at time t*. Theory predicts that $\gamma = 0$; there is no particular reason to restrict the alternative here.

Probability, Statistics and Econometrics. http://dx.doi.org/10.1016/B978-0-12-810495-8.00023-3

Example 20.3. (c) Structural change

$$y = \alpha + \beta x_t + \gamma D_t + \varepsilon_t$$

$$D_t = \begin{cases} 0, & t < 1974 \\ 1, & t \geq 1974. \end{cases}$$

Would like to test $\gamma = 0$.

20.2 TEST OF A SINGLE LINEAR HYPOTHESIS

We wish to test the hypothesis $c^{\mathsf{T}}\beta = \gamma$, e.g., $\beta_2 = 0$. Suppose that $y \sim N(X\beta, \sigma^2 I)$. Then,

$$\frac{c^{\mathsf{T}}\widehat{\beta} - \gamma}{\sigma\sqrt{c^{\mathsf{T}}(X^{\mathsf{T}}X)^{-1}c}} \sim N(0, 1).$$

We don't know σ and must replace it by an estimate. There are two widely used estimates:

$$\widehat{\sigma}^2_{mle} = \frac{\widehat{\varepsilon}^{\mathsf{T}}\widehat{\varepsilon}}{n}$$

$$s^2_* = \frac{\widehat{\varepsilon}^{\mathsf{T}}\widehat{\varepsilon}}{n - K}$$

The first estimate is the maximum likelihood estimator of σ^2, which can be easily verified. The second estimate is a modification of the MLE, which happens to be unbiased. Now define the test statistic

$$T = \frac{c^{\mathsf{T}}\widehat{\beta} - \gamma}{s\sqrt{c^{\mathsf{T}}(X^{\mathsf{T}}X)^{-1}c}}.$$

Theorem 20.1. *Suppose that A4 and H_0 hold. Then, $T \sim t(n - K)$.*

Proof. We show that:

$$\frac{n - K}{\sigma^2}s^2_* \sim \chi^2(n - K) \tag{20.2}$$

$$s^2_*, c^{\mathsf{T}}\widehat{\beta} - \gamma \text{ are independent.} \tag{20.3}$$

This establishes the theorem by the defining property of a t-random variable, see Theorem 10.2 (4). Recall that

$$\frac{\varepsilon^{\mathsf{T}}\varepsilon}{\sigma^2} = \sum_{i=1}^{n}\left(\frac{\varepsilon_i}{\sigma}\right)^2 \sim \chi^2(n).$$

But $\widehat{\varepsilon}$ are residuals that use K parameter estimates. Furthermore, $\widehat{\varepsilon}^{\mathsf{T}}\widehat{\varepsilon} = \varepsilon^{\mathsf{T}} M_X \varepsilon$ and

$$E[\varepsilon^{\mathsf{T}} M_X \varepsilon] = E[\operatorname{tr} M_X \varepsilon \varepsilon^{\mathsf{T}}] = \operatorname{tr} M_X E(\varepsilon \varepsilon^{\mathsf{T}})$$
$$= \sigma^2 \operatorname{tr} M_X = \sigma^2 (n - \operatorname{tr} P_X)$$
$$= \sigma^2 (n - K)$$
$$\operatorname{tr}(X(X^{\mathsf{T}}X)^{-1}X^{\mathsf{T}}) = \operatorname{tr} X^{\mathsf{T}} X (X^{\mathsf{T}}X)^{-1} = \operatorname{tr} I_K = K.$$

These calculations show that $E\,\widehat{\varepsilon}^{\mathsf{T}}\widehat{\varepsilon} = n - K$, which suggests that $\widehat{\varepsilon}^{\mathsf{T}}\widehat{\varepsilon}$ cannot be $\chi^2(n)$ [and incidentally that $Es_*^2 = \sigma^2$]. Note that M_X is a symmetric idempotent matrix, which means that it can be written $M_X = U\Lambda U^{\mathsf{T}}$, where $UU^{\mathsf{T}} = I$ and Λ is a diagonal matrix of eigenvalues, which in this case are either zero (K times) or one ($n - K$ times). Furthermore, by a property of the normal distribution, $U\varepsilon = \varepsilon^*$ has exactly the same distribution as ε [it has the same mean and variance, which is sufficient to determine the normal distribution]. Therefore,

$$\widehat{\varepsilon}^{\mathsf{T}}\widehat{\varepsilon} = \sum_{i=1}^{n-K} \varepsilon_i^{*2} \tag{20.4}$$

for some i.i.d. standard normal random variables ε_i^*. Therefore, (20.4) is $\chi^2(n - K)$ by the definition of a chi-squared random variable.

Furthermore, under H_0, $c^{\mathsf{T}}\widehat{\beta} - \gamma = c^{\mathsf{T}}(X^{\mathsf{T}}X)^{-1}X^{\mathsf{T}}\varepsilon$ is uncorrelated with $\widehat{\varepsilon} = M_X \varepsilon$, since

$$E[M_X \varepsilon \varepsilon^{\mathsf{T}} X (X^{\mathsf{T}}X)^{-1}c] = \sigma^2 \underbrace{M_X X (X^{\mathsf{T}}X)^{-1}c}_{=0} = 0.$$

Under normality, uncorrelatedness is equivalent to independence. $\qquad\square$

We can now base test of H_0 on

$$T = \frac{c^{\mathsf{T}}\widehat{\beta} - \gamma}{s^* \sqrt{c^{\mathsf{T}}(X^{\mathsf{T}}X)^{-1}c}},$$

using the $t(n - k)$ distribution for an exact test under normality. Can test either one-sided and two-sided alternatives, i.e., reject if $|T| \geq t_{\alpha/2}(n - K)$ [two-sided alternative] or if $T \geq t_\alpha(n - K)$ [one-sided alternative].

Above is a general rule, and would require some additional computations in addition to $\widehat{\beta}$. Sometimes one can avoid this: if computer automatically prints out results of hypothesis for $\beta_i = 0$, and one can redesign the null regression suitably. For example, suppose that

$$H_0 : \beta_2 + \beta_3 = 1.$$

Substitute the restriction in to the regression $y_i = \beta_1 + \beta_2 x_i + \beta_3 z_i + \varepsilon_i$, which gives the restricted regression $y_i - z_i = \beta_1 + \beta_2(x_i - z_i) + \varepsilon_i$. Now test whether $\beta_3 = 0$ in the regression $y_i - z_i = \beta_1 + \beta_2(x_i - z_i) + \beta_3 z_i + \varepsilon_i$.

20.3   TEST OF MULTIPLE LINEAR HYPOTHESIS

We now consider a test of the multiple hypothesis $R\beta = r$. Define the quadratic form

$$
\begin{aligned}
F &= (R\widehat{\beta} - r)^{\mathsf{T}} \left[s_*^2 R(X^{\mathsf{T}}X)^{-1} R^{\mathsf{T}} \right]^{-1} (R\widehat{\beta} - r)/q \\
&= \frac{(R\widehat{\beta} - r)^{\mathsf{T}} \left[R(X^{\mathsf{T}}X)^{-1} R^{\mathsf{T}} \right]^{-1} (R\widehat{\beta} - r)/q}{(n - K)s_*^2/(n - K)}.
\end{aligned}
\tag{20.5}
$$

If $y \sim N(X\beta, \sigma^2 I)$, then

$$
F = \frac{\chi^2(q)/q}{\chi^2(n - K)/(n - K)} \sim F(q, n - K)
$$

under H_0. The rule is that if

$$
F \geq F_\alpha(q, n - K),
$$

then reject H_0 at level α. Note that we can only test against a two-sided alternative $R\beta \neq r$ because we have squared value in (20.5).

Example 20.4. Standard F-test, which is outputted from computer, is of the hypothesis

$$
\beta_2 = 0, \ldots, \beta_K = 0,
$$

where the intercept β_1 is included in the regression but exempt from the restriction. In this case, $q = K - 1$, and $H_0 : R\beta = 0$, where

$$
R = \begin{bmatrix} 0_{K-1} & I_{K-1} \end{bmatrix}.
$$

The test statistic is compared with critical value from the $F(K - 1, n - K)$ distribution.

Example 20.5. Structural Change. Null hypothesis is $y = X\beta + \varepsilon$. Alternative is

$$
\begin{aligned}
y_1 &= X_1\beta_1 + \varepsilon_1, & 1 \leq i \leq n_1, \\
y_2 &= X_2\beta_2 + \varepsilon_2, & n_1 < i \leq n,
\end{aligned}
$$

where $n = n_1 + n_2$. Let

$$y = \begin{pmatrix} y_1 \\ y_2 \end{pmatrix}, \ X = \begin{bmatrix} X_1 & 0 \\ 0 & X_2 \end{bmatrix}, \ \beta = \begin{pmatrix} \beta_1 \\ \beta_2 \end{pmatrix}_{2K \times 1}, \ \varepsilon = \begin{pmatrix} \varepsilon_1 \\ \varepsilon_2 \end{pmatrix}_{n \times 1}.$$

Then, we can write the alternative regression as

$$y = X\beta + \varepsilon.$$

Consider the null hypothesis $H_0 : \beta_1 = \beta_2$. Let $R_{K \times 2K} = [I_K \vdots -I_K]$. Compare with $F(K, n - 2K)$.

A confidence interval is just a critical region centred not at H_0, but at a function of parameter estimates. For example,

$$c^\mathsf{T}\widehat{\beta} \pm t_{\alpha/2}(n - K)s\{c^\mathsf{T}(X^\mathsf{T}X)^{-1}c\}^{1/2}$$

is a two-sided confidence interval for the scalar quantity $c^\mathsf{T}\beta$. One can also construct one-sided confidence intervals and multivariate confidence intervals, which are ellipses geometrically.

20.4 TEST OF MULTIPLE LINEAR HYPOTHESIS BASED ON FIT

The idea behind the F test is that under H_0, $R\widehat{\beta} - r$ should be stochastically small, but under the alternative hypothesis it will not be so. An alternative approach is based on fit. Suppose we estimate β subject to the restriction $R\beta = r$, then the sum of squared residuals from that regression should be close to that from the unconstrained regression when the null hypothesis is true [but if it is false, the two regressions will have different fitting power]. To understand this we must investigate the restricted least squares estimation procedure.

1. Unrestricted regression:

$$\widehat{\beta} = \arg\min_b (y - Xb)^\mathsf{T}(y - Xb),$$

and let $\widehat{\varepsilon} = y - X\widehat{\beta}$ and $Q = \widehat{\varepsilon}^\mathsf{T}\widehat{\varepsilon}$.
2. Restricted regression:

$$\beta^* = \arg\min_b (y - Xb)^\mathsf{T}(y - Xb) \ \text{s.t.} \ Rb = r,$$

and let $\varepsilon^* = y - X\beta^*$ and $Q^* = \varepsilon^{*\mathsf{T}}\varepsilon^*$.

To solve the restricted least squares problem we use the Lagrangian method. We know that β^* and λ^* solve the first order condition of the Lagrangian

$$\mathcal{L}(b, \lambda) = \frac{1}{2}(y - Xb)^\mathsf{T}(y - Xb) + \lambda^\mathsf{T}(Rb - r).$$

The first order conditions are:

$$-X^\mathsf{T} y + X^\mathsf{T} X \beta^* + R^\mathsf{T} \lambda^* = 0 \tag{20.6}$$

$$R\beta^* = r. \tag{20.7}$$

Now, from (20.6), $R^\mathsf{T}\lambda^* = X^\mathsf{T} y - X^\mathsf{T} X\beta^* = X^\mathsf{T}\varepsilon^*$, which implies that

$$(X^\mathsf{T} X)^{-1} R^\mathsf{T} \lambda^* = (X^\mathsf{T} X)^{-1} X^\mathsf{T} y - (X^\mathsf{T} X)^{-1} X^\mathsf{T} X \beta^* = \widehat{\beta} - \beta^*$$

and

$$R(X^\mathsf{T} X)^{-1} R^\mathsf{T} \lambda^* = R\widehat{\beta} - R\beta^* = R\widehat{\beta} - r.$$

Therefore, $\lambda^* = \left[R(X^\mathsf{T} X)^{-1} R^\mathsf{T} \right]^{-1} (R\widehat{\beta} - r)$, and

$$\beta^* = \widehat{\beta} - (X^\mathsf{T} X)^{-1} R^\mathsf{T} \left[R(X^\mathsf{T} X)^{-1} R^\mathsf{T} \right]^{-1} (R\widehat{\beta} - r). \tag{20.8}$$

This gives the restricted least squares estimator in terms of the restrictions and the unrestricted least squares estimator. From this relation we can derive the statistical properties of the estimator β^*.

We now return to the testing question. The idea is that under H_0, $Q^* \sim Q$, but under the alternative the two quantities differ. The following theorem makes this more precise.

Theorem 20.2. *Suppose that A4 and H_0 hold. Then,*

$$\frac{Q^* - Q}{Q} \frac{n - K}{q} = F \sim F(q, n - K).$$

Proof. We show that

$$Q^* - Q = (R\widehat{\beta} - r)^\mathsf{T} \left[R(X^\mathsf{T} X)^{-1} R^\mathsf{T} \right]^{-1} (R\widehat{\beta} - r)$$

Then, since $s_*^2 = Q/(n - K)$ the result is established.

First, write $\beta^* = \widehat{\beta} + \beta^* - \widehat{\beta}$ and

$$\begin{aligned}
(y - X\beta^*)^\mathsf{T}(y - X\beta^*) &= [y - X\widehat{\beta} - X(\beta^* - \widehat{\beta})]^\mathsf{T}[y - X\widehat{\beta} - X(\beta^* - \widehat{\beta})] \\
&= (y - X\widehat{\beta})^\mathsf{T}(y - X\widehat{\beta}) + (\widehat{\beta} - \beta^*)^\mathsf{T} X^\mathsf{T} X (\widehat{\beta} - \beta^*) \\
&\quad - (y - X\widehat{\beta})^\mathsf{T} X(\beta^* - \widehat{\beta}) \\
&= \widehat{\varepsilon}^\mathsf{T}\widehat{\varepsilon} + (\widehat{\beta} - \beta^*)^\mathsf{T} X^\mathsf{T} X (\widehat{\beta} - \beta^*)
\end{aligned}$$

using the orthogonality property of the unrestricted least squares estimator. Therefore,

$$Q^* - Q = (\widehat{\beta} - \beta^*)^\mathsf{T} X^\mathsf{T} X (\widehat{\beta} - \beta^*).$$

Substituting our formulae for $\widehat{\beta} - \beta^*$ and λ^* obtained above and cancelling out, we get

$$Q^* - Q = (R\widehat{\beta} - r)^{\mathsf{T}} \left[R(X^{\mathsf{T}}X)^{-1}R^{\mathsf{T}} \right]^{-1} (R\widehat{\beta} - r)$$

as required. $\qquad\qquad\qquad\qquad\qquad\qquad\qquad\qquad\qquad\qquad\qquad\qquad$ $\square$

An intermediate representation is

$$Q^* - Q = \lambda^{*\mathsf{T}} R(X^{\mathsf{T}}X)^{-1}R^{\mathsf{T}}\lambda^*.$$

This brings out the use of the Lagrange Multipliers in defining the test statistic, and lead to the use of this name.

Importance of the result: the fit version was easier to apply in the old days, before fast computers, because one can just do two separate regressions and use the sum of squared residuals.

Example 20.6. Zero restrictions

$$\beta_2 = \cdots = \beta_K = 0$$

Then restricted regression is easy. In this case, $q = K - 1$. Note that the R^2 can be used to do an F-test of this hypothesis. We have

$$R^2 = 1 - \frac{Q}{Q^*} = \frac{Q^* - Q}{Q},$$

which implies that

$$F = \frac{R^2/(K-1)}{(1-R^2)/(n-k)}. \qquad\qquad (20.9)$$

Example 20.7. Structural change. Allow coefficients to be different in two periods. Partition

$$y = \begin{pmatrix} y_1 \\ y_2 \end{pmatrix} \begin{matrix} n_1 \\ n_2 \end{matrix}$$

$$\left. \begin{matrix} y_1 = X_1\beta_1 + \varepsilon_1 \\ y_2 = X_2\beta_2 + \varepsilon_2 \end{matrix} \right\} \quad \text{or} \quad y = \begin{bmatrix} X_1 & 0 \\ 0 & X_2 \end{bmatrix} \begin{pmatrix} \beta_1 \\ \beta_2 \end{pmatrix} + \varepsilon.$$

Null is of no structural change, i.e., $H_0 : \beta_1 = \beta_2$, $R = (I \vdots -I)$.

Consider the more general linear restriction

$$\beta_1 + \beta_2 - 3\beta_4 = 1$$
$$\beta_6 + \beta_1 = 2.$$

Harder to work with. Nevertheless, can always reparameterize to obtain restricted model as a simple regression.

Example 20.8. Chow Tests: Structural change with intercepts. The unrestricted model is

$$
\begin{pmatrix} y_1 \\ y_2 \end{pmatrix} = \begin{bmatrix} i_1 & 0 & x_1 & 0 \\ 0 & i_2 & 0 & x_2 \end{bmatrix} \begin{pmatrix} \alpha_1 \\ \alpha_2 \\ \beta_1 \\ \beta_2 \end{pmatrix} + \begin{pmatrix} \varepsilon_1 \\ \varepsilon_2 \end{pmatrix},
$$

and let $\theta = (\alpha_1, \alpha_2, \beta_1, \beta_2) \in \mathbb{R}^{2K+2}$. Different slopes and intercepts allowed. The first null hypothesis is that the slopes are the same, i.e., for some $\beta \in \mathbb{R}^K$

$$
H_0 : \beta_1 = \beta_2 = \beta. \tag{20.10}
$$

The restricted regression is

$$
\begin{pmatrix} y_1 \\ y_2 \end{pmatrix} = \begin{bmatrix} i_1 & 0 & x_1 \\ 0 & i_2 & x_2 \end{bmatrix} \begin{pmatrix} \alpha_1 \\ \alpha_2 \\ \beta \end{pmatrix} + \begin{pmatrix} \varepsilon_1 \\ \varepsilon_2 \end{pmatrix}.
$$

The test statistic is

$$
F = \frac{(\varepsilon^{*\top}\varepsilon^* - \widehat{\varepsilon^\top\varepsilon})/K}{\widehat{\varepsilon^\top\varepsilon}/(n - (2K+2))},
$$

which is compared with the quantiles from the $F(K, n - 2K - 2)$ distribution.

Example 20.9. The second null hypothesis is that the intercepts are the same, i.e.,

$$
H_0 : \alpha_1 = \alpha_2 = \alpha. \tag{20.11}
$$

Restricted regression $(\alpha, \beta_1, \beta_2)$

$$
\begin{pmatrix} y_1 \\ y_2 \end{pmatrix} = \begin{bmatrix} i_1 & x_1 & 0 \\ i_2 & 0 & x_2 \end{bmatrix} \begin{pmatrix} \alpha \\ \beta_1 \\ \beta_2 \end{pmatrix} + \begin{pmatrix} \varepsilon_1 \\ \varepsilon_2 \end{pmatrix}.
$$

Now suppose that $n_2 < K$. The restricted regression is ok, but the unrestricted regression runs into problems in the second period because n_2 is too small. In fact, $\widehat{\varepsilon}_2 \equiv 0$. In this case we must simply acknowledge the fact that the degrees of freedom lost are n_2 not K. Thus

$$
F = \frac{(Q^* - Q)/n_2}{Q/(n_1 - K)} \sim F(n_2, n_1 - K)
$$

is a valid test in this case.

20.5   LIKELIHOOD BASED TESTING

We have considered several different approaches which all led to the F test in linear regression. We now consider a general class of test statistics based on the Likelihood function. In principle these apply to any parametric model, but we shall at this stage just consider its application to linear regression.

The Likelihood is denoted $L(y, X; \theta)$, where y, X are the observed data and θ is a vector of unknown parameter. The maximum likelihood estimator can be determined from $L(y, X; \theta)$, as we have already discussed. This quantity is also useful for testing. Consider again the linear restrictions

$$H_0 : R\theta = r,$$

where R is of full rank q. The maximum likelihood estimator of θ is denoted by $\widehat{\theta}$, while the restricted MLE is denoted by θ^*, [this is maximizes L subject to the restrictions $R\theta - r = 0$]. Now define the following test statistics:

$$\text{LR}: 2\left[\log \frac{L(\widehat{\theta})}{L(\theta^*)}\right] = 2\{\log L(\widehat{\theta}) - \log L(\theta^*)\}$$

$$\text{Wald}: (R\widehat{\theta} - r)^{\mathsf{T}} \left\{ R\left[-\frac{\partial^2 \log L}{\partial\theta\partial\theta^{\mathsf{T}}}\bigg|_{\widehat{\theta}}\right]^{-1} R^{\mathsf{T}} \right\}^{-1} (R\widehat{\theta} - r)$$

$$\text{LM}: \frac{\partial \log L}{\partial\theta}\bigg|_{\theta^*}^{\mathsf{T}} \left[-\frac{\partial^2 \log L}{\partial\theta\partial\theta^{\mathsf{T}}}\bigg|_{\theta^*}\right]^{-1} \frac{\partial \log L}{\partial\theta}\bigg|_{\theta^*}.$$

The Wald test only requires computation of the unrestricted estimator, while the Lagrange Multiplier only requires computation of the restricted estimator. The Likelihood ratio requires computation of both. There are circumstances where the restricted estimator is easier to compute, and there are situations where the unrestricted estimator is easier to compute. These computational differences are what has motivated the use of either the Wald or the LM test. The LR test has certain advantages; but computationally it is the most demanding. Under the null hypothesis we may show that

$$T \xrightarrow{D} \chi^2(q) \tag{20.12}$$

for all three test statistics, which yields an asymptotic test. In some cases, the exact distribution of T is known and we may perform an exact test.

In the linear regression case, $\theta = (\beta, \sigma^2)$. We consider the case where the restrictions only apply to β, so that $R\beta = r$. Furthermore, we can replace the derivatives with respect to θ by derivatives with respect to β only [this requires an additional justification, which we will not discuss here]. The log-likelihood is repeated here

$$\log L(\theta) = \frac{-n}{2} \log 2\pi - \frac{n}{2} \log \sigma^2 - \frac{1}{2\sigma^2} \varepsilon(\beta)^\mathsf{T} \varepsilon(\beta),$$

and its derivatives are

$$\frac{\partial \log L}{\partial \beta} = \frac{1}{\sigma^2} X^\mathsf{T} \varepsilon(\beta)$$

$$\frac{\partial \log L}{\partial \sigma^2} = -\frac{n}{2\sigma^2} + \frac{1}{2\sigma^4} \varepsilon(\beta)^\mathsf{T} \varepsilon(\beta)$$

$$\frac{\partial^2 \log L}{\partial \beta \partial \beta^\mathsf{T}} = \frac{-1}{\sigma^2} X^\mathsf{T} X$$

$$\frac{\partial^2 \log L}{(\partial \sigma^2)^2} = \frac{n}{2\sigma^4} - \frac{2}{2\sigma^6} \varepsilon(\beta)^\mathsf{T} \varepsilon(\beta)$$

$$\frac{\partial^2 \log L}{\partial \beta \partial \sigma^2} = -\frac{1}{\sigma^4} X^\mathsf{T} \varepsilon(\beta).$$

The Wald test is

$$W = (R\widehat{\beta} - r)^\mathsf{T} \left[R(X^\mathsf{T} X)^{-1} R^\mathsf{T} \widehat{\sigma}^2 \right]^{-1} (R\widehat{\beta} - r) = \frac{Q^* - Q}{(Q/n)}, \qquad (20.13)$$

where $\widehat{\sigma}^2 = Q/n$ is the MLE of σ^2, and so is very similar to the F-test apart from the use of $\widehat{\sigma}^2$ instead of s_*^2 and a multiplicative factor q. In fact,

$$W = q F \frac{n}{n - k}.$$

This is approximately equal to $q F$ when the sample size is large.

The Lagrange Multiplier or Score or Rao test statistic is

$$LM = \frac{\varepsilon^{*\mathsf{T}} X}{\sigma^{*2}} \left\{ \frac{X^\mathsf{T} X}{\sigma^{*2}} \right\}^{-1} \frac{X^\mathsf{T} \varepsilon^*}{\sigma^{*2}} \qquad (20.14)$$

where $\sigma^{*2} = Q^*/n$. This can be rewritten in the form

$$\frac{\lambda^{*\mathsf{T}} R(X^\mathsf{T} X)^{-1} R^\mathsf{T} \lambda^*}{\sigma^{*2}},$$

where λ^* is the vector of Lagrange Multipliers evaluated at the optimum [Recall that $X^\mathsf{T} \varepsilon^* = R^\mathsf{T} \lambda^*$]. Furthermore, we can write the score test as

$$LM = \frac{Q^* - Q}{(Q^*/n)} = n \left(1 - \frac{Q}{Q^*} \right).$$

When the restrictions are the standard zero ones, the test statistic is n times the R^2 from the unrestricted regression.

The unrestricted and restricted Likelihoods are

$$\log L(\widehat{\beta}, \widehat{\sigma}^2) = -\frac{n}{2} \log 2\pi - \frac{n}{2} \log \widehat{\sigma}^2 - \frac{1}{2\widehat{\sigma}^2} \widehat{\varepsilon}^{\mathsf{T}} \widehat{\varepsilon}$$

$$= -\frac{n}{2} \log 2\pi - \frac{1}{2\widehat{\sigma}^2} \log \frac{\widehat{\varepsilon}^{\mathsf{T}} \widehat{\varepsilon}}{n} - \frac{n}{2}$$

$$\log L(\beta^*, \sigma^{*2}) = -\frac{n}{2} \log 2\pi - \frac{n}{2} \log \sigma^{*2} - \frac{1}{2\sigma^{*2}} \varepsilon^{*\mathsf{T}} \varepsilon^*$$

$$= -\frac{n}{2} \log 2\pi - \frac{n}{2} \log \frac{\varepsilon^{*\mathsf{T}} \varepsilon^*}{n} - \frac{n}{2}.$$

These two lines follow because $\widehat{\sigma}^2 = \widehat{\varepsilon}^{\mathsf{T}} \widehat{\varepsilon}/n$ and $\sigma^{*2} = \varepsilon^{*\mathsf{T}} \varepsilon^*/n$. Therefore,

$$LR = 2 \log \frac{L(\widehat{\beta}, \widehat{\sigma}^2)}{L(\beta, \sigma^2)} = n \left[\log \frac{Q^*}{n} - \log \frac{Q}{n} \right] = n[\log Q^* - \log Q].$$

Note that W, LM, and LR are all *monotonic* functions of F, in fact

$$W = F \frac{qn}{n-k}, \quad LM = \frac{W}{1 + W/n}, \quad LR = n \log \left(1 + \frac{W}{n} \right). \tag{20.15}$$

If we knew the exact distribution of any of them we can obtain the distributions of the others and the test result will be the same. However, in practice one uses asymptotic critical values, which lead to differences in outcomes. We have

$$LM \leq LR \leq W,$$

so that the Wald test will reject more frequently than the LR test and the LM tests, supposing that the same critical values are used.

20.6 BAYESIAN APPROACH

In the Bayesian approach we require a prior distribution for the unknown parameters β, σ^2. Combining the prior and the likelihood we obtain the posterior for β, σ^2 from which we can do inference. We just consider the simplest case where we treat σ^2 as known for which the algebra is simple. We have the following result.

Theorem 20.3. *Suppose that A4 holds with σ^2 known, and that the prior for β is $N(\beta_0, \Sigma_0)$ for some vector β_0 and covariance matrix Σ_0. The posterior* *distribution of $\beta | y$, X is $N(b, \Omega)$ with*

$$b = \left(\frac{1}{\sigma^2} X^\mathsf{T} X + \Sigma_0^{-1} \right)^{-1} \left(\frac{1}{\sigma^2} X^\mathsf{T} y + \Sigma_0^{-1} \beta_0 \right)$$

$$\Omega = \left(\frac{1}{\sigma^2} X^\mathsf{T} X + \Sigma_0^{-1} \right)^{-1}.$$

This result allows one to provide a Bayesian confidence interval or hypothesis test by just inverting the posterior distribution. For example, for $c^\mathsf{T} \beta$, the posterior is normal with mean $c^\mathsf{T} b$ and variance $c^\mathsf{T} \Omega c$ and so the Bayesian confidence interval is $c^\mathsf{T} b \pm z_{\alpha/2} \sqrt{c^\mathsf{T} \Omega c}$, which has Bayesian coverage probability $1 - \alpha$.

It is possible to derive explicit results also for the case that σ^2 is unknown and has a prior distribution such as a Gamma distribution on $\mathbb{R}_+$, however the algebra is more complicated. It is not clear where the normal prior comes from, nor for example why β_0, Σ_0 are themselves known and not subject to uncertainty like β, σ^2. It is possible to further "priorize" these quantities, but at some point one has to take something we might call a parameter as a fixed known quantity.

Chapter 21

Omission of Relevant Variables, Inclusion of Irrelevant Variables, and Model Selection

21.1 OMISSION OF RELEVANT VARIABLES

Suppose that

$$y = X_1\beta_1 + X_2\beta_2 + \varepsilon,$$

where Assumption A1 holds. However, we regress y on X_1 only, perhaps because we did not observe X_2. Then,

$$\begin{aligned}
\widetilde{\beta}_1 &= (X_1^\mathsf{T} X_1)^{-1} X_1^\mathsf{T} y \\
&= (X_1^\mathsf{T} X_1)^{-1} X_1^\mathsf{T} (X_1\beta_1 + X_2\beta_2 + \varepsilon) \\
&= \beta_1 + (X_1^\mathsf{T} X_1)^{-1} X_1^\mathsf{T} X_2\beta_2 + (X_1^\mathsf{T} X_1)^{-1} X_1^\mathsf{T}\varepsilon,
\end{aligned}$$

so that

$$E(\widetilde{\beta}_1 | X) = \beta_1 + (X_1^\mathsf{T} X_1)^{-1} X_1^\mathsf{T} X_2\beta_2 = \beta_1 + \beta_{12},$$

where $\beta_{12} = (X_1^\mathsf{T} X_1)^{-1} X_1^\mathsf{T} X_2\beta_2$. In general $\widehat{\beta}_1$ is biased and inconsistent; the direction and magnitude of the bias depend on β_2 and on $X_1^\mathsf{T} X_2$.

Example 21.1. Some common examples of omitted variables: (1) Seasonality; (2) Dynamics; (3) Nonlinearity; (4) Endogeneity. Wages on education get positive effect but are omitting ability. If ability has a positive effect on wages and is positively correlated with education this would explain some of the positive effect. Wages on race/gender (discrimination). Omit experience/education.

What about the variance? In general, the conditional variance given X is

$$\text{var}(\widetilde{\beta}_1 | X) = (X_1^\mathsf{T} X_1)^{-1} X_1^\mathsf{T} \Sigma(X) X_1 (X_1^\mathsf{T} X_1)^{-1},$$

which should be compared with

$$\text{var}(\widehat{\beta}_1 | X) = (X_1^\mathsf{T} M_2 X_1)^{-1} X_1^\mathsf{T} M_2 \Sigma(X) M_2 X_1 (X_1^\mathsf{T} M_2 X_1)^{-1},$$

Probability, Statistics and Econometrics. http://dx.doi.org/10.1016/B978-0-12-810495-8.00024-5

which is the variance of the estimator of β_1 taking account of X_2. In the homoskedastic case, this amounts to comparing $(X_1^\mathsf{T} X_1)^{-1}$ with $(X_1^\mathsf{T} M_2 X_1)^{-1}$, which clearly ends in favour of the first variance. The MSE comparison in this case is

$$(X_1^\mathsf{T} X_1)^{-1} X_1^\mathsf{T} X_2 \beta_2 \beta_2^\mathsf{T} X_2^\mathsf{T} X_1 (X_1^\mathsf{T} X_1)^{-1} + (X_1^\mathsf{T} X_1)^{-1} \quad \text{versus} \quad (X_1^\mathsf{T} M_2 X_1)^{-1}$$

and there is no necessary ranking between these two performance measures. However, in large samples, we expect the variance components to the MSE both to shrink, so in that case one should unambiguously prefer the estimator of β_1 taking account of X_2.

We also consider the effect on inference of this misspecification in the case of homoskedasticity. The standard estimated variance is $s_*^2 (X_1^\mathsf{T} X_1)^{-1}$, where

$$
\begin{aligned}
s_*^2 &= \frac{y^\mathsf{T} M_1 y}{n - K_1} = \frac{(X_2 \beta_2 + \varepsilon)^\mathsf{T} M_1 (X_2 \beta_2 + \varepsilon)}{n - K_1} \\
&= \frac{\varepsilon^\mathsf{T} M_1 \varepsilon}{n - K_1} + \frac{\beta_2^\mathsf{T} X_2^\mathsf{T} M_1 X_2 \beta_2}{n - K_1} + 2 \frac{\varepsilon^\mathsf{T} M_1 X_2 \beta_2}{n - K_1}.
\end{aligned}
$$

This has conditional expectation, under homoskedasticity,

$$\sigma^2 \mid \frac{\beta_2^\mathsf{T} X_2^\mathsf{T} M_1 X_2 \beta_2}{n - K_1} \geq \sigma^2,$$

where the inequality follows because M_1 is a positive semi-definite matrix. It follows that the estimated variance of $\widehat{\beta}_1$ is upwardly biased. Note also that the exact distribution of s_*^2 is not chi-squared under A4, and so the exact distribution of the t-statistic is not t any more.

If $X_1^\mathsf{T} X_2 = 0$, then $\widehat{\beta}$ is unbiased, but the OLS standard errors are still biased. In this special case, one can also show that the t-ratio is downward biased and so t-tests are less likely to reject the null hypothesis than they should. More generally, the t-ratio could be upward or downward biased depending of course on the direction of the bias of $\widehat{\beta}_1$.

In practice we might suspect that there are always going to be omitted variables. The questions is: is the magnitude large and the direction unambiguous?

We consider the simple case where we have omitted variables due to the true regression function being nonlinear. For example, suppose that x is scalar and that

$$y_i = \alpha + \beta x_i + \gamma x_i^2 + \varepsilon_i.$$

Then the OLS estimators ignoring the quadratic term are biased with

$$E\widehat{\beta} = \beta + \gamma \frac{\sum_{i=1}^{n}(x_i - \overline{x})x_i^2}{\sum_{i=1}^{n}(x_i - \overline{x})^2}$$

$$E\widehat{\alpha} = \alpha + \gamma \left[\frac{1}{n}\sum_{i=1}^{n}x_i^2 - \overline{x}\frac{\sum_{i=1}^{n}(x_i - \overline{x})x_i^2}{\sum_{i=1}^{n}(x_i - \overline{x})^2} \right].$$

In the special case that $\overline{x} = 0$, the bias of the slope depends on the skewness of the regressors and the value of γ, whereas the bias of the intercept depends on γ and the sample variance of the covariate. The magnitude and direction of the bias depend on unknown quantities.

21.2 INCLUSION OF IRRELEVANT VARIABLES/KNOWLEDGE OF PARAMETERS

Suppose now that A1 and A2 hold with

$$y = X_1\beta_1 + \varepsilon,$$

but we regress y on both X_1 and X_2. Then

$$\widehat{\beta}_1 = (X_1^\mathsf{T} M_2 X_1)^{-1} X_1^\mathsf{T} M_2 y = \beta_1 + (X_1^\mathsf{T} M_2 X_1)^{-1} X_1^\mathsf{T} M_2 \varepsilon$$
$$E(\widehat{\beta}_1|X) = \beta_1 \text{ all } \beta_1$$
$$\mathrm{var}(\widehat{\beta}_1|X) = \sigma^2 (X_1^\mathsf{T} M_2 X_1)^{-1}.$$

Compare this with the variance of y on X_1, which is only $\sigma^2(X_1^\mathsf{T} X_1)^{-1}$. Now

$$X_1^\mathsf{T} X_1 - X_1^\mathsf{T} M_2 X_1 = X_1^\mathsf{T} P_2 X_1 \geq 0 \Rightarrow (X_1^\mathsf{T} X_1)^{-1} - (X_1^\mathsf{T} M_2 X_1)^{-1} \leq 0.$$

One is always better off, as far as variance is concerned, with the smaller regression.

We can generalize the above discussion to the case where we have some linear restrictions $R\beta = r$. If we estimate by restricted least squares, we get smaller variance, and this is true whether or not the restrictions are true.

To summarize, there is a trade-off between bias and variance, which is a common theme in statistical modelling: a big model typically has low bias but high variance, while a small model may yield a small variance but large bias. Depending on the purpose we may take different positions on the bias variance trade-off.

The same result is true if the full model is valid but we know β_2 so that we regress $y - X_2\beta_2$ on X_1. In this case we learn that knowledge of the subvector β_2 is valuable. In a Gaussian likelihood context (A4), we might say that the information matrix is not block diagonal between β_1 and β_2.

21.3 MODEL SELECTION

Let $\mathcal{M}$ be a collection of *linear* regression models obtained from a given set of K regressors $X = (X_1, \ldots, X_K)$. For example: X, X_1, (X_2, X_{27}), etc. There are a total of $(2^K - 1)$ different subsets of X, and hence different regression models that can be counted as submodels. Suppose that the true model lies in $\mathcal{M}$, and that

$$y = X\beta + \varepsilon,$$

where $\varepsilon \sim N(0, \sigma^2 I_n)$. Some of the β_i could be zero, which would denote that the true model was a strict submodel of the general model.

We now consider how to select among different submodels when $K < n$, in which case all submodels can be estimated (assuming that there are no collinearity issues). Indeed in this case, we typically can estimate the full vector β by OLS

$$\widehat{\beta} = (X^{\mathsf{T}} X)^{-1} X^{\mathsf{T}} y.$$

Let K_j be the number of explanatory variables in a given regression (with some selection of K_j regressors), and let $\widehat{\varepsilon}_j$ denote the vector of residuals, where we drop the dependence on the particular choice of covariates in the notation. The unbiased estimator of error variance

$$s_{*j}^2 = \frac{\widehat{\varepsilon}_j^{\mathsf{T}} \widehat{\varepsilon}_j}{n - K_j}$$

makes a trade-off between goodness of fit and parsimony. We can see this by expanding it out around the average sum of squared residuals $\widehat{\varepsilon}_j^{\mathsf{T}} \widehat{\varepsilon}_j / n$, which just measures goodness of fit, i.e., gets smaller the more we add variables in, that is,

$$s_{*j}^2 = \frac{\widehat{\varepsilon}_j^{\mathsf{T}} \widehat{\varepsilon}_j}{n - K_j} = \frac{\widehat{\varepsilon}_j^{\mathsf{T}} \widehat{\varepsilon}_j}{n \left\{ 1 - \frac{K_j}{n} \right\}} = \underbrace{\overbrace{\frac{\widehat{\varepsilon}_j^{\mathsf{T}} \widehat{\varepsilon}_j}{n}}^{\text{goodness of fit}}}_{s_j^2} \left(1 + \overbrace{\frac{K_j}{n}}^{\text{penalty for no. of regressors}} + \cdots \right).$$

Can see that minimizing s_{*j}^2 over all possible models is equivalent to maximizing the "adjusted R^2"

$$\overline{R}_j^2 = 1 - \frac{n-1}{n-K_j}(1 - R_j^2) = 1 - \frac{n-1}{n-K_j} \frac{\widehat{\varepsilon}_j^{\mathsf{T}} \widehat{\varepsilon}_j}{\overline{\varepsilon}^{\mathsf{T}} \overline{\varepsilon}}. \tag{21.1}$$

Other criterion include:

$$PC_j = \frac{\widehat{\varepsilon}_j^{\mathsf{T}}\widehat{\varepsilon}_j}{n - K_j}\left(1 + \frac{K_j}{n}\right) \quad \text{Prediction criterion} \quad (21.2)$$

$$AIC_j = \ln\frac{\widehat{\varepsilon}_j^{\mathsf{T}}\widehat{\varepsilon}_j}{n} + \frac{2K_j}{n} \quad \text{Akaike criterion} \quad (21.3)$$

$$BIC_j = \ln\frac{\widehat{\varepsilon}_j^{\mathsf{T}}\widehat{\varepsilon}_j}{n} + \frac{K_j\log n}{n} \quad \text{Bayesian Information criterion,} \quad (21.4)$$

which should all be minimized for a good model. These criteria allow one to compare models with different numbers of covariates and perforce to compare models with the same number of covariates. The method involves computing these quantities for all candidate models and choosing the model with the best score. It has been shown that all these methods have the property that the selected model is larger than or equal to the true model with probability tending to one; only BIC_j correctly selects the true model with probability tending to one. This is to do with the larger penalty that BIC imposes on the number of parameters. An alternative model selection strategy is to choose a large initial model and perform a sequence of t-tests to eliminate redundant variables, this may be called the **Oxford School of Econometrics**. We shall not consider this further except to record a well known result that links the properties of the regression t test and the adjusted R squared.

Theorem 21.1. $\overline{R}^2$ *falls (rises) when the deleted variable has $t > (<)1$*

21.3.1 Problems and Issues

1. $\mathcal{M}$ may be large and searching exhaustively over 2^K regressions is computationally infeasible. In practice some directed search is needed. Either one starts small and works up, or starts big and works down (General to Specific or GtS).
2. The true model may not be in $\mathcal{M}$, but the procedure is guaranteed to find a best model. This used to be called data mining. White's (2000) **Reality Check** paper describes this phenomenon well. Suppose you consider all regressions with two predictor variables from a large set of predictors, a total of $K(K-1)/2$ distinct regressions. The degrees of freedom of each regression is the same. The best fitting such regression will have a high in sample R^2 even if the variables are all mutually independent. You can test this by drawing $K+1$ normal independent random variables and then searching over all the regressions. We show below the maximal value of R^2 obtained across simulations for the cases with $n = 1000$ and $K = 10, 100, 1000$. The

numbers are not large but the general message is consistent with the infinite monkey theorem...

$K = 10$	$K = 100$	$K = 1000$
0.018	0.030	0.042

3. Other criteria are important, especially for nonexperimental data.
   a. Consistency with economic theory elasticities the right sign? Demand slopes down?
   b. Consistency with data, e.g., suppose dependent variable is food share $\notin [0, 1]$, then ideally don't want a model that predicts outside this range.
   c. Residuals should be approximately random, i.e., pass diagnostic checks for serial correlation, heteroskedasticity, nonlinearity, etc. This signifies that the model is not grossly misspecified.
   d. How well the model performs out-of-sample. This is often used in time series analysis where it has been often observed that in sample performance is not necessarily followed by good prediction.

21.4 LASSO

We next discuss the so-called Lasso method, Tibshirani (1996), which is an alternative model selection procedure that addresses some of the issues raised above. Suppose that we have n observations on candidate covariates $x_1, x_2, \ldots, x_K$ and an outcome variable y, where $K > n$ and could be much larger than n. In this case we cannot compute the OLS estimator using all the regressors. One solution is to compute the **ridge regression** estimator

$$\widehat{\beta}_R = \left(X^\mathsf{T} X + \lambda I_K\right)^{-1} X^\mathsf{T} y, \tag{21.5}$$

where $\lambda > 0$ is some small positive number, as this will always exist because $X^\mathsf{T} X \geq 0$ implies $X^\mathsf{T} X + \lambda I_K > 0$. We can show that the ridge regression is the solution to the penalized least squares criterion

$$\min_{b_1, b_2, \ldots, b_K} \sum_{i=1}^n (y_i - b_1 - b_2 x_{2i} - b_3 x_{3i} - \ldots - b_K x_{Ki})^2 + \lambda \sum_{j=1}^K b_j^2,$$

which follows by direct application of constrained optimisation techniques. However, we may believe that the true model is of much smaller dimension, i.e., many of the β_i are zero, it is just that we don't know which ones are relevant. The ridge estimator will typically set all elements of $\widehat{\beta}_R$ to be nonzero, and so we are back to a further model selection step. When K is very large it is not feasible to search over all possible submodels, it is just too time consuming.

We now suppose that most of the covariates are known to have zero effect, i.e., not to belong in the regression model. In particular, suppose that

$$E(Y|X_1, \ldots, X_K) = \sum_{k=1}^{K_0} \beta_{j_k} X_{j_k},$$

for some $K_0 \leq K$. Denote the **active set** by

$$A = \{j : \beta_j \neq 0\}$$

and the inactive set by its complement in $\{1, \ldots, K\}$. The assumption that K_0 is much smaller than n is called **sparsity**. This says that only a small number of covariates actually matter.

The Lasso method solves the following constrained minimization problem

$$\min_{b_1, b_2, \ldots, b_K} \sum_{i=1}^{n} (y_i - b_1 - b_2 x_{2i} - b_3 x_{3i} - \ldots - b_K x_{Ki})^2 + \lambda \sum_{j=1}^{K} |b_j|,$$

where the penalty here is "L_1" not the usual L_0 penalty that is associated with classical model selection methods nor the L_2 penalty that defined the ridge regression. Unlike ridge regression there is no closed form solution to this problem. However, the computation of the lasso solutions is a quadratic programming problem, and can be tackled by standard numerical analysis algorithms. The problem can be equivalently written as

$$\min_{b_1, b_2, \ldots, b_K} \sum_{i=1}^{n} (y_i - b_1 - b_2 x_{2i} - b_3 x_{3i} - \ldots - b_K x_{Ki})^2 \text{ s.t. } \sum_{j=1}^{K} |b_j| \leq s$$

for some given s. The bound "s" is a tuning parameter. When "s" is large enough, the constraint has no effect and the solution is just the usual multiple linear least squares regression of y on $x_1, x_2, \ldots, x_K$. However when for smaller values of s ($s \geq 0$) the solutions are "shrunken" versions of the least squares estimates – many of the chosen coefficients $\hat{\beta}_j$ are exactly zero. Choosing "s" is like choosing the number of predictors to use in a regression model, and **cross-validation** is a good tool for estimating the best value for "s".

Define the selected set

$$\widehat{A} = \{j : \widehat{\beta}_j \neq 0\}.$$

It has been shown under some conditions that

$$\Pr(\widehat{A} = A) \longrightarrow 1.$$

That is, the Lasso selects the correct model with probability tending to one.

Chapter 22

Asymptotic Properties of OLS Estimator and Test Statistics

22.1 THE I.I.D. CASE

For this purpose we shall assume a random design, and moreover suppose that (x_i, ε_i) are i.i.d. We consider the regression model

$$y_i = \beta^\mathsf{T} \tilde{x}_i + \varepsilon_i, \quad \tilde{x}_i = (x_{i1}, \ldots, x_{iK})^\mathsf{T}.$$

Note the new notation with $\tilde{x}_i$ being a $K \times 1$ vector compared with x_k, which was an $n \times 1$ vector.

Assumption B. *We suppose that $(\tilde{x}_i, \varepsilon_i)$ are i.i.d. and that*

1. $E(\tilde{x}_i \varepsilon_i) = E(\varepsilon_i) = 0$ and $E\left[|x_{ji}\varepsilon_i|\right] < \infty$, $j = 1, \ldots, K$, and for some pd $K \times K$ matrix M

$$E\left[\tilde{x}_i \tilde{x}_i^\mathsf{T}\right] = M$$

2. For some finite pd $K \times K$ matrix Ω

$$E(\tilde{x}_i \tilde{x}_i^\mathsf{T} \varepsilon_i^2) = \Omega.$$

We also consider the homoskedastic special case where $E(\varepsilon_i^2 | \tilde{x}_i) = \sigma^2$ for some σ^2 in which case

$$\Omega = \sigma^2 M. \tag{22.1}$$

Note that under the i.i.d. framework, our earlier assumptions A1 and A2 imply B1 and B2.

In B1, we assume the **unconditional moment** condition

$$\mathrm{cov}(\tilde{x}_i, \varepsilon_i) = E(\tilde{x}_i \varepsilon_i) = 0,$$

which suffices for the asymptotic properties we derive. However, this condition is typically considered to be insufficient for the proper interpretation of the model as a regression. In that case, we are finding the Best Linear Predictor that we discussed in Chapter 7. Furthermore, it does not ensure that the OLS estimator is unbiased.

Probability, Statistics and Econometrics. http://dx.doi.org/10.1016/B978-0-12-810495-8.00025-7

297

We might assume the stronger **conditional moment** conditions that

$$E(\varepsilon_i | \tilde{x}_i) = 0$$
$$E(\varepsilon_i^2 | \tilde{x}_i) = v(\tilde{x}_i), \quad \Omega = E\left[v(\tilde{x}_i)\tilde{x}_i \tilde{x}_i^\mathsf{T}\right]$$

which does ensure the validity of the regression interpretation. This condition implies $E(\tilde{x}_i \varepsilon_i) = 0$ but is not implied by it.

Example 22.1. $\tilde{x}_i = \sin(\theta_i)$ and $\varepsilon_i = \cos(\theta_i)$, where $\theta_i \sim [0, 2\pi]$. We have

$$E(\tilde{x}_i \varepsilon_i) = 0$$

but clearly knowing $\tilde{x}_i$ tells you ε_i and it is not always zero. Actually, I think that $E(\varepsilon_i | \tilde{x}_i) = 0$.

Conditional moment condition also ensures that the OLS estimator is unbiased because

$$\widehat{\beta} = \beta + (X^\mathsf{T}X)^{-1}(X^\mathsf{T}\varepsilon) = \beta + \left(\sum_{i=1}^{n}\tilde{x}_i \tilde{x}_i^\mathsf{T}\right)^{-1}\sum_{i=1}^{n}\tilde{x}_i \varepsilon_i$$

$$E(\widehat{\beta}|X) = \beta + \left(\sum_{i=1}^{n}\tilde{x}_i \tilde{x}_i^\mathsf{T}\right)^{-1}\sum_{i=1}^{n}\tilde{x}_i E(\varepsilon_i | \tilde{x}_i) = \beta$$

We assume B1 and B2 in the sequel and are concerned with large sample properties. We require higher moments for some of the results below.

Theorem 22.1. *Suppose that B1 holds. Then we have*

$$\widehat{\beta} \xrightarrow{P} \beta.$$

Proof. We have

$$\widehat{\beta} - \beta = (X^\mathsf{T}X/n)^{-1}(X^\mathsf{T}\varepsilon/n) = \left(\frac{1}{n}\sum_{i=1}^{n}\tilde{x}_i \tilde{x}_i^\mathsf{T}\right)^{-1}\frac{1}{n}\sum_{i=1}^{n}\tilde{x}_i \varepsilon_i$$

and the result follows by applying law of large numbers to both terms and then apply the Slutsky theorem. □

These conditions are often regarded as unnecessary and perhaps strong, and we shall weaken them below for fixed design settings. We now turn to the limiting distribution of the least squares estimator.

Theorem 22.2. *Suppose that B1 and B2 hold. Then*

$$\sqrt{n}(\widehat{\beta} - \beta) \xrightarrow{D} N\left(0, M^{-1}\Omega M^{-1}\right).$$

Proof. We have

$$\frac{X^{\mathsf{T}}X}{n} = \frac{1}{n}\sum_{i=1}^{n}\widetilde{x}_i\widetilde{x}_i^{\mathsf{T}} \xrightarrow{P} M$$

using LLN element by element. Then for any $c \in \mathbb{R}^K$

$$\frac{c^{\mathsf{T}}X^{\mathsf{T}}\varepsilon}{\sqrt{n}} = \frac{1}{\sqrt{n}}\sum_{i=1}^{n}c^{\mathsf{T}}\widetilde{x}_i\varepsilon_i \xrightarrow{D} N\left(0, c^{\mathsf{T}}\Omega c\right)$$

by the CLT for i.i.d. random variables. Then apply the Crámer–Wald, the Mann–Wald, and the Slutsky Theorems. $\qquad\square$

In the special case of homoskedasticity, (22.1), we have

$$M^{-1}\Omega M^{-1} = M^{-1}\sigma^2 M M^{-1} = \sigma^2 M^{-1}.$$

We here consider further applications of the tools of asymptotic theory to standard errors and test statistics.

We first consider the usual unbiased standard error

$$s_*^2 = \frac{\widehat{\varepsilon^{\mathsf{T}}\varepsilon}}{n-K} = \frac{1}{n-K}\sum_{i=1}^{n}\widehat{\varepsilon}_i^2 = \frac{1}{n-K}\varepsilon^{\mathsf{T}}M_X\varepsilon$$

Theorem 22.3. *Suppose that B1 and B2 hold and let $\sigma^2 = E\varepsilon_i^2 < \infty$. Then*

$$s_*^2 \xrightarrow{P} \sigma^2.$$

Proof. We have

$$
\begin{aligned}
s_*^2 &= \frac{1}{n-K}\varepsilon^{\mathsf{T}}M_X\varepsilon \\
&= \frac{1}{n-K}\left[\varepsilon^{\mathsf{T}}\varepsilon - \varepsilon^{\mathsf{T}}X(X^{\mathsf{T}}X)^{-1}X^{\mathsf{T}}\varepsilon\right] \\
&= \left(\frac{n}{n-K}\right)\frac{\varepsilon^{\mathsf{T}}\varepsilon}{n} - \frac{n}{n-K}\frac{\varepsilon^{\mathsf{T}}X}{n}(X^{\mathsf{T}}X/n)^{-1}X^{\mathsf{T}}\varepsilon/n \\
&\xrightarrow{P} \sigma^2.
\end{aligned}
$$

This follows by the law of large numbers applied to $X^{\mathsf{T}}\varepsilon/n$, $\varepsilon^{\mathsf{T}}\varepsilon/n$, and $X^{\mathsf{T}}X/n$. $\qquad\square$

Note that this result does not require homoskedasticity, although its relevance and interpretation do.

Now what about the t statistic and F-statistic? Suppose that R is of full rank q and define:

$$t = \frac{\sqrt{n} c^{\mathsf{T}} \widehat{\beta}}{s_* \sqrt{c^{\mathsf{T}} \frac{(X^{\mathsf{T}} X)^{-1}}{n} c}}$$

$$F = n(R\widehat{\beta} - r)^{\mathsf{T}} \left[s_*^2 R \left(\frac{X^{\mathsf{T}} X}{n} \right)^{-1} R^{\mathsf{T}} \right]^{-1} (R\widehat{\beta} - r)/q.$$

Theorem 22.4. *Suppose that B1 and B2 hold and that (22.1) holds. Then, under H_0, as $n \to \infty$*

$$t \xrightarrow{D} N(0, 1)$$

$$qF \xrightarrow{D} \chi^2(q).$$

Proof. It follows from the above that under H_0

$$\frac{c^{\mathsf{T}} \widehat{\beta} - \gamma}{\sqrt{\operatorname{var}\left(c^{\mathsf{T}} \widehat{\beta} - \gamma\right)}} = \frac{\sqrt{n} c^{\mathsf{T}} (\widehat{\beta} - \beta)}{\sigma \sqrt{c^{\mathsf{T}} \frac{(X^{\mathsf{T}} X)^{-1}}{n} c}} \xrightarrow{D} N(0, 1).$$

Then (and using Slutsky and Mann–Wald)

$$t = \frac{\sqrt{n}(c^{\mathsf{T}} \widehat{\beta} - \gamma)}{\sigma \sqrt{c^{\mathsf{T}} \frac{(X^{\mathsf{T}} X)^{-1}}{n} c}} \times \overbrace{\frac{\sigma}{s_*}}^{\text{converges to one in P}} \xrightarrow{D} N(0, 1).$$

Similarly for the F-test. □

It follows from (20.15) that

$$W, LR, LM \xrightarrow{D} \chi^2(q)$$

by applying delta method and Slutsky theorem.

If the homoskedasticity condition fails, then $t \xrightarrow{D} N(0, v)$ for some $v \neq 1$, and the testing strategy would use the wrong critical values. Likewise the Wald statistic would not have the claimed chi-squared distribution.

We consider the general case that does not impose heteroskedasticity, i.e., we work with conditions B1 and B2. In this case, the asymptotic variance of $\widehat{\beta}$ involves both M and the matrix Ω,

$$\Omega = E(\tilde{x}_i \tilde{x}_i^{\mathsf{T}} \varepsilon_i^2).$$

How do we estimate Ω? We take

$$\widehat{\Omega} = \frac{1}{n} \sum_{i=1}^{n} \widetilde{x}_i \widetilde{x}_i^{\mathsf{T}} \widehat{\varepsilon}_i^2.$$

Then the matrix

$$\widehat{H} = \left(\frac{1}{n} \sum_{i=1}^{n} \widetilde{x}_i \widetilde{x}_i^{\mathsf{T}} \right)^{-1} \widehat{\Omega} \left(\frac{1}{n} \sum_{i=1}^{n} \widetilde{x}_i \widetilde{x}_i^{\mathsf{T}} \right)^{-1} = \left(\widehat{H}_{j,k} \right)_{j,k=1}^{K}$$

contains all the estimators of $\mathrm{var}(\sqrt{n}\widehat{\beta}_k)$ and $\mathrm{cov}(\sqrt{n}\widehat{\beta}_j, \sqrt{n}\widehat{\beta}_k)$.

In this case, we consider robust test statistics (White, 1980):

$$t_R = \frac{c^{\mathsf{T}}\widehat{\beta}}{\sqrt{c^{\mathsf{T}}(X^{\mathsf{T}}X)^{-1}\widehat{\Omega}(X^{\mathsf{T}}X)^{-1}c}} \tag{22.2}$$

$$W_R = (R\widehat{\beta} - r)^{\mathsf{T}} \left[R \left(X^{\mathsf{T}}X \right)^{-1} \widehat{\Omega} \left(X^{\mathsf{T}}X \right)^{-1} R^{\mathsf{T}} \right]^{-1} (R\widehat{\beta} - r), \tag{22.3}$$

where

$$\widehat{\Omega} = \frac{1}{n} \sum_{i=1}^{n} x_i x_i^{\mathsf{T}} \widehat{\varepsilon}_i^2 = \frac{1}{n} X^{\mathsf{T}} S X,$$

where S is the $n \times n$ diagonal matrix with typical element $\widehat{\varepsilon}_i^2$.

Theorem 22.5. *Suppose that B1 and B2 hold. Suppose also that* $E|x_{ij}x_{ik}x_{il}x_{ir}| < \infty$, $E|x_{ij}x_{ik}x_{il}\varepsilon_i| < \infty$ *and* $E(x_{ij}x_{ik}\varepsilon_i x_{il}) = 0$. *Then*

$$t_R \xrightarrow{D} N(0, 1)$$

$$W_R \xrightarrow{D} \chi^2(q).$$

Proof. We have

$$\widehat{\Omega} = \frac{1}{n} \sum_{i=1}^{n} x_i x_i^{\mathsf{T}} \varepsilon_i^2 - 2\frac{1}{n} \sum_{i=1}^{n} x_i x_i^{\mathsf{T}} \varepsilon_i x_i^{\mathsf{T}} (X^{\mathsf{T}}X)^{-1} X^{\mathsf{T}} \varepsilon$$

$$+ \frac{1}{n} \sum_{i=1}^{n} x_i x_i^{\mathsf{T}} x_i^{\mathsf{T}} (X^{\mathsf{T}}X)^{-1} X^{\mathsf{T}} \varepsilon \varepsilon^{\mathsf{T}} X (X^{\mathsf{T}}X)^{-1} x_i,$$

where $\widehat{\varepsilon}_i = \varepsilon_i - x_i^{\mathsf{T}}(X^{\mathsf{T}}X)^{-1}X^{\mathsf{T}}\varepsilon$. We have

$$\frac{1}{n} \sum_{i=1}^{n} x_i x_i^{\mathsf{T}} \varepsilon_i x_i^{\mathsf{T}} (X^{\mathsf{T}}X)^{-1} X^{\mathsf{T}} \varepsilon = \frac{1}{n} \sum_{i=1}^{n} x_i x_i^{\mathsf{T}} \varepsilon_i x_i^{\mathsf{T}} (X^{\mathsf{T}}X/n)^{-1} (X^{\mathsf{T}}\varepsilon/n) \xrightarrow{P} 0,$$

since $E(|x_{ij}x_{ik}x_{il}\varepsilon_i|) < \infty$:

$$\frac{1}{n}\sum_{i=1}^{n} x_{ij}x_{ik}\varepsilon_i x_{il} \xrightarrow{P} 0,$$

while

$$\frac{1}{n}\sum_{i=1}^{n} x_i x_i^\mathsf{T} x_i^\mathsf{T} (X^\mathsf{T}X)^{-1} X^\mathsf{T}\varepsilon\varepsilon^\mathsf{T} X(X^\mathsf{T}X)^{-1} x_i$$

$$= \frac{1}{n}\sum_{i=1}^{n} x_i x_i^\mathsf{T} x_i^\mathsf{T} (X^\mathsf{T}X/n)^{-1}(X^\mathsf{T}\varepsilon/n)(\varepsilon^\mathsf{T} X/n)(X^\mathsf{T}X/n)^{-1} x_i \xrightarrow{P} 0,$$

because $X^\mathsf{T}X/n \xrightarrow{P} M$ and $X^\mathsf{T}\varepsilon/\sqrt{n} \Longrightarrow N(0, \Omega)$, while for any j, k, l, r

$$\frac{1}{n}\sum_{i=1}^{n} x_{ij}x_{ik}x_{il}x_{ir} \xrightarrow{P} E\left[x_{ij}x_{ik}x_{il}x_{ir}\right].$$

It follows that $\widehat{\Omega} \xrightarrow{P} \Omega$. □

22.2 THE NON-I.I.D. CASE

We next consider the "fixed" design setting of Assumption A above and make general assumptions on the matrix X. These conditions work in more general sampling schemes including trending variables.

Theorem 22.6. *Suppose that Assumptions A1–A2 hold and that with probability one*

$$\lambda_{\max}(X^\mathsf{T}\Sigma X)\lambda_{\min}^2(X^\mathsf{T}X) \to 0 \text{ as } n \to \infty. \tag{22.4}$$

Then, $\widehat{\beta} \xrightarrow{P} \beta$.

Proof. We show that $c^\mathsf{T}\widehat{\beta} \xrightarrow{P} c^\mathsf{T}\beta$ for all vectors c. First, with probability one

$$E(c^\mathsf{T}\widehat{\beta}|X) = c^\mathsf{T}\beta$$

$$\mathrm{var}(c^\mathsf{T}\widehat{\beta}|X) = c^\mathsf{T}(X^\mathsf{T}X)^{-1}X^\mathsf{T}\Sigma X(X^\mathsf{T}X)^{-1}c.$$

We have

$$c^{\mathsf{T}}(X^{\mathsf{T}}X)^{-1}(X^{\mathsf{T}}\Sigma X)(X^{\mathsf{T}}X)^{-1}c = c^{\mathsf{T}}c\frac{c^{\mathsf{T}}(X^{\mathsf{T}}X)^{-1}X^{\mathsf{T}}\Sigma X(X^{\mathsf{T}}X)^{-1}c}{c^{\mathsf{T}}c}$$

$$\leq c^{\mathsf{T}}c \max_{u\in\mathbb{R}^K} \frac{u^{\mathsf{T}}(X^{\mathsf{T}}X)^{-1}X^{\mathsf{T}}\Sigma X(X^{\mathsf{T}}X)^{-1}u}{u^{\mathsf{T}}u}$$

$$\leq c^{\mathsf{T}}c\lambda_{\max}((X^{\mathsf{T}}X)^{-1}X^{\mathsf{T}}\Sigma X(X^{\mathsf{T}}X)^{-1})$$

$$= c^{\mathsf{T}}c\lambda_{\max}((X^{\mathsf{T}}X)^{-1})\lambda_{\max}(X^{\mathsf{T}}\Sigma X)$$

$$\times \lambda_{\max}((X^{\mathsf{T}}X)^{-1})$$

$$= c^{\mathsf{T}}c\lambda_{\max}(X^{\mathsf{T}}\Sigma X)\lambda^2_{\min}((X^{\mathsf{T}}X)),$$

and provided (22.4) is true, $\text{var}(c^{\mathsf{T}}\widehat{\beta}) \to 0$. $\qquad\square$

When $\Sigma = \sigma^2 I_n$, it suffices that $\lambda_{\min}(X^{\mathsf{T}}X) \to \infty$.

If we do have a random design then the conditions and conclusion should be interpreted as holding with probability one in the conditional distribution given X. Deterministic design settings arise commonly in practice, either in the context of trends or dummy variables.

Example 22.2. Suppose that

$$X = \begin{pmatrix} 1 & D_1 \\ \vdots & \vdots \\ 1 & D_n \end{pmatrix}$$

$$D_i = \begin{cases} 1 & \text{if } i \in I \subset \{1,\ldots,n\} \\ 0 & \text{else.} \end{cases}$$

Here, I is the set defining the dummy variable. For example, it could classify time series observations according to whether they are on the weekend or during the working week. For example, they could classify the cross sectional observations according to whether the individual is in a union or not. For example, in an **event study**, they could classify observations as to whether they are in the "event window" or out of it. In this case

$$X^{\mathsf{T}}X = \begin{pmatrix} n & \sum_{i=1}^n D_i \\ \sum_{i=1}^n D_i & \sum_{i=1}^n D_i \end{pmatrix} = \begin{pmatrix} n & n_I \\ n_I & n_I \end{pmatrix},$$

where n_I is the number of observations in the set I, because $D_i^2 = D_i$. Therefore,

$$\left(X^{\mathsf{T}}X\right)^{-1} = \frac{1}{(n-n_I)n_I}\begin{pmatrix} n_I & -n_I \\ -n_I & n \end{pmatrix}.$$

In this case (I used Mathematica)

$$\lambda_{\min}(X^\mathsf{T} X) = \frac{1}{2}n_I + \frac{1}{2}n - \frac{1}{2}\sqrt{5n_I^2 - 2n_In + n^2}$$

$$= \frac{1}{2}n_I + \frac{1}{2}n\left(1 - \sqrt{5\frac{n_I^2}{n^2} - 2\frac{n_I}{n} + 1}\right).$$

If $n_I \to \infty$ as $n \to \infty$, then $\lambda_{\min}(X^\mathsf{T} X) \to \infty$. This is the usual case say for day of the week dummies. On the other hand, if n_I is fixed, then we can see that $\lambda_{\min}(X^\mathsf{T} X) \to n_I/2$ as $n \to \infty$ and $\widehat{\beta}$ is not consistent. However, even in this case, the first component is consistent because

$$\left((X^\mathsf{T} X)^{-1}\right)_{11} = \frac{1}{n - n_I} \to 0$$

but the second component is inconsistent. One can't estimate consistently the effect of a dummy variable when it only effects a relatively small number of observations.

Example 22.3. Trends. Suppose that

$$X = \begin{pmatrix} 1 & 1 \\ \vdots & \vdots \\ 1 & n \end{pmatrix},$$

which says that there is potentially a linear trend in the data. In this case,

$$X^\mathsf{T} X = \begin{pmatrix} n & \sum_{i=1}^n i \\ \sum_{i=1}^n i & \sum_{i=1}^n i^2 \end{pmatrix} = \begin{pmatrix} n & \frac{1}{2}n(n+1) \\ \frac{1}{2}n(n+1) & \frac{1}{6}n(n+1)(2n+1) \end{pmatrix},$$

which you know from A level mathematics. Furthermore, (by Mathematica)

$$\lambda_{\min}(X^\mathsf{T} X) = \frac{7}{12}n - \frac{1}{2}n\sqrt{\frac{1}{9}n^4 + \frac{1}{3}n^3 + \frac{25}{36}n^2 + \frac{7}{6}n + \frac{61}{36} + \frac{1}{4}n^2 + \frac{1}{6}n^3}.$$

This looks nasty, but it can be shown by very tedious work that this goes to infinity. It is easier to see that

$$\left((X^\mathsf{T} X)^{-1}\right)_{11} = \frac{\frac{1}{6}n(n+1)(2n+1)}{\frac{1}{12}n^4 - \frac{1}{12}n^2} \to 0$$

$$\left((X^\mathsf{T} X)^{-1}\right)_{22} = \frac{n}{\frac{1}{12}n^4 - \frac{1}{12}n^2} \to 0.$$

Example 22.4. Consider the high-low method for determining average cost

$$\beta_{H-L} = \frac{y_H - y_L}{x_H - x_L},$$

where x_H, x_L are the highest and lowest values achieved by the covariate respectively, and y_H, y_L are the "concomitants", that is, the corresponding values of the outcome variable. This estimator is conditionally unbiased as discussed above and satisfies

$$\text{var}(\beta_{H-L}|X) = \frac{2\sigma^2}{(x_H - x_L)^2}.$$

For consistency, it suffices that $x_H - x_L \to \infty$ as the sample size increases. This happens for example if the covariates have support the whole real line, say are normally distributed.

Example 22.5. Suppose that the regressors are orthogonal meaning $X^\mathsf{T} X = I_K$ but that $K = K(n)$ is large. Then consider a linear combination $c^\mathsf{T} \widehat{\beta}$. We have

$$\text{var}(c^\mathsf{T}\widehat{\beta}) = \frac{\sigma^2}{n} c^\mathsf{T} c = \frac{\sigma^2 K(n)}{n} \frac{1}{K} \sum_{k=1}^{K} c_k^2.$$

This says that the individual estimates ($c_k = 1$, $c_j = 0$ for $j \neq k$) are consistent provided $K(n)/n \to 0$.

We next consider the limiting distribution of $\widehat{\beta}$. We shall suppose that the covariates are nonrandom, possibly containing trends or dummy variables, but the error terms are independent. We make the following assumptions.

Assumptions R. 1. u_i *are independent random variables with mean zero and variance* σ_i^2 *such that* $0 < \underline{\sigma}^2 \leq \sigma_i^2 \leq \overline{\sigma}^2 < \infty$ *and* $E\left(|u_i|^{2+\delta}\right) \leq C < \infty$ *for some* $\delta > 0$.

2. *X is non-stochastic and full rank and satisfy for all* $j = 1, \ldots, K$

$$d_j^2 = \sum_{i=1}^{n} x_{ij}^2 \longrightarrow \infty$$

$$\frac{\max_{1 \leq i \leq n} x_{ij}^2}{\sum_{i=1}^{n} x_{ij}^2} \longrightarrow 0$$

3. *The* $K \times K$ *matrices below satisfy for positive definite matrices* M, Ψ

$$M_n = \Delta^{-1} X^\mathsf{T} X \Delta^{-1} \longrightarrow M$$

$$\Psi_n = \Delta^{-1} X^\mathsf{T} \Sigma X \Delta^{-1} \longrightarrow \Psi,$$

where $\Delta = \text{diag}\{d_1, \ldots, d_K\}$ *and* $\Sigma = \text{diag}\{\sigma_1^2, \ldots, \sigma_K^2\}$.

Theorem 22.7. *Suppose that Assumptions R1–R3 hold. Then*

$$\Delta \left(\widehat{\beta} - \beta\right) \xrightarrow{D} N\left(0, M^{-1}\Psi M^{-1}\right).$$

Proof. We write

$$\Delta(\widehat{\beta} - \beta) = (\Delta^{-1}X^{\mathsf{T}}X\Delta^{-1})^{-1}\Delta^{-1}X^{\mathsf{T}}u = M_n^{-1}r_n.$$

By assumption, M_n converges to M. We consider for any $c \in \mathbb{R}^K$

$$c^{\mathsf{T}}\Delta^{-1}X^{\mathsf{T}}u = \sum_{j=1}^{K} c_j d_j^{-1} \sum_{i=1}^{n} x_{ij}u_i = \sum_{i=1}^{n} w_{ni}u_i,$$

where $w_{ni} = \sum_{j=1}^{K} c_j d_j^{-1} x_{ij}$. We next apply the Lindeberg CLT (generalized to **triangular arrays** – w_{ni} depends on n). We show that the standardized random variable

$$T_n = \frac{\sum_{i=1}^{n} w_{ni}u_i}{\left(\sum_{i=1}^{n} w_{ni}^2 \sigma_i^2\right)^{1/2}}$$

converges to a standard normal random variable.

For any i we have

$$E\left[u_i^2 1\left(w_{ni}^2 u_i^2 > \epsilon s_n^2\right)\right] \leq E\left[|u_i|^{2+\delta}\left(\frac{w_{ni}^2}{\epsilon s_n^2}\right)^{\delta/2} 1\left(u_i^2 > \frac{\epsilon s_n^2}{w_{ni}^2}\right)\right]$$

$$\leq \left(\frac{w_{ni}^2}{\epsilon s_n^2}\right)^{\delta/2} E\left[|u_i|^{2+\delta}\right]$$

$$\leq C\left(\frac{w_{ni}^2}{\epsilon s_n^2}\right)^{\delta/2},$$

where $s_n^2 = \sum_{i=1}^{n} w_{ni}^2 \sigma_i^2$. Therefore, provided

$$\frac{\max_{1 \leq i \leq n} w_{ni}^2}{s_n^2} \longrightarrow 0, \tag{22.5}$$

we have

$$\frac{1}{\sum_{i=1}^{n} w_{ni}^2 \sigma_i^2} \sum_{i=1}^{n} w_{ni}^2 E\left[u_i^2 1\left(w_{ni}^2 u_i^2 > \epsilon s_n^2\right)\right]$$

$$\leq \frac{\sum_{i=1}^{n} w_{ni}^2}{\sum_{i=1}^{n} w_{ni}^2 \sigma_i^2} \times C\left(\frac{1}{\epsilon^{\delta/2}}\right) \times \left(\frac{\max_{1 \leq i \leq n} w_{ni}^2}{s_n^2}\right)^{\delta/2} \to 0.$$

We have by R1, R2, and R3 and the Cauchy–Schwarz inequality

$$
\frac{\max_{1\leq i\leq n}\left(\sum_{j=1}^{K}c_j d_j^{-1}x_{ij}\right)^2}{\sum_{i=1}^{n}\left(\sum_{j=1}^{K}c_j d_j^{-1}x_{ij}\right)^2\sigma_i^2}
$$

$$
\leq \frac{\left(\sum_{j=1}^{K}|c_j|\max_{1\leq i\leq n}\left|d_j^{-1}x_{ij}\right|\right)^2}{\underline{\sigma}^2\sum_{i=1}^{n}\left(\sum_{j=1}^{K}c_j d_j^{-1}x_{ij}\right)^2}
$$

$$
= \frac{\left(\sum_{j=1}^{K}|c_j|\max_{1\leq i\leq n}\left|d_j^{-1}x_{ij}\right|\right)^2}{\underline{\sigma}^2 c^\mathsf{T}\Delta^{-1}X^\mathsf{T}X\Delta^{-1}c}
$$

$$
\leq \frac{K\times c^\mathsf{T}c\times \max_{1\leq j\leq K}\max_{1\leq i\leq n}\left|d_j^{-2}x_{ij}^2\right|}{\underline{\sigma}^2\times c^\mathsf{T}c\times(\lambda_{\min}(M)+o(1))}\longrightarrow 0.
$$

It follows that $T_n \xrightarrow{D} N(0,1)$ for any $c\neq 0$ and hence $\Delta^{-1}X^\mathsf{T}u \xrightarrow{D} N(0,\Psi)$. We apply the multivariate version of continuous mapping and Slutsky theorem to conclude. ☐

The scaling matrix Δ allows there to be different rates of convergence across the covariates. The theory allows for a wide range of trending variables that could for example be required in modelling climate change. Different growth rates need to be normalized differently.

Example 22.6. Suppose that $x_{i1}=1$, $x_{i1}=i$, and $x_{i1}=i^2$, and u_i are i.i.d. with variance σ^2. Then

$$
\Delta = \begin{pmatrix} \sqrt{n} & 0 & 0 \\ 0 & \sqrt{\sum_{i=1}^{n}i^2} & 0 \\ 0 & 0 & \sqrt{\sum_{i=1}^{n}i^4} \end{pmatrix} \simeq \begin{pmatrix} \sqrt{n} & 0 & 0 \\ 0 & n^{3/2}/\sqrt{3} & 0 \\ 0 & 0 & n^{5/2}/\sqrt{5} \end{pmatrix}
$$

$$
M = I.
$$

The negligibility conditions are easily satisfied, for example, if $x_i = i$,

$$
\frac{\max_{1\leq i\leq n}i^2}{\sum_{j=1}^{n}j^2} = \frac{n^2}{O(n^3)} \to 0.
$$

In this case, even though the largest element is increasing with sample size many other elements are increasing just as fast. We have

$$
\begin{pmatrix}
\sqrt{n}\left(\widehat{\beta}_1 - \beta_1\right) \\
n^{3/2}\left(\widehat{\beta}_1 - \beta_1\right) \\
n^{5/2}\left(\widehat{\beta}_1 - \beta_1\right)
\end{pmatrix}
\xrightarrow{D}
N\left(0, \sigma^2
\begin{pmatrix}
1 & 0 & 0 \\
0 & 3 & 0 \\
0 & 0 & 5
\end{pmatrix}
\right).
$$

Example 22.7. Consider the dummy variable example $x_i = D_i$, then

$$
\max_{1 \le i \le n} \frac{x_i^2}{\sum_{j=1}^n x_j^2} = \frac{1}{\sum_{j=1}^n D_j},
$$

which goes to zero if and only if $\sum_{j=1}^n D_j \to \infty$.

Example 22.8. An example, where the CLT would fail is

$$
x_i =
\begin{cases}
1 & \text{if } i < n \\
n & \text{if } i = n.
\end{cases}
$$

In this case, the negligibility condition fails and the distribution of the least squares estimator would be largely determined by the last observation.

We next consider the robust t and Wald statistics in this environment. We let

$$
\widehat{\Psi} = \Delta^{-1} X^{\mathsf{T}} S X \Delta^{-1}, \tag{22.6}
$$

where S is the $n \times n$ diagonal matrix with typical element $\widehat{\varepsilon}_i^2$. We can write

$$
t_R = \frac{c^{\mathsf{T}} \Delta^{-1} \Delta \widehat{\beta}}{\sqrt{c^{\mathsf{T}} \Delta^{-1} (\Delta^{-1} X^{\mathsf{T}} X \Delta^{-1})^{-1} \widehat{\Psi} (\Delta^{-1} X^{\mathsf{T}} X \Delta^{-1})^{-1} \Delta^{-1} c}}.
$$

Define

$$
\dot{x}_i = (\dot{x}_{i1}, \dots, \dot{x}_{iK})^{\mathsf{T}} \quad ; \quad \dot{x}_{ij} = \frac{x_{ij}}{\sqrt{\sum_{i=1}^n x_{ij}^2}}.
$$

Assumption R3 says that $\sum_{i=1}^n \dot{x}_i \dot{x}_i^{\mathsf{T}}$ converges to a positive definite matrix. We make the further assumption

R4. *For $j, k, l, r = 1, \dots, K$*

$$
\sum_{i=1}^n \dot{x}_{ij}^2 \dot{x}_{ik}^2, \quad \sum_{i=1}^n \dot{x}_{ij}^2 \dot{x}_{ik}^2 \dot{x}_{il}^2, \quad \sum_{i=1}^n \left| \dot{x}_{ij} \dot{x}_{ik} \dot{x}_{il} \dot{x}_{ir} \right| \to 0.
$$

R5. *For some $C < \infty$,*

$$
E\left[\left(\varepsilon_i^2 - \sigma_i^2 \right)^2 \right] \le C
$$

Theorem 22.8. *Suppose that R1–R5 hold. Then, under H_0*

$$t_R \xrightarrow{D} N(0, 1)$$

Proof. We have

$$
\widehat{\Psi} = \Delta^{-1} \sum_{i=1}^{n} x_i x_i^\mathsf{T} \widehat{\varepsilon}_i^2 \Delta^{-1} - 2\Delta^{-1} \sum_{i=1}^{n} x_i x_i^\mathsf{T} \Delta^{-1} \varepsilon_i x_i^\mathsf{T} (X^\mathsf{T} X)^{-1} X^\mathsf{T} \varepsilon
$$

$$
+ \Delta^{-1} \sum_{i=1}^{n} x_i x_i^\mathsf{T} \Delta^{-1} x_i^\mathsf{T} (X^\mathsf{T} X)^{-1} X^\mathsf{T} \varepsilon \varepsilon^\mathsf{T} X (X^\mathsf{T} X)^{-1} x_i
$$

$$
= \widehat{\Psi}_1 + \widehat{\Psi}_2 + \widehat{\Psi}_3,
$$

where $\widehat{\varepsilon}_i = \varepsilon_i - x_i^\mathsf{T} (X^\mathsf{T} X)^{-1} X^\mathsf{T} \varepsilon$. We have

$$
\widehat{\Psi}_2 = \Delta^{-1} \sum_{i=1}^{n} x_i x_i^\mathsf{T} \Delta^{-1} \varepsilon_i x_i^\mathsf{T} \Delta^{-1} (\Delta^{-1} X^\mathsf{T} X \Delta^{-1})^{-1} \left(\Delta^{-1} X^\mathsf{T} \varepsilon \right)
$$

$$
= \sum_{i=1}^{n} \varepsilon_i \dot{x}_i \dot{x}_i^\mathsf{T} \dot{x}_i^\mathsf{T} (\Delta^{-1} X^\mathsf{T} X \Delta^{-1})^{-1} \left(\Delta^{-1} X^\mathsf{T} \varepsilon \right) \xrightarrow{P} 0,
$$

since: $(\Delta^{-1} X^\mathsf{T} X \Delta^{-1})^{-1} \left(\Delta^{-1} X^\mathsf{T} \varepsilon \right) \xrightarrow{D} W \in \mathbb{R}^K$, say, while for any $j, k, l = 1, \ldots, K$ we have

$$
E \left(\sum_{i=1}^{n} \varepsilon_i \dot{x}_{ij} \dot{x}_{ik} \dot{x}_{il} \right) = 0
$$

$$
\mathrm{var} \left(\sum_{i=1}^{n} \varepsilon_i \dot{x}_{ij} \dot{x}_{ik} \dot{x}_{il} \right) = \sum_{i=1}^{n} \dot{x}_{ij}^2 \dot{x}_{ik}^2 \dot{x}_{il}^2 \sigma_i^2
$$

$$
\leq \bar{\sigma}^2 \sum_{i=1}^{n} \dot{x}_{ij}^2 \dot{x}_{ik}^2 \dot{x}_{il}^2 \longrightarrow 0.
$$

Likewise

$$
\widehat{\Psi}_3 = \sum_{i=1}^{n} \dot{x}_i \dot{x}_i^\mathsf{T} \dot{x}_i^\mathsf{T} (\Delta^{-1} X^\mathsf{T} X \Delta^{-1})^{-1} \Delta^{-1} X^\mathsf{T} \varepsilon \varepsilon^\mathsf{T} X
$$

$$
\times \Delta^{-1} (\Delta^{-1} X^\mathsf{T} X \Delta^{-1})^{-1} \dot{x}_i \xrightarrow{P} 0,
$$

because $(\Delta^{-1}X^{\mathsf{T}}X\Delta^{-1})^{-1}\Delta^{-1}X^{\mathsf{T}}\varepsilon\varepsilon^{\mathsf{T}}X\Delta^{-1}(\Delta^{-1}X^{\mathsf{T}}X\Delta^{-1})^{-1} \xrightarrow{D} WW^{\mathsf{T}}$, and the fact that $\sum_{i=1}^{n}|\dot{x}_{ij}\dot{x}_{ik}\dot{x}_{il}\dot{x}_{ir}| \to 0$. Likewise, for any j,k

$$E\left(\sum_{i=1}^{n}\dot{x}_{ij}\dot{x}_{ik}\left(\varepsilon_i^2 - \sigma_i^2\right)\right) = 0$$

$$\mathrm{var}\left(\sum_{i=1}^{n}\dot{x}_{ij}\dot{x}_{ik}\left(\varepsilon_i^2 - \sigma_i^2\right)\right) = \sum_{i=1}^{n}\dot{x}_{ij}^2\dot{x}_{ik}^2 E\left[\left(\varepsilon_i^2 - \sigma_i^2\right)^2\right]$$

$$\leq C\sum_{i=1}^{n}\dot{x}_{ij}^2\dot{x}_{ik}^2 \longrightarrow 0.$$

Therefore,

$$\widehat{\Psi} \xrightarrow{P} \Psi.$$

We have

$$t_R \xrightarrow{D} \left(\lim_{n\to\infty}\frac{c^{\mathsf{T}}\Delta^{-1}\left(M^{-1}\Psi M^{-1}\right)^{-1/2}}{\sqrt{c^{\mathsf{T}}\Delta^{-1}M^{-1}\Psi M^{-1}\Delta^{-1}c}}\right) \times Z = a^{\mathsf{T}}Z,$$

where $Z \sim N(0, I_K)$ and a is such that $a^{\mathsf{T}}a = 1$ and the result follows. □

Note that a may possess many zeros, so only a few components of Z contributed to the limiting distribution.

Example 22.9. In the case where $x_{ij} = i$ and $x_{ik} = i^2$ we have

$$\sum_{i=1}^{n}\dot{x}_{ij}^2\dot{x}_{ik}^2 = \frac{\sum_{i=1}^{n}i^6}{\sum_{i=1}^{n}i^2\sum_{i=1}^{n}i^4} \longrightarrow 0.$$

Let's consider the robust Wald statistic, which can be written

$$W_R = \left(R\Delta^{-1}\Delta(\widehat{\beta} - \beta)\right)^{\mathsf{T}}\left[R\Delta^{-1}\left(\Delta^{-1}X^{\mathsf{T}}X\Delta^{-1}\right)^{-1}\right.$$
$$\left. \times \widehat{\Psi}\left(\Delta^{-1}X^{\mathsf{T}}X\Delta^{-1}\right)^{-1}\Delta^{-1}R^{\mathsf{T}}\right]^{-1}R\Delta^{-1}\Delta(\widehat{\beta} - \beta).$$

We have $\Delta(\widehat{\beta} - \beta) \xrightarrow{D} \left(M^{-1}\Psi M^{-1}\right)^{1/2} \times x$, where $x \sim N(0, I_K)$ so replacing $\widehat{\Psi}$ by its probability limit we have

$$W_R \xrightarrow{D} x^\mathsf{T} \left(M^{-1}\Psi M^{-1}\right)^{1/2}$$
$$\times \lim_{n\to\infty} \left(\Delta^{-1}R^\mathsf{T}\left[R\Delta^{-1}M^{-1}\Psi M^{-1}\Delta^{-1}R^\mathsf{T}\right]^{-1}R\Delta^{-1}\right)$$
$$\times \left(M^{-1}\Psi M^{-1}\right)^{1/2} \times x.$$

The main issue is that we can't guarantee this limit exists, because the matrix $R\Delta^{-1}$ can be of deficient rank in large samples even when R is full rank.

Example 22.10. Suppose that $M = \Psi = I_3$ and

$$\Delta = \mathrm{diag}\left(n^{1/2}, n^{3/2}, n^{5/2}\right) \quad ; \quad R = \begin{pmatrix} 1 & 1 & 1 \\ 1 & 0 & 0 \end{pmatrix}.$$

Then

$$R\Delta^{-1} = \begin{pmatrix} n^{-1/2} & n^{-3/2} & n^{-5/2} \\ n^{-1/2} & 0 & 0 \end{pmatrix}$$

$$R\Delta^{-1}\Delta^{-1}R^\mathsf{T} = \begin{pmatrix} n^{-1}+n^{-3}+n^{-5} & n^{-1} \\ n^{-1} & n^{-1} \end{pmatrix},$$

and the matrix $nR\Delta^{-1}\Delta^{-1}R^\mathsf{T}$ is asymptotically singular. In this case, if c is the first row of R we have $a^\mathsf{T} = (1,0,0)$ so the t-statistic is only driven by the first component.

Intuitively, when there are restrictions across variables that are driven by different trend rates, it is the slowest rate that prevails. See Phillips (2007) for further discussion of regression with trending regressors and some of the pitfalls that may occur and the possible remedies.

Chapter 23

Generalized Method of Moments and Extremum Estimators

23.1 GENERALIZED METHOD MOMENTS

We suppose that there is i.i.d. vector data $\{Z_i\}_{i=1}^n$ from some population. It is known that there exists a unique $\theta_0 \in \mathbb{R}^p$ such that

$$E[g(Z_i, \theta_0)] = 0 \qquad (23.1)$$

for some vector of known functions $g(\cdot)$ $[q \times 1]$. For example, the first order condition from some optimization problem for the representative agent, see below. This is a **semiparametric model**, because the distribution of Z_i is unspecified apart from the q moments, but we are only interested in the parameters θ. There are several cases:

1. $p > q$; unidentified case
2. $p = q$; exactly identified case
3. $p < q$; overidentified case.

We next give some examples:

Example 23.1. Simultaneous Equations Model. Suppose that we observe $y_i \in \mathbb{R}^L$ and $x_i \in \mathbb{R}^K$, where

$$B(\theta)y_i = C(\theta)x_i + u_i,$$

where $B(\theta)$ is an $L \times L$ matrix and $C(\theta)$ is an $L \times K$ matrix of unknown quantities depending on unknown parameters $\theta \in \mathbb{R}^p$, while the error term $u_i \in \mathbb{R}^L$ satisfies the conditional moment restriction

$$E(u_i|x_i) = 0. \qquad (23.2)$$

The parameters of interest are B, C, which are not themselves identified unless the parameter vector θ encodes some restrictions (such as $B_{ij} = 0$). Notice that $E(y_i|x_i) = B(\theta)^{-1}C(\theta)x_i \equiv \Phi(\theta)x_i$ provided B is invertible, where $\Phi(\theta)$ is an

Probability, Statistics and Econometrics. http://dx.doi.org/10.1016/B978-0-12-810495-8.00026-9

$L \times K$ matrix, therefore, the parameters in Φ are identified provided $E(x_i x_i^\mathsf{T})$ is of full rank. However, it is the parameters in B and C that are fundamental to the economic interpretation and are therefore the quantities of interest. We will discuss the identification issue later. Let

$$g(Z_i, \theta) = (B(\theta)y_i - C(\theta)x_i) \otimes h(x_i),$$

where $h(x_i)$ is an $M \times 1$ vector of functions of x_i; here, for vectors $a \in \mathbb{R}^L$ and $b \in \mathbb{R}^M$, $a \otimes b$ means the $L \times M$ by 1 vector $(a_1 b^\mathsf{T}, \dots, a_L b^\mathsf{T})^\mathsf{T}$ that contains all the cross products. This falls into the framework (23.1) with $Z_i = (y_i^\mathsf{T}, x_i^\mathsf{T})^\mathsf{T}$ and $q = L \times M$. The traditional approach here has been to assume the stronger condition that

$$u_i \sim N(0, \Sigma(\theta))$$

for some unknown covariance matrix Σ, in which case, $y_i | x_i \sim N(B(\theta)^{-1} \times C(\theta)x_i, B(\theta)^{-1}\Sigma(\theta)B(\theta)^{\mathsf{T}-1})$.

Example 23.2. (Hansen and Singleton, 1982) One of the most influential econometric papers of the 1980s. Intertemporal consumption/Investment decision: c_i consumption $u(\cdot)$ utility $u_c > 0$, $u_{cc} < 0$, $1 + r_{j,i+1}$, $j = 1, \dots, m$ is gross return on asset j at time $i + 1$. The representative agent solves the following optimization problem

$$\max_{\{c_i, w_i\}_{i=0}^\infty} \sum_{\tau=0}^\infty \beta^\tau E[u(c_{i+\tau})|I_i],$$

where w_i is a vector of portfolio weights and β is the discount factor. This is a dynamic programming problem. We assume that there is a unique interior solution; this is characterized by the following condition

$$u'(c_i) = \beta E[(1 + r_{j,i+1})u'(c_{i+1})|I_i], \quad j = 1, \dots, m.$$

Now suppose that

$$u(c_i) = \begin{cases} \frac{c_i^{1-\gamma}}{1-\gamma} & \text{if } \gamma > 0, \ \gamma \neq 1, \\ \log c_i & \gamma = 1. \end{cases}$$

Here, γ is the coefficient of relative risk aversion. Then

$$c_i^{-\gamma} = \beta E[(1 + r_{j,i+1})c_{i+1}^{-\gamma}|I_i],$$

and rearranging we get

$$E\left[1 - \beta\left\{(1 + r_{j,i+1})\left(\frac{c_{i+1}}{c_i}\right)^{-\gamma}\right\}\Bigg| I_i^*\right] = 0 \ , \quad j = 1, \ldots, m$$

where $I_i^* \subset I_i$ and I_i^* is the econometrician's information set. We want to estimate the parameters and test the theory given a dataset consisting of $c_i, r_{j,i+1}, I_i^*$. Let $\theta_{p \times 1} = (\beta, \gamma)$ and define the vector

$$g(Z_i, \theta) = \begin{bmatrix} \vdots \\ \left[1 - \beta\left\{(1 + r_{j,i+1})\left(\frac{c_{i+1}}{c_i}\right)^{-\gamma}\right\}\right] v_i \\ \vdots \end{bmatrix}_{q \times 1},$$

where $v_i \in I_i^*$, and $Z_i = (v_i, c_i, c_{i+1}, r_{1,i+1}, \ldots, r_{m,i+1})^\mathsf{T}$.

For any $\theta \in \Theta \subseteq \mathbb{R}^p$, let

$$G_n(\theta) = \frac{1}{n}\sum_{i=1}^{n} g(Z_i, \theta) \in \mathbb{R}^q.$$

Here, Θ is the parameter space or the set of allowable parameters. In the exactly identified case where $q = p$, we can hopefully solve the p equations in p-unknowns: $G_n(\theta) = 0$ exactly, possibly using some numerical methods. However, in the overidentified case when $p < q$, this will not be possible because we cannot simultaneously zero q functions with p controls. Define

$$Q_n(\theta) = G_n^\mathsf{T}(\theta) W_n(\theta) G_n(\theta) = \left\| G_n^\mathsf{T}(\theta) \right\|_{W_n}^2$$

where $W_n(\theta)$ is a $q \times q$ positive definite weighting matrix, and $\|x\|_A^2 = x^\mathsf{T} A x$. For example, $W_n(\theta) = I_{q \times q}$. Then let $\hat{\theta}_{GMM}$ minimize $Q_n(\theta)$ over $\theta \in \Theta \subseteq \mathbb{R}^p$. This defines a large class of estimators, one for each weighting matrix W_n. It is generally a nonlinear optimization problem like maximum likelihood; various techniques are available for finding the minimizer.

An alternative approach to using overidentifying information is to combine the estimating equations, that is let

$$G_n^\dagger(\theta) = A_n(\theta) G_n(\theta) \in \mathbb{R}^p, \tag{23.3}$$

where $A_n(\theta)$ is a full rank deterministic $p \times q$ matrix. Then find the value of $\theta \in \Theta \subseteq \mathbb{R}^p$ that solves $G_n^\dagger(\theta) = 0$. The two approaches are broadly equivalent: for a given choice of W_n there is an equivalent choice of A_n and vice versa.

Some authors argue that GMM includes MLE as a special case because for a correctly specified likelihood function we have $E[s(Z_i, \theta_0)] = 0$, where s is the score function. However, statistical parlance is to treat Z-estimators (estimators that zero some moment condition) differently from M-estimators (estimators that minimize some objective function), van der Vaart (1998). The reasons being that: (1) in some cases the true parameter lies on the boundary of the parameter space/and or the MLE is not defined by first order conditions, e.g., the uniform distribution; (2) in some cases, the identification conditions are weaker for the M estimation case because this contains more information.

23.2 ASYMPTOTIC PROPERTIES OF EXTREMUM ESTIMATORS

We consider the asymptotic properties of a general class of estimators $\hat{\theta}$ that minimize

$$Q_n(\theta) \text{ over } \theta \in \Theta \subseteq \mathbb{R}^p \tag{23.4}$$

for some general objective function $Q_n(\theta)$ that depends on the data. This includes GMM and Maximum Likelihood as special cases. The difficult part is consistency because in general the objective function is nonlinear in the parameters and does not have a closed form solution.

23.2.1 Consistency

There are many treatments of the asymptotic properties of extremum estimators, we give a standard version that rules out discontinuous criterion functions; there are versions that allow for discontinuity in θ, see below.

What we do is construct a sequence of functions, $\{Q_n(\theta)\}$, which for each finite n have some distribution, but which "converge to" $Q(\theta)$ in some sense as n grows large. If that sense is strong enough, then for n sufficiently large, the value of θ that minimizes Q_n will be the value that minimizes Q. *What do we need for this logic to make sense?*

1. Identification Condition. The first thing to note is that there must be only one "minimum" of $Q(\theta)$. More formally what we will require is that for every θ different from θ_0 (i.e., provided $\|\theta - \theta_0\| \geq \delta > 0$, $Q(\theta) - Q(\theta_0) \geq \epsilon(\delta) > 0$). If this were not true then there would be two distinct θ's that would minimize the objective function, and we have no way of distinguishing which one is the true θ_0 (alternatively there is no way of knowing whether the computational algorithm stops at the right one). Consequently this is a condition we will have to impose on the problem. We will refer to it as the **identification condition** for the nonlinear model. Of course, if there is another way to choose between different θ's, then the model could be identified even if this condition is not satisfied for Q.

2. Convergence. The second point here is that for the logic to make sense the convergence must be uniform over $\theta \in \Theta$, i.e., $\sup_{\theta \in \Theta} |Q_n(\theta) - Q(\theta)| = o_p(1)$. If this were not the case then, even if the identification condition were met, we could go to some θ different from θ_0, say θ_* and find that $Q_n(\theta)$ hovers about $Q_n(\theta_0)$ as θ circles around that θ_* even though $Q(\theta_*) - Q(\theta_0) \geq \delta > 0$. Since at any fixed θ, say θ_1, G_n is just a sample mean of mean zero *i.i.d.* deviates, a standard LLN establishes that $\|Q_n(\theta_*) - Q(\theta_*)\| = o_p(1)$. What we need for consistency is the stronger property that $\sup_{\theta \in \Theta} |Q_n(\theta) - Q(\theta)| = o_p(1)$, i.e., a "uniform law of large numbers".

These two properties, that is the ULLN and the identification condition seem to be the only properties used in the intuition underlying the consistency of the estimator. Indeed, as we show now they are more than enough to prove consistency. Note that neither of these properties have anything directly to do with smoothness of the objective function; i.e., of $Q_n(\cdot)$. So using them certainly does not rule out estimators based on objective functions that are not differentiable.

Theorem 23.1. *(Consistency). Suppose that the following conditions hold:*
(A) The parameter space Θ is a compact subset of Euclidean p-space.
(B) $Q_n(\theta)$ is continuous in $\theta \in \Theta$ for all possible samples and is a measurable function of the data for all $\theta \in \Theta$.
(C) There exists a nonstochastic function $Q(\theta)$ such that

$$\sup_{\theta \in \Theta} |Q_n(\theta) - Q(\theta)| \xrightarrow{P} 0, \tag{23.5}$$

as $n \to \infty$.
(D) The limit $Q(\theta)$ achieves a unique global minimum at $\theta = \theta_0$.
Then,

$$\widehat{\theta} \xrightarrow{P} \theta_0.$$

Proof. Conditions (A) and (B) guarantee that there exists a minimizer $\widehat{\theta}$. From (D), if $\|\theta - \theta_0\| > \delta$, then there is an $\epsilon(\delta) > 0$ such that $Q(\theta) - Q(\theta_0) \geq \epsilon(\delta)$. Consequently,

$$\Pr(\|\widehat{\theta} - \theta_0\| > \delta) \leq \Pr(Q(\widehat{\theta}) - Q(\theta_0) \geq \epsilon(\delta)),$$

and it is sufficient to prove that for any $\epsilon(\delta) > 0$, the latter probability goes to zero. By adding and subtracting terms we obtain

$$Q(\widehat{\theta}) - Q(\theta_0) = Q(\widehat{\theta}) - Q_n(\widehat{\theta}) + Q_n(\widehat{\theta}) - Q_n(\theta_0) + Q_n(\theta_0) - Q(\theta_0)$$
$$= I + II + III.$$

By the fact that $\widehat{\theta} \in \Theta$, we can bound the first and third times in absolute value by the left hand side of (23.5), i.e.,

$$|I|, |III| \leq \sup_{\theta \in \Theta} |Q(\theta) - Q_n(\theta)| \xrightarrow{P} 0,$$

where the convergence to zero is assumed in (C). Then by the definition of the estimator, $II \leq 0$. Together this implies that $\Pr(Q(\widehat{\theta}) - Q(\theta_0) \geq \epsilon(\delta)) \to 0$. $\square$

Condition (A) that the parameter space is compact (closed and bounded such as an interval) is not needed in linear regression since we automatically, under full rank condition, have the existence of an estimator, but a general criterion may not have a minimizer over the whole of $\mathbb{R}^p$.

23.2.1.1 Uniformity

The **Uniform Law of Large Numbers** (ULLN) condition in (C) is necessary for uncountable parameter spaces, as the following example illustrates.

Example 23.3. Consider the following family of functions $\{Q_n(\cdot), n = 1, 2, \ldots\}$, where

$$Q_n(\theta) = \begin{cases} \frac{\theta^2}{\theta^2 + (1-n\theta)^2} & 0 \leq \theta < 1 \\ 1/2 & \theta = 1. \end{cases}$$

Then, $|Q_n(\theta)| \leq 1$ and

$$\lim_{n \to \infty} |Q_n(\theta) - Q(\theta)| = 0$$

for all fixed $\theta \in [0, 1]$, where $Q(\theta) = 0$ for all θ with $0 \leq \theta < 1$ and $Q(1) = 1/2$. However,

$$\lim_{n \to \infty} \sup_{0 \leq \theta \leq 1} |Q_n(\theta) - Q(\theta)| \neq 0.$$

Furthermore,

$$Q_n\left(\frac{1}{n}\right) = 1 \quad \text{for all } n.$$

Thus the maximizing value of Q_n $[\theta_n = 1/n]$ converges to 0, while the maximizing value of Q is achieved at $\theta = 1$.

The ULLN condition is often satisfied because $Q_n(\theta)$ is typically a function of a sample average, i.e., of the form $f(n^{-1} \sum_{i=1}^{n} q_i(\theta))$, where q_i depends only on the ith observation. When the data are independent across i, or at least only weakly dependent, many results can be applied to verify the required convergence. Andrews (1994) gives suitable conditions for uniform law of large numbers to hold for sample averages $n^{-1} \sum_{i=1}^{n} q_i(\theta)$. Bernstein's inequality or its variants is often a key tool in establishing these results. In some cases, simple arguments apply

Example 23.4. [Normal linear regression model.] Suppose that $Q_n(\beta) = -n^{-1} \sum_{i=1}^{n} (y_i - \beta^\mathsf{T} \widetilde{x}_i)^2$. Then

$$-Q_n(\beta) = \frac{1}{n} \sum_{i=1}^{n} \left\{ \varepsilon_i - (\beta - \beta_0)^\mathsf{T} x_i \right\}^2$$

$$= \frac{1}{n} \sum_{i=1}^{n} \varepsilon_i^2 + (\beta - \beta_0)^\mathsf{T} \frac{1}{n} \sum_{i=1}^{n} x_i x_i^\mathsf{T} (\beta - \beta_0) + 2(\beta - \beta_0)^\mathsf{T} \frac{1}{n} \sum_{i=1}^{n} \varepsilon_i x_i.$$

But $n^{-1} \sum_{i=1}^{n} \varepsilon_i x_i \overset{P}{\longrightarrow} 0$, $\frac{1}{n} \sum_{i=1}^{n} x_i x_i^\mathsf{T} \overset{P}{\longrightarrow} M = E x_i x_i^\mathsf{T}$, and $n^{-1} \sum_{i=1}^{n} \varepsilon_i^2 \overset{P}{\longrightarrow} \sigma^2$. Therefore,

$$Q_n(\beta) \overset{P}{\longrightarrow} \sigma^2 + (\beta - \beta_0)^\mathsf{T} M (\beta - \beta_0) \equiv Q(\beta).$$

The convergence is uniform over $\beta \in B$, where B is a compact set because for example (take $K = 1$ and $B = [-b, b]$)

$$\sup_{\beta \in B} \left| (\beta - \beta_0) \frac{1}{n} \sum_{i=1}^{n} \varepsilon_i x_i \right| \leq \sup_{\beta \in B} |\beta - \beta_0| \times \left| \frac{1}{n} \sum_{i=1}^{n} \varepsilon_i x_i \right|$$

$$\leq 2b \times \left| \frac{1}{n} \sum_{i=1}^{n} \varepsilon_i x_i \right| \overset{P}{\longrightarrow} 0.$$

We next give a classic ULLN result.

Theorem 23.2. *(Glivenko, 1933; Cantelli, 1933)*

$$\sup_{x \in \mathbb{R}} |F_n(x) - F(x)| \overset{P}{\longrightarrow} 0.$$

Proof. We assume for simplicity that F is continuous and strictly monotonic. Let x_{jk} be the value of x that satisfies $F(x_{jk}) = j/k$ for integer j, k with $j \leq k$. For any x between x_{jk} and $x_{j+1,k}$,

$$F(x_{jk}) \leq F(x) \leq F(x_{j+1,k}) \quad ; \quad F_n(x_{jk}) \leq F_n(x) \leq F_n(x_{j+1,k}),$$

while $0 \leq F(x_{j+1,k}) - F(x_{jk}) \leq 1/k$, so that

$$F_n(x) - F(x) \leq F_n(x_{j+1,k}) - F(x_{jk}) \leq F_n(x_{j+1,k}) - F(x_{j+1,k}) + \frac{1}{k}$$

$$F_n(x) - F(x) \geq F_n(x_{j,k}) - F(x_{j+1,k}) \geq F_n(x_{j,k}) - F(x_{j,k}) - \frac{1}{k}.$$

Therefore, for any x and k,

$$|F_n(x) - F(x)| \leq \max_{1 \leq j \leq k} \left| F_n(x_{jk}) - F(x_{jk}) \right| + \frac{1}{k}. \tag{23.6}$$

Since the right hand side of (23.6) does not depend on x, we can replace the left hand side by $\sup_{-\infty < x < \infty} |F_n(x) - F(x)|$.

Let $\epsilon > 0$ be fixed and take $k = \lfloor 1/2\epsilon \rfloor$. It suffices to show that $\max_{1 \leq j \leq k} \left| F_n(x_{jk}) - F(x_{jk}) \right| \xrightarrow{P} 0$. Now let $A_{jk}(\epsilon) = \left\{ \omega : |F_n(x_{jk}) - F(x_{jk})| \geq \epsilon \right\}$ and

$$A_k(\epsilon) = \bigcup_{j=1}^{k} A_{jk}(\epsilon) = \left\{ \omega : \max_{1 \leq j \leq k} \left| F_n(x_{jk}) - F(x_{jk}) \right| \geq \epsilon \right\}.$$

We have for any $\delta > 0$ there exists n_j such that for all $n \geq n_j$, $\Pr\left(A_{jk}(\epsilon)\right) \leq \delta$. Therefore,

$$\Pr\left(\max_{1 \leq j \leq k} \left| F_n(x_{jk}) - F(x_{jk}) \right| \geq \epsilon \right) = \Pr(A_k(\epsilon)) \leq k\delta$$

for all $n \geq \max_{1 \leq j \leq k} n_j$. It follows that for any δ' we can find δ such that $\delta' = k\delta$ and n' such that for all $n \geq n'$

$$\Pr\left(\max_{1 \leq j \leq k} \left| F_n(x_{jk}) - F(x_{jk}) \right| \geq \epsilon \right) \leq \delta.$$

The result follows.

An alternative proof. We take $k = \log n$, which ensures that

$$\sup_{x \in \mathbb{R}} |F_n(x) - F(x)| \leq \max_{1 \leq j \leq k} \left| F_n(x_{jk}) - F(x_{jk}) \right| + o(1)$$

as $n \to \infty$. For any $\epsilon > 0$, let $A_j = \{ \left| F_n(x_{jk}) - F(x_{jk}) \right| > \epsilon - 1/k \}$ and

$$A = \cup_{j=1}^{k} A_j = \{ \max_{1 \leq j \leq k} \left| F_n(x_{jk}) - F(x_{jk}) \right| > \epsilon - 1/k \}.$$

Then for large enough n, $\epsilon - 1/k \geq \epsilon/2$ and

$$\Pr(A) \leq \sum_{j=1}^{k} \Pr(A_j)$$

$$\leq \sum_{j=1}^{k} \frac{4E\left(\left| F_n(x_{jk}) - F(x_{jk}) \right|^2 \right)}{\epsilon^2}$$

$$= \sum_{j=1}^{k} \frac{4F(x_{jk})(1 - F(x_{jk}))}{\epsilon^2 n}$$

$$\leq \frac{\log n}{\epsilon^2 n},$$

because $F(x)(1 - F(x)) \leq 1/4$ for all x. The first inequality follows by the Bonferroni inequality, while the second one uses the Chebychev or Markov inequality. Now $\log n / n \to 0$ so that $\Pr(A) \to 0$ as $n \to \infty$, which implies the result. $\qquad\square$

The asymptotic properties of the empirical c.d.f. have been established in 1933 in two separate papers by Glivenko and Cantelli; in fact they showed the strong law version (convergence with probability one). The only 'condition' in their result is that X_i are i.i.d., although note that since F is a distribution function it has at most a countable number of discontinuities, is bounded between zero and one and is right continuous. Note also that the supremum is over a non-compact set – in much subsequent work generalizing this theorem it has been necessary to restrict attention to compact sets. The proof of this theorem exploits some special structure: specifically that for each x, $1(X_i \leq x)$ is Bernoulli with probability $F(x)$. This proof is very special and uses the structure of the empirical c.d.f. quite a lot. Much work has gone into establish ULLN's for more general settings.

23.2.1.2 Identification

Often more difficult to establish is condition (D). For the MLE the following lemma is available.

Lemma 23.1. *Suppose that θ_0 is identified, i.e., for any $\theta \in \Theta$ with $\theta \neq \theta_0$ we have with positive probability $f(X|\theta) \neq f(X|\theta_0)$. Suppose also that for all $\theta \in \Theta$, $E\{|\ln f(X|\theta)|\} < \infty$. Then, $Q(\theta) = E\{\ln f(X|\theta)\}$ has a unique maximum at θ_0.*

Proof. For all $\theta \neq \theta_0$,

$$Q(\theta_0) - Q(\theta) = E\left[-\ln\left\{\frac{f(X|\theta)}{f(X|\theta_0)}\right\}\right] > -\ln\left[E\left\{\frac{f(X|\theta)}{f(X|\theta_0)}\right\}\right] = 0,$$

by Jensen's inequality. $\qquad\square$

Example 23.5. [Normal linear regression model.] Suppose that $Q_n(\beta) = -n^{-1}\sum_{i=1}^{n}(y_i - \beta^\mathsf{T}x_i)^2$. Then we have

$$Q(\beta) = \sigma^2 + (\beta - \beta_0)^\mathsf{T} M(\beta - \beta_0).$$

Provided $M > 0$, the function $Q(\beta)$ is uniquely minimized at $\beta = \beta_0$.

Example 23.6. The simultaneous Equation system. The normalized negative likelihood function is

$$Q_n(\theta) = \log \det(B(\theta))$$

$$+ \frac{1}{2n} \sum_{i=1}^{n} (B(\theta)y_i - C(\theta)x_i)^{\mathsf{T}} \Sigma(\theta)^{-1} (B(\theta)y_i - C(\theta)x_i).$$

Under the assumption that $E(y_i|x_i) = \Phi(\theta_0)x_i$ and $\text{var}(y_i|x_i) = B(\theta_0)^{-1} \times \Sigma(\theta_0)B(\theta_0)^{\mathsf{T}-1}$ for some $\theta_0 \in \Theta$, $Q_n(\theta)$ has the probability limit

$$Q(\theta) = \log \det(B(\theta)) + \frac{1}{2}\text{tr}\left(M\,(C(\theta_0) - C(\theta))^{\mathsf{T}} \Sigma(\theta)^{-1} (C(\theta_0) - C(\theta))\right)$$

$$+ \frac{1}{2}\text{tr}\left(B(\theta_0)^{-1}\Sigma(\theta_0)B(\theta_0)^{\mathsf{T}-1}B(\theta)^{\mathsf{T}}\Sigma(\theta)^{-1}B(\theta)\right)$$

for each $\theta \in \Theta$. We have

$$Q(\theta_0) = \log \det(B(\theta_0)) + \frac{L}{2}.$$

The question is, whether there exists any other $\theta \in \Theta$ such that $Q(\theta) = Q(\theta_0)$. In the case where $\theta \in \mathbb{R}^{L^2+KL+L(L+1)/2}$ is unrestricted, then the answer is positive, meaning the model is not identified. This is because the triple $B^* = FB$, $C^* = FC$, and $\Sigma^* = F\Sigma F^{\mathsf{T}}$, where F is any nonsingular $L \times L$ matrix, will yield exactly the same $Q(\theta)$ because

$$B^{*-1}C^* = B^{-1}F^{-1}FC = B^{-1}C$$

$$B^{*-1}\Sigma^* B^{*\mathsf{T}-1} = B^{-1}F^{-1}F\Sigma F^{\mathsf{T}}F^{\mathsf{T}-1}B^{\mathsf{T}-1} = B^{-1}\Sigma B^{\mathsf{T}-1}.$$

23.2.2 Asymptotic Normality

Once we have consistency we can confine ourselves to "local conditions" to prove subsequent limit properties of the estimator. That is if we now can prove that provided that any $\widehat{\theta}$ that is eventually within a δ neighbourhood of θ_0 will have a particular property, then our estimator will have that property with probability tending to one (since our estimator will be in that neighbourhood with probability tending to one). This allows us to focus in on conditions on Q_n and Q in a neighbourhood of θ_0, and ignore entirely the behaviour of these functions outside of this neighbourhood. This is in distinct contrast to consistency, which is generally thought of as a "global" property; it depends on the properties of Q_n and Q over all of Θ. That is the conditions we need for consistency are global, but once we have consistency, the additional conditions we need for asymptotic normality are local. The literature often goes one step further than this in its discussion of local properties.

Theorem 23.3. *Suppose that* $\widehat{\theta} \longrightarrow \theta_0$. *Then there exists a sequence* $\{\delta_n\}$ *with* $\delta_n \to 0$, *such that*

$$\lim_{n \to \infty} \Pr(\|\widehat{\theta} - \theta_0\| > \delta_n) = 0.$$

Proof. Consistency implies that for all $\epsilon > 0$ and for all positive integers J, there exists a positive integer $n_0(J)$ such that for all $n \geq n_0(J)$

$$\Pr\left(\|\widehat{\theta} - \theta_0\| > 1/J\right) \leq \epsilon.$$

For every J, let $n^*(J)$ be the smallest value of n that satisfies this condition, so that $n^*(J)$ is an increasing sequence. Then set

$$\delta_n = 1/J \text{ for } n^*(J) < n \leq n^*(J+1).$$

Clearly, $\lim_{n \to \infty} \delta_n = 0$. Therefore, by construction, for all $n \geq n^*(1/\delta_n)$

$$\Pr\left(\|\widehat{\theta} - \theta_0\| > \delta_n\right) \leq \epsilon. \qquad \square$$

The sequence δ_n can go to zero arbitrarily slowly depending on the case. The discussion of subsequent properties can confine itself to conditions that need only hold in "shrinking neighbourhoods" of θ_0; i.e., neighbourhoods of θ_0 that can get arbitrarily small as n grows large, and still we know that our estimator will have that property with probability tending to one. Define the event $\Theta_n = \{\|\widehat{\theta} - \theta_0\| \leq \delta_n\}$. Then, for any event A, we have

$$\Pr(A) = \Pr(A \cap \Theta_n) + \Pr(A \cap \Theta_n{}^c)$$
$$\leq \Pr(A \cap \Theta_n) + \Pr(\Theta_n^c) \leq \Pr(A \cap \Theta_n) + \epsilon.$$

Since ϵ is arbitrary, we can effectively assume that Θ_n is true.

We next consider the asymptotic distribution of the optimization estimator.

Theorem 23.4. *(Asymptotic Normality). Suppose that the following conditions hold:*
(A) $\widehat{\theta} \xrightarrow{P} \theta_0$;
(B) θ_0 *is an interior point of* Θ
(C) $\frac{\partial^2 Q_n}{\partial \theta \partial \theta^\top}(\theta)$ *exists and is continuous in an open convex neighbourhood of* θ_0.
(D) There exists a finite nonsingular matrix A, such that

$$\sup_{|\theta - \theta_0| < \delta_n} \left| \frac{\partial^2 Q_n}{\partial \theta \partial \theta^\top}(\theta) - A \right| \xrightarrow{P} 0$$

for any sequence $\delta_n \to 0$.
(E) $n^{1/2} \frac{\partial Q_n}{\partial \theta}(\theta_0) \xrightarrow{D} N(0, B)$ *for some positive definite matrix B.*

Then with $V(\theta) = A(\theta)^{-1}B(\theta)A(\theta)^{-1}$ and $V = V(\theta_0)$ we have

$$n^{1/2}(\widehat{\theta} - \theta_0) \xrightarrow{D} N(0, V). \tag{23.7}$$

Proof. Conditions A and B ensure that with probability tending to one, $\widehat{\theta}$ satisfies the first order condition. By the Mean Value Theorem

$$0 = \frac{\partial Q_n}{\partial \theta}(\widehat{\theta}) = n^{1/2}\frac{\partial Q_n}{\partial \theta}(\theta_0) + \frac{\partial^2 Q_n}{\partial\theta\partial\theta^\mathsf{T}}(\theta^*)n^{1/2}(\widehat{\theta} - \theta_0).$$

where θ^* is intermediate between $\widehat{\theta}$ and θ_0, i.e., $\|\theta^* - \theta_0\| \leq \|\widehat{\theta} - \theta_0\|$. Actually, we need a different such θ^* for each row, but each will satisfy the contraction condition. By assumption D we can replace $\frac{\partial^2 Q_n}{\partial\theta\partial\theta^\mathsf{T}}(\theta^*)$ by the limiting matrix A with probability tending to one, and obtain that

$$n^{1/2}(\widehat{\theta} - \theta_0) = -A^{-1}n^{1/2}\frac{\partial Q_n}{\partial \theta}(\theta_0) + R_n,$$

where the remainder term $R_n \xrightarrow{P} 0$. Then apply Assumption E and Slutsky's theorem to conclude the result (23.7). $\qquad\square$

The uniformity condition (B) is needed, i.e. it is not generally sufficient that

$$\frac{\partial^2 Q_n}{\partial\theta\partial\theta^\mathsf{T}}(\theta_0) \xrightarrow{P} A.$$

In the linear regression case, the usual least squares objective function satisfies

$$\frac{\partial^2 Q_n}{\partial\beta\partial\beta^\mathsf{T}}(\beta) = -X^\mathsf{T}X$$

for all parameter values β and so this condition is automatically satisfied.

Condition B is needed because otherwise $\widehat{\theta}$ may not satisfy the first order condition.

Example 23.7. Suppose that $X \sim N(\mu, 1)$, where $\mu \in \Theta = [\underline{\mu}, \overline{\mu}]$. The maximum likelihood estimator in this case can be shown to be

$$\widehat{\mu} = \begin{cases} \overline{\mu} & \text{if } \overline{X} \geq \overline{\mu} \\ \overline{X} & \text{if } \overline{X} \in [\underline{\mu}, \overline{\mu}] \\ \underline{\mu} & \text{if } \overline{X} \leq \underline{\mu}. \end{cases}$$

This will satisfy

$$\sum_{i=1}^{n}(X_i - \widehat{\mu}) = 0 \tag{23.8}$$

only when $\overline{X} \in (\underline{\mu}, \overline{\mu})$, i.e., the constraint is not binding. If the true parameter $\mu_0 = \overline{\mu}$, then we can see that only 50% of the time will (23.8) occur. In fact, $\widehat{\mu}$ is not asymptotically normal in this case. See the exercise.

The precise form of the limiting distribution depends on the details of Q_n. We consider the main leading cases separately.

Correctly Specified Likelihood. The score function and Hessian are sample averages of independent variables (under the i.i.d. sampling) and thus satisfy the appropriate CLTs and ULLNs under some regularity conditions. By virtue of the information matrix equality, $A = B = \mathcal{I}$, the asymptotic variance has the simpler form $\mathcal{I}^{-1}$.

A number of different methods exist for estimating the asymptotic covariance matrix using either the Hessian or outer product:

$$\frac{1}{n}\frac{\partial^2 \ell}{\partial\theta\partial\theta^\mathsf{T}}(\widehat{\theta}) \quad \text{or} \quad \frac{1}{n}\sum_{i=1}^{n}\frac{\partial \ell_i}{\partial\theta}\frac{\partial \ell_i}{\partial\theta^\mathsf{T}}(\widehat{\theta}).$$

Misspecified Likelihood. Clearly, the meaning of the limit θ_0 is not obvious when the model is not correct, since these parameters may have nothing to do with the true distribution of the data. However, under regularity conditions, θ_0 is the parameter value that minimizes the Kullback–Liebler distance between the distribution of the data and the specified model. Under partial misspecification, one may retain consistency. For example, in a regression model if the mean is correctly specified but the distribution of the errors is not normal or the heteroskedasticity is ignored. In these cases the (pseudo or quasi) ML estimates of the mean parameters can be consistent. In the general case, the limiting variance is of the sandwich form $A^{-1}BA^{-1}$. One can carry out robust inference by allowing for this more general structure when estimating the asymptotic covariance matrix. The leading example here is when the parametric model is linear regression with normal homoskedastic errors but the distribution of the data has heteroskedasticity. In this case, $A = X^\mathsf{T}X$ and $B = X^\mathsf{T}\Sigma X$, which can be estimated by replacing the diagonal matrix Σ by the diagonal matrix whose elements are the squared least squares residuals. For a general (pseudo) likelihood criterion, we estimate the covariance matrix robustly by

$$\widehat{V} = \left\{\frac{1}{n}\sum_{i=1}^{n}\frac{\partial^2 \ell_i}{\partial\theta\partial\theta^\mathsf{T}}(\widehat{\theta})\right\}^{-1}\left\{\frac{1}{n}\sum_{i=1}^{n}\frac{\partial \ell_i}{\partial\theta}\frac{\partial \ell_i}{\partial\theta^\mathsf{T}}(\widehat{\theta})\right\}\left\{\frac{1}{n}\sum_{i=1}^{n}\frac{\partial^2 \ell_i}{\partial\theta\partial\theta^\mathsf{T}}(\widehat{\theta})\right\}^{-1}.$$

See White (1982) for a comprehensive discussion of this theory.

Generalized Method of Moments. Suppose that $W_T \xrightarrow{P} W > 0$ and that the moments are correctly specified. Then

$$\sqrt{n} \left(\hat{\theta}_{GMM} - \theta_0 \right) \xrightarrow{D} N(0, (\Gamma^\mathsf{T} W \Gamma)^{-1} \Gamma^\mathsf{T} W \Omega W \Gamma (\Gamma^\mathsf{T} W \Gamma)^{-1}),$$

$$\Omega = \mathrm{var} \sqrt{n} G_n(\theta_0) = \frac{1}{n} \sum_{i=1}^{n} E \left(g(Z_i, \theta_0) g(Z_i, \theta_0)^\mathsf{T} \right)$$

$$\Gamma = E \left(\frac{\partial G_n(\theta_0)}{\partial \theta} \right).$$

If $p = q$, then $(\Gamma^\mathsf{T} W \Gamma)^{-1} \Gamma^\mathsf{T} W \Omega W \Gamma (\Gamma^\mathsf{T} W \Gamma)^{-1} = \Gamma^{-1} \Omega \Gamma^{\mathsf{T}-1}$, and the asymptotic variance simplifies. We estimate Γ and Ω by

$$\hat{\Gamma} = \frac{\partial G_n(\hat{\theta})}{\partial \theta} \quad ; \quad \hat{\Omega} = \frac{1}{n} \sum_{i=1}^{n} g(Z_i, \hat{\theta}) g(Z_i, \hat{\theta})^\mathsf{T}$$

and hence $\hat{V} = (\hat{\Gamma}^\mathsf{T} W_n \hat{\Gamma})^{-1} \hat{\Gamma}^\mathsf{T} W_n \hat{\Omega} W_n \hat{\Gamma} (\hat{\Gamma}^\mathsf{T} W_n \hat{\Gamma})^{-1}$ is used to estimate $V = (\Gamma^\mathsf{T} W \Gamma)^{-1} \Gamma^\mathsf{T} W \Omega W \Gamma (\Gamma^\mathsf{T} W \Gamma)^{-1}$.

Example 23.8. A simple example, linear regression $y = X\beta + \varepsilon$. In this case, the moment conditions are

$$E[\tilde{x}_i \varepsilon_i(\beta_0)] = 0.$$

Here there are K conditions and K parameters, it corresponds to the exactly identified case. In this case, there exists a unique $\hat{\beta}$ that satisfies the empirical conditions provided X is of full rank.

Example 23.9. Instrumental variables. Suppose now $E[\tilde{x}_i \varepsilon_i(\beta_0)] \neq 0$ because of omitted variables/endogeneity. However, suppose that

$$E[z_i \varepsilon_i(\beta_0)] = 0$$

for instruments $z_i \in \mathbb{R}^J$, with $J > K$. In this case, we can't solve uniquely for $\hat{\beta}_{IV}$ because there are too many equations which can't all be satisfied simultaneously. Take

$$G_n(\theta) = \frac{1}{n} \sum_{i=1}^{n} g_i(\theta) g_i(\theta)^\mathsf{T} \quad ; \quad g_i(\theta) = z_i \varepsilon_i(\beta_0) = z_i \left(y_i - \tilde{x}_i^\mathsf{T} \beta_0 \right).$$

If we take weighting matrix $W_n = (Z^\mathsf{T} Z)^{-1}$, where Z is the $n \times J$ matrix of instruments, then the objective function becomes

$$Q_n(\beta) = (y - X\beta)^\mathsf{T} Z (Z^\mathsf{T} Z)^{-1} Z^\mathsf{T} (y - X\beta) = \| P_Z(y - X\beta) \|^2$$

where $P_Z = Z(Z^\mathsf{T} Z)^{-1} Z^\mathsf{T}$. This has a closed form solution

$$\widehat{\beta}_{GMM} = ((P_Z X)^\mathsf{T} P_Z X)^{-1} (P_Z X)^\mathsf{T} (P_Z y) = (X^\mathsf{T} P_Z X)^{-1} X^\mathsf{T} P_Z y,$$

i.e., it is an instrumental variables estimator with instruments $X^* = P_Z X$. We require Z to be full rank.

23.3 QUANTILE REGRESSION

The quantile regression model is of the form

$$y_i = \widetilde{x}_i^\mathsf{T} \beta + u_i, \tag{23.9}$$

where the conditional α-quantile of u_i given x_i is zero. Therefore, the conditional quantile function satisfies $Q_{y_i | \widetilde{x}_i} (y_i | \widetilde{x}_i; \alpha) = \widetilde{x}_i^\mathsf{T} \beta$. The quantile restriction can be expressed as

$$E(\psi_\alpha(u_i) | \widetilde{x}_i) = 0,$$

where $\psi_\alpha(x) = \mathrm{sgn}(x) - (1 - 2\alpha)$, which is a conditional moment restriction. To estimate β we may consider the objective function

$$Q_n(\beta) = \frac{1}{n} \sum_{i=1}^n \rho_\alpha(y_i - \widetilde{x}_i^\mathsf{T} \beta), \quad \text{where}$$

$$\rho_\alpha(x) = x(\alpha - 1(x < 0)),$$

or its first order condition

$$G_n(\beta) = \frac{1}{n} \sum_{i=1}^n \widetilde{x}_i \psi_\alpha(y_i - \widetilde{x}_i^\mathsf{T} \beta), \quad \text{where}$$

is the check function. The median corresponds to the case $\rho_{1/2}(x) = |x|$ and $\psi_{1/2}(x) = \mathrm{sgn}(x)$.

The solution is not generally unique. Note that the objective function is not differentiable (at one point) and the first order condition is not even continuous at the same point, so that typically different methods have to be employed to study the large sample properties. Nevertheless, the consistency theorem can be applied directly. In fact, conditions A and B are unnecessary, because one can show that the objective function is globally convex and so there exists a minimizing value $\widehat{\beta} \in \mathbb{R}^K$ although it won't generally be unique.

We have the following result (an adaptation of Koenker (2005)).

Assumptions Q. *Q1.* *Suppose that u_i, x_i are i.i.d. and $u_i | x_i$ is continuous with density $f_{u|x}$ and α-quantile 0 such that $0 < \inf_x f_{u|x}(0|x) \leq \sup_x f_{u|x}(0|x) < \infty$.*

Q2. *The matrices* $M = E\left[x_i x_i^\mathsf{T}\right]$ *and* $M_\alpha = E\left[x_i x_i^\mathsf{T} f_{u|x}(0|x_i)\right]$ *exist and are positive definite.*

Theorem 23.5. *Suppose that assumptions Q1 and Q2 hold. Then*

$$\sqrt{n}\left(\widehat{\beta} - \beta\right) \xrightarrow{D} N\left(0, \alpha(1-\alpha)M_\alpha^{-1}MM_\alpha^{-1}\right).$$

Proof. We just give some heuristics. We may show that for any $\beta \in \mathbb{R}^K$ that

$$G_n(\beta) = \frac{1}{n}\sum_{i=1}^{n}\widetilde{x}_i\psi_\alpha(y_i - \widetilde{x}_i^\mathsf{T}\beta) \xrightarrow{P} G(\beta) = E\left[\widetilde{x}_i\psi_\alpha(u_i - \widetilde{x}_i^\mathsf{T}(\beta - \beta_0))\right].$$

There are special arguments that make use of the convexity of the objective function that guarantees that this convergence is uniform. We suppose for convenience of notation that x is continuously distributed. We can write

$$G(\beta) = \int \left[x\psi_\alpha(u - x^\mathsf{T}(\beta - \beta_0))\right]f_{u|x}(u|x)f_x(x)dudx$$

$$= \int \left[x\,\mathrm{sgn}(u - x^\mathsf{T}(\beta - \beta_0))\right]f_{u|x}(u|x)f_x(x)dudx - (1 - 2\alpha)$$

$$= \int \left[x\,\mathrm{sgn}(v)\right]f_{u|x}(v + x^\mathsf{T}(\beta - \beta_0)|x)f_x(x)dvdx - (1 - 2\alpha)$$

$$- \int \int_0^\infty xf_{u|x}(v + x^\mathsf{T}(\beta \quad \beta_0)|x)f_x(x)dvdx$$

$$- \int \int_{-\infty}^0 xf_{u|x}(v + x^\mathsf{T}(\beta - \beta_0)|x)f_x(x)dvdx - (1 - 2\alpha)$$

$$= \int x\left[1 - F_{u|x}(x^\mathsf{T}(\beta - \beta_0)|x)\right]f_x(x)dx$$

$$- \int xF_{u|x}(x^\mathsf{T}(\beta - \beta_0)|x)f_x(x)dx - (1 - 2\alpha)$$

$$= \int x\left[1 - 2F_{u|x}(x^\mathsf{T}(\beta - \beta_0)|x)\right]f_x(x)dx - (1 - 2\alpha),$$

where we used the change of variable $u \mapsto v = u - x^\mathsf{T}(\beta - \beta_0)$. The function $G(\beta)$ satisfies $G(\beta_0) = 0$ and it is differentiable with

$$\frac{\partial G}{\partial \beta}(\beta_0) = -2\int xx^\mathsf{T}f_{u|x}(0|x)f_x(x)dx = -2E\left[xx^\mathsf{T}f_{u|x}(0|x)\right],$$

which we will assume below is non-zero. This implies that at least in a neighbourhood of β_0 there can be no other zero of $G(\beta)$ and indeed $Q(\beta_0) < Q(\beta)$ for all such β, where $Q(\beta) = EQ_n(\beta)$. Consistency follows. Regarding the asymptotic normality, the tricky part is to show that the estimator satisfies the condition

$$n^{1/2}(\widehat{\beta} - \beta_0) = \left[\frac{\partial G}{\partial \beta}(\beta_0)\right]^{-1} n^{1/2} G_n(\beta_0) + R_n, \qquad (23.10)$$

where $R_n \xrightarrow{P} 0$. Note that we have $\partial G/\partial \beta$ not $E \partial G_n/\partial \beta$, which is not well defined due to the discontinuity of G. Once this is established, the result follows by the Slutsky theorem etc. since

$$n^{1/2} G_n(\beta_0) = \frac{1}{\sqrt{n}} \sum_{i=1}^{n} \widetilde{x}_i \psi_\alpha(u_i)$$

satisfies a CLT because by assumption $E(\psi_\alpha(u_i)|\widetilde{x}_i) = 0$. $\qquad \square$

Quantile regression is robust in the sense that nowhere in the above theory have we required $E(u_i^2) < \infty$ or even $E(|u_i|) < \infty$, which contrasts with the theory for OLS. The monotone equivariance property implies that

$$Q_{\Lambda(y_i)|\widetilde{x}_i}(\Lambda(y_i)|\widetilde{x}_i; \alpha) = \Lambda(\widetilde{x}_i^\mathsf{T} \beta)$$

for any strictly increasing transformation Λ such as the logarithm. This property says for example that we can infer the effect of $\widetilde{x}_i$ on say $\log(y_i)$ from the quantile regression of y_i on $\widetilde{x}_i$.

Chapter 24

A Nonparametric Postscript

We consider an example of recent work on nonparametric identification, which goes beyond the parametric framework we have mostly considered. Suppose that we observe continuous random variables Y_1, Y_2, X, where

$$Y_1 = h_1(Y_2, X, \varepsilon_1, \varepsilon_2)$$
$$Y_2 = h_2(Y_1, X, \varepsilon_1, \varepsilon_2),$$

where ε_1 and ε_2 are unobserved shocks, and h_1 and h_2 are unknown structural functions of interest.

Example 24.1. Y_1 is the wage and Y_2 is a measure of investment in schooling. The unobserved shocks $\varepsilon_1, \varepsilon_2$ represent fortune in the labour market and ability respectively. The parameters of interest here would include the return to schooling $\partial h_1(Y_2, X, \varepsilon_1, \varepsilon_2)/\partial Y_2$.

The model reflects the simultaneous determination of the endogenous variables Y that is at the heart of market equilibrium. It generalizes the linear simultaneous equation system we saw earlier by allowing for nonlinearity in a general way. That is, we are not requiring the functions h_1 and h_2 to be linear or in fact possess any simple functional form. The reason this line of work is important is because of Manski's **law of decreasing credibility**. The strong parametric assumptions that we have focussed on lead to estimates that are not robust to certain often arbitrary assumptions needed to justify likelihood theory or even GMM theory. Why should the functions we are interested in be linear? Instead, we make minimal assumptions and ask what can be learnt about the structural functions in that case. The model implies a particular form for the joint conditional c.d.f. $F_{Y_1, Y_2 | X}(y_1, y_2 | x)$ for the observable variables, that is, given the distribution of $\varepsilon_1, \varepsilon_2$ and the functions h_1, h_2 we can, under some minimal restrictions obtain the reduced form $Y_1 = g_1(X, \varepsilon_1, \varepsilon_2)$ and $Y_2 = g_2(X, \varepsilon_1, \varepsilon_2)$ for functions g_1 and g_2 and the distribution function $F_{Y_1, Y_2 | X}(y_1, y_2 | x)$.[1] We

---

1. Provided h_1, h_2 are continuously differentiable in all their arguments, we can invoke the implicit function theorem to the equation $H = 0$, where $H : \mathbb{R}^5 \longrightarrow \mathbb{R}^2$ with $H = (Y_1 - h_1(Y_2, X, \varepsilon_1, \varepsilon_2), Y_2 - h_2(Y_1, X, \varepsilon_1, \varepsilon_2))$, to guarantee the existence of an inverse mapping $Y = G(X, \varepsilon_1, \varepsilon_2)$, where $G : U \longrightarrow V \subset \mathbb{R}^2$ with $G = (g_1, g_2)$ that is also differentiable.

Probability, Statistics and Econometrics. http://dx.doi.org/10.1016/B978-0-12-810495-8.00027-0

can estimate the quantity $F_{Y_1,Y_2|X}(y_1, y_2|x)$ from a random sample using non-parametric methods and this quantity is uniquely identified. However, it is not clear whether we can identify the structural functions h_1 and h_2 without strong functional form restrictions such as linearity along with further exclusion restrictions, that is, do there exist h_1^*, h_2^* with $h_1^*, h_2^* \neq h_1, h_2$ that delivers exactly the same distribution for the observables? It is clear that in general the functions h_1 and h_2 are not unique. This is the critical issue, because although we may be able to learn the reduced form functions, the parameters of interest are to be found inside the structural functions instead.

Suppose that we have a **triangular system**, i.e.,

$$Y_1 = h_1(Y_2, X, \varepsilon_1, \varepsilon_2) \tag{24.1}$$

$$Y_2 = h_2(X, \varepsilon_2), \tag{24.2}$$

whereby Y_2 does not depend directly on Y_1 or ε_1. The model is still very general. Note that in this case

$$E(Y_1|X = x) = \int h_1(h_2(x, e_2), x, e_1, e_2) f(e_1, e_2|x) de_1 de_2$$

$$= \int g_1(X, e_1, e_2) f(e_1, e_2|x) de_1 de_2,$$

where $f(e_1, e_2|x)$ is the conditional density of $\varepsilon_1, \varepsilon_2|X = x$. In general, $E(Y|X = x)$ does not tell us anything useful except in vary special cases. Chesher (2003) shows how to use conditional quantiles to identify features of the structural functions.

Assumptions CH. CH1. *Eqs (24.1) and (24.2) determine a unique value of Y_1, Y_2, that is, $Y_1 = g_1(X, \varepsilon_1, \varepsilon_2)$ and $Y_2 = g_2(X, \varepsilon_1, \varepsilon_2)$*

CH2. *The functions h_1, h_2 are differentiable in all arguments; X is continuously distributed*

CH3. $\partial h_i(Y_2, X, \varepsilon_1, \varepsilon_2)/\partial \varepsilon_j \neq 0$

CH4. *The distribution of $\varepsilon_1, \varepsilon_2$ given X is continuous and this distribution is differentiable in X*

CH5. *Quantile insensitivity:* $\partial Q_{\varepsilon_2|X}(\varepsilon_2|x; \beta)/\partial x = 0$ *and* $\partial Q_{\varepsilon_1|\varepsilon_2,X}(\varepsilon_1|\varepsilon_2, x; \alpha)/\partial x = 0$

Theorem 24.1. *Suppose that assumptions CH1–CH5 hold. Let e_1 and e_2 be given and define α, β such that $e_1 = Q_{\varepsilon_1|\varepsilon_2,X}(\varepsilon_1|e_2, x; \alpha)$ and $e_2 = Q_{\varepsilon_2|X}(\varepsilon_2|x; \beta)$. Then*

$$h_1(y_2, x, e_1, e_2) = Q_{Y_1|Y_2,X}(Y_1|Q_{Y_2|X}(Y_2|x; \beta), x; \alpha)$$

$$h_2(x, e_2) = Q_{Y_2|X}(Y_2|x; \beta).$$

After the identificational foreplay one can proceed to estimation using nonparametric or parametric estimates of the conditional quantiles. Following (7.4) we let

$$\widehat{F}_{Y_2|X}(y|x) = \frac{\frac{1}{n}\sum_{i=1}^{n} 1\,(Y_{2i} \leq y)\,1\,\{X_i \in [x - \epsilon, x + \epsilon]\}}{\frac{1}{n}\sum_{i=1}^{n} 1\,\{X_i \in [x - \epsilon, x + \epsilon]\}}$$

for some small ϵ that is called the **bandwidth**. From this we may obtain estimates of the conditional quantiles by the analogue definition

$$\widehat{Q}_{Y_2|X}(y|x; \beta) = \inf\left\{y : \widehat{F}_{Y_2|X}(y|x) \geq \beta\right\}.$$

This estimator is consistent under some conditions including that $\epsilon = \epsilon(n) \to 0$. In conclusion, it is possible to estimate parameters of interest in general structural models without imposing strong restrictions.

Chapter 25

A Case Study

In this chapter we consider a case study, that is, we analyze a dataset with a view to illustrating some of the concepts and definitions introduced in the book. We consider data from the 2016 summer Olympics. The number of athletes submitted by country and the number of medals (Gold, Silver, and Bronze) won by each country. There were a total of 11249 athletes and 974 medals. We might suppose that this is a repeatable random experiment with random variable $X = 1$ if athlete wins a medal and $X = 0$ if athlete does not, and suppose the true probability of $X = 1$ was p. We have a sample of $n = 11249$ and $k = 974$ so we could estimate p by 0.087. Is this a good assumption/model here? Athletes can win more than one medal and the probability of Usain Bolt, say, winning a medal is obviously higher than other athletes. Finally, if athlete i wins a medal, then the chance of athlete j winning a medal is diminished slightly. So one might question the applicability of the random experiment model.

There were a total of 208 countries entered, although Kuwait submitted no athletes, so was dropped from the sample. Suppose that we assume that all athletes come from the same homogeneous population, and that the independence is a good assumption. Then we can calculate the probability that India wins no medal given they submitted 124 athletes would be

$$(1 - 0.087)^{124} = 0.0000125.$$

In fact they won 2 medals. The probability that they would exactly win two medals is also quite low, around 0.00087. In any case, we may think that the equal likelihood of all athletes across all countries is just not a good assumption, and prefer to partition by countries.

Consider X_i to be the number of athletes entered by country i and Y_i to be the number of medals won by country i. There are only 87 countries for which $Y_i \geq 1$ so most countries did not win a thing. The data are integer valued but cover a wide range ($1 \leq Y_i \leq 121$) and ($0 \leq X_i \leq 552$), which makes the data hard to categorize as discrete or continuous. At the low end there is quite a bit of discreteness, meaning multiple countries taking the same value

Probability, Statistics and Econometrics. http://dx.doi.org/10.1016/B978-0-12-810495-8.00028-2

$k =$	0	1	2	3	4	5
Y	120	21	10	6	6	3
X	0	1	9	10	11	18

However, even for Y at the low end, the Poisson distribution does not seem too good. It should satisfy that

$$k \times \frac{\Pr(Y = k)}{\Pr(Y = k - 1)} = \lambda$$

is a constant, but this seems far from the case. There are too many zeros. Indeed the Poisson distribution would not be a good fit for the whole distribution. The sample mean of X is 54.0 and the sample standard deviation is 95.4 so that this is a gross violation of the mean-variance law of the Poisson. The median is 10. This is even more the case when considering Y, where mean is 4.7 and standard deviation is 13.0, and of course there are very many zeros such that the median is 0. The frequency count shows the sparsity of X, most cells contain zero entries and the second most common count is one. There are many models for discrete data that can address some of these issues.

We next look at the top end of the distribution. Recall that for discrete Zipf distribution or Pareto distribution we have

$$\ln \Pr(X > x) = a + b \ln(x)$$

for constants a, b, where the discrete Zipf's law applies only to integers whereas the Pareto distribution is for continuous variation. We just consider this for $x > 150$ for which there are 20 observations. We compute this regression and find $b = -2.3$, which says that $\Pr(X > x) \sim x^{-2.3}$ for large x; this decay rate is higher than has been found for cities and stock volume ($b \sim -1$). The Gini coefficients are 0.71 for X and 0.85 for Y, which indicates a highly unequal distribution (according to the World Bank, the Gini coefficient for worldwide income was 0.68 in 2005).

We next consider the association between X and Y. There does seem to be a positive relationship between X and Y. We run the regression with all the observations $n = 207$. The usual OLS estimate yields R-squared of 0.729 and parameter estimates

	est	se	wse
constant	−1.5914	0.5427	0.6635
Athletes	0.1166	0.0050	0.01944

The t-statistics are very significant. The scatter plot in Fig. 25.1 shows the raw data and the regression line.

There must be some heteroskedasticity here because when X is small Y must also be small. We compute the White's standard errors (wse) in the table, which

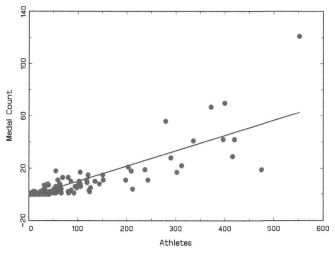

FIGURE 25.1 Medal count against athletes

are larger than the OLS standard errors but the coefficients are still statistically significant.

We might believe that the regression goes through the origin because when $X = 0$ we must have $Y = 0$. In this case we obtain parameter estimate 0.1094 with se 0.0044. This doesn't change very much.

We might believe there is a host country advantage, so we include a dummy variable for Brazil. The fit improves slightly to R^2 of 0.768. The host country dummy is negative and statistically significant. Relative to the number of athletes they submitted, Brazil underperformed.

	est	se	wse
constant	−1.873	0.5062	0.6336
Host	−38.6195	6.6429	8.2857
Athletes	0.1252	0.0048	0.01869

Perhaps it is better to work with logarithms. In that case we must drop the countries that did not win any medals. The scatter plot appears to be more homoscedastic, but there is still an issue with an oversupply of zeros (which were the ones in the previous model).

A common approach in econometrics to dealing with zero values is censored regression. In that case assume that

$$y_i^* = \beta^\mathsf{T} \widetilde{x}_i + \varepsilon_i$$

for some variable y_i^* and that we observe $y_i = y_i^* 1(y_i^* > 0)$, which would account for the large number of zeros observed. In this case, $E(y_i | \widetilde{x}_i)$ is a nonlinear function of $\widetilde{x}_i$ that depends on the error distribution.

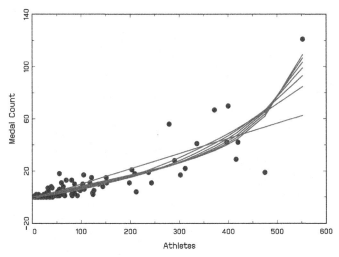

FIGURE 25.2 Alternative regression models. (For interpretation of the references to colour in this figure, the reader is referred to the web version of this chapter.)

We investigate whether a linear relationship is correct here, specifically, we consider polynomials. In fact, we estimated the linear regression with covariates $1, x, \ldots, x^k$ for $k = 1, 2, \ldots, 7$ and show the fitted lines along with the raw data. See Fig. 25.2. The $k = 1$ case is shown in red, while the higher order polynomials are all in blue.

The polynomial fitting leads to an improvement in fit mostly with regard to how it takes account of the right most observation, the USA, which is a substantial positive **outlier** relative to the linear regression fit. The BIC criterion selected $k = 7$ (out of $k = 1, 2, \ldots, 14$).

One might wonder whether the linear regression (or polynomial regression) is well specified here. We might think that over time the number of athletes a country submits is related to the number of medals they have won in the previous Olympics and therefore X and Y are jointly determined. However, from the point of view of predicting the number of medals obtained in an Olympics, the number of athletes submitted by each country is known sometime in advance and can be treated as given for the prediction exercise of the coming games.

There is a substantial betting market on outcomes of various sorts in the Olympics. Goldman Sachs and PwC have published articles that describe their methodology for predicting Olympic success. They essentially do regressions of win percentage (number of medals won divided by total number of available medals) on a variety of covariates. The choice of dependent variable doesn't change the essentials of the linear regression but it does make for comparability across Olympics where the total number of available medals has grown over time. In our case, we might regress win percentage on the ratio of number of athletes submitted by country to total number of athletes. The linear transformations will not change the R-squared but will change the coefficients. It might also make the analysis more relevant for future Olympics where there is likely to be a further inflation of both totals. GS and PwC also included GDP, population, and past performance as regressors. Our analysis has not included those variables in which case they might be considered omitted variables and our coefficients to be biased estimates.

We also regress the ratio of gold medals to total medals on the number of athletes and find almost no linear relationship.

Chapter 26

Exercises and Complements

Exercise. If x is an n-dimensional column vector of random variables with mean vector μ, prove that the covariance matrix of x, $\Sigma = E\left[(x - \mu)(x - \mu)^{\mathsf{T}}\right]$ is positive semidefinite, by using the fact that the scalar $c^{\mathsf{T}}x$ has a non-negative variance. If Σ is not positive definite, what does this imply about x?

Exercise. Write the following expressions in matrix/vector notation:

a. $\sum_{i=1}^{n} a_i b_i$;

b. $a_i b_j, i = 1, \ldots, n; j = 1, \ldots, J$;

c. $\sum_{j=1}^{J} a_{ij} x_j, i = 1, \ldots, n$;

d. $\sum_{j=1}^{J} a_{ij} b_{jk}, i = 1, \ldots, n; k = 1, \ldots, K$;

e. $\sum_{j=1}^{J} \sum_{k=1}^{K} a_{ij} b_{kj} c_{km}, i = 1, \ldots, n; m = 1, \ldots, M$;

f. $\sum_{i=1}^{n} \sum_{j=1}^{J} a_{ij} x_i x_j$.

Exercise. Prove that if A and B are matrices such that AB and BA both exists, then AB and BA have the same sum of diagonal elements, i.e. $\operatorname{tr}(AB) = \operatorname{tr}(BA)$. Extend the result to show that

$$\operatorname{tr}(ABC) = \operatorname{tr}(CAB) = \operatorname{tr}(BCA),$$

provided the matrices are conformable. Show that however $\operatorname{tr}(BAC)$ and $\operatorname{tr}(ACB)$ may be different.

Exercise. Suppose that A is $n \times n$, B is $K \times K$, and C is $n \times K$ are given matrices. Consider the system of equations in $n \times K$ matrices X:

$$AXB = C. \tag{26.1}$$

Show that this system of equations is linear and solve for X.

Solution. This equation is linear in X, because for any X, X^* of same dimensions

$$AXB + AX^*B = A(X + X^*)B$$

If A, B are invertible, then we have a unique solution

$$X = A^{-1}CB^{-1}.$$

Probability, Statistics and Econometrics. http://dx.doi.org/10.1016/B978-0-12-810495-8.00029-4

Special case $K = 1$. We have $axb = c$, which implies that $x = c/ab$. Question: Suppose that $K = n$

$$AX^{-1}B = C$$

then solve for X. $\qquad\qquad\qquad\qquad\qquad\qquad\qquad\qquad\qquad\qquad$ □

Exercise. If X is a non-zero matrix of order $T \times K$, prove that $X^\mathsf{T}X$ is:
(a) symmetric and
(b) positive semi-definite;
(c) Under what conditions on X is $X^\mathsf{T}X$ positive definite.

Exercise. For a real symmetric $n \times n$ matrix A, prove:
(a) $\det(A) = \prod\limits_{j=1}^{n} \lambda_j$, where λ_j are the eigenvalues of A;
(b) $\operatorname{tr}(A) = \sum_{j=1}^{n} \lambda_j$, where λ_j are the eigenvalues of A;
(c) A is positive definite, if and only if its eigenvalues are positive;
(d) A is positive definite, if and only if A^{-1} is positive definite;
(e) If A is positive definite, then there exists an $n \times n$ matrix P such that $A = PP^\mathsf{T}$.

Exercise. A square matrix A is idempotent if $A = A^2$. Prove that:
(a) The eigenvalues of A are either zero or one;
(b) $\operatorname{rank}(A) = \operatorname{tr}(A)$.

Exercise. Suppose that X is a real symmetric matrix, calculate the eigenvectors and eigenvalues of the matrix X^2 in terms of the eigenvalues and eigenvectors of the matrix X. Now consider the matrix quadratic equation

$$2X^2 - 3X + I_n = 0_n,$$

where $X, I_n, 0_n$ are $n \times n$ matrices. Find real valued matrix solutions to this equation, i.e., find the X that solves this equation.

Solution. If X is symmetric

$$X = U \Lambda U^\mathsf{T},$$

where $UU^\mathsf{T} = I$. It follows that

$$2U\Lambda^2 U^\mathsf{T} - 3U\Lambda U^\mathsf{T} + I_n = 0_n.$$

Collecting terms we have

$$U \begin{bmatrix} 2\lambda_1^2 - 3\lambda_1 + 1 & & 0 \\ & \ddots & \\ 0 & & 2\lambda_n^2 - 3\lambda_n + 1 \end{bmatrix} U^\mathsf{T} = 0_n.$$

Consider the quadratic equation

$$2x^2 - 3x + 1 = 0$$

This can be factorized as

$$(2x - 1)(x - 1) = 0$$

so that the set of solutions includes all matrices of the form

$$\{ X = U \Lambda U^\mathsf{T} : \lambda_i \in \{1, 1/2\}, \ i = 1, \ldots, n,$$
$$\text{where } U \text{ is any orthonormal matrix} \}$$ □

Exercise. Suppose that the matrix A has characteristic polynomial

$$\lambda^2 - a\lambda - b = 0.$$

Using the Cayley Hamilton theorem shows that

$$A^{-1} = \frac{1}{b} (A - aI).$$

Exercise. Show that the matrix $I - Z(Z^\mathsf{T} Z)^{-1} Z^\mathsf{T}$, where Z is any $n \times K$ matrix of full rank K, is idempotent and find its rank.

Exercise. An $n \times K$ matrix X is partitioned column-wise

$$X = (X_1, X_2),$$

where X_1 is $n \times K_1$ and X_2 is $n \times K_2$ where $K_1 + K_2 = K$. Write the cross-product matrix $X^\mathsf{T} X$ in terms of X_1 and X_2. An $n \times K$ matrix W is partitioned column-wise

$$W = \begin{pmatrix} W_1 \\ W_2 \end{pmatrix},$$

where W_1 is $n_1 \times K$ and W_2 is $n_2 \times K$ where $n_1 + n_2 = n$. Write the cross-product matrix $W^\mathsf{T} W$ in terms of W_1 and W_2.

Exercise. If u is an n-dimensional vector of random variables distributed as $N(0, \sigma^2 I_n)$, and A is a symmetric, idempotent matrix of order n and rank p, show that $u^\mathsf{T} A u / \sigma^2$ is distributed as χ^2 with p degrees of freedom.

Exercise. If u is an n-dimensional vector of random variables distributed as $N(0, \Sigma)$, where Σ is non-singular, show that $u^\mathsf{T} \Sigma^{-1} u$ is distributed as χ^2 with n degrees of freedom.

Exercise. Consider the matrix

$$A = \mathrm{diag}(s) - ss^\mathsf{T},$$

where $s = (s_1, \ldots, s_n)^\mathsf{T}$ is such that $i^\mathsf{T} s \neq 0$ and $s_i \neq 0$ for $i = 1, \ldots, n$. Is this matrix symmetric? Show that its inverse is

$$A^{-1} = \mathrm{diag}(1/s_1, \ldots, 1/s_n) + \frac{1}{1 - i^\mathsf{T} s} ii^\mathsf{T}$$

Exercise. Verify that the matrix

$$U = \begin{pmatrix} \cos(\theta) & -\sin(\theta) \\ \sin(\theta) & \cos(\theta) \end{pmatrix}$$

is orthonormal for any $\theta \in \mathbb{R}$.

Exercise. For any skew symmetric matrix A (such that $A^\mathsf{T} = -A$), let

$$U = (I + A)(I - A)^{-1}.$$

Show that U is orthonormal.

Exercise. Suppose that $Y \in \mathbb{R}^{d_y}$, $X \in \mathbb{R}^{d_x}$ with

$$X \sim N(\mu_x, \Sigma_x)$$
$$Y | X = x \sim N(a + Bx, \Sigma_y),$$

where B is $d_y \times d_x$. Prove that

$$X | Y = y \sim N(\mu_{x|y}, \Sigma_{x|y}) \tag{26.2}$$
$$\mu_{x|y} = \Sigma_{x|y} \left(B^\mathsf{T} \Sigma_y (y - a) + \Sigma_x \mu_x \right)$$
$$\Sigma_{x|y} = \Sigma_x^{-1} + B^\mathsf{T} \Sigma_y^{-1} B$$

Exercise. Suppose that

$$y_i = \beta x_i + \varepsilon_i,$$

where (x_i, ε_i) are i.i.d. with ε_i independent of x_i with mean zero but with unknown distribution. Suppose that $x_i \sim N(0, 1)$. Then claim that

$$t = \frac{\widehat{\beta}}{s \left(\sum_{i=1}^{n} x_i^2\right)^{-1/2}} \sim t_{n-1},$$

where s is the usual standard error. That is, the exact t-test is valid as before even though the distribution of ε could be anything.

Solution. We have

$$\widehat{\beta} - \beta_0 = \frac{\sum_{i=1}^{n} x_i \varepsilon_i}{\sum_{i=1}^{n} x_i^2}$$

$$t = \frac{\sum_{i=1}^{n} x_i \varepsilon_i}{\sqrt{\sum_{i=1}^{n} \varepsilon_i^2}} \times \sqrt{\frac{\sum_{i=1}^{n} \varepsilon_i^2}{\frac{1}{n-1}\sum_{i=1}^{n} x_i^2 \sum_{i=1}^{n} \widehat{\varepsilon}_i^2}}$$

Note that conditional on $\varepsilon_1, \ldots, \varepsilon_n$

$$\sum_{i=1}^{n} x_i \varepsilon_i \sim N\left(0, \sum_{i=1}^{n} \varepsilon_i^2\right)$$

so that conditionally and unconditionally

$$\frac{\sum_{i=1}^{n} x_i \varepsilon_i}{\sqrt{\sum_{i=1}^{n} \varepsilon_i^2}} \sim N(0, 1).$$

Furthermore, we can write

$$(n-1)s_*^2 \frac{(x^\mathsf{T} x)}{(\varepsilon^\mathsf{T}\varepsilon)} = \frac{(x^\mathsf{T} x)}{(\varepsilon^\mathsf{T}\varepsilon)} \sum_{i=1}^{n} \widehat{\varepsilon}_i^2$$

$$= \frac{(x^\mathsf{T} x)}{(\varepsilon^\mathsf{T}\varepsilon)}\varepsilon^\mathsf{T}\varepsilon - \frac{(x^\mathsf{T} x)}{(\varepsilon^\mathsf{T}\varepsilon)}\varepsilon^\mathsf{T} x(x^\mathsf{T} x)^{-1}x^\mathsf{T}\varepsilon$$

$$= (x^\mathsf{T} x) - \varepsilon^\mathsf{T} x(\varepsilon^\mathsf{T}\varepsilon)^{-1}x^\mathsf{T}\varepsilon$$

$$= x^\mathsf{T} M_\varepsilon x,$$

which is distributed as a chi-squared random variables with $n-1$ degrees of freedom conditional on $\varepsilon_1, \ldots, \varepsilon_n$. Moreover, they two terms are independent. Voila! □

Exercise. Derive the equation of the regression line, the R^2 and the t-statistics for the slope coefficient for each of the following datasets (X_i, Y_{ji}), $i = 1, \ldots, 11$ and $j = 1, 2, 3$. Graph the data and comment on your findings.

X	Y_1	Y_2	Y_3
10.0	8.04	9.14	7.46
8.0	6.95	8.14	6.77
13.0	7.58	8.74	12.74
9.0	8.81	8.77	7.11
11.0	8.33	9.26	7.81
14.0	9.96	8.10	8.84
6.0	7.24	6.13	6.08
4.0	4.26	3.10	5.39
12.0	10.84	9.13	8.15
7.0	4.82	7.26	6.42
5.0	5.68	4.74	5.73

Exercise. Consider the regression model

$$Y_i = \alpha + \beta X_i + \varepsilon_i,$$

where $\varepsilon_i \sim N(0, \sigma^2)$, and X_i are fixed numbers. Let $\theta = (\alpha, \beta, \sigma^2)$. Provide the Lagrange Multiplier, Wald, and Likelihood Ratio statistics [and give their asymptotic distribution] for testing the null hypothesis that $\sigma^2 = 1$ versus (a) the two sided alternative $\sigma^2 \neq 1$; (b) the one-sided alternative $\sigma^2 < 1$.

Solution. The t-test is straightforward. The log likelihood

$$\log L(\alpha, \beta, \sigma^2) = \frac{-n}{2} \log 2\pi - \frac{n}{2} \log \sigma^2 - \frac{1}{2\sigma^2} \sum_{i=1}^{n} (Y_i - \alpha - \beta X_i)^2$$

$$\log L(\alpha, \beta, 1) = \frac{-n}{2} \log 2\pi - \frac{1}{2} \sum_{i=1}^{n} (Y_i - \alpha - \beta X_i)^2.$$

In this case, the estimates of α, β are unaffected by the restriction. Therefore, since

$$\widehat{\sigma}^2 = \frac{1}{n} \sum_{i=1}^{n} \widehat{\varepsilon}_i^2$$

$$\text{LR} = 2\{\log L(\widehat{\theta}) - \log L(\theta^*)\} = -n \log \widehat{\sigma}^2 + n(\widehat{\sigma}^2 - 1).$$

Now this looks complicated. But write $\widehat{\delta} = \widehat{\sigma}^2 - 1$ and then

$$\text{LR} = -n \left(\log \left(1 + \widehat{\delta} \right) - \widehat{\delta} \right).$$

Consider the function $f(x) = -\ln(1 + x) + x$ plotted below

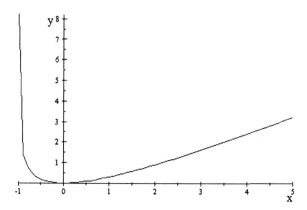

for $x \geq -1$.

We now apply the fact that $\ln(1 + \varepsilon) - \varepsilon \simeq \varepsilon^2/2$ for small ε so that

$$\text{LR} \simeq n \left(\widehat{\sigma}^2 - 1 \right)^2.$$

Formally apply the delta method. Then further approximate by

$$n \left(\frac{1}{n} \sum_{i=1}^{n} \varepsilon_i^2 - 1 \right)^2 \xrightarrow{D} \chi^2(1).$$

In this case, we reject the null that $\sigma^2 = 1$ against the two-sided alternative if $\text{LR} > \chi_\alpha^2(1)$. To test the one sided alternative we consider the signed likelihood ratio test with

$$\text{LR}_+ = -n \left(\log \left(1 + \widehat{\delta} \right) - \widehat{\delta} \right) \times 1(\widehat{\delta} > 0). \qquad \square$$

Exercise. Consider the regression model $Y_i = \beta X_i + \varepsilon_i$, where X_i is i.i.d., while ε_i are i.i.d. with mean zero and variance σ^2. Discuss the consistency and asymptotic normality of $\widehat{\beta}$, where $\widehat{\beta}$ minimizes

$$\sum_{i=1}^{n} (Y_i - \beta X_i)^4.$$

Discuss the case $E(\varepsilon_i^3) = 0$ and the case $E(\varepsilon_i^3) \neq 0$.

Solution. Let

$$Q_n(\beta) = \frac{1}{n} \sum_{i=1}^{n} (Y_i - \beta X_i)^4.$$

We can write

$$Q_n(\beta) = \frac{1}{n} \sum_{i=1}^{n} (\varepsilon_i + (\beta_0 - \beta)X_i)^4$$

$$= \frac{1}{n} \sum_{i=1}^{n} \varepsilon_i^4 + 4(\beta_0 - \beta) \frac{1}{n} \sum_{i=1}^{n} \varepsilon_i^3 X_i + 6(\beta_0 - \beta)^2 \frac{1}{n} \sum_{i=1}^{n} \varepsilon_i^2 X_i^2$$

$$+ 4(\beta_0 - \beta)^3 \frac{1}{n} \sum_{i=1}^{n} \varepsilon_i X_i^3 + (\beta_0 - \beta)^4 \frac{1}{n} \sum_{i=1}^{n} X_i^4.$$

Then provided fourth moments exist we have

$$Q_n(\beta) \xrightarrow{P} Q(\beta) = a_0 + a_1(\beta_0 - \beta) + a_2(\beta_0 - \beta)^2 + a_3(\beta_0 - \beta)^3 + a_4(\beta_0 - \beta)^4.$$

This convergence is uniform in β over a compact set because of the separation of the random variables from the parameters. When $E(\varepsilon_i^3) = 0$, we have

$$Q(\beta) = a_0 + a_2(\beta_0 - \beta)^2 + a_4(\beta_0 - \beta)^4.$$

This function is uniquely minimized at $\beta = \beta_0$ because $a_2, a_4 > 0$. In general a_1, a_3 may not be zero, and then the analysis is more complicated. $\quad\square$

Exercise. Suppose that

$$y_i = \sin \beta x_i + \varepsilon_i,$$

where $E(\varepsilon_i | x_i) = 0$. Suppose also that x_i is uniformly distributed on $[a, b]$ for some a, b. The conditional moment restriction implies that $E\varepsilon_i h(x_i) = 0$ for any measurable function h. Consider two choice $h(x) = 1$ and $h(x) = x \cos \beta x$. Check the identification issue for the GMM method with these two choices of instruments in the case that $\beta = 0$.

Solution. We have to check that

$$Eh(x_i) \sin \beta x_i = 0$$

if and only if $\beta = 0$. The if part always works by assumption. We compute the above expectation for different h and a, b. First, suppose that $[a, b] = [0, \pi]$. Then

$$\frac{1}{\pi} \int_0^\pi \sin \beta x \, dx = -\frac{1}{\pi} \frac{\cos \pi \beta - 1}{\beta}$$

$$\frac{1}{\pi} \int_0^\pi x \cos \beta x \sin \beta x \, dx = \frac{1}{4\pi} \frac{-2\pi\beta \cos^2 \pi \beta + \cos \pi \beta \sin \pi \beta + \pi \beta}{\beta^2}.$$

These two functions are graphed below on the range $-4 \leq \beta \leq 4$:

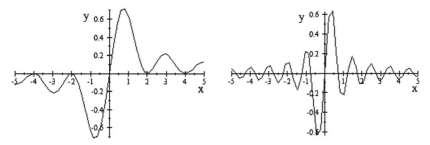

They both have very similar behaviour, namely many isolated zeros. However, in the first graph, the zeros are at points where the derivative is zero, which suggests that these points do not correspond to a minimum (of whatever criterion function). In the second graph there are some zeros where the derivative is also positive, which suggests that these points correspond to local minima. It turns out that the zero at $\beta = 0$ corresponds to the global minimum of the nonlinear least squares criterion function, which can be checked by looking at the quantity

$$\frac{1}{\pi} \int_0^\pi (\sin(\beta x))^2 dx = \frac{1}{2\pi} \frac{-\cos \pi\beta \sin \pi\beta + \pi\beta}{\beta},$$

which is plotted below

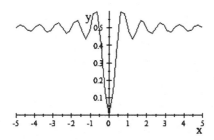

Finally, we repeat the exercise for the case where $[a, b] = [-\pi/2, \pi/2]$. In this case,

$$\frac{1}{\pi} \int_{-\pi/2}^{\pi/2} \sin(\beta x) dx = 0$$

$$\frac{1}{\pi} \int_{-\pi/2}^{\pi/2} \sin(\beta x) x \cos(\beta x) dx = -\frac{1}{4\pi} \frac{2\pi\beta \cos^2 \frac{1}{2}\pi\beta - 2\cos \frac{1}{2}\pi\beta \sin \frac{1}{2}\pi\beta - \pi\beta}{\beta^2}$$

$$\frac{1}{\pi} \int_{-\pi/2}^{\pi/2} (\sin(\beta x))^2 dx = \frac{1}{2\pi} \frac{-2\cos \frac{1}{2}\pi\beta \sin \frac{1}{2}\pi\beta + \pi\beta}{\beta}.$$

Now of course, the instrument $h = 1$ is totally useless, while the nonlinear least squares instruments still work, as can be seen from the graph below of the first order condition and the least squares criterion

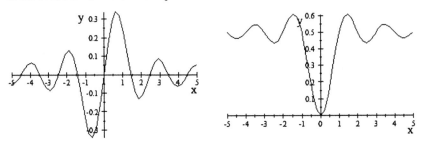

Exercise. How long is the coastline of Britain? Lewis Fry Richardson conjectured that the length of the coastline L was related to the length of the ruler G by

$$L = MG^{1-D},$$

where M, D are constants with $D \geq 1$. Suppose that you have a sample of observations $\{L_i, G_i\}_{i=1}^{n}$ how would you test the hypothesis that the length is finite against the alternative that it is infinite (i.e., as $G \to 0$)?

Exercise. Suppose that you want to measure the sides of a table, i.e., length (L) and width (W). However, your research assistant reports to you only the area (A). Luckily, she was trained at Oxford and so makes an error in each measurement. Specifically,

$$L_i = L + \varepsilon_i \quad ; \quad W_i = W + \eta_i,$$

where ε_i, η_i are mutually independent standard normal random variables. The RA reports $\{A_i\}_{i=1}^{n}$, where $A_i = L_i W_i$. Suggest Method of Moments estimators of L, W based on the sample information. Now suppose that ε_i and η_i are both $N(0, \sigma^2)$ for some unknown σ^2. Show how to estimate L, W, and σ^2 from the sample data $\{A_i\}_{i=1}^{n}$.

Solution. We have

$$E(A_i) = E\left[(L + \varepsilon_i)(W + \eta_i)\right] = LW$$

$$E(A_i^2) = E\left[(L + \varepsilon_i)^2 (W + \eta_i)^2\right] = L^2 W^2 + L^2 + W^2 + 1.$$

$$\text{var}(A_i) = L^2 + W^2 + 1$$

These are two moment conditions in two unknowns. In fact by substitution $L = E(A)/W$ we get the quadratic equation

$$\theta^2 + (1 - E(A))\theta + E^2 A = 0$$

where $\theta = W^2$. Note that the coefficient on θ is negative and the intercept is positive. We have

$$\theta = \frac{E(A) - 1 \pm \sqrt{(1 - E(A))^2 - 4E^2 A}}{2}$$

assuming this is well defined. We need

$$(1 - E(A))^2 - 4E^2 A \geq 0,$$

which will be satisfied because we can expand out and find this quantity is $(L^2 - W^2)^2$. We should take the positive root. Therefore, we estimate using sample mean and sample variance of the area measurements to obtain $\widehat{\theta}$ and then estimate $\widehat{W} = \sqrt{\widehat{\theta}}$ and $\widehat{L} = \widehat{E}(A)/\sqrt{\widehat{\theta}}$. □

Exercise. Consider the following regression model

$$y = X_1 \beta_1 + X_2 \beta_2 + \varepsilon,$$

where X_j is an $n \times K_j$ matrix of non-random regressors for $j = 1, 2$. The disturbance term ε satisfies

$$E(\varepsilon) = X_1 \gamma$$

for some non-zero vector γ, and further suppose that

$$E\left[(\varepsilon - E(\varepsilon))(\varepsilon - E(\varepsilon))^{\mathsf{T}} \right] = \sigma^2 I_n.$$

Calculate $E(\widehat{\beta}_1)$ and $\text{var}(\widehat{\beta}_1)$.

Exercise. True, False, or Indeterminate, and Explain.
(a) Let X and Y be two mean zero random variables. Then, $E(X|Y) = 0$ and $E(Y|X) = 0$ if and only if X and Y are uncorrelated. *This is false. If $E(Y|X) = 0$ or $E(X|Y)$, then X and Y are uncorrelated, but not vice versa;*
(b) Two events A and B with $P(A) = 1$ and $P(B) = 1$ must be mutually independent. *True. We have*

$$P(A \cap B) = P(A) + P(B) - P(A \cup B) \geq P(A) + P(B) - 1 = 1$$

so $P(A \cap B) = P(A)P(B)$.
(c) Whenever the cumulative distribution function is discontinuous, the median is not well-defined. *False. The cumulative distribution function could be discontinuous at some points but be continuous at the median.*

Exercise. True, False, or Indeterminate, and Explain.
(a) The Cramér–Rao Theorem says that with normally distributed errors the maximum likelihood estimator is Best Unbiased. *The CR theorem says that any unbiased estimator has variance greater than or equal to the inverse information. In the normal case, the MLE is unbiased and achieves the CR lower bound.*
(b) Suppose that for some estimator $\widehat{\theta}$, we have as $n \to \infty$

$$n(\widehat{\theta} - 2\pi) \xrightarrow{D} N(0, 1),$$

where n is the sample size. Then

$$n \sin \widehat{\theta} \xrightarrow{D} N(0, 1).$$

This is true from a simple application of the delta method with $f(x) = \sin(x)$ has derivative $\cos(x)$, which is equal to 1 when $x = 2\pi$;
(c) Suppose that A, B are symmetric real matrices. The eigenvalues of $A + B$ are the same as the eigenvalues of $B + A$. *True because $A + B = B + A$.*

Exercise. Consider the linear regression model

$$Y = X\beta + \varepsilon,$$

where $Y = (y_1, \ldots, y_n)^\mathsf{T}$ and X is the $n \times K$ matrix containing the regressors. Suppose that the classical assumptions hold, i.e., ε_i are i.i.d. with $\varepsilon_i \sim N(0, 1)$ and independent of X. Consider the reverse regression estimator $\widehat{\beta}^R = (\widehat{\beta}_1^R, \ldots, \widehat{\beta}_K^R)^\mathsf{T}$, where

$$\widehat{\beta}_j^R = \left(Y^\mathsf{T} Y\right)^{-1} Y^\mathsf{T} X_j,$$

where X_j are $n \times 1$ vectors containing the observations on the jth regressor. Let x_i be the $K \times 1$ vector containing the ith observations on the regressors, and let $\widehat{x}_i = \widehat{\beta}^R y_i$ and $\widehat{u}_i = x_i - \widehat{x}_i$. Which, if any, of the following hold and why:
(i) $n^{-1} \sum_{i=1}^{n} x_i \widehat{u}_i = 0$;
(ii) $n^{-1} \sum_{i=1}^{n} \widehat{u}_i = 0$;
(iii) $n^{-1} \sum_{i=1}^{n} y_i \widehat{u}_i = 0$. *This is the only necessarily true answer, because the OLS procedure is constructed to make the right hand side variable, in this case y, orthogonal to the residual $\widehat{u}$.*
(iv) $X^\mathsf{T} y = X^\mathsf{T} X \widehat{\beta}^R$
Derive the probability limit of $\widehat{\beta}_R$ as n gets large. State clearly any additional assumptions you need to make. *Consider the scalar case ($K = 1$). Then*

$$\widehat{\beta}^R = \frac{Y^\mathsf{T} X}{Y^\mathsf{T} Y} = \frac{\frac{1}{n} X^\mathsf{T} Y}{\frac{1}{n} Y^\mathsf{T} Y}.$$

We have

$$\frac{1}{n}X^\mathsf{T}Y = \beta\frac{1}{n}X^\mathsf{T}X + \frac{1}{n}X^\mathsf{T}\varepsilon$$

$$\frac{1}{n}Y^\mathsf{T}Y = \beta^2\frac{1}{n}X^\mathsf{T}X + 2\beta\frac{1}{n}X^\mathsf{T}\varepsilon + \frac{1}{n}\varepsilon^\mathsf{T}\varepsilon.$$

We apply law of large numbers to show that

$$\frac{1}{n}X^\mathsf{T}X \xrightarrow{P} Ex_i^2$$

$$\frac{1}{n}X^\mathsf{T}\varepsilon \xrightarrow{P} 0$$

$$\frac{1}{n}\varepsilon^\mathsf{T}\varepsilon \xrightarrow{P} 1,$$

provided x_i are i.i.d. with finite variance. We then apply Slutsky theorem to establish

$$\hat{\beta}^R \xrightarrow{P} \frac{\beta Ex_i^2}{\beta^2 Ex_i^2 + 1}.$$

Exercise. Consider the regression model

$$Y_i = \alpha + \beta X_i + \varepsilon_i,$$

where $\varepsilon_i \sim N(0, \sigma^2)$ and are independent of X_i, which you may treat as fixed numbers. Let $\{Y_i, X_i, i = 1, \ldots, n\}$ be the observed sample, and let $\theta = (\alpha, \beta, \sigma^2)$ be unknown parameters. Provide the Likelihood Ratio statistic for testing the null hypothesis that $\sigma^2 = 1$ versus the two sided alternative $\sigma^2 \neq 1$. Derive its large sample distribution under the null hypothesis. You may use the expansion $\log(1 + x) = x - x^2/2 + x^3/3 + \ldots$ for $x \in (-1, 1)$.

Solution. The t-test is straightforward. The log likelihood

$$\log L(\alpha, \beta, \sigma^2) = \frac{-n}{2}\log 2\pi - \frac{n}{2}\log\sigma^2 - \frac{1}{2\sigma^2}\sum_{i=1}^{n}(Y_i - \alpha - \beta X_i)^2$$

$$\log L(\alpha, \beta, 1) = \frac{-n}{2}\log 2\pi - \frac{1}{2}\sum_{i=1}^{n}(Y_i - \alpha - \beta X_i)^2.$$

In this case, the estimates of α, β are unaffected by the restriction. Therefore, since

$$\hat{\sigma}^2 = \frac{1}{n}\sum_{i=1}^{n}\hat{\varepsilon}_i^2$$

$$LR = 2\{\log L(\widehat{\theta}) - \log L(\theta^*)\} = -n \log \widehat{\sigma}^2 + n(\widehat{\sigma}^2 - 1).$$

Now this looks nasty. But write $\widehat{\delta} = \widehat{\sigma}^2 - 1$ and then

$$LR = -n \left(\log \left(1 + \widehat{\delta} \right) - \widehat{\delta} \right).$$

We now apply the fact that $\ln(1 + \varepsilon) - \varepsilon \simeq \varepsilon^2 / 2$ for small ε so that

$$LR \simeq n \left(\widehat{\sigma}^2 - 1 \right)^2$$

and then approximate by

$$n \left(\frac{1}{n} \sum_{i=1}^{n} \varepsilon_i^2 - 1 \right)^2 \xrightarrow{D} \chi^2(1) \qquad \square$$

Exercise. Suppose that $X \sim N(\mu, 1)$, where $\mu \geq c$ for some $c \in \mathbb{R}$. That is, the parameter space is $\Theta = \{x : c \leq x < \infty\}$. The maximum likelihood estimator in this case can be shown to be $\widehat{\mu} = \max\{\overline{X}, c\}$. Derive the limiting distribution of this estimator when the true parameter $\mu_0 = c$.

Exercise. Suppose that

$$y_i = \beta x_i + \varepsilon_i,$$

where ε_i, x_i are i.i.d. and mutually independent with $\varepsilon_i, x_i \sim N(0, 1)$. Consider the Rogoff–Satchell estimator. The idea is to remove observations in such a way as to change the sign of the estimator. One version of this is defined as follows:

$$\widehat{\beta}_{RS} = \frac{\sum_{i=1}^{n} x_i y_i 1(x_i y_i \widehat{\beta} < 0)}{\sum_{i=1}^{n} x_i^2 1(x_i y_i \widehat{\beta} < 0)}.$$

Note that $x_i y_i \widehat{\beta} < 0$ if either $\widehat{\beta} > 0$ and $x_i y_i < 0$ or $\widehat{\beta} < 0$ and $x_i y_i > 0$. We have $x_i y_i < 0$ if either $x_i < 0$ and $y_i > 0$ or $x_i > 0$ and $y_i < 0$. Essentially this keeps only the data in quadrants opposite to the least squares slope and then fits least squares to them. This estimator is nonlinear and it is biased. Derive the properties of this estimator in two cases:
(a) $\beta \neq 0$;
(b) $\beta = 0$.

Solution. When $\beta \neq 0$ we have

$$\widetilde{\beta}_{R-S} = \widetilde{\beta}_{R-S}^* + o_p(n^{-1/2})$$

$$\widetilde{\beta}_{R-S}^* = \frac{\sum_{i=1}^{n} x_i y_i 1 (x_i y_i \beta < 0)}{\sum_{i=1}^{n} x_i^2 1 (x_i y_i \beta < 0)}$$

and this can be treated by standard arguments. When $\beta = 0$, we argue as follows. Firstly, we may show that

$$\sqrt{n}\widehat{\beta} \xrightarrow{D} Z,$$

where Z is standard normal. Then we have

$$\widetilde{\beta}_{R-S} = \widetilde{\beta}_{R-S}^{\$} + o_p(n^{-1/2})$$

$$\widetilde{\beta}_{R-S}^{\$} = \frac{\sum_{i=1}^n x_i y_i 1(x_i y_i Z < 0)}{\sum_{i=1}^n x_i^2 1(x_i y_i Z < 0)}.$$

Since Z is independent of the data we may condition on it. Furthermore, note that if $Z > 0$ then $x_i y_i < 0$ to ensure 1 and vice versa. We have

$$\frac{1}{n} \sum_{i=1}^n x_i y_i 1(x_i y_i Z < 0) \xrightarrow{P}_{Z>0} E\left[x_i y_i 1(x_i y_i < 0) \right]$$

$$\frac{1}{n} \sum_{i=1}^n x_i y_i 1(x_i y_i Z < 0) \xrightarrow{P}_{Z<0} E\left[x_i y_i 1(x_i y_i > 0) \right].$$

Similarly

$$\frac{1}{n} \sum_{i=1}^n x_i^2 1(x_i y_i Z < 0) \xrightarrow{P}_{Z>0} E\left[x_i^2 1(x_i y_i < 0) \right]$$

$$\frac{1}{n} \sum_{i=1}^n x_i^2 1(x_i y_i Z < 0) \xrightarrow{P}_{Z<0} E\left[x_i^2 1(x_i y_i > 0) \right].$$

Therefore, when $Z > 0$

$$\widetilde{\beta}_{R-S}^{\$} \xrightarrow{P}_{Z>0} \frac{E\left[x_i y_i 1(x_i y_i < 0) \right]}{E\left[x_i^2 1(x_i y_i < 0) \right]}$$

but when $Z < 0$

$$\widetilde{\beta}_{R-S}^{\$} \xrightarrow{P}_{Z<0} \frac{E\left[x_i y_i 1(x_i y_i > 0) \right]}{E\left[x_i^2 1(x_i y_i > 0) \right]}.$$

This shows that

$$\widetilde{\beta}_{R-S} \xrightarrow{D} W = \begin{cases} \frac{E\left[x_i y_i 1(x_i y_i < 0) \right]}{E\left[x_i^2 1(x_i y_i < 0) \right]} & \text{if } Z > 0 \\[2mm] \frac{E\left[x_i y_i 1(x_i y_i > 0) \right]}{E\left[x_i^2 1(x_i y_i > 0) \right]} & \text{if } Z < 0, \end{cases}$$

which is a two point distribution. $\qquad\square$

Exercise. Establish whether the following statements are True, False, or Indeterminate. Explain your reasoning.

(i) If X_n is a discrete random variable for each n, and if $X_n \xrightarrow{P} 0$, then $Pr(X_n = 0) \to 1$. *False. For example, $X_n = \pm 1/n$ with probability 1/2. However, if support of X_n is fixed then this is true.*

(ii) The Gauss–Markov theorem says that with normally distributed errors the ordinary least squares estimator is Best Linear Unbiased. *True, but don't need normality, unnecessary condition*

(iii) Suppose that A, B are symmetric real matrices. Let λ be a nonzero eigenvalue of AB, then λ^2 is an eigenvalue of $(AB)^2$. *This is true. Suppose that*

$$ABx = \lambda x.$$

Then

$$ABABx = \lambda ABx = \lambda^2 x.$$

Exercise. Suppose that you observe data $\{Y_i, X_i, i = 1, \ldots, n\}$ with $X_i \in \mathbb{R}^K$. You believe that the linear regression model holds, so that

$$Y_i = \alpha + \beta^{\mathsf{T}} X_i + \varepsilon_i$$

where $\beta \in \mathbb{R}^K$ is an unknown parameter vector and $\alpha \in \mathbb{R}$ is an unknown scalar parameter. Explain how you would test the following hypotheses. In your answer, be clear about what additional assumptions you make and what role the assumptions have in making the test valid. Also give the test statistics and the critical values you would use (no table work).

(i) The null hypothesis that $\alpha = 0$ versus the alternative that $\alpha > 0$.

(ii) The null hypothesis that $\beta = 0$ versus the alternative that $\beta \neq 0$.

(iii) The null hypothesis that $\alpha = 0$ and $\beta = 0$ versus the alternative that $\alpha \neq 0$ or $\beta \neq 0$.

Appendix

A   SOME RESULTS FROM CALCULUS

1. Limits. For a function f

$$\lim_{x \to x_0} f(x) \quad ; \quad \lim_{x \downarrow x_0} f(x) \quad ; \quad \lim_{x \uparrow x_0} f(x)$$

$$f'(x) = \lim_{h \to 0} \frac{f(x+h) - f(x)}{h}$$

2. Fundamental Theorem of Integral Calculus. If $F(x) = \int_a^x f(t)dt$, where f is continuous in $[a, b]$, then $F'(x) = f(x)$.

3. Rolle's Theorem. If a function f is continuous on a proper closed interval $[a, b]$, differentiable on the open interval (a, b), and $f(a) = f(b)$, then there exists at least one c in the open interval (a, b) such that $f'(c) = 0$.

4. Mean Value theorem. For $y \in (x, x + h)$

$$f'(y) = \frac{f(x+h) - f(x)}{h}$$

$$f(x+h) = f(x) + hf'(y)$$

5. Integration by Parts. Let $u(x) = U'(x)$ and $v(x) = V'(x)$, then

$$\int_a^b U(x)v(x)dx = U(b)V(b) - U(a)V(a) - \int_a^b u(x)V(x)dx.$$

6. Change of variables. Letting $u = g(t)$, we have

$$\int_a^b f(u)du = \int_\alpha^\beta f(g(t))g'(t)dt \quad ; \quad g(\alpha) = a \text{ and } g(\beta) = b.$$

7. Interchanging limits. When can you say that for example

$$\lim_{x \to x_0} \lim_{y \to y_0} f(x, y) = \lim_{y \to y_0} \lim_{x \to x_0} f(x, y).$$

Need either Monotone or Dominated convergence.

357

8. Partial Derivatives

$$\frac{\partial f(x, y)}{\partial x} = \lim_{h \to 0} \frac{f(x + h, y) - f(x, y)}{h}$$
$$\frac{\partial f(x, y)}{\partial y} = \lim_{h \to 0} \frac{f(x, y + h) - f(x, y)}{h}$$

B   SOME MATRIX FACTS

B.1   Matrix Operations Satisfy Certain Mathematical Laws

$A + (B + C) = (A + B) + C$ (associative law for addition)

$A(BC) = (AB)C$ (associative law for multiplication)

$A + B = B + A$ (commutative law)

$c(A + B) = cA + cB$, where c is a scalar (distributive law for scalar products)

$C(A + B) = CA + CB$, provided the products are defined (distributive law for matrix multiplication)

B.2   Transpose of a Matrix

$(A^\mathsf{T})^\mathsf{T} = A$

$(A + B)^\mathsf{T} = A^\mathsf{T} + B^\mathsf{T}$

$(AB)^\mathsf{T} = B^\mathsf{T} A^\mathsf{T}$

B.3   Inverse

We only define for square matrix

$(A^{-1})^{-1} = A$

$(AB)^{-1} = B^{-1} A^{-1}$

$(A^\mathsf{T})^{-1} = (A^{-1})^\mathsf{T}$

B.4   Trace of a Matrix

We only define for square matrix

$\mathrm{tr}(A + B) = \mathrm{tr}(A) + \mathrm{tr}(B)$

$\mathrm{tr}(AB) = \mathrm{tr}(BA)$

B.5   Determinant of a Matrix

We only define for square matrix

For diagonal matrix $D = \mathrm{diag}\{d_1, \ldots, d_n\}$, $\det(D) = d_1 \times \cdots \times d_n$

$\det(AB) = \det(A)\det(B)$

A matrix is nonsingular if and only if $\det(A) \neq 0$

B.6   Rank of a Matrix

Defined also for rectangular matrices A, $n \times K$

$\text{rank}(A) \leq \min\{n, K\}$

$\text{rank}(A^\mathsf{T}) = \text{rank}(A)$

$\text{rank}(AB) = \min\{\text{rank}(A), \text{rank}(B)\}$

B.7   Eigenvalues of Real Symmetric Matrix

$\det(A) = \lambda_1 \times \cdots \times \lambda_n$

$\text{tr}(A) = \lambda_1 + \cdots + \lambda_n$

AB and BA have the same eigenvalues (but not the same eigenvectors)

A^2 has the same eigenvectors as A but the eigenvalues are squared

B.8   Positive Definiteness

We only define for square matrix

Identity matrix is pd

If A is psd, then $-A$ is nsd

If A is psd, then A^T is psd, A^{-1} is psd, and A^2 is psd

If A, B are psd, then $A + B$ is psd

For any $n \times K$ matrix X, the matrix $X^\mathsf{T}X$ is psd

Bibliography

Aldrich, J., 1997. R.A. Fisher and the making of maximum likelihood 1912–1922. Statistical Science 12 (3), 162–176.

American Statistical Association, 2016. Statement on Statistical Significance and P-Values.

Andrews, D.W., 1994. Empirical process methods in econometrics. In: Engle, R.F., McFadden, D.L. (Eds.), Handbook of Econometrics, vol. IV. Elsevier Science, Amsterdam, pp. 2248–2296.

Bahadur, R.R., Savage, L.J., 1956. The nonexistence of certain statistical procedures in nonparametric problems. Annals of Mathematical Statistics 27 (4), 1115–1122.

Bernoulli, D., 1738. Specimen theoria novae de mensura sortis. Commentarii Academiae Scientarum Imperialis Petropolitane 5, 175–192.

Bickel, P.J., Freedman, D.A., 1981. Some asymptotic theory for the bootstrap. Annals of Statistics 9 (6), 1196–1217.

Billingsley, P., 1986. Probability and Measure, 2nd ed. Wiley, New York.

Blyth, C.R., 1986. Approximate binomial confidence limits. Journal of the American Statistical Association 81 (395), 843–855.

Brown, B.H., 1933. American Mathematical Monthly 40 (10), 607.

Cantelli, F.P., 1933. Sulla determinazione empirica delle leggi di probabilita. Giornale Dell'Istituto Italiano Degli Attuari 4, 221–424.

Casella, G., Berger, R.L., 2002. Statistical Inference. Duxbury, Pacific Grove, CA.

Chesher, A., 2003. Identification in nonseparable models. Econometrica 71 (5), 1405–1441.

Chung, K.L., 1974. A Course in Probability Theory, 2nd ed. Academic Press, New York.

Cox, D.R., 2005. Frequentist and Bayesian statistics: a critique. In: Louis, L., Unel, M.K. (Eds.), Proceedings of the Statistical Problems in Particle Physics, Astrophysics and Cosmology. Imperial College Press, UK. http://www.physics.ox.ac.uk/phystat05/proceedings/default.htm.

Cox, D.R., Hinkley, D.V., 1979. Theoretical Statistics. Chapman and Hall, London.

Dawid, A.P., 2002. Sally Clark Appeal, Statement of Professor A.P. Dawid. http://www.statslab.cam.ac.uk/~apd/.

Efron, B., 1986. Why isn't everyone a Bayesian? The American Statistician 40 (1), 1–5.

Engle, R.F., Hendry, D.F., Richard, J.F., 1983. Exogeneity. Econometrica 51 (2), 277–304.

Gallant, A.R., 1997. An Introduction to Econometric Theory. Princeton University Press, Princeton.

Glivenko, V., 1933. Sulla determinazione empirica della legge di probabilita. Giornale Dell'Istituto Italiano Degli Attuari 4, 92–99.

Goldberger, A.S., 1991. A Course in Econometrics. Harvard University Press, Cambridge, MA.

Hansen, L.P., Singleton, K.J., 1982. Generalized instrumental variables estimation of nonlinear rational expectations models. Econometrica 50 (5), 1269–1286.

Hogg, R.V., Craig, A.T., 1978. Introduction to Mathematical Statistics. Macmillan, New York.

Ioannidis, J.P.A., 2005. Why most published research findings are false. PLoS Medicine 2 (8), 696–701.

Johnson, N.L., Kotz, S., 1994. Continuous Univariate Distributions, vol. 1, 2nd ed. Blackwell.

Koenker, R., 2005. Quantile Regression. Cambridge University Press, New York.

Koenker, R., Bassett, G., 1978. Regression quantiles. Econometrica 46, 33–50.

Leamer, E.E., 1978. Specification Searches. Wiley, New York.

Levy, H., 2016. Stochastic Dominance: Investment Decision Making Under Uncertainty, 3rd ed. Springer, Berlin.

Manski, C., 2007. Identification for Prediction and Decision. Harvard University Press, Cambridge and London.

Mood, A.M., Graybill, F.A., Boes, D.C., 1974. Introduction to the Theory of Statistics. McGraw-Hill, New York.

NASA, 2016. Nasa Space Place, http://spaceplace.nasa.gov/starfinder2/en/.

Pearson, K., 1901. On Lines and Planes of Closest Fit to Systems of Points in Space. Philosophical Magazine 2 (6), 559–572.

Phillips, P.C., 2007. Regression with slowly varying regressors and nonlinear trends. Econometric Theory 23 (04), 557–614.

Romano, J.P., 2004. On non-parametric testing, the uniform behaviour of the t-test, and related problems. Scandinavian Journal of Statistics 31 (4), 567–584.

Rothenberg, T.J., 1971. Identification in parametric models. Econometrica 39 (3), 577–591.

Rothenberg, T.J., 2005. Incredible structural inference. In: Andrews, D.W.K., Stock, J.H. (Eds.), Identification and Inference for Econometric Models, Essays in Honor of Thomas Rothenberg. Cambridge University Press.

Roy, A.D., 1952. Safety first and the holding of assets. Econometrica 20 (3), 431–449.

Sachs, G., 1999. Die Akte Astrologie (in Dutch), revised ed. Goldmann, München.

Silverman, B.W., 1986. Density Estimation for Statistics and Data Analysis. Monographs on Statistics and Applied Probability. Chapman and Hall, London.

Tibshirani, R., 1996. Regression shrinkage and selection via the lasso. Journal of the Royal Statistical Society: Series B 58 (1), 267–288.

Trafimow, D., Marks, M., 2015. Editorial in Basic and Applied Social Psychology 37, 1–2.

Tucker, H.G., 1967. A Graduate Course in Probability. Academic Press, New York.

Tukey, J.W., 1977. Exploratory Data Analysis. Addison-Wesley, Reading, Mass.

Tufte, E.R., 2001. The Visual Display of Quantitative Information. Graphics Press, Cheshire, CT.

van der Vaart, A.W., 1998. Asymptotic Statistics. Cambridge University Press, New York.

White, H., 1980. A heteroskedasticity-consistent covariance matrix estimator and a direct test for heteroskedasticity. Econometrica 48 (4), 817–838.

White, H., 1982. Maximum likelihood estimation of misspecified models. Econometrica 50 (1), 1–25.

White, H., 2000. A reality check for data snooping. Econometrica 68 (5), 1097–1126.

Index

A

Algebra, 5, 21, 239, 287, 288
Alternative hypothesis, 119, 182, 183,
    185, 189, 193, 281
Approximation, 4, 58, 108, 170, 173, 177,
    195, 216, 251
Asymptotic distribution, 213, 223, 224,
    323, 346
Asymptotic normality, 205, 322, 323,
    329, 347

B

Bayes rule, 12, 14, 77, 83
Bayes theorem, 12, 68, 147, 148
Bayesian, 142, 146, 148, 149
Bayesian approach, 146, 149, 287
Bayesian confidence interval, 208, 288
Best linear fit, 78–80, 252
Bias, 147, 163, 164, 289–291
Binomial distribution, 55, 58, 59, 227
Bivariate, 77, 80, 82, 83, 86, 91, 145, 261
Bootstrap, 213, 217–219
Borel sigma algebra, 6, 22, 63

C

c.d.f., 23, 24, 27–33, 35, 40, 41, 48, 49,
    53, 56, 58, 59, 61, 63, 64, 67, 91,
    106–108, 113, 115–117, 137, 151,
    209, 321, 331, 351
Cauchy, 45, 47, 50, 60, 74, 100, 137, 173
Cauchy distribution, 160, 173
Cauchy–Schwarz inequality, 70, 93, 168,
    307

Central Limit Theorem, see CLT
Characteristic function, 51, 52, 88, 100,
    140, 245
Chebychev's inequality, 94, 95, 128
Chi-squared distribution, 140, 191, 201
CLT, 59, 100, 101, 103–105, 127, 179,
    181, 191, 194, 195, 202, 219, 299,
    308, 325, 329
Coefficient, 227, 256, 268, 283, 295, 314,
    337, 339, 351
    Gini, 30, 336
Computation, 160–162, 174, 256, 279,
    285, 295
Conditional distribution, 19, 66, 68, 72,
    80–82, 86, 144, 146, 245, 268,
    269, 303
Conditional expectation, 72, 73, 77, 80,
    120, 290
Conditional probability, 11–14, 16, 112
Confidence interval, 125, 144, 199–202,
    205–207, 209, 210, 217, 227, 268,
    269, 281
Confidence set, 199, 204, 205, 209
Continuous random variable, 23, 26, 27,
    41, 51, 53, 54, 65, 74, 85, 114
Convergence, 96–100, 102, 106, 307,
    317–319, 321, 328, 348
Copula, 90, 91
Correlation, 71, 76, 264
Covariance, 69–72, 77
Covariance matrix, 244–246, 264, 287,
    325, 341
    conditional, 83, 245, 267

Covariate, 146, 254, 260, 261, 264, 271, 291–293, 295, 305, 307, 338
Coverage, 199, 205, 217
two-sided, 200, 201, 206
Critical region, 175, 181, 187, 188, 227, 281
Critical value, 176–178, 181, 204, 213, 217, 218, 280, 287, 300, 356
Cumulative distribution function, see c.d.f.

D

Data distribution, 172, 173, 176
Degrees of freedom, 140, 141, 153, 284, 293, 344, 345
Density, 31–33, 45, 48, 54, 60, 68, 69, 72, 84, 85, 129, 136, 142, 145, 147, 148, 209, 217
conditional, 67, 68, 113, 114, 125, 147, 332
joint, 65, 67, 68, 82, 114, 245
marginal, 65, 67, 68, 90, 113, 125, 147
Density function, 32, 33, 36–38, 59, 61, 64, 66, 91, 113, 128, 136, 142, 145, 151, 269, 270
Dependence, 15, 16, 18, 90, 91, 135, 292
Diagonal matrix, 233, 241, 254, 268
Dimension, 231, 232, 234, 237, 239, 240, 249, 256, 341
Direction, 15, 16, 18, 19, 66, 238, 289–291
Distribution
bootstrap, 213, 219
discrete, 4, 55
empirical, 151, 152, 212, 213, 219
estimated, 149, 212
exact, 189, 268, 285, 287, 290
Gaussian, 44, 59, 173
income, 50, 60
joint, 66, 88–90, 97, 106, 121, 122, 146, 221, 222
large sample, 138, 204, 353
limiting, 171, 189, 192, 205, 298, 305, 310, 325, 354

marginal, 64, 88–91, 106, 146, 221
normal, 4, 35, 36, 44, 49, 50, 59, 76, 83, 84, 91, 101, 140, 141, 159, 178, 223, 224, 268, 279
Pareto, 163, 336
Poisson, 57, 58, 227, 336
prior, 13, 147–149, 208, 287, 288
true, 173, 325
unconditional, 84, 269
uniform, 36, 44, 158, 223, 316
unknown, 142, 345
Distribution function, 26, 27, 90, 124, 212, 321
empirical, 136, 152, 153
Dummy variables, 254, 257, 268, 303–305, 337

E

Eigendecomposition, 240, 242–244, 253
Eigenvalue, 237–243, 249, 253, 279, 342, 352, 356, 359
distinct, 239, 240
largest, 243, 246
Eigenvector, 237–241, 246, 248, 255, 342, 359
Estimation, 151, 173, 174, 269, 273
Event, 4, 9, 11, 12, 15–17, 19, 27, 48, 57, 64, 66–68, 107, 112, 117, 121, 225, 323, 351
independent, 15, 17, 18
Expectation, 43–47, 52, 72, 73, 81, 93, 119, 120, 138, 164, 268, 272, 348

F

Frequentist, 142, 143, 146, 147, 149
Full rank, 234, 236, 243, 244, 249, 252–254, 258, 260, 268, 271, 274, 285, 300, 305, 311, 314, 326, 327, 343
Full rank matrix, 235, 343
Function
continuous, 26, 32, 35
moment generating, 51, 55, 140
monotonic, 37–39, 287

nonlinear, 71, 73, 270
scalar, 243, 272

G

Generalized Method of Moments, see GMM

GMM, 174, 271, 316, 326

H

Hessian, 156–158, 169, 325
Homoskedastic, 265, 268, 269, 290, 297
Homoskedasticity, 175, 273, 290, 299, 300
Hypothesis, 100, 111, 119, 175, 179, 184, 188, 193, 196, 197, 205, 218, 227, 277–280, 283, 350, 356

I

Identification, 143, 144, 226, 321
Identification condition, 316, 317
Income, 27, 30, 179, 180
Independence, 14–18, 66, 68, 69, 71, 76, 88, 139, 141, 175, 181, 279, 335
conditional, 18, 19
pairwise, 18
Inference, 12, 144, 146, 197, 287, 290
Integer, 96, 112, 219, 319, 335, 336
Intercept, 257, 280, 284, 291, 351
Invariant, 50, 70, 238, 253, 261
Inverse, 27, 37, 88, 89, 232, 233, 244, 248, 268, 344, 358

L

Lagrange multiplier, 223, 283, 285, 286, 346
Large sample, 163, 172, 177, 183, 196, 205, 211, 290, 311
Law of Large Numbers, see LLN
Law of total probability, 12, 13, 37, 99, 107
Lebesgue measure, 6, 7, 31, 32, 35, 65, 148, 209
Likelihood, 13, 15, 45, 111, 143, 146, 147, 155, 157, 158, 161, 162, 173, 183, 270, 285, 287

Likelihood function, 142–144, 155, 156, 158, 159, 221, 223, 285
Likelihood ratio, 181, 183, 187, 190, 223, 285, 346, 353
Linear approximation, 78, 79
Linear regression, 277, 285, 318, 325, 326, 338
LLN, 100, 101, 105, 179, 211, 298
Local power function, 190, 191, 193, 195
LR test, 182, 188, 285, 287
LRT, 182, 183, 204

M

Magnitude, 70, 289–291
Markov chain, 19
Maximum likelihood, 151, 153, 155, 174, 315, 316
Maximum likelihood estimator, see MLE
Mean squared error, see MSE
Measurable function, 23, 35, 46, 69, 76, 77, 80, 136, 317, 348
Median, 27, 28, 45, 47, 50, 52–54, 81, 147, 152, 173, 327, 336, 351
conditional, 69, 80, 83
Method of Moments, see MoM
Minimizer, 53, 119, 120, 152, 315, 317, 318
unique, 52, 152
MLE, 143, 144, 147, 153, 155, 160, 162, 163, 165, 169, 170, 172–174, 181, 182, 223, 247, 270, 274, 278, 285, 286, 316, 321, 324, 352, 354
MoM, 151, 153, 174
Moment, 45, 49, 52, 53, 58, 85, 151, 153, 166, 195, 264, 298, 313, 326, 348
MSE, 52, 76, 164, 165, 167, 170, 171, 272, 273, 290
Multivariate, 21, 63, 72, 157, 161, 245, 268, 272, 273

N

Null hypothesis, 175–186, 189, 190, 192–197, 200, 207, 223, 277, 280, 281, 285, 290, 346, 353, 356

O

Objective function, 77, 80, 104, 152, 316, 317, 324, 326–328

Observation, 135, 148, 222, 225, 226, 254, 256, 294, 303, 304, 336, 338, 350, 352, 354

OLS, 251, 263, 267, 271, 274, 290, 292, 329, 337

OLS estimator, 267, 271, 273, 291, 294, 297, 298

Omitted variable, 289, 290, 339

Ordinary Least Squares, see OLS

P

p.d.f., 31, 43, 55, 60, 64, 65, 67, 85, 116, 120

p.m.f., 31, 43, 55, 64, 65, 67, 69, 72, 85, 221

Parameter point, 143, 156

Parameter space, 142, 144, 156, 167, 200, 205, 209, 272, 315, 317, 318, 354
  natural, 158

Parameter value, 142, 172, 212, 221, 225, 226, 272, 324, 325

Parameters of interest, 142, 151, 154, 313, 331, 332

Partition, 5, 38, 39, 128, 177, 245, 254, 255, 283

Payoff, 50, 103, 129, 130, 248

Poisson, 85, 158, 188, 193, 194, 336

Posterior, 13, 14, 146–148, 287, 288

Posterior density, 146–148, 208

Power, 184–187, 189, 190, 192, 194–196
  optimal, 189
  zero, 186, 194

Power set, 5, 22

Predictor, 76, 181, 202, 293, 295

Probability
  joint, 12, 64
  marginal, 11, 12, 64, 66
  positive, 248, 321

Probability density function, see p.d.f.

Probability mass function, see p.m.f.

Probability measure, 6, 11, 21, 23, 31, 38, 43, 63, 142, 144, 148

Property
  asymptotic, 170, 223, 297, 316, 321
  linearity, 73
  statistical, 163, 221, 267, 282

Q

Quantile, 27–30, 60, 151, 152, 213, 219, 228, 284, 327, 332, 333

Quantile function, 29, 30

R

Random sample, 125, 135, 138, 202, 221–223, 332

Random variable
  chi-squared, 279, 345
  discrete, 23, 26, 28, 69, 85, 183, 193, 356
  distributed, 40, 79, 116, 140
  independent, 71, 102, 127, 305
  independent standard normal, 116, 118, 155, 350
  multiple, 21, 63
  n-dimensional vector of, 344
  normal, 51, 59, 100, 140, 270
  sequence of, 96–99
  standard normal, 109, 279, 306
  transformed, 35, 85

Random vector, 106, 116, 244, 246

Rank, 234, 235, 253, 257, 273, 359

Real symmetric matrix, 240, 242, 243, 342, 359

Regression, 72, 73, 146, 256, 257, 260, 271, 280, 281, 283, 293, 297, 311, 336–338
  quantile, 327, 329
  restricted, 281, 283, 284
  ridge, 294, 295
  unrestricted, 281, 284, 287

Regression function, 72, 73, 76–78, 80, 113, 125

Regression model, 264, 292, 295, 297, 325, 346, 351, 353

Regressor, 291, 292, 294, 305, 311, 339, 352

Rejection probability, 180, 192, 227

S

Sample median, 152–154, 173, 271

Sample space, 3, 6, 8, 21, 22, 55, 63, 64, 144

Scalar, 36, 72, 78, 157, 161, 162, 167, 233, 234, 237, 239, 259, 272, 273, 290, 341, 352, 358

Score function, 156, 160, 161, 169, 316, 325

Score test, 182, 184, 286

Sigma algebra, 5, 6, 21, 22, 35, 63, 68, 72

Significance level, 176, 178, 181, 182, 184, 196, 208

Simpson's paradox, 19

Simulation, 40, 101, 212, 219, 293

Singular value decomposition, 241, 254

Slope, 79, 80, 284, 291, 294

Slutsky theorem, 139, 179, 298, 300, 307, 329, 353

Stock, 11, 12, 14, 15, 50, 60, 61, 70, 104, 137, 181, 202, 247

Strategy, 13, 46, 112, 120, 222

Structural change, 278, 280, 283, 284

Subsample, 137, 219

Subsampling, 219

T

t-distribution, 59, 209, 270

t-statistics, 226, 227, 290, 311, 336, 345

Test statistics, 143, 175, 185, 186, 189, 190, 193, 200, 206, 218, 219, 278, 280, 283–285, 287, 299, 356

Theorem
continuous mapping, 105, 106
infinite monkey, 17, 18, 181, 294
projection, 250, 251
transformation, 88–90

Theory, 38, 72, 183, 189, 190, 196, 210, 216, 273, 277, 307, 315, 325, 329
asymptotic, 93, 96, 299
large sample, 139, 218

Transformation, 35, 39, 85–87, 114, 128, 189, 238, 253
redundant, 85, 88, 89

U

ULLN, 317, 318, 321, 325

UMP, 186, 188, 189, 223

UMVUE, 167, 170

Unbiased estimator, 167, 168, 170, 273, 274, 292, 352

Uniform Law of Large Numbers, see ULLN

Uniformly Minimum Variance Unbiased Estimator, see UMVUE

Uniformly Most Powerful, see UMP

Unknown parameter, 118, 125, 142–144, 158, 201, 223, 270, 275, 285, 287, 313, 353

W

Wald statistic, 182, 184, 300, 308, 310

Wald test, 182, 226, 285–287

Z

Zipf's law, 57, 336

Printed in the United States
By Bookmasters